D1713370

Dancing Past the Light

UNIVERSITY PRESS OF FLORIDA

Florida A&M University, Tallahassee
Florida Atlantic University, Boca Raton
Florida Gulf Coast University, Ft. Myers
Florida International University, Miami
Florida State University, Tallahassee
New College of Florida, Sarasota
University of Central Florida, Orlando
University of Florida, Gainesville
University of North Florida, Jacksonville
University of South Florida, Tampa
University of West Florida, Pensacola

Dancing Past the Light

THE LIFE OF TANAQUIL LE CLERCQ

OREL PROTOPOPESCU

UNIVERSITY PRESS OF FLORIDA

Gainesville / Tallahassee / Tampa / Boca Raton

Pensacola / Orlando / Miami / Jacksonville / Ft. Myers / Sarasota

BALANCHINE is a Trademark of The George Balanchine Trust.
Writings by Lincoln Kirstein are © 2021 by the New York Public Library
(Astor, Lenox and Tilden Foundations)

Copyright 2021 by Orel Protopopescu
All rights reserved
Published in the United States of America

26 25 24 23 22 21   6 5 4 3 2 1

ISBN 978-0-8130-6902-9
Library of Congress Control Number: 2021930611

The University Press of Florida is the scholarly publishing agency for the State University
System of Florida, comprising Florida A&M University, Florida Atlantic University, Florida
Gulf Coast University, Florida International University, Florida State University, New College
of Florida, University of Central Florida, University of Florida, University of North Florida,
University of South Florida, and University of West Florida.

University Press of Florida
2046 NE Waldo Road
Suite 2100
Gainesville, FL 32609
http://upress.ufl.edu

To my husband and best friend, Șerban,
for his unconditional love for me, our daughters and
grandchildren, his careful readings of my drafts,
and his patience throughout the four years that I
was steeped in this project

And in memory of the celebrated New York City Ballet
principal dancer, Jacques d'Amboise (1934–2021), Le Clercq's
dance partner and friend, whose generous, ebullient spirit has
guided my work since the day we met at his National Dance
Institute in Harlem, NYC, in June 2018

Contents

Preface

I first saw Tanaquil Le Clercq dance fourteen years after her death. The place was the Elinor Bunin Munroe Film Center in Lincoln Center, New York City, across the plaza from the theater built to George Balanchine's specifications. The film was Nancy Buirski's *Afternoon of a Faun* (2014).

Le Clercq (1929–2000), Balanchine's last wife, a principal ballerina of the New York City Ballet and a legendary muse of Jerome Robbins as well as Balanchine, was paralyzed by polio on the European tour of 1956. I had heard her tragic story in the 1960s, when studying French with her father, Professor Jacques Le Clercq, in his waning years at Queens College, CUNY. But it was seeing Le Clercq dance on film that compelled me to write her biography. I had never seen a dancer so exquisite, a unique fusion of power and lightness, pathos and wit.

Another aspect of her life had particular resonance for me: Le Clercq was an artist at the forefront of social change. She and Arthur Mitchell broke the color barrier in classical ballet on a New York stage with a *pas de deux* in 1955. Even before Mitchell founded the Dance Theatre of Harlem, she accepted his invitation to teach students in a church basement. When she began that pioneering decade of teaching and coaching (1967–77), using hand gestures to convey steps while seated in a wheelchair, I was a college student, commuting from my home in Hempstead, Long Island. Nearly every White family, besides mine, had left my neighborhood by then, an experience that precipitated my early activism in civil rights. Researching Le Clercq's life for this book, I discovered that she shared my family's keen sense of social injustice in all its forms.

This work is the record of an exhilarating journey through thousands of letters, notes, scrapbooks, photos, films, audio and video recordings, articles, books, and the memories of Le Clercq's dance partners, students, and friends. Esteemed dance scholars generously made suggestions and corrections that saved me from many errors and enriched the book. I hope it conveys some portion of the joy exploring Tanaquil Le Clercq's remarkable life has given me.

1

Her Last Tour

At the start of the New York City Ballet's European tour in the last week of August 1956, Tanaquil Le Clercq, a principal dancer, already looked exhausted and perilously thin. She was facing a brutally fast-paced schedule that would prove to be harder than anyone had anticipated. No matter how she felt, Le Clercq kept dancing. She couldn't let the company down. It had no other ballerina like her—tall, yet delicate, with the long limbs of a gazelle. And she was beautiful, with a glow that could warm any audience, onstage or off.

Tanny (the nickname that just about everyone called her) had an unconventional beauty, paired with the aristocratic elegance of a fashion model. In 1953 she had posed for a feature article in *Cosmopolitan,* wearing a bright-pink coat and bending down to try on pointe shoes. Her sleek, intriguing image (captured by top photographers) appeared in a range of magazines, from high fashion to mass market, including *Vogue, Town and Country, Look, Life, Mademoiselle,* and *Good Housekeeping.* Who wasn't fascinated by the latest wife of George Balanchine, the world-famous choreographer whose passions fueled and ruled his ballet company?

But by the summer of 1956, her troubled marriage had sapped her energy and appetite. Rumors flew through the dance company that the couple had agreed to split up, although no official announcement had been made.[1]

Everyone knew that she would have preferred not to be on that tour. It was hard to put on a pair of pointe shoes and a smile, matinees and evenings, for adoring fans in thirteen cities over ten weeks when you felt like crawling under a warm duvet with a book. When a company soloist, Barbara Walczak, spoke of her joy at being in Salzburg, Austria, their first stop, Tanny confided, "You know, I didn't want to come. . . . I sense death here."[2]

There were few traces left in Salzburg of World War II, which had ended eleven years before. But Le Clercq still felt uneasy in German-speaking countries that had been part of Hitler's Third Reich, and the weather didn't help her mood. It was unusually cold and damp for late summer. On August 24, she heard Mozart's *Idomeneo*. The dancers had to wait for the three-hour opera to finish before they could rehearse because they were to perform on the same stage. The rehearsal lasted from 11:00 p.m. to 1:00 a.m. Worse than the hours were the heavy, monotonous meals of sausages and veal cutlets. "I'm on eggs now," Tanny wrote to a good friend, the pianist Robert "Bobby" Fizdale (half of the celebrated duo Fizdale and Gold).[3]

But she rose to the occasion, as always. The Austrian press praised "the dancing magic of these delightful Americans," the first ballet company to perform at the legendary Salzburg Music Festival. The New York City Ballet was proclaimed the hit of the entire event, and Le Clercq was singled out as one of three dancers who displayed a "rarely found understanding for their art." Her triumph is all the more impressive because she may have been dancing in spite of pain. From Venice, their stop after Vienna and Zurich, she had written "Dearest Bobby" Fizdale that she might not dance for two nights because "I have, not *one*, but *two* infected toes."[4]

The Venice engagement was followed, in rapid succession, by performances in Berlin and Munich. "I miss Italy," Tanny wrote to another close friend, the dancer/choreographer Jerome "Jerry" Robbins. "Germany scares me. Just can't feel the admiration George does. . . . So they are disciplined and work work work— it doesn't seem civilized to me."[5]

Winter seemed to have come early that year. "It is absolutely freezing unbearably cold—and wet . . . we are at the halfway mark—and I don't really want to go to Frankfurt Brussels or Antwerp. . . . Its [*sic*] started to sleet— I've finished breakfast and am sitting in bed under one of those feather quilts still my nose and hands are cold— the matinée starts at 4:00 evening at 8:00— Ugh—." She wondered whether they would see snow in Denmark. "I hate cold weather like this. I feel I could stay in bed all day long . . . from Munich to Frankfurt we dance the next day— no day in between. . . . I think this tour is starting to pall— is that a word? I say it but never write it and it looks very strange. I wonder where it comes from a-pall-ing maybe?"[6]

By mid-October, a few weeks after her twenty-seventh birthday, she arrived in France. It had been cold there, too, and now she was enduring a typically rainy fall day in Paris, her birthplace. On the thin airmail paper then commonly used to save postage, she wrote to Jerry Robbins that she would be filmed that Saturday morning, dance a Sunday matinee, and then leave for Cologne, Germany, the next day. Tanny felt more at home in France than

Germany, although she had German roots on her father's side. "My German stinks," she informed Jerry with self-mocking humor, "but I tell everyone that my father was born in Carlsbad so they love me— when I'm in France I say I'm French. What an insincere fake I am— love xxxxxT"[7]

She was counting the hours until the tour would be over. The late matinees, a concession to the European tradition of a long and copious midday meal, left little time for rest before evening performances. But the French food and Parisian shops cheered her. "I lost my head today," she confessed in one of many letters she sent to Robbins, almost daily, throughout that tour. "I spent 27,000 francs on perfume and gloves . . . but these are so adorable with embroidered roses— and then there is one pair with a tiny blue flower on the index finger." The perfume was a gift for Tamara Geva, the first of Balanchine's ex-wives, now their neighbor and friend. She had requested "an ounce of something," Tanny wrote, "so I felt generous and got her a *tremendous* bottle."[8]

In 1956, five hundred old French francs equaled about one U.S. dollar. She had spent a bit more than fifty dollars, but that was a substantial chunk of her weekly salary on the tour, which never topped $225. (Two older principal dancers, Maria Tallchief and André Eglevsky, received far more, most likely to keep them in the company.) The life of a famous ballet dancer may have appeared glamorous from the outside, but they were not paid like Hollywood or Broadway stars.[9]

In a film shot in Paris, Le Clercq is in superb form, strutting her way through the ballet, *Western Symphony,* as a high-kicking dance-hall girl in the Wild West of Balanchine's wilder imagination. She wore a ravishing costume by her husband's favorite designer, Russian-born Barbara Karinska (Varvara Jmoudsky). The critic B. H. Haggin had raved about Tanny's hat, "to say nothing of the way she wore it—alone worth the price of admission."[10]

The dancers got no extra pay for being filmed on their only day off in Paris. Tanny had the right to refuse. Thankfully, she didn't. Contemporary audiences around the world can watch, online, her comical, elegant performance in the *Rondo* section of the ballet, aided by her partner, the towering powerhouse Jacques d'Amboise, just twenty-two years old. As she takes a saucy jump backward, Le Clercq fluffs up the back of her tutu with both hands. Her practiced smile verges on laughter.

The company could not afford costumes the first time the pair had danced their *pas de deux,* two years earlier, so Balanchine had told them to wear whatever they wished. All the same, they had triumphed at the 1954 premiere.

Tanaquil Le Clercq posed in an arabesque, *Western Symphony,* photo by George Platt Lynes, March 11, 1955. Used with Permission of The George Balanchine Trust and The George Platt Lynes Estate. Choreography by George Balanchine ©The George Balanchine Trust. Jerome Robbins Dance Division, The New York Public Library for the Performing Arts.

Edwin Denby, an influential critic, wrote, "Tanaquil Le Clercq and Jacques d'Amboise were the special heroes of the first night."[11]

Other great ballerinas appear in the color film, including the principal dancer Diana Adams, but Le Clercq stands out. She flits about the stage like a weightless sprite, prancing, whirling and leaping, her scissor legs slicing great, saucy arcs in the air, her face radiating impish joy, as if to let us in on a joke.

Her swagger makes visible the rhyme of sashay and ballet. She shows no signs of being ill, although she is at her thinnest—sheer muscle, nerves, and bone. But there is nothing thin about her personality. It fills the stage. She seems to soak up all the available light until she's lit from within.[12]

By the time they had arrived at the tour's next stop, Cologne, Le Clercq and d'Amboise both had bronchitis, he recalled. But they had passionate fans in Europe who'd bought tickets far in advance. Nobody else in the ballet company could do the variety of roles that Le Clercq took on—witty, laugh-out-loud comedy, tender, lyric romance, and harrowing tragedy. She *had* to dance. As d'Amboise wrote in his memoir, at the end of their final performance together, they were both wheezing. He hugged her goodbye onstage and flew home for the birth of his first child, skipping a party given for the company by a Mrs. Ellen Few, the wife of the American cultural attaché. Tanny rarely enjoyed these formal occasions and would occasionally play sick to get out of attending one. Not this time. Later, Mrs. Few came to a performance but was not feeling well. Tanny didn't discover, until she met her again the following spring in Warm Springs, Georgia, that their hostess had contracted paralytic polio.[13]

The last week in October, the company left for Copenhagen, where Tanny was eager to explore a shop that Jerry had recommended for its vintage, rare finds. At a rehearsal, the dancers were instructed to bow in unison toward the queen of Denmark in her box at the Royal Opera House, before bowing to the public. Members of the Danish royal family were sure to attend at least one performance.[14]

Le Clercq had to push herself through rehearsals, resisting what she thought might be the start of a flu. But she danced on opening night, Friday, October 26, and throughout the rest of that weekend. Two giants of ballet choreography, George Balanchine and Jerome Robbins, had made roles expressly for her. How could she let them and her public down?

On Saturday night, October 27, she put on a short, belted, pale-blue tunic, applied her makeup, tied her pointe shoes, and waited for her entrance. The stage set looked like an enchanted ballet studio, with curtains billowing in the breeze. Robbins had choreographed *Afternoon of a Faun* in 1953 for her face as much as her limbs and torso, especially her big, wide-spaced, changeable eyes, which could seem gray or green or watery blue, depending on the light.

He had imagined how she would stare at the audience while she performed the steps. That was where Robbins had finally decided to place the invisible

Tanaquil Le Clercq, photo by Cris Alexander, ca. 1953. Courtesy of NYCB Archive.

mirror of his imaginary studio, in the "fourth wall" separating the performers and their audience, a brilliant choice. Pretending to watch herself dancing, coolly appraising her own image with beguiling concentration, Le Clercq would captivate everyone watching her.

Robbins had used her unique qualities in the dance—her almost translucent presence, delicate flexibility, dramatic allure, and the long hair that she'd had in 1953. It had been cut four months before the 1956 tour, a snap decision that she'd immediately regretted. Her role required no other adornment. No costumes beyond exercise clothes were needed to portray the elusive nymph and the boy faun who is drawn to her. But in Robbins's version of the classic Nijinsky ballet, the boy and girl weren't mythological creatures, just two young dancers discovering themselves, and then each other, as they warmed up and practiced combinations.[15]

Making her entrance on the stage of Copenhagen's Royal Opera House, Le Clercq tried not to let the audience see how much her body ached. She rose with the music, stretching out a long leg to one side, an invitation to Francisco "Frank" Monción, her partner that day, to lift her over his head. Monción had been her first partner in this dance, but he'd never imagined that he would be the last.

She flowed over his back like water, first her golden-brown hair and then the rest of her, as if the music were a stream that could take her anywhere. She stood on pointe, all her weight on one foot, her other leg raised high in arabesque, as he spun her around in a measured whirl, punctuated by her

Tanaquil Le Clercq and Francisco Monción, *Afternoon of a Faun*, choreography by Jerome Robbins, photo by Fred Melton, 1953. Courtesy of Christopher Melton. Jerome Robbins Dance Division, The New York Public Library for the Performing Arts.

wide-open arms. With his support, she did a slow bend on her left leg, descending all the way down with perfect control. He was a superb partner, like d'Amboise, who could make her feel gloriously at ease.

Monción had known Le Clercq since her ballet school days. Whenever he held her aloft, he recalled, decades later, "she used to look down maybe just with a half-smile . . . then kicking her feet gently as if enjoying the whole thing just like a cat."[16]

Tanaquil Le Clercq and Francisco Monción, *Afternoon of a Faun,* choreography by Jerome Robbins, photo by Fred Melton, 1953. Courtesy of Christopher Melton. Jerome Robbins Dance Division, The New York Public Library for the Performing Arts.

In Copenhagen, nearly three and a half years since her first performance of *Faun,* she must have been relieved that the ballet was over. Bowing as the applause washed over her, had she masked her agony with a smile? Le Clercq had always been as great an actress as a dancer.

She had one more performance that evening, the fast, *Rondo* section of *Western Symphony.* Now the ballet studio was gone, replaced on the stage by a backdrop of rickety-looking storefronts out of an old Western. Prancing on the tips of her pointe shoes, she danced a jaunty jig, in rhythm with the lighthearted pastiche of American folk songs. She'd always made it look so easy, landing again and again as lightly as if she had invisible wings. During the filming in Paris, she had seemed like a creature of the air. But that last Saturday in Copenhagen, it was far from easy, even with the support of a gifted young partner, high-flying Arthur Mitchell.

Arthur Mitchell in cowboy costume, *Western Symphony,* ca. 1955, photo by JPC staff photographer Moneta Sleet Jr. Johnson Publishing Company Archive. Choreography by George Balanchine ©The George Balanchine Trust. Courtesy Ford Foundation, J. Paul Getty Trust, John D. and Catherine MacArthur Foundation, Andrew W. Mellon Foundation, and Smithsonian Institution.

Barely a year before, their first *pas de deux* in this ballet at the City Center in New York, months after the landmark *Brown v. Board of Education* Supreme Court decision, had provoked an audible outburst, although Mitchell was not the first African American dancer to partner her. In 1950, performing the role of *Sacred Love* in Sir Frederick Ashton's *Illuminations,* Le Clercq had been "handed about by a ring" of four "youths, with naked torsos and tight satin trousers," among them a Black dancer, Arthur Bell, a guest artist with Balanchine's company.[17]

Before going onstage in Copenhagen, Le Clercq had told Mitchell that she felt stiff. He had suggested that she stretch her muscles. She did some exercises on her dressing-room floor, then struggled into her costume and through the ballet. Right after the curtain closed, Leon Barzin, music director of the company, saw her backstage. She was feverish. "I came up and put my scarf around her," he recalled, "she was so wringing wet."[18]

At the Sunday 3:00 p.m. matinee, October 28, Le Clercq was scheduled to perform the role of Odette, the Swan Queen, in Balanchine's *Swan Lake.* "I ache from head to toe," she told Barbara Horgan, his personal assistant, who was backstage handing out travel information to the dancers. They would be finishing the tour in Sweden at the end of that week. Barbara ran to get her some Miltown (meprobamate), a tranquilizer that dancers in the company used for muscle aches. Odette was a taxing role, but Le Clercq managed to make it through this ordeal and one more performance of *Afternoon of a Faun.* Trying to gather whatever strength she had left for the evening, she rested on her dressing-room floor.[19]

She was scheduled to perform only once that Sunday night, in *Bourrée Fantasque,* a ballet that Balanchine had made expressly for her and Robbins. The word *bourrée* comes from a French folk dance with quick, skipping steps; to *bourrée* means to move rapidly on the tips of the toes, a motion that resembles gliding.

For the four parts of this ballet, Balanchine had selected four works by a French Romantic composer, Emmanuel Chabrier. The first movement was a comical *pas de deux* for a tall woman and a small man in wild, frustrated pursuit of her. She goes one way and he another. His kisses miss their target. Her whirling foot lands on the back of his head twice, and each time he doesn't realize what hit him. She sits on his proffered knee, facing him, but shakes her head "No, no, no!" as he leans in, enthusiastically nodding "Yes!"[20]

As Deborah Jowitt wrote in her biography of Robbins, "Had Balanchine been a fortune-teller, he couldn't have expressed more clearly the relationship that would shortly develop between Robbins and Le Clercq . . . not unlike a pair of talented, ambitious, and very smart siblings." They had made such a madcap romp of their teasing, affectionate dance at the 1949 premiere that audiences had laughed aloud, again and again. Le Clercq had "proved," the critic Lillian Moore marveled, that "it is possible to be simultaneously beautiful and funny."[21]

At the frenetic, galloping start of the short first movement, set to Chabrier's *Marche joyeuse,* the ballerina had to brandish a fan while jumping, prancing, hopping, and pirouetting, much of it on the tips of her toes. Knowing that she had not been feeling well, a good friend, the ballerina Patricia "Pat" Wilde, dropped by her dressing room to check on her.[22]

"Oh, Pat, come in," Tanny said. "Look at my back. It feels strange." Wilde didn't see any problem, but she offered to replace her. Le Clercq said that since she was already in her costume and makeup, she might as well dance. But just before the 8:00 p.m. curtain rose, she felt too exhausted and asked her friend Diana Adams, who usually danced in the lyrical second movement, a romantic *pas de deux,* to switch roles and costumes with her. (Tanny normally wore an exquisite, black-and-gold tutu designed by Karinska. Diana's costume was a long, flowing gown.) As Le Clercq explained to a friend, the writer Holly Brubach, years later, this part was "slower and, I thought, easier than to crash in with the fan and do the fast stuff."[23]

She got through it, never far from another frequent partner, Nicholas "Nicky" Magallanes, whose role was to support her turns, leaps, and lyrical arabesques until, near the end, he danced offstage and she had to make her winding way, on tiny, rapid *bourrée* steps, through the corps de ballet and offstage, alone. "Then I went back to the hotel and I still wasn't feeling well, but I was still walking."[24]

Tanaquil Le Clercq never danced again. It was not the flu. It was polio. Within a few days, she could not lift her legs. Two months later, barely able to move her hands, she scrawled a note to Jerry Robbins: "The past makes me cry. It seems so wonderful." Dancing had been her life ever since she could remember. If only she could go back, be whole again . . . [25]

2

---◯◯◯---

Starting Out "Like a Real Ballerina..."

On both sides of her family, Tanaquil Le Clercq's immediate ancestors were prosperous and socially well-connected, advantages to which she attached little importance. Her mother, Edith Whittemore Le Clercq, had been a glamorous debutante, the "premiere danseuse of St. Louis's Junior League," where she probably excelled at ballroom dancing. Edith had longed to be a ballerina, Tanny told a reporter, but "in St. Louis, nice girls didn't." Discouraged from choosing what seemed to people of her class an unsettled, disreputable way of life, Edith had pursued her passion for dance through her daughter. "Nobody in my family had ever been a dancer," Le Clercq declared in 1955, "but my mother decided I could be one."[1]

Born in St. Louis on December 16, 1895, Edith began her education at Mary Institute, a school founded by William Greenleaf Eliot, T. S. Eliot's grandfather, the founder of Washington University. She went on to Miss Porter's School in Farmington, Connecticut. (Jacqueline Bouvier Kennedy Onassis was a graduate.) A Miss Porter girl, one of the First Lady's biographers wrote, "was expected to rise to the occasion, to put her best foot forward, to do what was right—even in times of crisis—and to display, as the chaplain often said at the nondenominational Sunday services, 'guts and gumption.'" Edith had plenty of both, as did her only child.[2]

Edith's father, Frederick Whittemore Churchill Sr., the head of an insurance firm, had installed his young family at 10 Hortense Place in the Central West End of St. Louis, five blocks from Forest Park, with its theater, art museum, ice rink, and other attractions constructed for the 1904 World's Fair. The Whittemore's turn-of-the-century red-brick home, built in 1902, was approximately seven thousand square feet, but it was dwarfed by the limestone-faced castle at 9 Hortense Place, inhabited by the family of a Jewish banker, Jacob Goldman, who had named the street for a deceased daughter. Since in 1900 Jews (among other minorities) were not welcome in this exclusive, gated neighborhood, he had developed the street of mansions himself. Housing "covenants" kept "persons not of Caucasian race" out of majority White neighborhoods until these unconstitutional practices were overturned by the U.S. Supreme Court in 1948. But unwritten covenants still prevailed throughout the United States.[3]

Privileged as she was, Edith was subject to the restrictions then imposed upon girls of her class. When she was past twenty-one, she wrote a letter to her father pleading for permission to remain in New York and take a job doing war work. His answer is not known, but she did manage to stay in the city for an extended time, at least until March 1919.[4]

Sometime after her husband's death in 1920 at the age of fifty-five, Edith's mother, Elenore, must have sold the house on Hortense Place. Suddenly, her life became more adventurous, as did her only daughter's. Elenore lived for long stretches at hotels in St. Louis, Paris, and elsewhere. She rented cottages for the summer in New Hampshire, the Michigan shore, and Santa Barbara. The society pages of the St. Louis newspapers in the 1920s were full of the widow's travels, most often with Edith. By then Elenore had only one other living child, Edith's younger brother, Robert. An older son had died young.[5]

Given the social strictures of the time, it was probably mutually convenient for the women to live together for the sake of propriety, if not economics. Edith had income from a trust established by her father, although payments probably varied with the stock market. Whatever its origins, her deep bond with her mother, well into adulthood, was a model that Edith later tried to replicate with her only child, Tanaquil. At least once, however, Edith had attempted to break the chains that bound her to Elenore. In 1927, the *St. Louis Star and Times* reported that Edith had "expected to spend the winter in India" but gave up the trip "and will remain in New York until April or May when she and her mother will return to Paris, France, where they have been living for some years."[6]

Edith chose a more traditional way to achieve independence, although her choice of a mate was not conservative. On June 28, 1928, she married a hard-drinking, rather dashing, Franco-American scholar in the Chapel of Grace Church, on Broadway at Tenth Street, New York. Edith was thirty-two, an advanced age for a bride then. Her groom, Jacques Georges Clemenceau Le Clercq, had just turned thirty. Family members from both sides attended the "informal" reception at the Grosvenor Hotel on Fifth Avenue. The couple planned to sail for Europe on July 10 and were expected to remain there un-

Edith Le Clercq with Tanaquil Le Clercq, 1930. Courtesy of NYCB Archive.

til September, when Jacques would resume his duties as "a professor of languages at Columbia University." By the time his only child was born in Paris, France, on October 2, 1929, Jacques had probably returned to New York.[7]

The proud mother was aware of her daughter's balletic potential early on. She took a snapshot of Tanny at eleven months, already up on her toes and clinging to a supporting iron *barre.*

Jacques Le Clercq must have visited them, at least on holidays. Since childhood, he had been accustomed to going back and forth across the Atlantic. The son of a doctor from Dresden and his Irish American wife, Jacques had been born in Carlsbad, Bohemia, then part of the Austro-Hungarian Empire (now Karlovy Vary in the Czech Republic), on June 27, 1898.

His father, Dr. Frederic Schuman LeClercq (1854–1932), had completed his medical studies in Prague and established a practice in Carlsbad, a spa town. By the time of Tanny's birth, he had also practiced for brief intervals in Hot Springs, Virginia, and on a German steamer that plied the Atlantic from

Tanaquil Le Clercq at eleven months, Cannes, France, photo by Edith Le Clercq, 1930. Courtesy of NYCB Archive.

Madeira to Brazil. Dr. LeClercq was the son of a half-French, half-German professor of French literature, Eduard Schuman LeClercq (1820–1871), and his German American wife, Marie Regina Siegling (1824–1920), a performer and composer, the daughter of a German-born musician and instrument maker who had established one of the first music stores in Charleston, South Carolina, the Siegling Music House.[8]

Marie, Tanny's great-grandmother, had a self-proclaimed "dash of reck-lessness" in her nature. Hailed by her Italian singing teacher as "Charleston's Jenny Lind," she had played the harp and performed the lead role in Doni-zetti's *Lucia di Lammermoor* for the Spanish elite in Havana, where she'd ac-companied her father on a business trip in 1844. Later, she studied singing and composition in Europe, where she met Wagner and other celebrated mu-sicians, including Robert Schumann and his wife, Clara, "an intimate friend of the LeClercq family," and heard Liszt "improvise in a private circle." Returning to Charleston for her 1850 marriage to Professor LeClercq, for whom she had broken off a prior engagement, Marie Siegling Schuman LeClercq subsequently spent most of her married life in Dresden.[9]

Marie's oldest son, Tanny's grandfather, was a sophisticated, multilingual bon vivant. The doctor was just past forty when he was captivated by Margaret Hart, a twenty-year-old convent-educated heiress who had stopped in Carlsbad on a transcontinental tour with friends and family. The attraction was instantaneous and mutual. Margaret's parents had died, so she sent a telegram alerting her legal guardian, a Mr. Moore, the former business partner of her father: "I am in love—to hell with the money!" They married in 1895 at the American Consulate in Paris.[10]

Money, however, did not seem to be a problem. Mr. Moore sent her a generous monthly allowance, and Frederic, one of the first doctors to use insulin as a treatment for diabetes, had a thriving practice. A noted antiquarian, he had filled a historic three-story house in Carlsbad, "Die Koerner," purchased for his bride, with artifacts collected on his archaeological voyages in the Middle East and beyond. Margaret received political and artistic leaders, including Georges Clemenceau (later prime minister of France), a close friend, as well as a patient of her husband's. Returning to New York for the births of her five children, she assured American citizenship for each of them. Tanny's father, Jacques, was the middle child.[11]

Soon after the birth of his mother's fifth child, she fell madly in love once more, with a handsome Irish American, James Kilduff. The couple ran off together, a scandal that reverberated on both sides of the Atlantic. The effect this had on ten-year-old Jacques can be imagined. Frederic and Margaret divorced soon after the birth of her last child, Sybil Kilduff, but her romance with the child's father withered. Mr. Moore continued to send her three hundred dollars per month, a remarkable sum in those days, enough to enable visits with her children on both continents.[12]

Jacques spent his student years in the British Isles, France, and the United States, graduating from the University of California at Berkeley in 1921. Despite his known Allied sympathies, Tanny's grandfather had managed to keep his house throughout World War I by working out a deal with the Austrian army. He was responsible for the care of Allied prisoners of war. According to his son, Jacques, sometime before 1923 Dr. LeClercq was made a Chevalier de la Légion d'Honneur.[13]

On both sides, Tanny's immediate ancestors were adventurous, artistic, worldly, and liberal-minded for their times. This legacy was embodied in

Margaret Hart and Dr. Frederic Schuman LeClercq, 1895. Courtesy of NYCB Archive.

the middle names her father, Jacques Georges Clemenceau Le Clercq, had acquired from his godfather, Clemenceau, who died shortly after her birth. (Margaret Hart LeClercq Kilduff had died a few months before, at age fifty-three.) Jacques did not give his mother's name to his child, preferring one with historical resonance, that of Tanaquil, the Etruscan queen of Rome, also his pen surname. He had won the Yale Younger Poets Prize in 1922 for a book of rhyming, conventionally romantic poetry, *Attitudes*.[14]

On May 20, 1933, Tanaquil (age three) and Edith Le Clercq (thirty-four) arrived in New York on the *Acquitania*. Edith gave their address as "c/o U. S. Trust Company, 40 Wall St.," although Jacques must have had an apartment ready to receive them. He remained on the Columbia faculty until 1939 or 1940. Tanny seems to have believed that her father had been on sabbatical leave in Paris at the time of her birth, a story she'd probably gotten from her parents. But Jacques Le Clercq was never a full professor at Columbia, and universities do not commonly grant a paid sabbatical to an assistant professor or lecturer without tenure.[15]

Edith may have been the source of the equally false story that her husband had been on a three-year Guggenheim fellowship and that they'd all returned together when it expired. She most likely fed that falsehood to her hometown society page correspondents in order to preserve her family's reputation in St. Louis. (The Guggenheim Foundation doesn't give fellowships of more than one year, although in the early years they could be renewed.) Jacques was listed as a Creative Writing Fellow for 1930. At that time, the average Guggenheim grant was $2,500, then roughly the mean annual income of an American family with two wage earners.[16]

Why did the Le Clercqs live apart for so long? Their correspondence indicates that it had to do with money. When Tanny was fourteen months old, Edith wrote a letter to her "Darling" Jacques that expressed joy over his news of an imminent job offer from a company called Vanguard (most likely the publisher), which would free him from having to accept more translation work, presumably to supplement his income from Columbia. She hoped that "our complicated lives were going to straighten out at last and let us stay together for one year."[17]

The offer from Vanguard seems to have evaporated. In December 1931, Jacques applied for a certificate legitimizing his French studies in political sciences and law, stating that he had been doing research work in Paris since 1927. Perhaps he thought this document would help him to advance at Columbia. He did not receive his doctorate in letters from the University of Marseille until late in 1937, when he was thirty-nine, for a thesis on the poet Alfred de Vigny.[18]

Doctorates in France have varied levels of distinction, and finishing that late is not unusual. But the thesis did not win him tenure at Columbia. By the time Tanny was eleven and a student at the School of American Ballet, her father was teaching at Queens College, which became a campus of the newly formed City University of New York in 1960. Before Jacques received this tenure-track position, the family may have had some financial help from relatives, most likely on Edith's side, although it's likely that her fund at U.S. Trust Company and her mother's resources had been depleted by the 1929 stock market crash.[19]

No doubt Jacques's family had suffered losses, too. It was larger than Edith's and may not have been as wealthy, with five full siblings and one motherless half sibling to consider. Jacques must have received something from his father's estate that made bringing his wife and child to New York in 1933 feasible. An older sister, Marguerite, bought a new Packard limo with part of her inheritance. (On June 10, 1932, their father died days after he was struck by a motorcycle in Geneva. Up until his death at seventy-seven, Dr. LeClercq had been professionally active.)[20]

Edith Le Clercq soon had Tanny enrolled in classes at the King-Coit School, founded by two remarkable women, Edith King (1884–1975) and Dorothy Coit (1889–1976), who had met in 1911 when both were teaching at the Buckingham School in Cambridge, Massachusetts, where they'd collaborated on dramatic productions. King (a painter) handled the design elements, and Coit focused on storytelling and drama. Some of Edith King's methods (such as applying skin paint on bare flesh) alarmed puritanical Cambridge society. Even though King compromised by "painting just the parts of children's bodies that showed" and put tunics on the youngsters, "there were some complaints from those looking up at the stage from the front rows that they could see the children's 'private parts.'" Buttressed by influential champions, in 1923 the women left Cambridge and opened a school in more liberal-minded New York.[21]

For thirty-five years (1923–58) they offered children's theater and art classes on select weekday afternoons and weekends. Manners and poise were part of a curriculum that attracted elite patrons. When Tanny entered, classes for her age group (four to seven) were held on Wednesdays from 3:00 to 4:30 p.m. at the townhouse the women shared at 166 East Seventy-Third Street. She probably also attended the classes for all ages (four to fifteen-year-olds) on Saturday mornings.[22]

Hours were considerably longer during the six-week rehearsal periods, which could pose legal problems. Coit and King devised a clever way to combat the zealots charged with administering the city's strict child labor laws. They did a lot of "benefit" performances, did not sell tickets at the theater, and called all the children in their productions "understudies." The young actors had to learn every part, in case one was pulled out at the last minute, which had happened more than once. In 1940, Eleanor Roosevelt personally called Mayor Fiorello La Guardia on behalf of the school, "asking him to bend the rules a little."[23]

Although they were perfectionists, King and Coit considered their integrated, cross-curriculum process more important than the theatrical result. A play they'd premiered in Cambridge, *Nala and Damayanti,* had been inspired by Rajput miniatures from India's Mughal period and developed in consultation with the Boston Museum of Fine Arts. In preparation for remounting the production in New York, children were taken to the Metropolitan Museum of

Art to view the miniatures and then painted their own versions. Bits of these were incorporated into King's stage design for the show. Platforms at varied levels simulated the way the miniatures conveyed the passage of time, as well as outdoor and indoor spaces.[24]

Tanny received an education that encompassed the history, literature, myths, and customs of the place and period of any play under production, as well as its music and dance. For *Nala and Damayanti,* Miss Coit relied on a book of stylized Hindu theatrical gestures, *The Mirror of Gesture.* Some people found her approach too rigid, as she expected the youngsters to copy her exact movements and intonations.[25]

These were not children's plays designed for children. They attracted an audience of leading artists, philanthropists, and critics, and many alumni of the school had distinguished careers in the arts. Although King-Coit was considered an exclusive school, scholarships were available for the poor and not-so-poor. Tanny had one. The two-hundred-dollar-per-year tuition that others paid (October–May) didn't cover costs. Grant money from foundations and donations from wealthy individuals helped, as did a multitude of poorly paid or volunteer assistants. Edith Le Clercq, one of King-Coit's business managers, worked on their productions for a small salary. Perhaps she was earning Tanny's scholarship, as well as keeping a close eye on her daughter. And yet Edith was not above asking King and Coit to pay her "at least as much as they paid to the cleaning woman." Regardless of whether the school complied, Edith remained.[26]

At five, Tanny performed for the first time in a King-Coit production, as a swan in *Nala and Damayanti.* It was held in a real theater, most likely the "little jewel of a playhouse" on top of the old Cosmopolitan Club at 135 East Fortieth Street. Her costume of feathered headdress, beads, and long skirt was not exactly swanlike, but she created the illusion with her gestures.[27]

The dancer/choreographer Todd Bolender taught modern dance at the school on Fridays and Saturdays. He had choreographed a dance for the five-year-old Tanny that suggested classical Indian dance. Decades after they had worked together in Balanchine's company, he recalled "the sharpness of her ability to pick up whatever I'd do, as if she'd been trained."[28]

The day after her debut, she got her first review. "Mistress Tanaquil Le Clercq," exulted John Anderson in the *New York Evening Journal,* had danced her role as an "ethereal swan with entrancing effect." He reported that she had kept one eye on the audience throughout her performance, making her "my favorite actress!" Even then, she had known how to make an audience

Tanaquil Le Clercq, *Nala and Damayanti,* 1935. Courtesy of NYCB Archive.

her mirror. She had the same intent look in her eyes at five that other dancers noticed when, as a member of the New York City Ballet, she appraised her performance in the mirrors of a studio.[29]

By the time she was seven, Tanny was enrolled in Mikhail Mordkin's ballet school, located in the Carnegie Hall Building on West Fifty-Seventh Street. Mikhail Mikhailovich Mordkin (1880–1944), a former Bolshoi *premier danseur,* occasionally taught at King-Coit. One of the first Russians to perform in Western Europe, Mordkin had danced with Diaghilev's Ballets Russes in Paris in 1909 and partnered the legendary Russian ballerina Anna Pavlova in London and the United States the following year. (During one "contentious performance" of *Bacchanale,* she had given him a slap that was not part of the choreography.)[30]

Mordkin, a graduate of the Moscow Imperial Ballet School, was known

Mikhail Mordkin posed in costume as a Don Cossack, ca. 1920–29, Apeda Studio. Jerome Robbins Dance Division, The New York Public Library for the Performing Arts.

for his expressivity as a character dancer. His school, founded in 1927, offered classes in mime and drama as well as ballet. Although Italian dancers had brought the Cecchetti method of teaching ballet to New York, founding the Metropolitan Opera Ballet School in 1909, by the 1930s the most sought-after teachers in the city were from Russia. The art, from its beginnings in the courts of Western Europe, had quickly migrated from Renaissance Italy to

Tanaquil Le Clercq (*far right*), Mikhail Mordkin School, ca. 1937–39. Courtesy of NYCB Archive.

France, taking centuries to reach imperial Russia, and yet its French vocabulary had prevailed there: *glissade, jeté, plié.*[31]

Some King-Coit students found Mordkin's teaching methods odd, to say the least. He often spoke to them in French, a language few understood. With a small baton he would "lightly rap that part of the body sticking out." One former assistant called him a "dragon and a raving maniac as far as discipline was concerned." Coit supposedly asked him to stop swearing at the children (that he did in English).[32]

Mordkin did not commonly take children Tanny's age, but she had shown such promise at King-Coit that he made an exception for her. She had already been to see a ballet, and she'd liked it. "I was also taking piano lessons," she recalled, "which I was a dud at. I mean, you could tell right away, the kid can't play the piano, so it better be dancing." Five days a week, after Tanny's classes (in French) at the Lycée Français at 3 East Ninety-Fifth Street on the Upper East Side, Edith accompanied her daughter to the studio.[33]

Fifty-six by then, Mordkin still exuded the masculine authority that had entered the lexicon as an infinitive, "to Mordkin," which became "a popular reference to male dancing." At the same time, he had acquired a reputation for eccentricity, wearing vividly striped pajama tops instead of shirts. Nevertheless, Edith always made sure that her daughter was impeccably dressed for his classes. Tanny, the youngest in her class, wore a "stiffly starched pink dotted swiss ballet dress with white satin ballet slippers," according to a "special correspondent" for the *St. Louis Post-Dispatch* in March 1939 (quite possibly Edith herself), her "blond pigtails, tied with colored ribbons." Twenty years afterward, Le Clercq recalled "my first exciting sight of the rehearsal room with its bars along the wall and the smell of—well, sweat."[34]

Mordkin had a dance company that by 1939 had dissolved into Ballet Theatre. In June 1940, Tanny was scheduled to appear in his abbreviated production of *The Sleeping Beauty* on the stage of Carnegie Hall, a huge honor for a child. The heiress Lucia Chase (1897–1986), one of Mordkin's oldest students, had been performing the title role of Princess Aurora since 1937, on tour with the Mordkin Ballet, which she had joined that year.[35]

The dancer/choreographer Leon Danielian, another student of Mordkin's, was a charter member of the new company, Ballet Theatre. Tanny often saw him in her classes, as well as the ambitious Chase. By 1939 Chase had teamed up with Richard Pleasant, Mordkin's business manager, to transform the Mordkin Ballet into the repertory company Ballet Theatre (later American Ballet Theatre). Pleasant infuriated Mordkin by giving the direction of *Giselle* to the English dancer and choreographer Anton Dolin. Mordkin was so upset, Chase recalled, "He left the company before our first performance and never spoke to me again."[36]

To Danielian, Mordkin seemed more interested in performing than teaching, but by the time Tanny met him, he was only doing character parts. Danielian recalled how the imperious Mordkin "would walk into the classroom and all the students would have to stand at attention." When he appreciated the way a student moved, Mordkin shouted, "Maryinsky! [*sic*] Bolshoi!" or the name of a celebrated dancer like "Pavlova!" Mordkin used these names as a form of shorthand, perhaps because his English was so poor, giving few verbal instructions of any kind. He demonstrated steps and the students imitated.[37]

Tanny, adept at mimicry, made rapid progress. She was eager to get her first pair of toe shoes. At seven or eight, she recounted: "I used to stuff cotton into the toes of my bedroom slippers at home and, waiting until my mother was not around to stop me, practice standing on my toes, holding onto the dresser or the bed. It is a great moment in a dance student's life when she takes her first toe class; it is like an air cadet's first solo flight."[38]

She may have been soaring around her family's apartment (449 Park Avenue then, according to the above-mentioned "special correspondent") just before she wrote the following, formal apology to her mother in pencil: "Dear dear Mother! I broke the clock not bad but shall pay. Very sory hapend [*sic*] but accident. Love Tanaquil le Clercq" Although Edith is usually Ma or Mother in Tanny's early letters, even as a child she addressed her father as Jack, Jacky, and Jacques. Her mother was the parent she had always relied on, the one Tanny credited for her dance career. Behind many dazzling dancers, male and female, there's more often than not a ballet mother. Edith, a lifelong balletomane, was one of the most dedicated.[39]

Tanny was still too young for the School of American Ballet, founded by George Balanchine and Lincoln Kirstein in 1934. Girls had to be at least nine

Tanaquil Le Clercq with cat, Jacques, and Edith Le Clercq, ca. 1938. Courtesy of NYCB Archive.

to go to that school then, although boys, always in short supply, could start earlier. Jacques d'Amboise was eight when he began taking classes at Balanchine's school, but Tanny entered at eleven. By that time, her father and mother's relations had become strained. His excessive drinking had long been a problem. A family friend, the novelist and diarist Dawn Powell, would often run into Jacques Le Clercq at her favorite New York City watering holes, during and after Prohibition. In 1927, they were both at a place called Sam's when it was raided.[40]

After Edith entered Jacques's life, the Le Clercqs shared many congenial dinners and cocktail hours with Powell and her husband. But after March 31, 1940, Edith vanishes from Powell's diary. Not long after her father returned in 1946 from his prolonged war service in Europe, Tanny's parents separated.

Their marriage was not simply a war casualty. Dawn Powell had noted tension between the Le Clercqs back in 1934, when Tanny was five and a half. One evening at the Hotel Lafayette in Greenwich Village, a popular hangout for literary bohemians, the inebriated company was trading roguish stories around the table. "Jacques and Edith silently fought with each other over Jacques' 4th drink," Powell wrote in her diary. In another entry, from 1954, she mentioned encountering a woman named "Martha" at a party in Jacques's apartment and recognizing her as the one who had "put the riveting crack" in his marriage twenty years before, that is, close to the night of the silent duel.[41]

For years before their separation and the divorce legalized in 1956, Edith and Jacques had gone their separate ways in the summertime. Thanks to regular updates in the society pages of Edith's hometown paper, the *St. Louis Post-Dispatch,* you could learn that Jacques was off doing research in Mexico while Tanny and Edith visited the Whittemores of St. Louis, or that Tanny would be spending part of the summer with her mother's family and the rest on Cape Cod, Massachusetts, where Edith rented a cottage, nearly every summer, in the village of Dennis. As late as 1950, Tanny supported the fiction that she came "from a happy congenial home and family of which she is very proud." Nice girls had to keep up appearances, especially in the St. Louis society to which Edith had remained connected.[42]

Throughout the early 1940s, Jacques was listed in the New York City phone book at the same address as Tanny and Edith, 677 Madison Avenue. They had an apartment above a liquor store called Sherry's, three blocks north of the School of American Ballet. After Jacques moved out, he made regular appearances at the apartment, his daughter's friends recalled. But Edith was the primary caregiver. She never remarried and kept the name Le Clercq to the end of her life.

They may have already been living there by the early spring of Tanny's tenth year, 1940, when she played the part of the hero, Ferdinand, in a King-Coit production of *The Tempest,* a scaled-down version of Shakespeare's play, about an hour long, with original music by a seventeen-year-old composer, Lukas Foss. This event, held at the Guild Theater, New York, was a benefit for the Cape Cod Institute of Music. (Tanny was simultaneously understudying the role of the tipsy butler.) Edith helped with makeup and dressing the players in costumes designed by Karinska, which probably involved some adjusting and sewing. Tanny, already interested in fashion as a child, liked to watch her mother sew, Edith said in a 1981 interview.[43]

Dawn Powell attended the post-performance party at the Le Clercq apartment. With a skewering tone that says as much about Powell (like Jacques, an alcoholic) as her subjects, her diary describes how Tanny "arranges herself in an imitation of childish naturalness on the floor. She shows pictures of herself in other performances. 'I was just a baby in that,' she says. 'You can see how tiny I was.'" Powell caps this portrait with, "At bedtime, she must have her dilapidated doll, Charles, whom she insists "'isn't a boy doll. . . . This is Charles Boyer.'"[44]

On the same day Powell recorded these sniping snippets in her diary, the *St. Louis Post-Dispatch* published an account of the Guild performance that mentioned a brand-new ballet school Edith Le Clercq was helping to establish on the Cape. Muriel Stuart, a scout for Balanchine, taught there that summer and discovered Tanny. "All teachers who are successful must love people," she said to the author, John Gruen, in an interview long afterward. "I look for the artist—for the exciting personality." An elegant, English-born ballerina of Balanchine's generation, Stuart had studied with Pavlova in London and danced with her company. Now she taught at Balanchine's school.[45]

"It's either innate or it ain't," a student recalled her saying about a dancer's sense of rhythm. With Tanny, it was clearly innate. Stuart had encouraged her to audition for the School of American Ballet. It was considered *the* school to attend, and Edith Le Clercq was eager for her daughter to be accepted. Mordkin, who denigrated Balanchine for working in Hollywood, would not have been. He was probably jealous of the younger man and afraid to lose his most promising students to him.[46]

A dancer's career is short, so choreographers have to be constantly on the lookout for fresh talent. Balanchine was like a fine artist always looking for a vibrant new color. When, as chief judge of her audition for a place at his school, he saw Tanny for the first time, she appeared to him "like a real ballerina already, only very small, as if you were looking at her through the wrong end of a telescope."[47]

Stuart recalled her first impression of Tanny, too, "an absolutely beautiful girl—very, very thin, with a wonderful neck. She was the most delicate, the most musical of girls. She had a marvelous ear . . . one of the two or three most gifted students we've ever had. . . . [T]he only thing she had to do was slowly gain strength, because she was so delicate. But we got her young enough so that she was able to do that."[48]

Decades later, Le Clercq recalled, with pleased amusement, how "they put a number on you like a horse and then you came in and everybody looked at you." She remembered her number, 64, attached front and back, and that she had worn a starched tutu and a headband with flowers "sewn all across the top, like I was some grand ballerina." Edith had probably done the sewing.[49]

Whether or not the flowers caught his eye, Mr. B, as the ballet students respectfully called Balanchine, could see that moving with grace and speed came naturally to Tanny. He could not have failed to note her musicality and distinctive, lively personality. The competitors "hopped about, executed arabesques, and pirouetted for almost three hours before the winners were finally chosen," the *New York Times* reported in October 1940. It must have been her most prized birthday present. That week, she had turned eleven.[50]

Nearly sixty years later, with characteristic self-deprecation, she said that since she had taken Stuart's summer course, "She probably gave me all the steps we were going to do. Well, I'm sure she just threw it my way. And I won." She would have won in any case. Tanny's inborn talent was obvious to everyone. Balanchine offered her one of the first full scholarships to his school. He and its cofounder, Lincoln Kirstein, had planned to award only one, since their school had little money, but the quality was so high that five students were chosen.[51]

"It is a fine thing about ballet, that with a bit of talent, your education costs you nothing," Le Clercq told readers of the mass-market magazine *Good Housekeeping* in a 1955 article with the feel-good title, "Practically Anybody Can Become a Ballet Dancer." She added that for boys this was "especially true" as "there is always a shortage of male dancers, because of our American

School of American Ballet scholarship winners, 1941, *left to right:* Brunhilda Roque, Marie-Jeanne (a judge), Lee Joyce Mandel, Marjorie McGee, Sally Pearse, Tanaquil Le Clercq, Lincoln Kirstein. Courtesy of NYCB Archive.

feeling that ballet dancing, for men, is 'sissy.' In Europe nobody thinks anything of it when a young man decides to become a ballet dancer."[52]

At the School of American Ballet, there was never a shortage of aspiring females. In 1940, 103 girls competed for places. Tanny was one of the youngest scholarship winners.

3

Two Paths Converge

Tanny was placed in classes that included teenagers and adults since there were few children at her level. The first day, she was mortified because her mother "dressed me up in a pink organdy tutu, or short ballet skirt, and pink slippers; I walked in to find the other kids in severe, professional black practice tights and slippers. I rushed home in a fury and was fitted in black for the next day."[1]

Her first teacher, Kyra Blanc, one of several Russian exiles at the school, was a gentle person, generally well-liked, although some students found her teaching style too strict. Balanchine had hired many superbly trained Russians who had fled their country during or after the hardships of World War I, revolution, and civil war. He was an exile himself, born Georgi Melitonovich Balanchivadze in 1904, the son of a Georgian musician, Meliton Antonovich Balanchivadze, and a Russian mother, Maria Nikolayevna Vasilieva.[2]

In his early years, Georgi was a pampered child, thanks to his mother's lucky purchase of a savings bond lottery ticket in 1901 (worth two hundred thousand gold rubles) before his birth in St. Petersburg, the imperial capital. (A factory worker earned about five hundred rubles per year then.) Meliton, well-known in Georgia, earned little in Russia. Maria's winning ticket enabled the family to live in grand style in a bourgeois neighborhood in St. Petersburg until 1911, as well as to purchase a dacha in Lounatjoki, a rural area of Russia (now part of Finland).[3]

By the time Georgi was seven, his family was no longer affluent. Meliton, neither practical nor used to having money, had squandered a fortune on friends, relatives, and failed business ventures. He'd bought a fancy white horse and carriage, not knowing that the animal came from a circus. Hearing something that sounded like its cue to dance, the horse reared up on its hind legs, "smashing the carriage and shaking up the occupants."[4]

No longer able to afford their former lifestyle, the family had retreated to their big country house, registered in Maria's name. Meliton did not go with them. In Balanchine's recollection of the story, his father had gone to a debtors' prison for failing to pay taxes, but his mother told her children that he was off collecting folk songs. Andrei, two years younger than Georgi, thought that their father had rooms in town that he could not leave, but it was a comfortable house arrest. It may well have been, because the following year Meliton made a trip to Georgia to celebrate his fiftieth birthday with the two children from his first marriage, which may or may not have ended in divorce. (In some accounts, he was a widower. In others, he married Maria after their three children were born. He did not legally acknowledge them until 1906.)[5]

His family had initially envisioned a military career for Georgi, like an uncle and his Georgian, older half brother. Since Lounatjoki offered no educational opportunities, Maria took nine-year-old Georgi and Tamara, his eleven-year-old sister, on a long train trip to St. Petersburg in August 1913. Georgi was supposed to take the exam for the Naval Academy and Tamara, the one for the ballet section of the Imperial Theater School. But there was no place left at the Academy, so he had to go with his mother and sister. A school official who knew the family suggested that the boy audition, too, and Georgi's mother agreed.[6]

The children were examined for two days by an assortment of teachers, as well as given a medical exam. Georgi was asked to walk back and forth, without music, before judges who rated his appearance, energy, posture, and movement. The prima ballerina, Olga Preobrajenska, then near the end of a distinguished dance career, noticed this intense-looking, thin, rather aloof boy and picked him out for particular scrutiny. He wasn't even asked to dance, which is just as well because he didn't enjoy dancing then, Andrei recalled.[7]

Georgi, not his sister, was accepted to the ballet school that year, but unlike Tanny, he was not thrilled to be chosen. According to Andrei, Georgi "cried and screamed horribly" when he learned that his mother was going to leave him at the school. But he was now his parents' shining hope. How could he disappoint them by refusing room, board, and tuition from the government of the czar of Russia? (Minimal fees were required only the first year.)[8]

The first arrival in the empty dormitory, Georgi was so miserable that he ran away to a family member on his mother's side whom the children called Aunt Nadia. She lived close to the school, right next to Vladimir Cathedral. (They had stayed with her whenever they were in town, so Georgi had a fairly good idea how to find her.) A school official tracked him down there, and Aunt Nadia persuaded the boy to go back with him.[9]

"I didn't want to go back," he recalled. "But they brought me back. Somehow, I was unhappy for about a year." Georgi missed his beloved mother most of all, although some of her descendants later described her as "detached," even cold. Deprived of family and forced to do what seemed to him endless and pointless dance exercises, the lonely boy developed a tic that he never outgrew. It made him look like he was suffering from a constant cold or allergy. The first time Jacques d'Amboise saw him in class, "I couldn't take my eyes off Balanchine's nose. He was plagued by a nervous twitch, sniffing continually." That, plus his protruding front teeth, had earned him the nickname "Rat" at ballet school.[10]

On weekends and holidays, the school emptied out. According to his early biographers, Georgi Balanchivadze saw his family only once a year because they couldn't afford to send for him. But the school logbooks indicate that he was given frequent weekend leaves to see relatives in Petersburg and that his immediate family had hosted his classmates for a winter holiday party at their dacha in Lounatjoki, with his father present as a generous host. Throughout the year, Georgi saw family members at Aunt Nadia's place. And yet the sudden loss of daily contact with them was a huge shock to a boy whose education had been sporadic and informal up until his admission to the school.[11]

He was often alone on weekends in the empty school, where he practiced the piano for days on end in the reception hall. These solitary sessions may have provided some solace. His home had always been filled with music; both parents played the piano. Their lessons were augmented, from 1921 to 1924, by advanced studies in piano, music theory, and composition at the Petrograd State Conservatory of Music, where he learned to read orchestral scores and transcribe the notes so that he could play these works on a piano, a useful skill for a choreographer. At the same time, he was performing in ballets and discovering that he could invent them. This talent made him more and more popular, and by his teens, his classmates were eager to have him make dances for them. The ballet world had become his family and choreography his life's work.[12]

When he was thirteen years old, his studies had been interrupted by social unrest fueled by the deprivations of the war. The czar's own army turned against the monarchy, refusing to suppress increasingly violent uprisings of soldiers and workers. On February 27, 2017, a bullet came through a high window of the Imperial Theater School, one incident among many during a week that later came to be known as the February Revolution. On March 2, Czar Nicholas II abdicated in favor of a brother, who refused the honor, thus ending Romanov rule. Since the czar had been the patron of the school and its affiliated theater, the Mariinsky, his abdication left both in limbo for a time.[13]

Meliton seized an opportunity to escape the chaos of the city, now renamed Petrograd, and assure his family's future. He'd accepted a post as minister of culture in the short-lived Georgian republic and left Petrograd in March 1917. Tamara joined him months later, and Andrei left for Georgia in 2018. Their mother stayed behind with Georgi. Was she hoping, in spite of the fact that teachers were deserting the school, that he could resume his ballet studies?[14]

Young people grow up fast during years of violence and deprivation. Georgi got boils all over his body (thirty of them) from malnutrition. He found work stitching for a saddler and played piano in clubs and for silent films, just for food. Later, he and others blamed those hardship years for the tuberculosis that severely damaged his lungs. When the school reopened on November 1, 1918, the ballet students, living in freezing dormitories, tore up floorboards to burn for heat. Pneumonia was a constant hazard of performing for their new audiences of workers and soldiers in the equally freezing Mariinsky Theater, renamed the State Academic Theater of Opera and Ballet. And they were always hungry. At a time when looters were shot, the teenagers raided barges moored along the rivers of the city, stealing fish and anything else they could find. They ate rats that invaded the basement of their school. Stray cats might end up in a stew, perhaps prepared by Maria Balanchivadze, by all accounts an excellent cook.[15]

Contrast this with Tanaquil Le Clercq's comfortable childhood and adolescence, spent under the watchful eye of a "ballet mother" from a prosperous family. Passionate about ballet, Edith darned Tanny's pointe shoes and knit sweaters, tights, and skirts for her. Even before she had started classes at the School of American Ballet, Tanny had received her first pair of the coveted shoes. Today, budding ballerinas are advised to wait until they are twelve. (In Tanny's day, it was not common knowledge that the bones of the foot, ankle, and heel are not fully formed until puberty.)[16]

She might have never trained with Balanchine if he hadn't gotten a lucky break at age twenty, thanks to Vladimir Pavlovich Dmitriev, a wily former opera singer turned government casino croupier. In 1924, Dmitriev persuaded his well-placed contacts in the new regime that it would profit them to show-case Soviet artists abroad. He was granted permission to shepherd a summer tour of Germany for a dance collective of friends, the Young Ballet, for which Georgi Balanchivadze had been making classical and experimental dances for about a year. Dmitriev's feat is all the more astonishing because authorities at the former Mariinsky, now the State Theater, frowned on its company dancers performing with outside groups.[17]

The group included Tamara Geva (born Tamara Zheverzheeva), Balanchivadze's bride, an evening student at the school who had previously taken private ballet classes. A latecomer to an institution transformed by revolution, she had not been part of the original group and lacked the technical training of the others. But she was a beautiful, blue-eyed ash blond who could sing as well as dance. In addition to choreographing classic and avant-garde dances, Georgi accompanied her on piano while Tamara sang for their supper in clandestine, illegal clubs.

For a time, he kept his relationship with Geva hidden from their friends, even after they registered their marriage on October 24, 1922. Georgi Balanchivadze was eighteen and Tamara seventeen, although she later claimed to be three years younger, probably to extend her career, giving rise to a child-bride myth that persisted for decades.[18]

Until they found their own rooms, the couple lived in the five-story house occupied by Tamara's bohemian, cultivated parents, a Swedish singer (and former "high-class" courtesan) and a secular Muslim, half Turk and half Tatar, whose family had never approved of his wife. He had married her when Tamara was six, after the death of his father, from whom he had inherited a highly profitable business providing gold cloth and liturgical items for the Orthodox Church, hardly a booming business after the revolution. Tamara's father, Levko Zheverzheev, cared little for business. A music lover and arts patron, he had amassed a collection of avant-garde art, rich in theatrical memorabilia, which he had donated to the Soviet state. Because of that gift and his many prominent friends in the intelligentsia (including the poet Mayakovsky), the Zheverzheev family had been allowed to stay in their house, even after it was confiscated.[19]

Zheverzheev, who greatly admired his son-in-law, became a second father to him. According to Geva, Georgi's father came from Georgia with Andrei for the marriage ceremony, then returned to Tbilisi, but given the difficulties of travel then, this seems unlikely. By the time Georgi left Petrograd, his mother had already joined her family in Tbilisi. He never saw her, his sister, or his father again. He did not see his brother, Andrei, until 1962, when the New York City Ballet made its first tour of the Soviet Union.[20]

On July 4, 1924, Dmitriev's troupe, renamed the Soviet State Dancers, boarded the steamship *Prussia*. Balanchine later recalled how he had "almost wept" at the sight of bread and butter left unguarded on the dining tables. But joy was muted by tragedy. Seventeen days before, a beloved classmate, Lidia Ivanova, expected to be on the tour with them, had been reported drowned after a boating accident (one of two purported victims). Now they were departing from the very embankment on the Nevsky River where they had gone to view the recovered remnants of the small motorboat, smashed and sunk by a ferry, that she had been riding in.[21]

Lidia's friends and family were convinced that the young ballerina, a strong swimmer, had been murdered. After a prolonged search of the canals, no bodies had turned up. There was a growing suspicion that the boating accident had been staged, after the burial in a forest of her (possibly violated) body, but what, then, of the other missing victim? Not much is known beyond his last name, spelled Klemet, Kelmet, or Klement in newspaper accounts.[22]

Other boats had previously collided at that treacherous passage where the branches of the Neva River emptied into the Bay of Finland. It was a graveyard of sunken barges. Bodies, knocked unconscious, could have easily been trapped there or swept out to sea. What's more, the motorboat was not deemed seaworthy. The three "survivors" of the crash all said that its engine had overheated and stopped. They had not been able to row away from the ferryboat suddenly bearing down upon them in the dark. The Finnish captain of that steamer said that the small skiff had been motionless, unresponsive to his repeated whistles. He could not avoid hitting it.[23]

Alcohol may have played a part, at least among Lidia's party of young merrymakers. Nevertheless, rumors about motives for murder swirled, ranging from the jealousy of an aged prima ballerina or a spurned suitor, to the threat that Ivanova may have posed to some boss of the young Communists she'd been out with that evening. (Geva recounted a tense encounter with one, a few hours after the crash, at the theater where Ivanova had been expected to perform.)[24]

Most of her friends suspected some of the supposed survivors of being agents of the Bolshevik Cheka (secret police), acting on orders from those higher up who wanted Ivanova dead. Georgi Balanchivadze had never been persuaded by any accounts of the "accident" and believed that the trusting young woman had overheard some dark secret that someone did not want

George Balanchine on a vaporetto, Venice, photo by Boris Kochno, 1926. BALANCHINE is a Trademark of The George Balanchine Trust.

her to convey to the West. Long-awaited visas for their tour arrived soon after her death, augmenting his suspicions. This never-resolved mystery haunted Lidia's friends all their lives. Her ghost may have appeared decades later in several Balanchine ballets, according to the scholar Elizabeth Kendall, most notably in one of Tanaquil Le Clercq's signature roles, the doomed girl, courted by Death, in *La Valse*.[25]

In Germany, the troupe struggled. (Tamara Geva sold her hair so they could eat.) And yet, when ordered to return to the Soviet Union, not one dancer complied. Some were still shaken by Lidia's grim fate. All trusted their survival to Balanchivadze's artistic vision, and their faith was soon rewarded.[26]

He was recruited by the influential and innovative Russian-born impresario Serge Diaghilev to choreograph opera ballets, which assured work for the whole troupe. Soon after, Georgi made original works for Diaghilev's company, the Ballets Russes, based in Monte Carlo, a company that had become a magnet for the most inventive, avant-garde artists in Europe.

Diaghilev proposed a name change for his new ballet master in keeping with the French art of ballet: Georges Balanchine. Although Balanchine's position was eminent, his salary was not. Diaghilev paid his dancers a standard 1,500 francs a month (about sixty dollars), more for soloists, and just a bit more to Balanchine (2,500 francs), but they all had to give 20 percent to Dmitriev, as contracted. Balanchine didn't worry so long as he could work. He was in a period of nonstop invention and growth, enriched by collaborations with great dancers, artists, and musicians.[27]

None was more important to him than Igor Stravinsky, whose music he had long admired. Their first collaboration, *Apollon Musagète,* premiered in Paris on June 12, 1928; Balanchine called it "the turning point of my life." Making this classical/experimental ballet for Diaghilev's Ballets Russes, Balanchine was inspired above all by Stravinsky's lyrical, spare score, which he later credited with teaching him that he could "dare to not use all my ideas."[28]

The sudden death of Diaghilev, a diabetic, in 1929, generated a power struggle at the Ballets Russes. Abruptly let go by the new leadership, Balanchine accepted an offer from the Paris Opera Ballet. By then, Tamara Geva was working in New York, and Balanchine was living with a former classmate a year his senior, the prima ballerina Alexandra Danilova, often counted among his wives although they never legally married. (Getting a divorce from Geva finalized by the Soviet government from abroad was next to impossible at that time.)

And then, a year after Diaghilev's death, tuberculosis nearly killed Balanchine. He spent months in a Swiss sanitarium, refused a "pneumothorax operation" proposed by its doctors, and left with impaired lungs. Against the odds, he returned to work. Making new ballets for Danilova and the others, he eventually found limited backing for his own company, Les Ballets 1933. By then, Danilova had joined the Colonel Wassily de Basil Ballet Russe de Monte Carlo.[29]

Enter Lincoln Kirstein, twenty-six, the Harvard-educated son of a department store multimillionaire and prominent arts patron from Boston. Having seen Balanchine's work before, Kirstein was convinced of his genius. When they finally met in London in 1933, he was prepared to make his pitch, in French. Flush with a rather modest inheritance and a pledge of support from an even wealthier Harvard classmate, Edward M. M. Warburg (of the internationally prominent banking family), Kirstein offered to supply whatever

Balanchine would need to build an American dance company that could rival the best in the world. "First, a school," he replied, words Kirstein recollected at the fiftieth anniversary celebration of the founding of their school. Seeing Ginger Rogers dancing with Fred Astaire had convinced Balanchine that America was capable of producing marvels. He arrived in New York with Dmitriev on the steamship *Olympic* on October 18, 1933.[30]

In New York, Georges became George, an American. Multitalented Kirstein—writer, art connoisseur, editor, and founder of Harvard's literary quarterly *Hound and Horn,* a young man skilled at drawing and playing the piano—had another influential friend, A. Everett "Chick" Austin, director of the Wadsworth Athenaeum in Hartford, Connecticut. Kirstein proposed establishing the school there. But Balanchine and Dmitriev refused to set up shop in provincial Hartford, so Kirstein found space on the top floor of the Tuxedo Building at 637 Madison Avenue, near East Fifty-Ninth Street. Balanchine had the walls painted the Mariinsky shade of gray-blue, and the School of American Ballet was born.

Warburg, whose patronage would help to launch Balanchine's short-lived company American Ballet (1935–38), did not share Kirstein's passion for dance. He had never even seen a ballet. But out of friendship he agreed to support a venture unlikely to succeed, especially in the midst of an economic depression. Soon after he saw how much time, aggravation, and money it was going to continue costing him, he bowed out. His role, however, had been crucial in the early years; Balanchine's legendary first American ballet, *Serenade,* had its premiere at the Warburg estate in White Plains on June 10, 1934. George Balanchine was then thirty years old. Tanaquil Le Clercq was not yet five and hadn't begun ballet lessons. She had no idea that Balanchine's life story was going to become an inseparable part of hers.[31]

Mr. B popped into classes from time to time, demonstrating steps and making corrections. He stressed presentation—how a dancer came out onstage, presenting his or herself to an audience, or presenting a foot in a simple *tendu* (where a foot slides along the floor and then points). One didn't grab, one offered a hand and was accepted, and one acknowledged a hand before accepting it. Tanny, an exemplary student, was a product of all these edicts.

Although he was not dancing much anymore because of an old knee injury, Balanchine gave memorable performances in his classes, singing and humming the music when he didn't have a rehearsal pianist. By all accounts, he was a fantastic mime, communicating with moves and gestures, using his hands to show what feet could do. "Caress the floor, use the foot like a hand," he said. He thought that feet should be able to move as fast as hands, a lesson Tanny never forgot.[32]

Vera Zorina, Balanchine's second wife (whose classical dancing career suffered from a late start as well as long breaks for film and theatrical performances), came to realize by her mid-twenties that a new, impressive generation was overtaking her: "I could see it at the school. There was a whole class full of young, little bees—thin, ambitious, full of drive and talent, faster, lighter, more flexible, more daring." When she saw Tanny in class at age twelve, Zorina thought, "Aha, a buzzing little bee—*she* will be something."[33]

But Tanny's first adagio class, where the more advanced students learned to dance slowly and with partners, was something else. "I sat on a bench, in tights," she recalled, "and waited for a boy to offer to dance with me, to hold me up and throw me around. None came near me; I was younger than most of the students, and the boys didn't want to dance with so small a girl. I was told to wait another year and walked out crestfallen, feeling worse than a wallflower at a private party ever felt."[34]

Around this time, she was packed off to a summer camp in Vermont while her mother was caring for a sick relative in St. Louis (probably Edith's mother, who died a year and a half later, at the age of seventy-eight). Leaving Tanny with her father, even for a brief spell, seems to have been out of the question. Her frequent letters to her parents from camp ranged from cheerful to homesick: "I hate baseball its [*sic*] awful and I hurt my finger. . . . P.S. If you expect letters send stamps."[35]

At thirteen or fourteen, she posed for pictures, hoping for modeling jobs (probably her mother's idea). Those jobs didn't come until later, after public acclaim for her dancing. Around that time she had, perhaps, her most embarrassing experience so far. Tanny learned, from Balanchine himself, how not to be "floaty," a word used for a dancer who, as she put it, "is doing the little things badly and feeling very good about it all."[36]

She had stopped doing that, she confessed, the day Mr. B reprimanded her in class. "I was not always well-behaved," she recalled. "I went through a prima-donna period at thirteen, when I was dancing everything wrong and being proud and 'floaty' about it. I was bawled out on behalf of the school by George Balanchine. . . . He almost never raises his voice, but he did then, and it cured me." When Balanchine walked into her class, she'd started showing off, eager to please him. In front of everyone, in the words of Bernard Taper, Balanchine's official biographer (who got the story from Tanny), Balanchine said that she was "a naughty, saucy child, who was putting on gestures so

Tanaquil Le Clercq, ca. 1943. Courtesy of NYCB Archive.

mannered and affectedly pretty that he could not bear to look at her." Then he sent her out of the room. Mortified, Tanny (according to Taper) thought he was "something of an old fogy and a very dull teacher, and she could not see what was supposed to be so great about him." One can imagine her laughing with disbelief if anyone had predicted then that a decade later, she would marry him.[37]

Never discouraged for long, Tanny concentrated on perfecting her moves, practicing the same steps, over and over, with great discipline, but she liked to be silly, too. Tying her long legs into a pretzel, she walked on her knees, "a big clownish grin" on her face. Her dance teachers were not amused. Balanchine saw the pouting teenager in the hall. Tanny, around fourteen by then, was sitting on the floor, her arms folded. "Why not in class?" he asked, in his thick Russian accent.[38]

"Kicked out," she said. The old fogy sent her right back to class. As Tanny moved up from intermediate to advanced classes, she got more personal instruction from Mr. B. By then, they had changed their minds about each other. He had come to appreciate her impish sense of humor, onstage and off. Dancing his steps and following his advice, she had learned to value the man as well as the teacher.[39]

"He cannot help but do interesting combinations," she said, years later. "If he's working on turns, somehow it's an odd turn, it's a *cou-de-pied* back where you think it should be front. Anyone else would make a ballet out of his classroom steps, ten ballets. I've written some of the classes down; the steps are amazing, unpredictable, the way his choreography is onstage."[40]

As a ballet master, Balanchine was patient and gentle, although insistent. As a teacher, he was the same way, almost never losing his temper, especially with children. His harsh reprimand to Tanny, early in her training, seems so out of character that perhaps it was calculated rather than spontaneous. He may have imagined that stern words were required to discipline a student whose promise seemed limitless. If so, it didn't work. Tanny had too playful a nature. Whenever Mr. B dropped in to observe her class, she sometimes tried, slyly, to get his attention. She veered left when everyone else was going right, just to be sure that he would notice her. He certainly did, although her behavior did not attract the positive attention she had hoped for.[41]

Jacques d'Amboise, a scholarship student, had grown up on the tough streets of Washington Heights in upper Manhattan. Six years younger than Tanny, he'd started classes at the School of American Ballet a few years after her. He recalled that Edith Le Clercq presided over "the cabal of ballet mothers." She accompanied Tanny to her classes, sitting in the hallway outside the studio. Thanks to Edith's connections and his own mother's determination, Jacques was soon enrolled in the King-Coit School's after-school program, on scholarship. His mother (whom Jacques referred to as "The Boss") kept telling Edith that her daughter was too skinny: "She should eat more!"[42]

In Miss King and Miss Coit's school and productions, Tanny remained a top attraction, well into her teens, in what Jacques called "kindergarten play and games . . . taken to a sophisticated performing-arts level." Edith continued to assist at King-Coit. In addition to Tanny's scholarship, Dorothy Coit tutored her free of charge after she dropped out of school at age thirteen. Edith also worked as a manager for a Broadway producer and executive secretary for the ballet school she had helped to form on Cape Cod, but these activities were probably in service to her daughter's budding career, not her own personal ambition.[43]

Tanny did not disappoint. She worked hard to improve, taking at least one ninety-minute ballet class a day. She practiced her pirouettes, trying to balance a bit longer each time on the tip of a pointe shoe. Since early childhood, as Dawn Powell observed, Tanny had loved to make an impression. "Half of dancing is showing off," Le Clercq admitted, years later. She danced her best on the rare occasions someone came into class to observe, especially Mr. B and, in her teen years, "just a cute boy in uniform—wow, of course I danced better."[44]

After the Japanese attack on Pearl Harbor, there were more and more boys in uniform. Throughout Tanny's early teens, the United States was at war. Many adult males left the ballet school to join the war effort. Lincoln Kirstein enlisted in 1943. As an art expert, he was later assigned to a team, the Monuments Men, retrieving artworks stolen by the Nazis. Jacques Le Clercq, a veteran of World War I, had reenlisted. He used his bilingual skills at the U.S. Information Service in New York and France, where he had two floors of a villa in Marseille.[45]

The widening chasm between her parents must have been painful for Tanny, although there's no hint of discord in Jacques's many letters home. He seemed to have found it far easier to be a husband and father from a distance. Although he sent "lots of love" to his "Darling Ede," he stayed in France months past the end of the war, in part because of a traffic accident in the winter of 1946, which he blamed on wet pavement, not alcohol. During his recovery in a clinic in Toulouse, both his "Darlings" received long, chatty letters full of comical portraits of his civilian and military colleagues, as well as graphic details (less appreciated, perhaps) of his bouts of colitis, plus a hospital chart with the red and blue zigzagging lines of his pulse and rectal temperatures, which he thought might provide Tanny "choreographic inspiration" for steps.[46]

According to Robert L. Chapman, a distinguished linguist and lexicographer who had befriended Tanny's father while stationed in Toulouse, over "copious drafts of eau de vie," Jacques Le Clercq told the story of how he had known, very early, that his daughter would be a dancer. Around age four, she had burned her hand on the kitchen stove. Rather than screaming, she had pirouetted around the room, singing, "This is the dance of the lady who has just burned her hand on the stove."[47]

4

———— ∞ ————

A "Coltish" Muse

By the time she turned fifteen in 1944, everybody at the School of American Ballet could see that Tanny was extraordinary. Balanchine made a ballet for her to perform with other students at a benefit for the March of Dimes, a charity whose mission during the war years was the eradication of polio. The ballet was a minor work, but after 1956, it haunted him. A deeply superstitious man, Balanchine could never get over the feeling that he had doomed Tanny by casting her in the starring role of a child paralyzed by polio.

In 1944, prevention was the only way to combat the disease. There was no vaccine or cure. A highly contagious virus that entered the body through the mouth, via contaminated food or water, polio could cause paralysis and even death. Since children were more susceptible than adults, terrorized parents kept their progeny away from crowds, especially in the summer.

In Balanchine's ballet *Resurgence,* he danced the role of the Threat of Polio himself, wearing a large black cape in which he covered Tanny, as musicians played the slow part of Mozart's String Quintet in G Minor. She dropped to the floor when he touched her and reappeared, later in the dance, in a wheelchair where "she performed exquisite, pathetic variations to the music with her arms and upper body." Children tossed dimes at her, a shower of dimes, as the music picked up. Dramatically, Tanny rose out of her wheelchair, in rhythm with the now joyful music. She danced again, thanks to all those shiny silver contributions.[1]

And she kept on dancing. "I don't want people who *want* to dance," Balanchine once said. "I want people who *have* to dance." Tanny *had* to dance. She had stopped going to the Lycée Français because dancing took up so much time. "School was like the piano," she remembered, "absolutely not for me. I went to a thing called the New York Tutoring School for a few years, a real cop-out, but I never passed anything. I don't have a high school diploma.

My mother didn't care, but my father was a professor—He was translating books and had lots of degrees—so he was upset for a while."[2]

So was the man who had hired Jacques for the job at Queens College, Dr. Maurice Chazin, chair of the Department of Romance Languages. He and his wife blamed Edith for pushing Tanny's dance career to the detriment of her studies. Although Chazin had been impressed by her father's erudition and superlative translations of French poetry, by the 1950s Jacques Le Clercq's drinking had made him an unreliable teacher. Chazin was torn between concern for the professor's students and the needs of Tanny and Edith. "I can't fire him," he lamented to his wife. "They have no money."[3]

Tanny's father may have pleaded poverty in order to retain his job, even though he was not the family's sole source of income. When Le Clercq was touring Europe, from 1949 through the early 1950s, she availed herself of a J. P. Morgan line of credit, although she wrote her mother about these expenses and promised to pay her back during the dance seasons. It is not clear how much Edith and her brother inherited from the trust her father had established in 1918, but it's likely that their income grew substantially after January 1944, when their mother died. Until then, Jacques's salary at Queens College may have been essential to his family's survival in New York. Whatever Edith's personal means, her husband's precarious situation at work, coupled with his drinking and their marital problems, were more reasons for her to focus on Tanny.[4]

When Jacques Le Clercq realized what a brilliant dancer his daughter was, even he stopped insisting that she go back to school. "I don't care what my daughter does," he said, "as long as she does it well." He tried to tutor her in mathematics but soon gave up. The girl who could watch a complicated series of steps and then perform them perfectly could never remember the multiplication tables.[5]

She was done with formal schooling, except for rigorous ballet classes, but books remained a great pleasure for Tanny, who had a way with words and a wry wit that peppered her letters, although she often misspelled even simple words in English and French. Getting her high school diploma and going to college was not an option she or her mother considered for long. The career of a dancer, especially in classical ballet, was heartbreakingly short, and now was the time to take advantage of every opportunity.

Tanny took ballet classes every day and had rehearsals, too, after she joined Ballet Society and was cast in productions. Some days she danced from morning until night. Ballet took up so much time that just about all her friends were from the dance school. They could see that she was fast becoming Mr. B's prize pupil. "She had a magnetic quality," recalled her closest friend during their teen years, Patricia "Pat" McBride (later Lousada), not to be confused with the ballerina Patricia McBride. "She really could fascinate anybody that she wanted to."[6]

Pygmalion, in Ovid's version of the Greek myth, is a sculptor who carves a woman out of a piece of ivory and falls in love with her. His love seems hopeless, but Aphrodite takes pity on him and the sculpture comes to life. George Balanchine didn't need to mold his ideal woman from clay or carve her from stone or ivory or assemble her image from a palette of colors. His palette was alive, breathing, uncommonly strong, musical, and daring. His canvas was the space he filled with rhythmic, complex movements. He was more drawn to female dancers, although he made some marvelous solos for men, too.

Balanchine's romantic feelings were deeply wedded to the dance, perhaps because as a child, his ballet family had replaced his parents and siblings. Vida Brown, a company dancer who became its ballet mistress, described him as "married to the ballet." And he married only ballerinas, his muses, young women who were not only willing to follow his imaginative lead but who altered his vision with the force of their athleticism and personalities, the unique ways they moved to music and were moved by it. They inspired him to create, although he abhorred the word *create*. "God creates," Balanchine said. "I do not create. I assemble and I steal everywhere to do it—from what I see, from what the dancers can do, from what others do." It was a true imaginative collaboration.[7]

Throughout his life, dance and music nourished him. He painted the air with bodies, but the ways they moved didn't all come from him. He was no Pygmalion, looking for a passive creature born of his own desires. Attracted by personality as much as technical ability, he wanted to see someone move in ways he had never seen or imagined. Tanny showed him what she could do, inspiring Balanchine to "assemble" more and more ballets for her. She became one of his most important muses. That didn't stop him from criticizing her in class. Struggling to do the difficult *entrechat six,* beating her legs back and forth three times before she landed from a high jump, she heard him call out, "Tanny! Your legs look like asparagus— *cooked* asparagus!"[8]

He watched Tanny closely, interested in every aspect of her progress, even her friendships. She and Pat McBride, also a student at the ballet school, were inseparable. "She was a star when I was a beginner," Pat remembered.[9]

Mr. B cast them in a duet together, Élégie, in 1945, when Tanny was just sixteen. Pat was six months older. They wore blue and danced barefoot to a piece of music by Igor Stravinsky, Élégie for Solo Viola. An intimate *pas de deux* for two women was unusual then. Perhaps Mr. B had been inspired by the girls' friendship to develop a short ballet out of what Denby's review called, "two young girls with hands entwined, turning, rising, interlacing, spreading, crouching, and folding in a long, uninterrupted, beautiful adagio sequence."[10]

They danced in front of the curtain, a prologue to the main event. The contrast between these exquisite girls (Pat, a dark brunette, and the lighter-haired Tanny) was part of the choreography. Some people thought it was "a lesbian thing," Tanny said, but she found that idea a "bunch of junk." She thought the dance "very pretty. Two rather wild girls, just twining—bare feet, with hair flowing."[11]

"We were mainly sitting and winding," Pat McBride said, "holding on to each other; it was just this flow which we had to control and sustain. . . . I think it looked a bit odd— maybe a little lesbian." They performed the ballet only three times that season, receiving favorable attention from critics.[12]

Because Tanny lived in an apartment three blocks from the ballet school, the girls often went to her house for lunch, "usually delicious egg sandwiches," Pat recalled. Tanny suffered from anemia, so Edith prepared foods rich in iron to build up her strength.[13]

Pat invited Tanny to spend weekends at her parents' house in Bronxville, Westchester, just north of the city. It was a wealthy community, but the Mc-Brides struggled to make ends meet. Pat's father, Charles, an Irish-born broker, had lost just about everything in the market crash of 1929 and by the 1940s was working as a maintenance engineer. Her mother, Marie, a former opera singer from Italy, was a high-end seamstress with an upscale clientele (including Greta Garbo). Marie McBride worked constantly, to the point of exhaustion, outfitting weddings for her wealthy Bronxville customers. In spite of financial worries, the family was warm and welcoming, with a more casual lifestyle than Edith's. Tanny, who loved visiting them, "yearned to get away from the hothouse life her mother provided," Pat said.[14]

As Tanny got older, her mother "kept herself more in the wings and didn't appear as often at school. Tanny, I suspect, wouldn't have put up with it!" Pat observed. During the dance seasons, in spite of their busy schedules, Tanny and Pat "did all the usual things teenagers do— went to movies armed with a box of our favorite candy, Butternut Crunch," Pat remembered. They "talked about boys and dancers. And endlessly giggled and laughed together."[15]

Until the 1960s, newsreels were commonly shown in movie theaters before the main feature. In 1945, the girls watched one about the Nazi death camps, newly liberated by American soldiers—emaciated, hollow-eyed survivors, piles of dead bodies stacked like firewood. Tanny ran out of the theater before it was over. Pat found her in the ladies' room, sobbing inconsolably. Memories of that newsreel must have contributed to Tanny's sense of doom in Austria during the 1956 tour, a country that had capitulated to Hitler (born in Austria) and collaborated in his roundup of its Jews. At the Lycée many of her classmates, Jews and non-Jews, had been war refugees from Europe.[16]

On August 4, 1945, two days before the first atomic bomb fell on Hiroshima, Tanny appeared as a "guest artist" at the renowned Jacob's Pillow Dance Festival in Lee, Massachusetts, an extraordinary honor for a student. She danced solos from *Raymonda* and *Le Baiser de la Fée*. Miss Tanaquil Le Clercq, a student at the School of American Ballet, was already making a name for herself. After the last performance, she left for Cape Cod with her mother. Although the war had ended in Europe, Jacques Le Clercq was lingering with the USIS in Marseilles.[17]

Nancy Norman, another ballet school friend, also vacationed in Cape Cod. She was the only daughter of the photographer, activist, and writer Dorothy S. Norman and Edward A. Norman, the son of a founder of Sears, Roebuck. Mrs. Norman, her daughter recalled, looked forward to Tanny's visits, being "a tremendous admirer of her sharp wit and her comic sense."[18]

Nancy treasured the memories of those "golden summer days" when they were young women. At the formal tea parties Edith gave at her rented cottage in Dennis, Tanny and her friends were expected to wear white gloves. Whenever Tanny appeared at Nancy's place in Woods Hole, "every young man in the neighborhood fell in love with her."[19]

A year after *Élégie*, Balanchine cast Tanny in her first major role: Choleric in *The Four Temperaments*. This ballet was inspired by Paul Hindemith's Theme with Four Variations (According to the Four Temperaments) for String Orchestra and Piano, a work commissioned by Balanchine in 1938, for which he had paid only five hundred dollars. Each variation was named for one of the four temperaments. The ballet was loosely based on an idea that originated in the Middle Ages, that you could divide people into four basic personality types: melancholic (wise, thoughtful, quiet); sanguinic (enthusiastic, social, active); phlegmatic (relaxed, peaceful); and choleric (short-tempered, fast).[20]

Tanaquil Le Clercq, photo by Edith Le Clercq, ca. 1947. Courtesy of NYCB Archive.

By 1946, Balanchine was ready to make a ballet from the Hindemith piece for the launch of Ballet Society, the company he had founded with Lincoln Kirstein. (They had bought out Dmitriev's interest in 1940.) To fill seats, the ever-resourceful Kirstein decided to sell subscriptions, not single tickets. Even the press was required to subscribe. Ballet Society sold eight hundred subscriptions the first year, short of the twelve hundred needed, and subsequent sales did not cover costs. For fifteen dollars per year, "Participating Members" received one ticket per production. For fifty dollars per year, "Associate Members" got two tickets for all performances and invitations to special events and dress rehearsals. A dollar went far then. You could buy a Buick Sedan for less than two thousand dollars, a more luxurious convertible car for under three thousand. Rent and food were a lot cheaper, too, but most dancers still struggled to survive.[21]

The 4 T's, as the dancers called it, was on Ballet Society's first program, performed in a vocational high school auditorium because Balanchine had no theater yet. He had helped to finance the ballet with money he had earned in Hollywood and on Broadway. Its classical ballet steps were put together in ways new to traditional-minded balletomanes—pure dancing, not a literal enactment of the title.

The astonishing Maria Tallchief, twenty-one, Balanchine's third wife, had married him that summer. She inherited the role of Sanguinic, made for the beautiful, long lines of the ballerina Mary Ellen Moylan, after Moylan left Ballet Society in 1947. The part featured supported extensions, split-legged jumps (*grands jetés*), and the fast pointe work Balanchine favored. He had revolutionized the art form with off-center moves that required daring and speed in order to maintain balance. Maria's feet were so strong, Tanny once told a friend, that Balanchine would put a special emphasis on them in the roles made or tailored for her.[22]

Tanny, just seventeen, was memorable for her "personal dramatic intensity" in the role of Choleric. Announced by staccato chords on strings, followed by thundering arpeggios up and down the piano, she burst onto an empty stage. With a fury of jumps, long arms, and legs open wide, her body made a series of *X* marks in the air. In spite of her speed and exuberance, there was an uncommon grace in the way Tanny quickly folded and unfolded her arms and legs. Because she was so thin, at times her precise movements had an oddly mechanical, insect-like, weightless quality. And yet her steps never looked jarring or unnatural, no matter how complicated. She reminded Moylan of a "great blue crane in flight," an effect enhanced by "ribbonlike things flying off" her costume.[23]

Le Clercq relished this high-energy part of fast turns, high kicks, swiveling steps on pointe, split-legged leaps, as well as the varied, precise footwork of its slower sections, where she did unsupported arabesques on pointe and was lifted and turned by four male partners. But she hated the costume, designed by Kurt Seligmann, a Swiss American surrealist painter. It covered her hands, making it almost impossible to reach for support from a partner. Seligmann's costumes worked with the set, which he had also designed, if you saw the dancers as moving parts of paintings, but they were horrible to dance in. He had ignored the old maxim, *Dress opera singers; undress dancers!* The dancers wore mittens, breastplates, long skirts, and headdresses, "including bonnets that looked like sunbursts."[24]

If Balanchine had seen the costumes in advance, he probably would not have allowed his dancers to be so overdressed. At his ballet school, whenever he entered a class, bulky leg warmers and floppy exercise clothes were immediately discarded, so that he could see how bodies moved. Later, he got rid of the costumes that made it hard for people to see this great ballet, "with all that junk on top," as Tanny put it.[25]

Today, the ballet is always performed in practice clothes. It no longer has the Hollywood ending that Le Clercq had "adored" doing, but Kirstein disliked. It was like "a Busby Berkeley thing," she recalled. "We made a circle and then we got up and down so it looked like a wavy circle." There were actually three circles, with a tight knot of men (hidden, at first) at its center and female dancers comprising the two outer rings. A silent black-and-white film of a rehearsal shows how different parts of these circles slowly rise and descend in turn, an undulating wave punctuated by raised arms that seem to be the tentacles of a giant anemone. At the end of the ballet, a lone male dancer at the center of all the circles is lifted high, descending and rising, again and again, like water pulsing in a fountain. The whole ensemble moves as one, alive and beautiful. Even robbed of this spectacular ending, *The Four Temperaments* is a masterpiece that has remained in the repertoire of many companies. (Although many of his dancers have lamented Balanchine's lifelong propensity for changing his ballets.)[26]

The day of the premiere, the outlandish costumes arrived just thirty minutes before curtain time. Balanchine grabbed a pair of scissors and ran around snipping things. Tanny described the scene: "We all had wigs. I had a hip-length blue wig with a horn in the middle, like a unicorn. And then there were wings, which completely encased the fingers. Well, it was the most awful, suffocating thing, having all ten fingers wrapped up. Anyway, I was crying. . . . And Mr. B came over and said: 'What's the matter? What's the matter?'"[27]

"I said, 'Oh, I'm trapped. I haven't got my fingers. I can't do anything!' And he was very clever. He made a little slit with a scissor, and I put my middle finger through, so that the wings looked like they were right there on top of my hand, but I had this one finger that I could use for undoing my toe shoe or whatever I needed to do. So I fell in love right then and there, if I hadn't been before." (Did she mean romantic love? There's no hint of it in her letters before 1950.)[28]

Tanny was still tortured by the two silver breastplates she had to wear. They would knot up every time she crossed her arms. It was enough to drive one truly mad! In spite of this, she attacked her role with a decisiveness that nailed every step. High-spirited and strong-willed, she had already shown a flair for drama that excited Balanchine's imagination. That drive, emerging from such a fragile-seeming beauty, moved him to set more roles on her.

He cast her in a new ballet, *Divertimento,* set to a score by Alexei Haieff, a Russian-born American. Balanchine conducted the premiere in the Hunter College Playhouse on January 13, 1947. This ballet in five parts, a chamber work for a leading couple and four supporting couples, was praised by critics for its seamless fusion of classical ballet and popular dance. It included tricky, syncopated jumps and turns just behind the beat. This gave the classical steps a jazzy air that went with the music, a fusion of classical and American idioms closer to Copland than Gershwin. Balanchine's upper-body choreography is also percussive at times, with rhythmic, precise shifts of arms and hands, as well as fingers that open and close.[29]

Francisco Monción partnered Maria, who alternated in the lead role of the Ballerina with Mary Ellen Moylan, who had originated it. Tanny had one of the supporting roles. Speaking of the principal couple's part, Le Clercq said that it was "a blues *pas de deux* that is fabulous" with, for the ballerina, "a sort of pussy-cat step which was very pretty. Sometimes turned in, kind of floozy, like two tango dancers." Of her own part, she described "little solo moments, stepping out of the group. The tone of the ending was cute and perky."[30]

The ballet was less popular with Balanchine, who refused entreaties to revive it later. Even if he could remember all the steps, he was parenthetically quoted as saying, "he has used all the movements one way or another in his subsequent ballets and people would see that he has merely been cribbing from himself." Thanks to the memories of his dancers, *Divertimento* has been revived from time to time. In addition to the steps used in other ballets, it covers familiar Balanchine thematic territory: the loner. The fifth man out is alone at its start, until the female lead joins him. At the end, she dances offstage, leaving him alone again.[31]

That year, 1947, classical and modern dance choreographers competed to work with Le Clercq. John Taras cast her as Ariadne in *The Minotaur,* based on a scenario by Lincoln Kirstein, with a commissioned, eponymous score by Elliott Carter, an unpopular ballet with uncomfortable Grecian costumes. Tanny remembered little about it, although critics pronounced her "the find of the evening." She did a *pas de deux* with Taras (in the role of Theseus) and was tugged back and forth by a real string as Theseus struggled with the Minotaur in a stylized labyrinth. Although art and music critics also gave the carefully designed production favorable reviews, the ballet received only two performances.[32]

In the spring of 1947, the wildly modern choreographer and dancer Merce Cunningham chose her for a role in *The Seasons,* the first ballet he made for classically trained dancers. He was only ten years older than Le Clercq, who was seventeen. "She was astonishing to look at," Cunningham reminisced about their first meeting, "this tall slender creature" with "intelligence to match the look." Merce performed in his ballet, too, which opened at New York's Ziegfeld Theater. Tanny's friend Pat McBride had a part as well.[33]

The one-act ballet in nine sections had music by John Cage, the inventor of the "prepared piano," Cunningham's partner in every sense of the word. To change the sound of a piano, Cage would "prepare" it by putting things like screws or bolts or erasers on or between the strings. Whenever these objects got loose, the sound changed even more. That never bothered John Cage, who relished the unexpected. Influenced by Cage, Cunningham gradually introduced randomness into his working process as a way to free the imagination and make room for the unexpected. Music, dance, and the visual elements of a work could develop separately, he declared, coming together in the "common time" of a performance. Even when he had finished setting a dance, Cunningham's choreography, full of abrupt changes of direction, still embodied this idea of playful risk.

For *The Seasons,* more conventional than some of his later ballets, Cage had composed piano music that fit its "Indian" theme. Cunningham had been inspired by Native American art and legends of the U.S. Northwest about changing seasons, as well as Hindu philosophy. Just like the seasons, the light onstage began in darkness, grew, died, and revived. "For summer and spring," Le Clercq recalled, "the girls tied on little tails. That got a lot of laughs."[34]

The sets and costumes were by Isamu Noguchi. Dancers wore gray tights and leotards with uneven leg lengths. These were painted with swirling white lines that picked up even the dimmest light from the magnesium flashes on the stage. Small explosions, like lightning, punctuated the ballet, and the long prop list was unusual, too. It included birdlike hats, butterfly nets, and a kite.[35]

Other dancers found Cunningham aloof and difficult, but Le Clercq declared him "so nice to work with" and his instructions easy to follow. "He told you the counts and he really knew. It worked." She especially enjoyed doing this ballet "because we didn't have to wear toe shoes." *The Seasons* got a glowing review from John Martin, the tough critic of the *New York Times,* who likened it to Diaghilev's experiments of the 1920s. It was popular with most audiences, but some found it ridiculous. Cunningham became incensed during one performance where the laughter seemed particularly persistent and inappropriate to him. He grabbed Tanny's hand to stop her from taking a curtain call at the end. She held back as he wished but later said that at that moment she had been thinking, "It doesn't matter if they laughed, let's take a bow."[36]

Cunningham was in awe of her beauty, wit, and "brilliant theater sense." One day, at the beginning of their collaboration (which later blossomed into friendship), he had asked her how she liked to dance: "She stood on one leg, the other slightly bent and turned in, thought a moment, and then said, 'Well, I like to dance either very fast or very slow.'" Cunningham laughed as he recounted this story, many years later. He thought her answer was "marvelous."[37]

That important year, Tanaquil Le Clercq was awarded the first fellowship ever offered by Ballet Society. Her selection, by George Balanchine himself with "no hesitation," was announced on a special page of the souvenir program Ballet Society published to commemorate the 1946–47 season. Tanaquil, the brief article revealed, had also studied acting, drawing, and modeling. Clearly, she had other options than to remain in Balanchine's company. By selecting her out of all others, he had declared that she was the young dancer he valued most. Photos of the seventeen-year-old appeared in the program, including a glamorous portrait with her hair dressed in the fashion of the times, her look knowing and mature. The girl whom many critics and dancers had described as endearingly "coltish" had become an elegant young woman.[38]

Tanaquil Le Clercq, Ballet Society Souvenir Program, 1946–47. Jerome Robbins Dance Division, The New York Public Library for the Performing Arts.

5

---○○○---

The Ballet Society Years

Le Clercq had been invited to join Ballet Society at seventeen, right after she graduated from the School of American Ballet. She continued to take classes there, most often the company classes, sometimes taught by Balanchine, who also taught B and C classes (the latter being at a higher level). He was now artistic director of the Society and Lincoln Kirstein its general director.[1]

Kirstein, born in 1907, the second child of a prosperous and philanthropic Boston family, didn't have vast wealth himself. At twenty-one, he had received a guaranteed income of one thousand dollars per year, later augmented by trust fund money and dividends from stocks and securities. His father, who had made millions as a partner in Filene's department store, generously funded his son's artistic ventures and gave him a direct, yearly allowance of more than four thousand dollars. This money did not come without strings. Well into middle age, Kirstein repeatedly pleaded with his father for increases to his allowance to support his ventures. The poet W. H. Auden, a friend, called him "a very *poor* millionaire."[2]

Out of approximately $250,000 Kirstein received from his family over a six-year period, he put $173,000 into the ballet company, and only (briefly) took a modest salary of fifty dollars per week when his father made this a requirement of his continual support. In addition to donating millions of dollars from his own funds over the course of his life, Kirstein found other donors to keep the school and company going. "The only justification I have," he wrote in a letter to Lucia Chase in 1946, was to allow George Balanchine "to do exactly what he wants to do in the way he wants to do it." Balanchine said, with a nod to Kirstein's Jewish heritage and lack of religious convictions: "Lincoln is a true Christian, even though he won't admit it. He gives you money and runs away before you can thank him." A committed, secular leftist since at least the 1930s, Kirstein had a firm belief in art for the masses.[3]

Lincoln Kirstein and George Balanchine looking at prints and designs, photo by Tanaquil Le Clercq, 1955. BALANCHINE is a Trademark of The George Balanchine Trust. Jerome Robbins Dance Division, The New York Public Library for the Performing Arts.

During the two years of Ballet Society's existence (1946–48), the company ran deficits, as it continued to do after becoming the New York City Ballet. In the early years, Balanchine made many of the new dances himself and sometimes did without costumes and scenery. Influenced by experimental modern dancers since his youth, he had begun to show a taste for non-narrative works of pure movement where dancers wore simple rehearsal clothes, what Kirstein called, "the ballet's metaphor for nudity." It was a preference born only in part of necessity. Convinced that "the dance will speak for itself," Balanchine objected to program notes for any of his ballets, even the ones with stories, like *Orpheus,* a major triumph for Ballet Society in 1948.[4]

From the 1930s to the 1960s, Balanchine received no salary from the school or Ballet Society, subsisting on royalties from his work in theater, film, and other companies. In spite of Kirstein's initial fears of losing him for good to Broadway and Hollywood, Balanchine's primary loyalty was to his company and school. He expected the same of his dancers, even though they were paid a pittance, eighteen dollars per show and no pay for rehearsal time. As the dancer Carolyn George (later Mrs. Jacques d'Amboise) wrote in her diary in 1946: "Balanchine was our God. It's not so easy to explain. We didn't pray to him. We asked for help for our dancing because he was all knowing, all seeing, you believed with all your heart that what he saw in your dancing was absolutely true, and right. No one else I have ever known had such a clear vision of what we were each struggling to do."[5]

The first year, Ballet Society had no proper theater. The dancers performed in many venues, including the cramped, narrow stage of a vocational high school for the fashion industry, the Central High School for Needle Trades on West Twenty-Fourth Street. The company's first performance there, on November 20, 1946, a white-tie event that attracted prominent people, was the premiere of Balanchine's *Four Temperaments.* A few hours before curtain time, the dancers weren't sure they would get to perform, since the musicians had not been paid yet. "Kirstein was out on the town, scrounging dollars from the munificent," Esther Magruder Brooks, a corps member, recalled. "He arrived back just in time for the curtain to go up, with the full orchestra in the pit. From then on, through many crises, we were told to call ourselves *Dancers for Rockefeller,* and those old enough, were to vote for him."[6]

After months of rehearsals, that evening was the sole performance, a "one-night stand," as Esther put it. By 1947, Ballet Society had enough subscribers to move to the City Center for Music and Drama on West Fifty-Fifth Street, space they shared with the New York City Opera and traveling companies. Built in 1923 for the Shriners, a Masonic fraternity, City Center (previously called the Mecca Temple), looked like a Disneyesque, Arabian fantasy. The Shriners could not pay their city taxes, so New York City had confiscated the building and rented it out for five hundred dollars per performance, a huge expense for Ballet Society. Morton Baum, a musical, Harvard-educated tax attorney, chaired the finance committee that administered the space for the city. Although the venue was far better than a high school auditorium, its small stage, once used for secret Shriner ceremonies, was not ideal for opera or ballet. "I could do a couple of jumps and be past center stage," Jacques d'Amboise recalled.[7]

Dancers had to exercise a mindful restraint. Sometimes they crashed into the scenery when they leaped with legs wide open. The wings were so narrow, Maria Tallchief wrote in her memoir, that they allowed "just enough room to stand and breathe and be nervous in; trying out steps there required the talents of a contortionist." Stagehands were primed to catch dancers leaping offstage, to avert disaster. Stage left was particularly tight. Stage right, where Balanchine always stood, afforded no space to adequately warm up before going onstage either. Backstage facilities were less than ideal. There was no crossover from one side of the stage to the other, so dancers sometimes had to race behind the building, through snow, to reenter the theater on the other side.[8]

Some of the studio floors were riddled with splinters, others too slippery. Jacques remembered a large, windowless studio on the fifth floor "where the Masons used to hold their ceremonies. It wasn't well heated. The floor was slick, so we used to use Tide powder to keep from slipping. But if you sat down on the floor, when you got up you would have a white spot on your ass!" In hot weather, the dancers suffered under the house lights. "They used to deliver huge blocks of ice, the dancer Edward "Eddie" Villella reminisced, "and they would take it into the alley in the back, and that was the air conditioning."[9]

But the enormous hall offered advantages, too. Because its sections were not deep, there was an intimacy between performers and their fans. When the stage lights weren't too bright, dancers could make eye contact with audience members, even those seated in the balcony. And yet the width of the space allowed for huge crowds, appropriate for a former temple baptized "the people's theater." It held 2,250 people, although obstructing pillars made for partial views in a few notorious spots.[10]

In 1948, the top ticket price was $2.50. Even so, on most nights at least half the tickets went unsold. At some matinees, Jacques d'Amboise recalled, you could count more dancers onstage than people who had come to watch them. The audiences may have been small, but they were enthusiastic and as fascinating as the performers. Frank O'Hara, a regular, wrote an ode to Le Clercq, published in 1970. William Faulkner had been seen smoking his pipe in the lobby during intermission. Salvador Dalí, easily identifiable by his "mustache and gold cane," had "an aisle seat in Row R," and W. H. Auden came to the ballet "in his bedroom slippers (even when it was snowing outside)," d'Amboise wrote in his memoir. "Balanchine gave the impression he was unaware of the empty seats. Supremely confident, he never worried." When Lincoln Kirstein bemoaned the number of people who left after the first or second ballets, Balanchine reminded him of all the people who had stayed.[11]

More and more of them were there to see Le Clercq, who had vaulted over the usual steps on the way up to ballerina status. She had never danced in the corps de ballet, having distinguished herself so early. And her look was so distinctive that it's hard to imagine her blending into a group. Balanchine made dramatic and comic roles expressly tailored to her unique qualities. In Russia, he had grown up with short ballerinas with small hands and feet. Tanny's thin, elongated body was as striking as her stage presence.

When Jacques d'Amboise joined the company (by then renamed New York City Ballet) at the age of fifteen, it was clear to him that Le Clercq, just out of her teens, was Balanchine's latest muse. Little Eddie Villella, a few years younger than Jacques, had started studying at the school in 1946. Even as a kid, he had been intrigued, along with everyone else, by the question of which ballerina Balanchine would pick as his next source of inspiration. "I had the feeling," Villella wrote in his memoir, "all the ballet mothers sitting in the hall would have gladly thrown their twelve-year-old daughters at him on the chance he'd become entranced with one of them and make her a star." When Eddie was ten and Tanny seventeen, he spotted her sipping a drink with Balanchine at Schrafft's, a restaurant near the school. "He was oblivious of everyone but her. By then everyone knew he was in love with her." Everyone but Tanny, it seems.[12]

That didn't keep him from showing interest in others, although he was old-school, courtly, and respectful. One day in 1947, Balanchine invited Esther Magruder, beautiful, blond, and twenty-one, to lunch at Sammy's Deli on Madison Avenue, a popular ballet school hangout. She ordered *escargots,* which came on a plate with round hollows to hold the snail shells. When Esther started eating from the center of the plate, Balanchine protested that the proper way was to eat the outside circle first, working your way toward the center. Tanny might have laughed that off and gone on eating as she pleased. But to Esther, "tired of darning toe shoes and washing tights," it seemed a critical turning point, symbolizing more.[13]

Dancers in Balanchine's school and company (especially the females), knowing how jealously he demanded that they save their energy for *his* ballets, concealed their outside activities from him, even those not related to dance. Although they revered his genius, many chafed at his dictatorial

Left to right: Romana Kryzanowska, Esther Magruder, and Aline Du Bois, School of American Ballet students relaxing, ca. 1942. Jerome Robbins Dance Division, The New York Public Library for the Performing Arts.

nature. Esther had growing doubts about whether to spend her life in Balanchine's dance company. It could make you or break you, sometimes both at once. "We all loved him," she said, but Balanchine "had to have cogs for his machine." She thought it was "one of the greatest machines" for ballet ever made, but his dancers paid a steep price for being part of it. He told them what to eat, what books to read and what music to listen to. He insisted that they had to live for ballet, as he did. "I got to the point where I never wanted to see him again," she said. Without alerting Balanchine, Esther left Ballet

Society abruptly, returned to Paris, where she had spent her childhood, and danced for other companies.[14]

It took uncommon stamina to work with Balanchine. He had brought a Russian rigor to the training of American ballerinas, a discipline that was almost military. Although Georgi Balanchivadze hadn't made it into the Russian Naval Academy, Tamara Geva found in him "a combination of poet and general." When he and Kirstein started the School of American Ballet, they had joked about calling it the "West Point of dance." At the same time, there was nothing regimented about his choreography. It pushed the human body beyond the controlled movements of the classical ballets of his youth, toward whatever he imagined possible.[15]

Esther's friend Romana Kryzanowska, who had started at Balanchine's school in 1942, hoping to be "a very great ballerina," suffered from a problematic ankle. Balanchine referred her to his friend Joseph Pilates, a man he considered "a genius of the body." (Romana was so impressed by the treatment she received that she eventually became a renowned Pilates instructor and took over the running of the studio in New York after the deaths of Joseph and his widow, Clara.) In 1944, while still a ballet student, Romana left for Peru after marrying a Peruvian businessman she called the "Alpaca King," Pablo Mejia, but his prosperous family suffered business reversals due to changing wool markets and Peruvian politics. Returning to New York with her two children in 1958, Ramona taught ballet and Pilates. Her son, the dancer/choreographer Paul Mejia, joined Balanchine's company in 1964, at the age of seventeen. A soloist who performed principal roles, Mejia came to play, unwittingly, a role in Balanchine's personal history which resulted in his banishment from the company in 1969.[16]

Every dancer who left created space others had to fill, since Ballet Society was such a small company. During the dance seasons, the pace was intense. Le Clercq did two or three ballets a performance, which she preferred: "I would be scared doing just one, because one was like a warm-up. With two, if you disgrace yourself in something, you have a second chance."[17]

She was already having a powerful impact on Balanchine's aesthetic. In interviews, he expressed a growing preference for thin, tall female dancers with long necks and limbs. Tanaquil Le Clercq was the prototype of what came to be called "the Balanchine ballerina." Her naturally elegant line, coupled with a high extension, speeded the evolution of his taste. He was fusing the Petipa school of his youth and his off-center American style of ballet. "I like tall people," he said, when asked about this choice, decades after he had firmly established the New York City Ballet. "It's because you can see more."[18]

The tallest females he had ever worked with walked on four legs. In 1942, he had staged a *Ballet of the Elephants* (to a commissioned Circus Polka by Stravinsky) for a cast of fifty female dancers astride fifty elephants (in pale-blue tutus, earrings, and jeweled headbands) for the Ringling Bros. and Barnum & Bailey Circus. The elephants were the stars of the show, sharing the spotlight with Vera Zorina, who at one point was cradled and lifted by the trunk of the lead elephant.

As a child, Tanny may have seen that show, and most probably the hit movie On *Your Toes* (1939) in which Zorina performed a role that he had choreographed for Tamara Geva. The innovative musical, mixing ballet, jazz, and tap, was supposed to be a film from the start, starring Fred Astaire, Balanchine's favorite dancer. But he had turned the part down, so *On Your Toes* first came to life on a Broadway stage, where Geva was partnered by Ray Bolger, later the Scarecrow in *The Wizard of Oz.*

A Broadway star by the early 1930s, Geva had helped Balanchine find work soon after his arrival in New York. He made memorable dances for her that contributed to the transformation of choreography for the musical theater. By then, he and Danilova had gone their separate ways, but she always referred to herself as Balanchine's second wife, making for some confusion as to how to count Zorina, his second legal wife. Some sources count five wives, although Balanchine legally married four women, all dancers, Le Clercq being the final one.

In October 1940, the month she entered the School of American Ballet, a hit musical opened on Broadway, *Cabin in the Sky,* which Balanchine had worked on with Katherine Dunham, the founder of one of the first "Negro" dance companies in America. In 1945, Dunham opened a school at 220 West Forty-Third Street, near Times Square. Advertisements in the press offered classes in "Primitive Rhythm—Percussion—Ballet—Modern—Dunham Technique," some taught by dancers in her company. According to a teacher of Dunham Technique at the school, Walter Nicks, Tanny and her more adventurous friends would "sneak down" to the school to learn from him. "Studying Afro-Cuban dance at the Dunham school was a craze for a while," Jacques d'Amboise said, but he maintained that there was no need for concealment; Mr. B encouraged his students to take outside classes, as long as these weren't in ballet. Arthur Mitchell said that Balanchine even "sent some of the ballerinas to study at her school."[19]

Dunham's curriculum, like her choreography, was eclectic, sophisticated, and constantly evolving. Todd Bolender, who had choreographed Tanny's first public appearance at age five, taught ballet at the school. Arthur Mitchell took his first ballet classes with Karel Shook there in 1951. Many actors attended classes—including James Dean, Sidney Poitier, Shelley Winters, and Marlon Brando. Dunham's mix of ballet, modern, and Afro-Caribbean dance styles was as revolutionary for New York in the 1940s and 1950s as her racially integrated classes.[20]

Classic Dunham Technique, taught at the *barre,* involved bending the knees in a "hinge" position and then arching the back while keeping the knees bent. The pelvic movements taught at the school were radical for that time, "not just contracting forward and back, but also moving side to side, on the diagonal, in a circle, or in a figure eight," in the words of Dunham biographer Joanna Dee Das. "After the barre warm-up, students learned movements that traveled across the studio floor on the diagonal, called Progressions," including rhythmically complex Caribbean dance steps.[21]

By 1946, her school was called the Dunham School of Dance and Theatre and offered an array of classes that encompassed foreign languages, anthropology, philosophy, and history. Like Le Clercq's first teachers at King-Coit, Dunham was a multiculturalist open to many influences, including Indian classical dance, but her primary focus was on the historical and cultural roots of the African diaspora. Combining a wide second-position *plié* with a pelvic contraction was a defining part of the Dunham Technique.[22]

The way Tanny had learned to undulate her torso at Dunham's school must have informed her daring performance in Balanchine's *Orpheus* (1948), a ballet that is still occasionally revived by the New York City Ballet. Based on Ovid's version of the ancient Greek myth, its score, commissioned by Ballet Society, was composed by Stravinsky in close collaboration with Balanchine. Apart from the sections in which Le Clercq danced, the music was measured, stately, with a ritualistic, otherworldly solemnity. Isamu Noguchi designed the equally spare, abstract scenic elements and costumes. Maria Tallchief (born Elizabeth "Betty" Marie Tall Chief) won acclaim in the role of Eurydice, the bride of Orpheus bitten by a poisonous snake. At a rehearsal, Stravinsky asked Balanchine, "How long is it going to take Maria to die?" Answering himself, he asserted, "She must do it in five counts."[23]

Nicholas Magallanes gave a theatrically powerful performance as the grief-stricken Orpheus, the poet/musician who tries to rescue Eurydice from Hades. Le Clercq, in the smaller role of the leader of the Bacchantes, priestess

Katherine Dunham, January 1, 1950. Bettmann/Getty Images.

followers of the god of wine and ecstasy, Dionysius, made an indelible impression. At the end of the ballet, the Bacchantes tear Orpheus to pieces in a frenzied dance, their arrival announced with *grands battements,* legs raised high that quickly descend, resounding like thunder. This was a departure for Balanchine, who generally insisted that his ballerinas make their steps as quiet as possible.

Tanaquil Le Clercq, eighteen years old, was praised for her dramatic fierceness and the angularity of her movements. She danced in a pink, long-haired

Tanaquil Le Clercq and Nicholas Magallanes, *Orpheus,* photo by George Platt Lynes, 1948. Used with Permission of The George Balanchine Trust and The George Platt Lynes Estate. Choreography by George Balanchine ©The George Balanchine Trust. Jerome Robbins Dance Division, The New York Public Library for the Performing Arts.

wig (left over from *The Four Temperaments*) with a snake wrapped around one leg. In this dance, legs become weapons. Her high extension in a *grand battement,* crotch exposed, would have been considered vulgar in the Russian and European traditions that Balanchine inherited, where ballerinas did not customarily raise their legs higher than their waists. Moncíon said, years later, that in this role Le Clercq had never been equaled: "One of our gamest dancers—she had contractions of the torso that were straight out of modern dance, but it was with a style." Whether her inspiration came from Dunham directly or via Balanchine, Le Clercq shared with both of them a talent for taking ideas from anywhere and making them hers. Whatever she did was infused with her own forthright personality and theatricality. Critics applauded the jazzy American jauntiness of her dancing.[24]

It had taken her hours of rehearsal to make the simulation of tearing off Orpheus's arms look convincing. Magallanes said, "She was very fragile, very slim. This made her more ferocious, like a whiplash." To watch her knife-sharp movements was to hear every note of Stravinsky's nerve-jangling music. "George [Balanchine] counted it for me," Le Clercq recalled, necessary because of all the silences in the score, but soon she didn't need him to do it.[25]

She was still a soloist then, not yet a principal dancer like Maria Tallchief, four years older and the company's biggest box office draw. Tallchief, considered America's first major prima ballerina, was of Native American ancestry, on her father's side. Her great-grandfather was an Osage chief. Her father, Joseph Alexander Tall Chief, had been wealthy since childhood, ever since oil was discovered on the tribe's land in Oklahoma. Like Le Clercq, Tallchief had benefited from having a family with the means to pay for her dance and piano lessons. She was a talented pianist, too, with perfect pitch. This could be a liability if any musician in the orchestra was off-key. Then Maria might be "in agony," Tanny wrote.[26]

Tallchief had studied with Bronislava Nijinska, the celebrated sister of Nijinsky, considered the greatest male dancer of his time, but Balanchine's technique, extremely fast and often daringly off-balance, was new to her. The speed made his off-center moves possible as without it, the dancers risked falling. Balanchine had "begun to shake the nineteenth century out of twentieth-century dance," Todd Bolender said. Le Clercq had helped him to do it.[27]

Zorina, who had danced in the 1930s with Colonel Wassily de Basil's Ballet Russe de Monte Carlo, described the process of becoming a Balanchine dancer. It "mostly involved the hip—as if I was learning to move sideways after having kept my body straight up and down." His ballerinas displayed an extreme turnout (the rotation of the leg and foot to the side) that had been new to Tallchief as well, so Balanchine gave her private lessons. She had danced with a newer incarnation of the Ballet Russe de Monte Carlo before joining his company at eighteen. Le Clercq, too, worked to achieve maximum turnout, which rarely came naturally to dancers.[28]

When Maria first met Tanny, she saw "a coltish creature who still had to grow into her long, spindly legs. Those legs went on forever—it seemed as if her body could barely sustain them." Le Clercq was only five feet six and a half inches tall, but because a large part of her height came from her legs, she was often labeled "coltish" and soon tired of the word. Dance critics, she declared in an interview, decades later, "tend to pigeon-hole dancers when they are young, and sometimes fail to give them credit when they try to do something new in their artistic development. I, for example, was described early in my career as long-legged, coltish and a natural comedian. And for years afterwards I kept reading those descriptions, even about roles in which I was quite different, and long after I had ceased to be coltish, if I ever was!"[29]

Maria, a stylish woman who favored designer clothes, once she could afford them, admired Tanny's elegance. "She had the long, willowy look of a fashion model, dressed stylishly in long skirts and sweaters, and had a lovely presence . . . articulate, witty, and chic." To Ruth Gilbert, who joined the company at the age of fifteen in 1948, Le Clercq and Pat McBride "looked like they'd stepped out of the pages of *Vogue*."[30]

For her debut performance with Ballet Society, Tallchief had been paired with Le Clercq in *Symphonie Concertante,* based on a ballet that Balanchine had originally made for his students in 1945. The premiere of the revived and reimagined ballet, set to Mozart's Symphonie Concertante in E-Flat Major for Violin, Viola and Orchestra, took place in the new space at City Center on November 12, 1947. Le Clercq danced in all three movements, doing two *pas de deux* with Tallchief and, in the second, *Andante* movement, a *pas de trois* with Maria Tallchief and Todd Bolender, the lone male. The 1947 performances of the ballet had twenty-two women in the cast—six soloists, fourteen in the corps, plus Tanny and Maria. (Balanchine liked to give performance opportunities to as many of his students as possible.)

Three years later, *Symphonie* was well received on the company's first tour of England. It is a strictly classical ballet with innovative ideas. In the first movement, the corps members briefly link arms like chorus girls as they line up across three sides of the stage. At the end of the second movement, the six soloists surround the three principal dancers and sweep them offstage in a smooth wave of *bourrées.* The lone male dancer turns from one partner to the other, or kneels, back to the audience, to admire them both. Finally, he takes measured steps as he exits the stage, surrounded by a shimmer of tutus, as if carried off by a wave.

Balanchine contrasted Le Clercq and Tallchief, having them dance to separate musical lines, the violin (Le Clercq) and the deeper-toned viola

Tanaquil Le Clercq and Patricia McBride, late 1940s. Courtesy of NYCB Archive.

(Tallchief). At times the women's *bourrées, entrechats,* leaps, turns, and arabesques were synchronized, at other times they followed each other in an almost fugal pattern, or they each did a different series of steps. The language of the part made for Le Clercq is feather-light, filled with hopping arabesques and fluttering *entrechats,* a dance for a gazelle.

Although Balanchine's choreography seemed to come directly from his subconscious, the steps were developed in rehearsal. He didn't work them out, alone at home, apart from going over the music he had chosen until he could have conducted it or played it on the piano from his own reduction of the score, neither being an unusual feat for him. "Without dancers I cannot do anything," he said. "If I didn't have dancers I like to be with—because I like to look at them and show how they look and move—[t]hen I would never think of dance." He watched his dancers intently, imagining where he might take them even as he went wherever their qualities took him. (Quite often, they took him by surprise.)[31]

In *Symphonie Concertante,* for example, he may have subtly expressed his attraction to the delicate, dramatic Le Clercq and the more mature, powerful Tallchief. One can picture him turning from one exquisite ballerina to the other, marveling at being in the center of such beauty. And yet this ballet is pure dance, not high drama. The lone male dancer, back to the audience, briefly kneels before the two women, suggesting the position of the choreographer and spectators. It is a gesture easily eliminated, as it has been in some revivals.

Whether the male dances with the women separately or in a threesome, there is no implied rivalry. All is in service to the dance. He stretches out an arm to one, and then the other arm to the other, his head swiveling like a spotlight. They turn toward and away from him, and one or the other circles around the other two. He moves them about the stage like potted plants, unearthly flowers that turn with exquisite slowness on one thin stem.

There is no narrative, never any sense that he is struggling to make a choice. He does a brief *pas de trois* with two of the soloists as well as the principals, in classical steps that follow Mozart's music with a precision that is synesthetic: We see the music and hear the dance. The interchanging geometric patterns formed by rising and falling arms and legs (the corps members sometimes in sync and sometimes mirroring and/or echoing each other's steps and gestures) delineate the musical lines of the alternately stately and sprightly music. Occasionally the female soloists support each other, taking the traditional male role, joining hands as one does a turn on pointe or the other does an *arabesque penchée*. This is not a celebration of romantic love, but of Balanchine's love for Mozart. In the *Presto* the pace intensifies; the two principal females pop up like spring-loaded toys. The ballet ends with all the dancers raising their arms high, and then opening them wide to include the audience in a collective embrace.

Balanchine's *Symphony in C,* a year later, was a major critical success for the company in 1948. That may be why the New York City Ballet dropped *Symphonie Concertante* from its repertoire in 1952. It's similar to the more popular *Symphony in C* in the use of a large corps, dressed in gleaming tutus, lined up across the stage (sometimes in a three-sided position bordering the wings as well) and then divided into smaller groups. Its three movements are so challenging that some dancers called the ballet "Symphonie Concentrate."[32]

Mikhail Baryshnikov chose to reconstruct *Symphonie* for American Ballet Theatre from notation in 1983, and it was performed by the company many times since then. When Robbins saw the 1983 revival, he missed a gesture he recalled from the original: the entire company, including the principal "girls," as he called them, had crossed the stage, side to side, as they faced front, and flicked their hands, "turning them sharply from the wrists with each beat of the music . . . like sprinkling cold water or icy, little drops of spicy condiments on the rest of the ballet." This gesture was later restored, probably at his instigation.[33]

Maria Tallchief found the whole ballet "beautiful—just pure classical dancing and quite difficult." She considered it a vehicle for learning how to dance as if she had been a Balanchine ballerina from the start. Tanny liked the "pretty music, nice steps, nothing bravura." The ballet does contain a brief bravura solo for the male, who is used mainly for support. According to Suki Schorer, a ballerina who joined the company in 1959 and became a principal dancer and an eminent teacher and writer on Balanchine technique, he believed that support should be so subtle that "it should generally look as if the woman is turning with her own force, even when she turns a long time, and that she is on her own balance, almost completely by herself."[34]

Balance was one aspect of dancing Le Clercq struggled with at first. She was in awe of Tallchief's rigorous technique, the product of years of working with Nijinska and dancing with the Ballet Russe de Monte Carlo. As they rehearsed together, Tanny confessed, she was envious of the way Maria could effortlessly execute difficult classical steps, whipping off *fouetté* turns or beating her legs together rapidly in a perfect *entrechat-six*. "She was trying a particular step over and over, and every time she danced it, something went wrong," Tallchief recalled, until the teenager seemed about to burst into tears. Tallchief gave her some hard-won advice: "Tanny, I wouldn't get so upset. Something is always going to go wrong. You might as well get used to it." Soon Tanny was performing complicated moves with ease, and it was Maria's turn to be amazed. Not being originally trained by Balanchine, Tallchief was the one who had felt, at first, deficient. "I didn't understand the importance of feet and turnout until I met Balanchine," she said.[35]

Throughout 1947–48, Tanaquil Le Clercq was listed on every program, except for the odd special event. In the fall and winter seasons, she was often scheduled for three ballets a performance, matinees and evenings. If someone were sick or injured, she might be called upon as a last-minute substitute. Since the company was so small, even principal dancers like Maria thought nothing of filling in for a soloist or corps member. They all knew the steps. "I did not work like a dog," Tanny recollected, more than thirty years afterward. "I could have worked harder. But everything came easy to me." Even so, she added, "it was hard work." She's making a nuanced point, only superficially contradictory: her innate ability made hard work rewarding, not a strain, although she acknowledges that she could have pushed herself more. She worked hard to please the public as well as herself. "Later on I didn't care as much, but in the beginning, when I was starting, I'd get the newspapers the next morning to read the critics; it was really nice to be mentioned and to see that you were good."[36]

With modesty, Le Clercq explained the high number of roles created for her as partly luck. When the company began, they didn't have a lot of ballerinas. She was taller than most of the others, so "If you needed a body, I was the only one. . . . Ballet wasn't that popular; there weren't that many people training. . . . Today, every girl in the corps de ballet has fantastic legs and feet . . . like a master race, but they weren't screened then, and they didn't drop you unless you were eight feet tall—everybody was there. And then, I *was* more talented than the others, and I was a little interesting."[37]

Compared to ballet dancers today, she was not tall, but in pointe shoes, a ballerina can add five or six inches to her height. On pointe, she was taller than most of the male dancers in the company. That didn't matter, if they were skilled at partnering. "Partners make a great difference, definitely," she said. "They make you look better and they help you. . . . I danced with Jacques when he was just starting—when I was finishing, he was starting—and he was excellent, and Nicky [Magallanes] was a very good partner, and Frank [Moncion]."[38]

Balanchine, about five feet eight inches tall, according to himself and others, loved to demonstrate partnering. His male dancers grew tired of standing around in class, watching him lift his adored muses. If you are "fortunate enough, as I was, to be connected with the genius of Balanchine," Maria Tallchief told an interviewer, "then you are not only poetry in motion, but you are actually the music." It was a feeling shared by all of Balanchine's ex-wives, who regularly turned up for company classes.[39]

Vera Zorina was one, although wagging tongues had cast her as the treacherous woman who'd kicked Balanchine out of their apartment. Despondent on a Central Park bench, as the story went, he eventually found his way to a hotel. Katherine Dunham traced him there and arrived with food, champagne, and six beautiful dancers from her company. They danced and partied "all night!" Balanchine told Jacques d'Amboise, twenty years later. "I will never forget Dunham for this. She cured me." Zorina's version of their split was far less dramatic, a gradual falling away due to their diverging careers. "George has a way of telling stories," she said. "I loved George and thought he was a fantastically good and marvelous human being."[40]

In the year of their divorce, Balanchine had proposed marriage to Maria Tallchief. She had been startled by his offer, since she was twenty-one years younger than Balanchine and they'd never spent much time together outside of a dance studio. (She still called him Mr. Balanchine.) He had assured her, with a tender glow in his eyes, that it did not matter. Like any other marriage, theirs would work out or not. (The marriage, in 1946, lasted less than four years, although its official ending, an annulment, didn't come until 1952.)[41]

The Tallchief/Balanchine dance partnership endured far longer, although Tallchief left the company from time to time to accept offers as a guest artist for other ballet companies, with his approval. Mr. B rarely objected to the outside jobs his favored dancers took to survive. He created more work for some of them by staging ballets for operas, but the pay was no better and the opera seasons were just as short as the ballet ones.

After some childhood experiences, Tanny rarely performed in opera ballets where, in spite of Balanchine's efforts, singers got more attention than dancers. Modeling paid far better, helped to publicize the ballet company, and provided perks, most often free sample garments. Le Clercq posed for magazines and high-end stores, such as Saks Fifth Avenue, but she was in far greater demand after she became Mrs. Balanchine in 1952. Her husband shared her enthusiasm for fashion, one that she had most likely gotten from her glamorous debutante mother.

Francisco Monción modeled, too. Male and female dancers enjoyed the money and attention, as well as the designer clothes that they could not afford to buy for themselves. Manufacturers got lean, athletic bodies to display their wares and the cachet of being associated with a quintessentially elegant art form.

Shortly before the company's first tour of England in 1950, Phillip Bloom, its publicist, wrote to Eleanor Lambert of the Fashion Institute in New York. He wanted to know "the chances of getting a traveling suit and an evening dress and accessories" for the girls in the company, "pretty poor themselves," to be "given to them by some prominent manufacturers." The resultant publicity "would be well worth the money." Bathing suits that Jantzen had supplied for a new ballet, *Jones Beach,* he assured her, had yielded stories with color photographs in *Life* and *Look* magazines, "to be on the stands shortly."[42]

Jones Beach was popular, but the tour lasted only ten weeks and lost money. (In subsequent years, far more lucrative grand European tours would last for up to five months.) Tours were a financial necessity, since the length and timing of the ballet seasons in New York would vary from year to year. In January 1949, New York City Ballet presented its first independent season, only ten performances. It was not until 1955 that it enjoyed annual three-month winter seasons at City Center, buoyed by the popularity of Balanchine's *The Nutcracker.*

Because New York City owned City Center, ticket prices were kept low to make culture affordable for the masses. You could get a ticket for as little as a dollar. Even if you didn't have one, friendly ushers would sneak you in. Cheap tickets kept salaries low, too. In 1946, the weekly salary of a corps de ballet member, no matter how long they had been dancing, was no more than thirty-five dollars during rehearsal weeks and sixty-two dollars during performance weeks, far from starvation wages at the time, but less than a dancer might earn on Broadway. When the company toured, this increased by ten dollars to seventy-two dollars per week. Soloists and principals received a bit more, with individual salaries negotiated, but outside of the ballet seasons, nobody got paid. In 1950, Le Clercq's salary was thirty-three dollars per week during rehearsal weeks and $110 per week once a ballet opened. By then she was a principal dancer. Once the company began performing on a regular basis, the dancers were able to file for unemployment.[43]

Dancers at all levels were worse off than unionized low-skilled construction workers in New York in 1947, who averaged close to forty hours of work every week at about $1.31 per hour. Most ballet dancers earned less than unionized stagehands, even though they had a union of their own. Left-leaning Kirstein was most likely the prime mover behind the early unionization of Balanchine's company. Starting with the 1947–48 Ballet Society season, the company dancers had belonged to the American Guild of Musical Artists (AGMA), which was (and still is) the union for opera and ballet companies. By the early 1950s, a typical corps dancer, even one who did solos, earned no more than forty dollars per week during a rehearsal period. Principal dancers could negotiate for better contracts. Even by the late 1950s, corps de ballet members received less money for a week of rehearsals than they could expect to get from unemployment compensation. As early as 1949, Balanchine, who rarely wrote letters, had addressed the issue of the lack of government support for the arts in the United States compared to Europe and Cuba. In a letter to the Honorable William O'Dwyer, written with secretarial help, he expressed the hope that the "Mayor of the greatest city of the country, would take the lead in proving to the world that Americans are second to none in their recognition of artistic as well as commercial achievements." The situation did not appreciably improve until much later.[44]

When d'Amboise was already partnering Le Clercq, he was paid thirty-five dollars per week on his first tour of Europe in 1953, far from starvation wages. A week's pension, including breakfast, came to about ten to fifteen dollars per week then. Corps members routinely bunked together on tour, for companionship as well as to save money, and even principal dancers would share rooms. The best-paid managed to accumulate enough spare francs or lire to splurge on fashion, which mattered far more to them than fancy dinners, as it did to Balanchine. He set the tone for the company, onstage and off—always elegant, never sloppy. His ballerinas paid keen attention to how they looked at all times, to please themselves, the public, and the man around whom the entire company revolved.[45]

It's no coincidence that the women in Balanchine's orbit were partial to perfume, jewelry, and designer clothing. He had always been, Maria Tallchief wrote, "aware of what everyone wore." A trip to Christian Dior in Paris or his favorite jeweler in New York was de rigueur for a Balanchine wife (or a prospective one). When, months before her 1952 marriage to Balanchine, Tanny left behind on the plane home the suitcase that contained one of two Dior gowns he had purchased for her, he was "furious," the dancer Barbara Walczak recalled: "I don't think he ever forgave her." Although the gowns were "most likely model's samples," given his limited income, the cost would have mattered far less to him than the loss of something beautiful and rare.[46]

There's one gift that Balanchine gave to all his female dancers, as soon as he could afford to do so: free pointe shoes on demand. He remembered when he had danced in worn shoes and wanted his dancers to have an unlimited supply of the custom-made footwear. In the piece for *Good Housekeeping* published under her byline in 1955, Le Clercq said, "A pair of toe shoes lasts me for exactly one hard ballet; then they are too soft and must be thrown away." Hard ballets, indeed.[47]

Dancers used to other companies found it hard to adjust to Balanchine's demands. Judith "Gigi" Chazin had danced professionally for nine years with the Metropolitan Opera Ballet, the Joffrey Ballet, and other companies before she was accepted into New York City Ballet in 1961, at age twenty-four. Doing Balanchine's steps in classes and rehearsals, Judith began to have foot problems for the first time in her career. She tried working through the pain, but the problem worsened, so she returned to the Met, where the pointe work was less demanding.[48]

Le Clercq had her share of serious foot problems, too. These included swollen ankles, infected and bleeding toes, as well as Morton's neuroma, a thickening of the nerve tissue between the bones of the toes that was intensely painful. But she made light of her injuries in public, always putting her best foot forward, so to speak. In *Good Housekeeping* she declared, to an audience of potential recruits, that "toe dancing is not painful. Our satin ballet slippers have blocked, or glued, cloth shells built in at the tips, which hold the toes firmly. After one begins to dance professionally, the slipper manufacturer makes a mold of one's foot, around which he can build slippers accurately . . . if one toe is a little longer, it will turn under, and no harm done. We all darn the tips of our slippers with heavy buttonhole thread, making a sort of small mat, which prevents slipping and also deadens the sound as we dance."[49]

Others were more candid. Barbara Bocher, a young corps de ballet dancer and soloist in the company from 1949 to 1955, blamed injuries suffered by Balanchine's dancers on his dislike for starting class without a lengthy warm-up period at the *barre*. Nancy Reynolds, whose first ballet teacher at the King-Coit School was a teenaged Tanaquil Le Clercq, had a more comprehensive take on the issue. She spoke for many others when she said, "We always warmed up before George Balanchine's classes." Reynolds danced in the corps of New York City Ballet from 1957 to 1961 and later became a dance scholar and the company's historian. She attributed the problems some dancers endured to the fact that he "asked for extremes in general." The pointe shoes available then didn't help. Synthetic components like shock-absorbing foam have since been added to some shoes, lessening the stress, especially on the big toes that carry most of a dancer's weight.[50]

Publicly, Le Clercq minimized the sacrifices that a dancing career entailed. "Wherever we are, we dance, usually eight performances a week. . . . I gave up the whole wonderful teen-age life that young girls have in our country, the conversations and sodas at the corner shop (I was always hurrying off to ballet class) and the many teen-age dates (I never had time to make close friends). When I was fifteen or sixteen, well-meaning friends of the family introduced to me nice young college boys, who took me to dinner or the movies. I suppose the glamour of my profession attracted the boys; I was already dancing solo roles. The dates were always disasters. We never had anything to talk about, because the boys always seemed so young to me. I found it incredible that they did not even know what they were going to do when they grew up. . . . I had already been working at my trade for eight or nine years, and though the boys were several years older than I, they seemed like kids to me."[51]

And yet sometimes she daydreamed about getting off a train in a town where nobody knew her and getting a job in a store where she would "meet some man" and settle down. That fantasy of an imaginary domestic life she had most likely picked up from watching Hollywood movies. "But you go to a few parties, *with* boyfriends, and see the other life and you think, 'I don't think I'm missing so much anyway,'" she reminisced, decades later. Her real life—working with world-renowned choreographers and dancers—was far more exciting.[52]

6

Birth of the New York City Ballet

At nineteen, Tanaquil Le Clercq was made a principal dancer, a huge promotion for someone so young. She was working all the time now, dancing matinee and evening performances. As a younger Balanchine protégée, Allegra Kent, wrote in her memoir, Mr. B "knew how to send his ballerinas up like rockets, one after another, higher and higher." He sent "his chosen girls into ballerina space."[1]

The year Le Clercq became a principal, 1948, was a momentous one for Balanchine's company. Renamed the New York City Ballet, it had just become a constituent of City Center, like the New York City Opera. Morton Baum, who had engineered the move after seeing *Orpheus,* was so pleased with the company's first season under its new identity that he wrote to Lincoln Kirstein in November 1948, "In a short time, when the resident New York City Ballet Company will have achieved international fame, you will be able to take just pride in the realization of your vision." He vowed that "in future ballet seasons, the City Center will assume all the running expenses and meet any deficits."[2]

Baum wisely believed that as ambassadors of New York City, housed in its City Center, the ballet company could attract government help, although it took a few more years for this theory to become a reality, fueled by the Cold War competition with all things Soviet. Balanchine remained artistic director of the renamed company (although he preferred the title ballet master) and Kirstein, general director. Tallchief was still the company's biggest attraction, but Le Clercq was acquiring more and more followers. Their high expectations made her nervous. "I didn't have stage fright when I was young," she recollected. "When you're a nobody, you dance. And then you get discovered, and they start . . . applauding when you come out onstage, before you've done anything. . . . I know it's nice, but you think, 'Oh my God, just wait till I do it. Don't clap now.'"[3]

Holly Brubach, who had met Le Clercq long after her paralysis, wanted to know when she had first realized that Mr. B was interested in her as a dancer. Tanny didn't remember a specific moment. "It happened so slowly." Had he given her more corrections than he gave to others? "No," she answered. "When he taught class, I'd be the last one he'd correct." That's why she had deliberately gone the wrong way sometimes. "I could not get his attention. The only way would be to make a terrible mistake . . . then he'd wake up and see I was there."[4]

Once he scolded her and another scholarship winner, Marjorie McGee, for talking in class: "The teachers are giving corrections, you're both talking. Especially you." He pointed at Tanny. "You talk through the whole class. And you must stop mocking your teachers." She was instantly ashamed of her behavior because she knew he was right. Now she regretted getting laughs by imitating her teachers and decided then and there to stop talking and fooling around so much. "Of course, I danced the way he wanted me to, and I wanted to please him. But the truth is, I danced for myself. Because it felt so good to dance well."[5]

In 1948, Balanchine featured her in a new ballet, *The Triumph of Bacchus and Ariadne,* based on a text in rhymed verse by Lorenzo de' Medici (1449–1492), a ruler of fifteenth-century Florence who was called *The Magnificent.* The ballet was a love letter to Tanny, one that she probably did not read as such then, although the buildup to the opening was unprecedented. The *New York Times* announced the forthcoming ballet four times, starting in 1946. In December 1947, *Harper's Bazaar* published an article on the preparations for it. A book, never published, was said to be in the works, and the stage designs were part of an exhibit at the Museum of Modern Art that ran from January to April 1948. Le Clercq appeared in *Vogue,* wearing a costume designed by Corrado Cagli, who had also provided the scenery for the ballet and its conceptual framework. Openly gay and Jewish, Cagli had been a painter in Italy until the 1938 racial laws forced him to leave the country. He brought to Balanchine the idea of a ballet based on the Renaissance poem, staged as a carnivalesque celebration, as it had been in the fifteenth century. His designs for the costumes were inspired by Botticelli's painting *Primavera.*

Le Clercq liked the music for the new ballet, which used a large chorus, visible through the windows of the backdrop. In the lively allegro movement, the voices alternated like street performers at a carnival. The commissioned score was by Vittorio Rieti (a friend from Balanchine's days with the Ballets Russes), another Italian Jew who had fled fascism. Although Balanchine's first

Left to right: Corrado Cagli, Vittorio Rieti, Tanaquil Le Clercq, George Balanchine, photo by Irving Penn, 1948, *Vogue* ©Conde Nast. BALANCHINE is a Trademark of The George Balanchine Trust.

thought was to have the dancers perform to a recitation of the poem without music, he soon changed his mind. Irving Penn's photograph for *Vogue* shows designer, composer, and choreographer at Le Clercq's feet.[6]

In the ancient myth, as interpreted by de' Medici, after Ariadne (a Cretan princess) helps Theseus leave the labyrinth, he abandons her. But she is rescued by Bacchus, the god of wine and ecstatic revelry. The poem was a "triumph" in the Renaissance sense, originally performed in the streets of Florence with music. But the fanatical, ascetic friar Girolamo Savonarola burned the score and only the *carpe diem* text remained. It begins: "How beautiful is youth / and yet too soon it flees! /Let those who wish, be happy: / of tomorrow, nothing is sure." The last two lines are repeated throughout the work.[7]

The Triumph of Bacchus and Ariadne is a period piece, no longer performed. In 1948, it felt like a Bacchanalian postwar celebration. Le Clercq and Magallanes had a memorable *pas de deux* that he described as a "very pretty, leaves-in-the-hair, nude-looking, drapery kind of thing." In the "triumph" at the end, Bacchus and Ariadne were carried like royalty around the stage in a long processional sequence.[8]

Jacques d'Amboise recalled how, as a young teen, he sat in the front rows of City Center, watching his friend Tanny dance with Magallanes as her consort, Bacchus. Jacques was transfixed by her unconventional beauty. She was so light, he said, "she waved, like a blade of grass." She seemed "luminous" to him.[9]

The reviews, however, were tepid. Critics found the work to be mostly pageantry and rather dull, but John Martin of the *New York Times* declared the lively dance of the nymphs and satyrs (a tarantella with chorus) "brilliant." The choral voices alternate with a madcap *presto con brio* that has, at times, an almost comical effect. One can picture those cavorting satyrs.[10]

The ballet was presented once more, during the first New York City Ballet season, but it did not endure, which disappointed Rieti, who counted it among his best musical compositions (as did Hindemith, who attended the Ballet Society premiere). Rieti attributed its short life to the fact that it was so difficult to stage, requiring a large cast of singers and dancers, elaborately costumed. (And yet he revealed, in a 1985 interview, that he did not feel Balanchine and Cagli had done their best work in this ballet.)[11]

The Triumph was not Le Clercq's first time playing the mythical Ariadne. Just the year before, she had danced that role in *The Minotaur*, choreographed by John Taras. Balanchine had been expected to do it, but he had passed the job on to Taras. The costumes and set, modeled on ancient Greek

Tanaquil Le Clercq and Nicholas Magallanes, *The Triumph of Bacchus and Ariadne,* photo by George Platt Lynes, 1948. Used with Permission of The George Balanchine Trust and The George Platt Lynes Estate. Choreography by George Balanchine ©The George Balanchine Trust. Jerome Robbins Dance Division, The New York Public Library for the Performing Arts.

sculptures and architectural forms, had garnered more praise than the ballet, which had minimal dancing. Balanchine's far more lavish effort had also failed to triumph. Nevertheless, Le Clercq's rising star was blazing all the brighter now.[12]

In October 1948, just after her nineteenth birthday, she performed (with Francisco Monción) the adagio movement of *Symphony in C,* an exquisite ballet Balanchine had premiered the year before in Paris, where it was called *Le Palais de Cristal.* It was set to an exuberant masterpiece by Georges Bizet, written when he was only seventeen and a pupil of Charles Gounod at the Paris Conservatory. Balanchine had learned about this gem, a copy of which had been found in the Conservatory library in 1933, from Stravinsky.

Le Clercq, who struggled with balancing, was intimidated by the part, because she knew that Balanchine had first *made* the role, as dancers say, for the legendary "baby ballerina" Tamara Toumanova, whose debut in a children's ballet in Paris, at age ten, had astonished all who saw it in 1929. She was, Tanny said, "one of those dancers that you couldn't knock off pointe. That famous story—she's balancing, somebody goes out of the room to take a phone call, comes back and she's still balancing. So the role was handed to me from this fantastic balancer." And Toumanova had done the briefly unsupported balance on the raked stage (slanting downward toward the footlights) of the Paris Opera, the oldest national ballet company in the world. Balanchine offered to change the part for Le Clercq, to make it easier, but she had refused, wanting "to do it the original way—it's my stubbornness. So I did, but I was always scared."[13]

There was one on pointe balance she found particularly tough, when she had to do a *développé à la seconde,* lifting her bent working leg in second position and then opening it to the side in a movement that Balanchine said had to be as smooth as the unfolding of an elephant's trunk. He would illustrate this, in rehearsals, his biographer wrote, "with a gesture of the arm that at once made it uncannily both a leg and a trunk." When she was in this position, leg raised high and extended to the side, Tanny's partner would let go for a few seconds to go behind her and take her other hand. "If I could get through that balance, I was very happy," she said.[14]

The reviews were ecstatic, the ballet a sensation. The dancer Ruth Gilbert [Lawrence], interviewed fifty years later, recalled being struck by a "lightness about whatever she [Le Clercq] did." Ruth had never seen anything as perfect as Tanny's dancing in the slow second movement of *Symphony in C,* especially the supported *arabesque penchée.* On a brief clip from the trailer of Nancy Buirski's documentary *Afternoon of a Faun,* you can see the way Le Clercq suddenly falls backward into the arms of her partner (Moncíon), her arms up in fifth position, making her body seem even longer as she drops all the way down, straight as a seesaw, and then comes back up. Lifting her right leg in arabesque, she makes fast, high circles with her arms in fifth position as she dips forward in *penchée,* an unusual pinwheel *port de bras* that Nancy Lassalle thought Balanchine had invented for her.[15]

Maria Tallchief found Tanny "sublime" in the role. Extra performances were scheduled for the general public, who were clamoring for tickets. Le Clercq might have found failure easier to bear. The role made her queasy. "My whole dancing life," she admitted many years later, "I found it difficult."[16]

Her performance, according to Jerome Robbins, had a major impact on the subsequent history of the New York City Ballet. Robbins, already famous for his dancing and choreography for Ballet Theatre and Broadway shows, said that he'd decided to leave it all to work with Balanchine when he saw Le Clercq in *Symphony in C,* slowly letting herself fall back over Moncíon's arm. It was at once a fall and a turn, the two of them slowly spiraling down until she was bent all the way back over his knee. "Tanny Le Clercq made me cry when she fell backward at the end," Robbins said, "and I thought, 'Oh boy! I want to work with that company!'"[17]

Although he had seen her dance the role of Choleric in *The Four Temperaments,* the body-distorting costumes were so off-putting that the ballet didn't impress him. But the way Le Clercq had arched her back and let herself go with complete abandon in *Symphony in C,* trusting her partner to catch her, again and again, "left me in tears it was so beautiful," Robbins recalled. He was "just dissolved by it."[18]

Tanny had met him before, when she was fifteen, although he didn't remember. She had been with her mother at a Halloween party in Greenwich Village, a neighborhood that attracted artists, writers, and bohemian free spirits. Robbins, twenty-six then, had popped in and asked, "Is anyone bobbing for apples?" Nobody was, but as soon as he made the suggestion, everyone obeyed, Tanny recalled, "all together. I was thrilled and remember getting drenched with water."[19]

The thrill may have come, in some measure, from recognizing the handsome older dancer who had just made a much bigger splash at Lucia Chase's company, Ballet Theatre, with his choreography for *Fancy Free,* a startlingly American ballet, jazzy and brash, about three sailors on shore leave in New York City trying to pick up girls in a bar. It was Robbins's first collaboration

Jerome Robbins, *Fancy Free,* 1944 (second cast), *left to right:* Janet Reed, John Kriza, Jerome Robbins, Muriel Bentley, and Harold Lang, choreography by Jerome Robbins. Jerome Robbins Dance Division, The New York Public Library for the Performing Arts.

with the composer Leonard "Lenny" Bernstein. Even the notoriously tough critic of the *New York Times,* John Martin, had declared it a "smash hit" that was "ten degrees north of terrific."[20]

Robbins had mixed classical ballet steps with popular dance styles, soft shoe with bits of tap, comical antics and gestures (beer drinking, back and thigh slapping, playful purse snatching, somersaults, brawling, drumming on barstools and countertop, finger pointing, the tossing of gum wrappers, etc.). It was a crowd-pleasing, comical, sexy, and musical hit with three sensational male solos. He danced one of them, a swivel-hipped, Latin-style number that prefigured his work for the musical *West Side Story* in the late 1950s.

Fancy Free always remained one of Le Clercq's favorites in the Robbins repertoire, especially the way he danced "the finger-snapping rumba, lean and mean, slick and crisp, a know-it-all type of guy rather like Sinatra."[21]

Four years later, after seeing *Symphony in C,* Robbins wrote to Balanchine, asking if he could work for him. "I'll come as anything you need, anything you want. I can perform, I can choreograph, I can assist you." Balanchine immediately answered, "Come."[22]

That was the beginning of a long collaboration. Robbins was already a Broadway star, as a dancer and choreographer, but his love for ballet was primary. By the late 1940s, Ballet Theatre was near collapse and Balanchine was building one of the most daring ballet companies in the world. He had everything but money and hoped, along with Kirstein, that Robbins would bring in a whole new audience. Less than a year after he arrived, Balanchine gave Robbins the title of associate artistic director of the New York City Ballet.

The first ballet he created for the company was *The Guests,* about prejudice, a subject that had long preoccupied Robbins, a bisexual man with Russian-Jewish parents. He described the dance as a depiction of the struggles between in-groups and out-groups, welcome and unwelcome guests. Balanchine said it was about "The cluded." Asked what that meant, he replied, "The cluded. The in-cluded, the ex-cluded." Robbins danced the part of the host of the event where the guests met and failed to meet. The included were marked with dots on their foreheads, like Indian *bindis;* the excluded lacked them. The love affair of a "mixed" couple in the ballet prefigures his far more successful exploration of this theme in his musical inspired by Shakespeare's *Romeo and Juliet, West Side Story.*[23]

Tanny wasn't sure whether she was in- or excluded. Not having worked with Jerry Robbins before, she didn't know that he liked to have several people rehearsing the same role, so he could pick the best cast for the performance. He was often undecided until the last minute, a practice which did not endear him to dancers. Thinking she was just an understudy in *The Guests,* Tanny was "goofing off in the back" of the rehearsal studio, as she put it, when he told her, with a scowl, "You'd better learn this because you're going to dance it."[24]

She found the adagio, which she danced in a red tunic, "very pretty" but dubbed the punchy, nervous music for the ballet, by Marc Blitzstein, "horrible" and "cheap." Recollecting it, years later, she made a rapid series of plosive sounds."[25]

Blitzstein, who had worked closely with Robbins, developing the score as the ballet evolved, said, "It is a wild and perilous experience working with someone of [his] drive, imagination, and genius." That was an exceedingly diplomatic way to describe the experience. Most dancers in the company preferred to be cast in Balanchine's ballets, even though his steps could be fiendishly difficult. Although Robbins's ballets were physically easier to perform than Balanchine's, his volatile rehearsals were emotionally exhausting. He was a tormented soul, "gifted with wit—marbled with meanness," in the words of Jacques d'Amboise.[26]

How much was uncontrolled venting and how much part of Robbins's intense creative process? He had come to the company from Lucia Chase's Ballet Theatre, where he'd performed in ballets by the British choreographer Antony Tudor (1908–1987), born William Cook, the father of the so-called "psychological," or "Freudian," ballet. Tudor's approach, like Robbins's, resembled the method school of acting inspired by Stanislavsky. It involved breaking down the dancers emotionally, to get them to separate from their own egos so they could uncover feelings they could use onstage.

"He did this largely through humiliation, with cutting personal attacks and sexual remarks that pulled dancers into a spiral of self-hatred until they felt empty and blank," the dance historian Jennifer Homans wrote. It was a "deliberate strategy," not mere "run-of-the-mill directorial abuse." Robbins was generally easier on his principal dancers than the corps members, with whom he could be merciless. Equally merciless were the New York critics, who did not love his first effort for the company. The London critics were far more enthusiastic.[27]

Le Clercq could usually ride out his changes of mood and mind. The sparks between them rarely flared into anger. From the start, he adored Tanny, with whom he shared his passion for photography, at which they both came to excel. He found her to be an enticing subject, as did professional photographers. At twenty, she appeared in the first issue of *Flair,* a "high-minded cataclysm of a magazine" that lost millions in its only year of publication. Dancers were prominently featured in its pages, many of them photographed by Bert Stern, its first and only art director. He married Allegra Kent in 1959 and featured her and other dancers in the pages of *Vogue,* where he was a leading photographer in the late 1950s through the 1960s.[28]

The editor of *Flair,* Fleur Cowles, had a talent for attracting celebrated artists and for spending her husband's fortune. The short-lived magazine, which catered to elite tastes at a price to match, featured elaborate, expensive artwork and world-renowned writers. Tanaquil Le Clercq, one of the first flowers picked for the new magazine, was the stunning focus of a gathering captured in the garden of Café Nicholson, a "New Bohemian" mecca, then

Left to right: Tanaquil Le Clercq, Donald Windham, Virginia Reed (*rear*), Buffie Johnson, Tennessee Williams, Gore Vidal. Photo by Karl Bissinger, 1949, Courtesy of Zachary Fechheimer and Karl Bissinger Papers, University of Delaware Library, Museums and Press.

on East Fifty-Seventh Street. The group included the playwright Tennessee Williams, the artist Buffie Johnson, and the writers Donald Windham and Gore Vidal. Tanny's tall, lithe figure dominates the picture, even though she's on one side, looking tentative and shy, as if caught unawares.

The issue came out in February 1950, but the photo was taken the previous summer, when she was nineteen, just before or after her trip to Europe with a friend, the dancer Betty Nichols. That adventure proved to be a major turning point in both their lives.

7

Summer in Europe

George Balanchine was a pioneer of civil rights in the arts (albeit in an inconsistent fashion), and for his time remarkably open to unconventional casting. Afro-American music and dance styles (the jazzy steps, jutting hips, and flexed feet that Le Clercq had mastered at Dunham's school) influenced his ballet choreography. Balanchine did more than admire American tap and jazz dancers. He learned from them, working with Josephine Baker, the Nicholas Brothers, and Katherine Dunham, among others.

Lincoln Kirstein (like Robbins, Jewish and bisexual) had even stronger feelings on diversity. The gay male society he frequented had been racially inclusive since his Harvard days. Kirstein was enthusiastic about Balanchine's 1933 dream of founding an integrated dance company and may have been the one who had suggested it: sixteen Black dancers and sixteen White, evenly divided between males and females.

The New York City Ballet was already a diverse company, to some extent. Roles were set on Le Clercq by Jewish choreographer/dancers like Ruthanna Boris and Jerry Robbins (born Jerome Rabinowitz). At a time of open anti-Semitism (rarer among people in the arts), Balanchine advanced their careers. Although anti-Semitism had been common in czarist Russia, Balanchine seems to have been uninfected, as a friend of his youth, the Russian-born Jewish violinist Nathan Milstein, attested.[1]

Vladimir Dmitriev, whose business relationship with Balanchine had become more contentious since the advent of Lincoln Kirstein, was a notorious anti-Semite. But Balanchine had remained grateful to him for spiriting his fledgling troupe out of Russia. He did not fire him, not even in 1934 when Dmitriev told a student, Ruthanna Boris, to pack up and leave the ballet school. When the fifteen-year-old asked why, Dmitriev raged, "You are a Jew. Not be here. Go!" Balanchine assured her that he wanted her to stay. "It is good you are here," she recalled him saying. Touching his heart, he added: "Jews have here something warm, like the sun. I have here something sharp, you know, like dagger I keep in boot when I was son-of-a-bitch little Georgian boy." Ruthanna remained. By 1939 Dmitriev had departed, because of a heart ailment.[2]

Like Robbins, some Jewish dancers in the company had changed their names, a common practice in theatrical circles then, not only among Jews. Melissa "Milly" Hayden (born Mildred Herman) joined Balanchine's company in 1949, where she was a principal dancer (apart from brief periods dancing for other companies) until retiring in 1973. Allegra Kent (born Iris Margo Cohen) was a significant muse for Balanchine from an early age. Offered a scholarship to the School of American Ballet at fourteen, she had joined the New York City Ballet in 1953, at fifteen. There were many Jewish dancers in Balanchine's school and company in Le Clercq's era, including Barbara Milberg Fisher and Barbara Walczak, and two of Tanny's first dance partners were Hispanic. Francisco Monción, whose ancestry included some African roots, came to New York as a child from his native Dominican Republic. He had been one of the first students admitted to the School of American Ballet, along with Nicholas Magallanes, born in Mexico.

In her private correspondence, as well as published works and interviews, Le Clercq voiced her lifelong opposition to discrimination of all kinds, although she was never militant about it. She didn't use words like *racist* or *sexist* or *homophobic,* even when they became commonplace. The word *mean* sufficed to sum up how she felt about such behavior, a word that, in its childlike simplicity, seems far more expressive of the truth. It is all the more remarkable given the southern roots of her American ancestors on both sides, although her mother, grandmothers, and at least one great-grandmother, Marie Siegling (granddaughter of a slaveholder on her mother's side), were all Eurocentric sophisticates.

Le Clercq's natural inclusivity was sustained by lifelong friendships born, for the most part, in dance studios. Gay and bisexual male dancers were among her closest friends, and she was also friendly with a diverse group of ballerinas. Maria Tallchief was already dancing professionally when she first took classes with Tanny at the school. Betty Nichols, a versatile African American dancer, had performed in the hit musical *Carmen Jones.* Betty was "a beautiful dancer," Jacques d'Amboise remembered. "Balanchine liked her very much. So did Tanny."[3]

When offered a scholarship to Balanchine's School of American Ballet in

1943, Nichols quit Broadway to become the first Black dancer in the school. She had solo roles in two Ballet Society productions, neither of them choreographed by Balanchine: Todd Bolender's *Zodiac* in 1946 (as Virgo) and Lew Christensen's *Blackface* in 1947. These ballets did not win over critics or audiences, and each was performed only once. More acclaimed ballets suffered the same fate, given the precarious finances of Ballet Society. *Blackface,* a serious ballet about race relations in the antebellum South, featured Betty Nichols and Talley Beatty as the "Colored Couple." Christensen felt that it was ahead of its time and would have been better received decades later.[4]

Ballet Society "was not a big major company," Nichols recalled in an interview, long after she had retired from dancing. "It was like a family." But some family members were favored over others. Balanchine was focused on his wife, Maria, but more and more on his latest muse, Tanaquil Le Clercq. "Tanny had been fantastic in Ballet Society," Betty said. "We were just breathless because she was so beautiful. She had a very special thing, already when she was very young. She had wit. You didn't see it in ballet then. You don't see it much in ballet now. . . . She was unique. I would say, 'Kid, you're great.'"[5]

Le Clercq had been unforgettable in *Orpheus* as the fierce leader of the Bacchantes, who tear the poet to pieces. Apart from her amazing extension and unearthly lightness, she had a unique way of nailing every step, a deliberateness that underlined her movements, as if she hesitated for a fraction of a second before placing her foot. Her presence and attack gave a unique signature to her roles. Although she knew how lucky she was to be working with a genius like Balanchine, by the summer of 1949, Tanny was eager for a break. An opportunity presented: Betty Nichols had been planning a European vacation with first one, then another dancer. Both women had to drop out at the last minute when they got dancing jobs. (Most dancers, unless they had family support, grabbed whatever offers came their way, just to survive.) When she heard that a ticket was available, Tanny asked if she could go, and Betty readily agreed.

The two were in high spirits as they set out on their European adventure, unchaperoned. Elegantly dressed, they crossed the Atlantic on a ship called *De Graff,* nine luxurious days in a first-class cabin. Tanny was nineteen that summer and Betty twenty-four. Pavel Tchelitchew, a Russian-born surrealist painter close to Balanchine and Kirstein, was also on the ship. The young women knew Pavel because he designed sets and costumes for ballets. Tch-

Tanaquil Le Clercq and Betty Nichols on board ship, 1949. Courtesy NYCB Archive.

elitchew became their unofficial "godfather" on the trip, introducing them to everyone. "1949 was a fantastic year in Paris," Nichols remembered. "Everybody was there. It was recovering from the war fast."[6]

Tanny spoke French, of course, although never as perfectly as her erudite father would have liked. In Paris, she went to look at paintings by the impressionists and wrote to her friend Pat, back home, that it was "great to see paintings I've only seen in books or reproductions."

She had been equally impressed by the notes on the wall next to each painting, "so you can trace who impressed who," she joked.[7]

Tanny and Betty made an impression, too. They met some men who took them to a club in the Latin Quarter called Rouge et Noir (Red and Black). "Anyone comes up," Tanny wrote, "and asks you to dance. I danced with a lovely guy and before long he pressed a note in my palm that said I should meet him Sunday. Oh these men."[8]

Barely a week after the young women arrived, they bumped into Merce Cunningham, walking with John Cage, just outside the thirteenth-century Sainte Chapelle. With its stained-glass windows that threw a confetti of blues and reds and yellows on the mosaic-tiled floor, and its vaulted ceilings, shining with gold fleurs-de-lis on a deep-blue background, Tanny thought it "the most beautiful church in the world."[9]

She and Betty knew Cunningham, of course, from the School of American Ballet. Tanny had danced with him in *The Seasons* two years before. Cage and Cunningham invited them both to dinner and to perform on a makeshift stage in the studio of the artist Jean Hélion, lit by a skylight. Nichols hoped that someone important would see her and invite her to dance in a French company. Tanny thought that Betty had an excellent chance of finding work in France. "Her French is good," she wrote Pat. No one knew then whether Balanchine's company would manage to survive, and everyone knew that it was easier for what was then called a "colored" ballet dancer to find work in Europe than in the United States. Betty needed a good opportunity.[10]

Was this one? In rehearsal, she had trouble figuring out where to jump in, since the music, for prepared piano, seemed so strange. Betty didn't think she was doing her part the same way each time, but Cunningham told her, "You'll find it." Chance was an important component of Cage's compositions, and that had influenced Cunningham's approach to choreography. Nichols wasn't sure what to make of their ballet. "There was tremendous publicity about the program," she recalled. "It was the first time Paris had ever seen anything like that, and it was so astounding that they didn't know how to criticize it. So what they said was—they always fall back on this when they can't think of anything else—'It was so beautiful.'" Paris was charmed by the young Americans.[11]

Marianne Preger, an American drama student finishing a junior year abroad, attended the performance. Le Clercq, Nichols, and Cunningham performed *A Valentine Out of Season* (later called *Games*) dressed in rehearsal clothes, tights and sweaters, with ballet shoes. It was based on a work by that title composed by John Cage in 1944. Then Le Clercq and Cunningham performed a duet called *Amores* (*Loves*), also to music by Cage. It was nine minutes long, divided into four movements: a solo for prepared piano, a trio for nine tom-toms and a pod rattle, a trio for seven wood blocks, followed by another solo for prepared piano. Only eighteen notes on the piano were *pre-*

pared, using nine screws, eight bolts, two nuts, and three strips of rubber. Although Cunningham liked to use chance to free his imagination, sometimes drawing up a chart of potential movements and body parts, then using dice or the I Ching to determine a sequence, his early performances were not left to chance. Dancers were "bound by the results" of his experiments, according to Marianne, because once he had settled on a sequence of movements, it was fixed.[12]

Marianne had been captivated, above all, by the "unified flow, like the song of a bird" of a Cunningham solo, she wrote to a friend on July 15, 1949. The duet and trio had too many "static tableaux" for her taste, although she admired the women's "elegance" and training. As she said in her memoir, "balletic movement was familiar to me, whereas his [Merce's] personal style was so new and electric." After studying and performing with Cunningham until 1958, Marianne came to value the static quality she had deplored in 1949 and thought that the tableaux might have been "early indications of Merce's interest in stillness as part of movement."[13]

Alice B. Toklas and Alberto Giacometti were in the audience at Hélion's studio, too. Giacometti was already garnering recognition for his long, impossibly thin sculptures of people and animals, inspired by African sculptures he had seen in Paris, that looked like they didn't even have room for bones. People likened the three slim dancers to his sculptures. French dancer/choreographer Roland Petit, director of a fledgling company, the Ballets de Paris, came to the performance, as Betty had hoped. He had seen her dance before, in New York.

Roland was "*divine,* my dear—" Tanny wrote to Pat McBride, "how you would go for him. I think I know pretty well your taste. He said he would like to do a ballet for me, but he said if I leave for N.Y. what can he do? I said what about *next summer?* He said that still didn't give him time; also when I left there would be a ballet created for me, but *no me.* . . . He said if I could get Balanchine to manage something and get the orchestral score to it, he would have costumes made, etc. and would put it on. Ha, ha, can you just see Mr. B doing that?"[14]

Petit offered Nichols a role in one of his ballets. A girl had twisted her knee. "They got Betty in to do it. Isn't it *divine?*" Tanny reported. So much was happening for Betty in France that she had decided to stay longer, although she didn't plan to stay forever. Tanny said, "I'm going to stay with you." Why go home when she was having so much fun? She and Betty got along very well. There was no one else "except you," she had written to Pat, with whom she

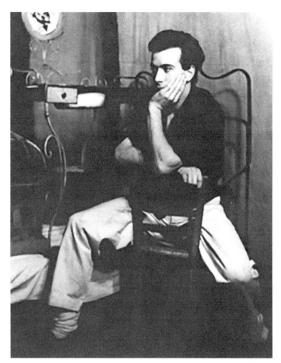
Roland Petit at rehearsal, 1949.

would rather be sharing this summer. Pat had planned to come on the trip but Balanchine had persuaded her to take a summer ballet course.[15]

The young dancers were constantly invited to parties and performances. They went to Bobby Fizdale and Arthur Gold's duo piano concert to hear music by Rieti, Cage, and Haieff. (Robbins had summoned Fizdale and Gold to his apartment just before her trip, expressly so they could meet Le Clercq, since they would all be in Paris at the same time.) Rieti was also at the concert, and afterward, he, Bobby, and Arthur invited Tanny and Betty to stay with them in Rome, where they had rented a house, a tempting prospect.

It would have been a blissful day except for an annoying fellow ("E") who showed up at the concert and, Tanny wrote to Pat, "Got frightfully offended. Well, he began it all by saying he hadn't seen me in two days and had I thought about him. So I said *no*. Well, anyway he kept tagging along after us. I didn't pay any attention (there are so many *new* people) and the first thing I knew he was furious. I just can't help it. . . . Wish you were here like crazy."[16]

Friends ran into friends until Le Clercq and Nichols had an entourage in Paris. They relished a picnic on the Seine River near a beautiful castle. After seeing the play *Ondine,* with spectacular sets and costumes by Pavel Tchelitchew, they went with fifteen other people, including Cunningham and Cage, to a restaurant where they ate *pâté* and steak with wine and mushroom sauce and *fraises des bois* (wild strawberries). "They are so little and sweet, it's like eating perfume," Tanny wrote Pat. The two men gave them gifts—a bottle of champagne for Betty, a box of pastries for Tanny—as well as "their repertoire of funny stories."[17]

Tanny wrote her "Dear Ma" that they had been to the palace of Versailles where "the fountains were playing— oh so beautiful." She described a "mad Montmartre artists ball" where nude models paraded around for hours and "They danced nude too— Ballroom that is— The men had on just underwear."[18]

Paris was so enticing that Tanny had second and third thoughts about returning home. In August, they were invited by the surrealist painter Roberto Matta to make the trip to Italy in his car, the sort of invitation that glamorous young ballerinas got all the time. They *did* get to Italy and most likely stayed with their musician friends in the Rome rental. But there, Le Clercq's mood abruptly changed. She wrote to her father, whom she addressed as "Jacques," that she didn't like Rome, its gilded, marble grandiosity, and wondered if she were missing something. Minor irritations of tandem travel had begun to chafe. Tanny complained that Betty was "continually putting on an act—I'll admit I do, so does everyone one way or another." She simply wanted Betty to admit it, as she did, to say something like "gee what an act." She doubted that Betty even realized when she was being theatrical.[19]

Complaints are rare in Le Clercq's letters to family and friends, before or after polio, although she didn't hide her feelings, especially in her youth. "Pat [McBride] and I always talked about the narrow little ballet world, the small minds, how confining, how prejudiced etc. how nice it would be to do *other* things. . . . I think I'd get very warped and confused if I didn't do *one* thing," she wrote to Robbins in 1951. "Maybe it's what keeps me going."[20]

From an early age, Le Clercq had been extremely self-aware. Her close friends came to appreciate her exacting standards for herself and others, in life as in work. Even at her peak as a ballerina, "She had doubts about how good she was, always questioning herself," Jacques d'Amboise recalled, "but also questioning everything and everybody. . . . She had by her nature a need, as well as a wit and ability, to puncture a hole in the pomposity of people, so she would zero in on a flaw." And yet, Jacques declared, "I never met anyone who didn't love Tanny." Her wit could be "biting, but always fun, never mean." Of course, strong personalities always have detractors. The dance historian and critic Joel Lobenthal met several company members who found Le Clercq decidedly less endearing. As a former soloist, Barbara Milberg Fisher, wrote in her memoir: "Tanny could be exclusive and bitchy and withdrawn. She could be friendly, entertaining, and surprisingly warm, especially with people she was close to."[21]

As quickly as it had descended, her teenage pique evaporated. She and Betty went their separate ways, and the brief break seemed to have done them both good. Tanny, who was so enraptured by Botticelli's painting *The Birth of Venus* that it made her feel "weak," decided to stay an extra day in Florence. Betty went off to Venice with a friend.[22]

After the women reunited, Le Clercq was in a much better mood. But now she had new concerns, far more crucial than whether people close to her were being real or phony. According to those who saw her over those six weeks in Europe, she was itching to break free from the grueling routine of a Balanchine ballerina's life, although what she had seen of Petit's company had not impressed her. She wrote to Pat: "There is no fluidity as we know it. They are, none of them, light or ethereal. Of course this is only one company, but I think our dancing and dancers far superior."[23]

Cunningham had reached the same conclusion. He said, in a 1949 *Dance Observer* essay, that much as he adored Paris, "I've seen no dancing that even touches what takes place in the United States." On the other hand, Ballet Society's short seasons (only three to four weeks of ten to sixteen performances each) were frustrating for a dancer at her peak, not giving her as much stage experience as she desired. Le Clercq would rehearse for a long time and then get only two performances, without much of a chance to improve if she messed up.[24]

This was not the first time that she had contemplated leaving. In 1946 Lincoln Kirstein had written to her mother, "I hope she stays around this year, simply because there are a number of things for her to do of considerable interest." That was an understatement. In 1946 Le Clercq had performed solo roles in *Resurgence, The Spellbound Child,* and *The Four Temperaments.*[25]

But three years later, studio time still dwarfed stage time. By 1949 there were many more companies in Europe than in the war's immediate aftermath, although some of the most celebrated did not hire foreign nationals. Now she was weighing an offer from John Taras, who had worked with Balanchine and had become choreographer and ballet master of the Grand

Ballet de Monte Carlo, directed by the Marquis de Cuevas, a company that toured widely. An eccentric, cultivated Chilean who had dubbed himself Marquis George de Cuevas, the founder of the company had acquired a fortune by marrying a granddaughter of John D. Rockefeller. His company was real; his title, probably self-invented. Maria's sister, Marjorie Tallchief, was a reigning star. Bronislava Nijinska, the company's ballet mistress, also taught and staged works for it. Tanny wrote to her mother in September: "John Taras begs me madly to join their company. Am confused and quite tempted. It is odd that neither Balanchine nor Kirstein nor Eddy [Bigelow] have bothered to write— Do they take me for granted, or don't they care?" (Edward Bigelow, a company dancer, had become an administrator, although he still did character roles.)[26]

In the same letter, she outlined the pros and cons of accepting the offer. On the plus side, she would be "assured of work" with the "chance to *support* myself." If she joined Taras's company, she expected to be given more "varied roles," although there were several ballerinas in the company (including Marjorie Tallchief and another part Native American dancer, Rosella Hightower) who would be stiff competition. But interestingly, she listed this increased competition on the plus side of her tally. "Responsibilities and worries" were a plus, too, part of "caring for myself," something Tanny felt that she could "face better and more to my advantage here and alone." (Not only would she be escaping Balanchine, but her mother's vigilance, too.) Furthermore, she wrote, she could use a "change of scenery," reminding her mother that she had been at the school since she was ten: "Our school, our teachers, Balanchine's guidance, Balanchine ballets—Purely Balanchine attack, style, type dancer."[27]

However, there was a decidedly negative side to working with Taras: "Bad crummy repertoire. Boring dull ballets." There would only be John Taras to guide her, too, and he was only a decade older than Le Clercq. She judged him too young and immature for the job. There would be a dearth of good ballet teachers as well, and, perhaps the biggest negative of all, this move could be a final rupture for her: "Maybe break with Mr. B permanently. Never will be the same. . . . It is confusing isn't it," she concluded. The decision was urgent, she let her mother know, because Taras was starting his season that October. She ended her letter on a softer note: "Thanks for your marvelous letters."[28]

In a letter to Pat McBride, Tanny expressed the same doubts. "Things are really confused, don't know what I'm doing, whether to turn in the passage or not." For years, she had done whatever her mother and Balanchine wanted. Already a great dancer, Tanaquil Le Clercq was also a young woman, not quite twenty, enjoying her first taste of freedom. She had no steady boyfriend, just an admirer she referred to as her "Persistent Beau" in a letter to Pat. (Maybe the disgruntled "E"?) He called her every day. Alas, she couldn't even picture herself enjoying a meal with him. "I would choke. Well, there is one more guy down the drain." She had met a "nice guy" through this fellow but could not imagine finding a way to see him alone.[29]

There is absolutely no hint in her letters or the recollections of friends of any romantic dreams about Mr. B. And whatever *his* feelings for the nineteen-year-old Tanny, conscious or not, in 1949 Balanchine was still married to Maria Tallchief. Ostensibly, Le Clercq was free to follow her own instincts, but the girl longing for a European lifestyle was in conflict with the dedicated dancer. Then a telegram came from the school, plus a letter from her mother: Tanny was "the great hope of the school," and she *had* to return immediately. Had Edith communicated with Kirstein, Balanchine, Bigelow, or others in the administration?[30]

Poised on the knife-edge of decision, Le Clercq agonized, but she obeyed the call to come home. "Tanny cried," Betty recalled. "She wanted to stay so badly." External pressure from her mother and the school had played a part, of course, but there was surely internal pressure, too. Opportunities were limited in Europe. The Paris Opera only hired French nationals. To join England's renowned Sadler's Wells company, you had to be from Great Britain or a Commonwealth country. And there was no ballet company in the world that felt as exciting to a young American dancer at that time as Balanchine's.[31]

Betty Nichols remained in Europe far longer than she had imagined she would. Tanaquil Le Clercq returned to New York and the rigorous life of a Balanchine dancer. She seemed to have had no idea that, within a year, her relationship with her mentor and guide would become an intimate one.[32]

A "Balanchine Ballerina"

That fall, 1949, the New York City Ballet enjoyed its first great popular success, Balanchine's one-act *Firebird*. Balanchine used Stravinsky's 1945 third ballet suite, not the original score (divided into two tableaux, plus an introduction) that Diaghilev had commissioned in 1910. The costumes and hand-painted sets were by Marc Chagall, from the 1945 Ballet Theatre production. The impresario, Sol Hurok, had paid $25,000 for the sets, but he sold them to his friend Morton Baum for $4,200.[1]

As the mythical bird, Tallchief seemed to fly across the stage before landing, upside down, in Monción's arms. Her performance, Balanchine told Maria's daughter decades later, had secured the company's future. To meet the demand for tickets, extra performances were scheduled. Le Clercq, a gazelle with a sharp sense of humor, did not see herself as a firebird. She had never coveted Maria's bravura, crowd-pleasing roles. *Firebird* "was done for Maria," she said, "it was one thousand turns, and I wasn't a turner. . . . I had enough to do of my own."[2]

On December 1, 1949, a week after Tallchief's triumph, Le Clercq won plaudits in the first movement of Balanchine's new ballet, *Bourrée Fantasque*, set to four rousing pieces by Emmanuel Chabrier. Making use of Tanny's scissor-quick legs, as well as her gift for mime, Balanchine played, to comical effect, with the height difference between her and her partner, Jerry Robbins. On pointe, she towered over Robbins, which prompted him to suggest a mental image to guide her performance: A "lady of high fashion out walking her poodle." After he stopped dancing the role, the breed changed with each new partner: "This one is a Pekinese," she would think, "no, a pug-basset."[3]

She liked the elegant costumes by Karinska, "a chic hat for me, a beret for Jerry." He was "a good partner and great fun to dance with." The day after the opening, Walter Terry of the *New York Herald Tribune* proclaimed them both

Tanaquil Le Clercq and Jerome Robbins, *Bourrée Fantasque,* photo by Walter E. Owen, ca. 1949–50. Choreography by George Balanchine ©The George Balanchine Trust. Courtesy of NYCB Archive.

"nothing short of triumphant," citing Tanny's witty use of her "wide and innocent eyes and her long legs," a perfect foil for Jerry, who was "agile as a lepre-
chaun and twice as mischievous." John Martin, the dour critic of the *New York
Times,* gave the ballet a tepid review but called the partners "irresistibly funny
in the most completely stylish terms" and Le Clercq, "particularly delicious."[4]

Watching from a wing of the City Center stage, Maria thought the pair "the
epitome of elegance. Everyone was surprised on opening night when they got
laughs." Not everyone, least of all George Balanchine. He had created a ballet
that was also a spoof of classical ballet. In one step, Le Clercq had to swing
her leg up behind her, knee bent in attitude, and lightly tap her partner on the
back of the head as she completed a supported turn in front of him. "When
I was mad at Jerry," she said, "I would whack him very hard on the head." He
complained afterward, "'What are you *doing?* You'll knock my teeth out.'"[5]

In spite of the teasing, or because of it, their friendship grew. Jerry, she
reminisced, decades later, "had a wicked sense of humor, and he wanted to
see everything, go everywhere. . . . We used to go to parties together, to Wa-
termill, to Fire Island. . . . Jerry was very good at games." He could improvise
his own on the spot. They often involved the punning wordplay she excelled
at. They called each other Charlie Brown and Lucy, after characters in *Peanuts,* a comic strip they adored. He called her "Baby" and matched her wit.
After she was stricken with polio, he wrote, in one of many tender letters to
her, "I love you so for just that quality which really is very honest and always
makes me blink at its directness and acuteness."[6]

In that momentous year, 1949, Le Clercq had the great good fortune to begin
studying with the legendary Felia Doubrovska (1896–1981), "a tall dancer in
the days when most ballerinas were quite small," she wrote in a profile of
her teacher. Eight years older than Balanchine, Doubrovska was a product
of the Imperial School in St. Petersburg. She had left Russia after the Revolution and later performed in ballets Balanchine choreographed for the Ballets
Russes (she was the Siren in *Prodigal Son,* 1929) and for other companies.
Doubrovska and her husband, the virtuoso dancer Pierre (Piotr) Vladimirov
(1893–1970), eventually settled in New York. Vladimirov had taught at the
School of American Ballet from its start. Now that his wife had retired from
dancing, Balanchine invited her to teach there, too, joining a distinguished
faculty that included another former star of the Mariinsky, Anatole Obuk-
hov (1896–1962). Doubrovska was delighted to accept. "Mr. Balanchine could
make a piece of wood dance," she told her students.[7]

A shy person, Doubrovska never forgot her first teaching day at the school in 1949. Balanchine had "personally ushered her into the studio, his arm linked in hers," Barbara Walczak recalled. But Doubrovska found it harder to face that class than to go onstage to perform: "My knees were shaking. The students were already in the room. But what was really terrifying was the fact that, leaning against the window, were Tamara Geva, Danilova, Zorina, and Maria Tallchief. All of Mr. Balanchine's wives were standing there!"[8]

Most likely, a wife-to-be was in the studio that day as well, Tanaquil Le Clercq. Many years later, she spoke of Doubrovska in an interview that became part of the soundtrack of the documentary film *Felia Doubrovska Remembered*. "She was a modest person, which I liked," Tanny said, in her throaty, deep post-polio voice. Doubrovska was "very chic, very elegant, what I would like to look like." Even the way Felia Doubrovska entered a classroom was graceful. She would slip in shyly, yet command everyone's attention, and she was the only teacher Le Clercq remembered seeing in pointe shoes. She taught pointe well into her eighties, having retained her slender legs, all muscle, and amazing posture. By emulating her, the students acquired a more elegant line. Decades later, speaking of her, they all sat up a little straighter.[9]

For nearly forty years, Doubrovska taught a series of exquisite ballerinas—her form always impeccable. "She corrected very quietly," Tanny remembered. "She was more the kind who'd call you over to the corner after class was finished. You had the feeling she was well brought up. She didn't want to hurt anyone's feelings." Students finished every Doubrovska pointe class in the old Imperial style, with a *révérence,* a deep curtsey, and then applause for their teacher.[10]

A rehearsal with Jerry Robbins rarely garnered applause from his dancers. He was maddening because he could never make up his mind. Tanaquil Le Clercq had the only principal female role in his first major ballet for the company, *Age of Anxiety,* its title taken from the book-length, Pulitzer Prize–winning poem by W. H. Auden that had inspired the music, Symphony No. 2 for Piano and Orchestra, "Age of Anxiety," by Leonard Bernstein. The young composer, like Robbins, was a Russian-Jewish American born in 1918 who had begun a brilliant career. Provoking anxiety may have been part of Robbins's method of wresting tortured performances from the dancers to suit the theme of "the frightened souls of an anguished era," as Walter Terry, dance critic of the *New York Herald Tribune,* described the four main roles in his opening-night review.[11]

Le Clercq danced in every section, along with the three other protagonists,

Francisco Moncíon, Todd Bolender and Robbins, who had an understudy solely to help the choreographer envision his own part. Tanny liked doing her *pas de deux* with Moncíon on pointe in practice clothes, but she found her costume "ugly" and the ballet "very long." The rehearsal process was long, too. Robbins kept changing the steps and spent a lot of time discussing character motivation. But, Le Clercq affirmed in an optimistic present tense, decades after her career ended, "He's good at using you." For instance, she explained, if he wants you to be hurt, he doesn't have to tell you how to *act* hurt. He's already chosen you for the part "because you can be hurt in the right way."[12]

Robbins had insisted that all his principal dancers read the poem. Unlike Balanchine, he wanted to discuss the feelings and ideas in a piece with his dancers, as in a theater workshop. Bolender remembered that they all knew the story well and "would often speak of ourselves as those characters." But Le Clercq said that reading the text hadn't helped her a bit with her role as one of those anguished souls, sharing their fears while wrestling with existential questions, who find brief, muted relief in each other.[13]

The ballet began with the protagonists entering and facing each other in a tight circle. Bolender told Deborah Jowitt: "And then we reached out and touched each other this way (formally and reticently, yet inquisitively). And then we did a grand plié, all four of us, with knees straight forward. . . . And then we rose up and we dropped our arms and then we would look—I would look at you and you would look away from me. . . . Then we started to back away from each other and then one person would start off in one direction and another and another and another." The solidarity of the group had evaporated.[14]

In one striking section, the "Seven Stages," the corps de ballet dancers, dressed in red and wearing fencing masks, acted as antagonists, mimicking the protagonists' gestures at stage rear. Robbins said he had gotten the idea by watching the understudies learning their parts. (Terry commended Robbins's "skillful use of repeated gesture" to convey the "alliterative nature of the poem.") Moncíon compared the corps to hurdles, alleys, and turnstiles "we had to break through" in several of the six sections of the forty-minute ballet. At one point, "they lined up in various directions and we had to find our way out of the maze; they shifted directions, which caught us against the wall."[15]

Bolender appreciated the way Robbins "seemed to focus the very word *anxiety* in his movement—jagged, almost unrelated things, like tics sometimes, throughout the body." During rehearsals, he would always "talk and

Francisco Moncíon, Jerome Robbins, Tanaquil Le Clercq, and Roy Tobias, *The Age of Anxiety*, choreography by Jerome Robbins, photo by Friedman-Abeles, 1950 ©The New York Public Library for the Performing Arts.

talk and talk, and at the end you may not be able to repeat what he has said, but you'll have a vivid impression of what he wants."[16]

Le Clercq thought of Robbins as her first "method" dance partner. To work with him, she recalled, was always "a mental process." They rehearsed *Age of Anxiety* "to death," she said, and "Jerry changed it all the time. Version A, Version B, Version C." He was known to complicate things further (if not in this ballet, in others) by adding numbers, too. He would call out combinations of letters and numbers, 1A, 2B, etc., expecting dancers to show him moves that they thought he had discarded. Whenever he got frustrated, which happened with gut-churning frequency, he screamed at everyone and anyone—even the esteemed Russian rehearsal pianist, Balanchine's old friend, Nicholas Kopeikine, who "could sight-read a Stravinsky orchestral score, transposing for piano as he went." Most often, Robbins chewed out the corps de ballet. When he worked with dancers, Robbins said in a 1988 interview, he was a "wanted wasp," that is, "the sound in the air" that "keeps everything moving." The wasp was not always wanted. His behavior stirred up more than he might have wished, creating deep hostilities.[17]

There is a famous true story: Robbins had a habit of watching a rehearsal from near the edge of the stage, his back to the orchestra pit. On the set of a Broadway musical (probably *Million Dollar Baby*), soon after one of his screaming fits, he took several slow steps backward, still facing the group onstage. Nobody warned him. They watched him move backward, step by step, toward the edge of the stage. Not one person broke the ferocious silence of the group. Even after he fell into the orchestra pit, "No one went to his aid," one of the performers recalled. Luckily, he wasn't injured. Dancers learn, early on, how to fall.[18]

"He used to have an annoying way of saying, 'Well, you've lost it,'" Le Clercq recalled. "And you'd say, 'Lost what?' 'You had a certain feeling, a quality, and you've lost it.' And you'd think, 'Oh my God! . . . What quality? What was it I lost?'" She remembered how, rehearsing *Age of Anxiety,* he "would keep us four after the rest of the cast had left and keep us at it until we got a little goofy from fatigue." They rehearsed in a studio on the fourth floor of the Madison Avenue building that housed the School of American Ballet. "There was no elevator service on weekends, when we were often rehearsing, so it seemed we were endlessly tramping up and down those stairs!"[19]

Davie Lerner, a dancer with Ballet Society, one of thirty World War II vets who had studied at the school on the GI Bill, ran into Tanny after one of those exhausting rehearsals. "Aren't you proud?" he asked her. "Proud of what?" she replied. "That Robbins chose you as the lead in his ballet," he said. (There were four leads, but Tanny was the only female.) "She looked me straight in the eye," Davie recalled, "and out of the perfect oval of her face came, 'I don't give a shit. I'm going home to soak my feet.'"[20]

Later Jerry Robbins had fond recollections of those rehearsals, as well as the group's downtime at a nearby coffee shop afterward, feelings probably not shared by the dancers. At the ballet's opening in February 1950, Terry in the *New York Herald Tribune* reported that "A large and distinguished audience received the new work with cheers and dozens of curtain calls." The ballet won favor from critics not for its ideas but for its dramatic use of space. In fact, John Martin of the *New York Times* advised people not to read the text before going to the theater, as it had little to do with what they would see, although he lauded Robbins's "uncompromising vision" and proclaimed his new work "completely fascinating." Terry found the ballet "an enormously compelling work of art" and praised the "superb" performers.[21]

Age of Anxiety perished under the glare of repeated viewings. What had seemed so startling and new rapidly lost its freshness. It's a *lost* ballet that exists only in a brief silent film, a handful of reviews, and the recollections of those privileged to have seen it. Jeanne Thomas Fuchs, a student at the ballet school who later became a good friend of Le Clercq's, remembered that "Tanny alternated the female role with Melissa Hayden and they were both spectacular in it." Jeanne could not understand why the ballet was *lost,* as she found it "powerful and one of Jerry's best." She was not the only one. A special correspondent to the *New York Times* reported that this ballet, more than any other presented at the company's first London appearance at the Royal Opera House, Covent Garden, "aroused the greatest enthusiasm of the audience, which shouted its approval, bringing Tanaquil Le Clercq, Francisco Monción, Todd Bolender and Jerome Robbins back for repeated curtain calls." London's *Daily Herald* proclaimed Le Clercq "the star of the evening."[22]

Less than a week after the premiere of *Age of Anxiety,* she had a leading role in Frederick Ashton's *Illuminations,* a work that also attempted to translate poetry into dance. With words by the poet Arthur Rimbaud and music by the contemporary British composer Benjamin Britten (Les Illuminations for Tenor and Strings), it was Ashton's first work for Balanchine's company. More pageant than ballet, *Illuminations* elicited a long, polite, but unenthusiastic review from John Martin, touching more on the ideas of the ballet than the dance elements. Martin, perhaps the toughest critic in New York at that time, found the costumes "too pretty" and the music "cold." He deemed Magallanes, torn between Sacred Love (Le Clercq) and Profane Love (Melissa Hayden), too "sweetly unhappy" to convey the more sordid adventures of Rimbaud. (By the 1950s Martin had mellowed, especially in regard to Balanchine's work.)[23]

At first, the prospect of portraying Sacred Love delighted Tanny. She imagined being freed from heavy costuming. "When I was little, you see, I used to puzzle over a reproduction of the famous painting Sacred and Profane Love, wondering which was which. Was it the nude that was sacred, or the figure fully attired? I had to be told that the exposed epidermis symbolized virtue." She was looking forward to the role, until she saw that Cecil Beaton had designed for her "a calf-length costume, tights, toe shoes, sleeves, neck-ruff, and even a hat, while Profane Love cavorted around the stage bare-legged and minus one toe shoe. What heaven! How I envied her the part—one slipper off—what a relief to the toes." Her envy was misplaced. Profane Love, "in the heat of the role" grew forgetful, rising more than once on the wrong, unshod foot, and "bruising all five nails."[24]

Le Clercq found working with the leading British choreographers, Frederick Ashton and Antony Tudor, difficult when it came to music, she revealed in a 1974 interview, although she didn't say why. She relied on private coaching from Balanchine to help her through any ballet. "I never really felt lost with the music," she averred, "because I had Balanchine. . . . With him, you're absolutely secure no matter what. You could dance to a drippy faucet with nothing left to chance. It's like your technique; there's nothing left to chance and you know it, which makes you very secure."[25]

Photos in *Cosmopolitan* magazine showed her applying makeup and donning a crown for the long adagio sequence of *Illuminations* called "Being Beauteous," in which she was "partnered in a number of precarious balances, lifts, and turns by four men, including a series of arabesque turns on pointe with a partner catching her by one arm." Balanchine, not Ashton, gave her technical help for this section.[26]

One of the men was Arthur Bell, the first Black dancer to perform with the New York City Ballet. Ashton said: "I think I was perhaps the first person to put a colored boy on the ballet stage. This was an allusion to Rimbaud's devoted Ethiopian servant, and it was also to suggest Rimbaud's African life." It is telling that Ashton felt that Bell's presence on that stage required a narrative framework. There was an aesthetic of symmetry (of colors and body types) that dominated ballet throughout the twentieth century and beyond, dashing the hopes of many gifted African American dancers.[27]

A guest artist, Bell was never invited to join Balanchine's company. The school had become slightly more diverse by the 1950s, but not the company. Another Black dancer, Janet Collins, became a prima ballerina of the Metropolitan Opera and danced on Broadway. She began teaching modern dance at the School of American Ballet in 1949, but not ballet, and never danced for the company, which did not have an African American ballerina until Debra Austin accepted Balanchine's offer in 1971. Black dancers fared better with Jerome Robbins, whether in his Broadway productions or at the New York City Ballet.[28]

In the spring of 1950, Balanchine and Robbins collaborated for the first time. The ballet was *Jones Beach,* named for a huge public beach on the

South Shore of Long Island. The score Balanchine chose was Symphony no. 1 of the *Berkshire Symphonies* by Jurriaan Andriessen, a Dutch composer, just twenty-five, who had come to the United States on an international arts and student exchange program. Although he came from a family of distinguished artists and musicians, at that time Andriessen's work was within the City Ballet's tight budget. As an additional cost-cutting measure, Mr. B outfitted his dancers in the brightly colored swimsuits donated by Jantzen, which may have spurred his initial idea to make this ballet. The stripped-down look of most of his later ballets, however, had little to do with money. "George wanted his choreography to be seen, and not have his work spoiled unnecessarily," Zorina wrote.[29]

The two-piece suit that Le Clercq wore was modest, not a true bikini, a style that didn't catch on in the United States until the 1960s. Dancing on the

Jurriaan Andriessen with George Balanchine, 1950. BALANCHINE is a Trademark of The George Balanchine Trust. Courtesy of NYCB Archive.

City Center stage in bathing suits, skimpy or not, was provocative enough in 1950. Balanchine and Robbins choreographed some sections of the ballet together and divided the rest, an exhilarating experience for both of them. "Keep doing and doing," the older man advised, "and every so often you'll do a great one."[30]

Andriessen had been about to return to Holland, having run out of funds, when he received a Rockefeller fellowship to spend two years in New York. Kirstein or Balanchine had probably made at least one call on his behalf, helping to launch the young man's career as a world-renowned composer for theater and film.[31]

Robbins and Balanchine worked together on the first part of the ballet, "Sunday," as well as the last part, "Hot Dogs," where the dancers mimed the cooking of hot dogs over the orchestra pit. Robbins choreographed a comical dance for three boys attacked by girls cast as mosquitoes. (He later credited the idea to Balanchine, although Le Clercq said, "The scherzo is all Jerry's.") The girls buzzed around, miming stinging, while the boys slapped them away. Jerry danced in that section, wearing a striped suit that Tanny called "that little zebra job."[32]

Balanchine did most of the slow middle section, "Rescue," where Le Clercq was a swimmer saved by artificial respiration. Her partner was Nicholas Magallanes, whom she had enthusiastically destroyed at the end of *Orpheus*. Now he was cast as her savior.

She revived and expressed her gratitude in a playfully seductive *pas de deux* before feigning unconsciousness again, an incarnation of female surrender just before the stage went black. It was, by one account, "unexpectedly moving." Deborah Jowitt wrote, in her biography of Robbins, that even from the still photographs that provide the only visual record of Le Clercq's performance, one can see that she was "bewitchingly limp . . . and her rescuer is making love to her even as he engages in artificial respiration."[33]

Years later, Tanny remembered this "divine adagio" as her best moment in the ballet. In 1950, the critic Doris Hering wrote that Le Clercq's "rag-doll dance (with Magallanes tucking her hands between her shoulder blades and breathing into her mouth) seemed sweetly sad."[34]

Jones Beach was the last new ballet of that short season, which closed on March 19. The opening night, March 9, 1950, attracted an unusual mix of dignitaries. Officials from the Dutch consulate attended, in honor of the composer, as well as New York City's commissioner of parks, Robert Moses, the prime mover behind the monumental project of creating Jones Beach itself.

Nicholas Magallanes and Tanaquil Le Clercq, *Jones Beach,* photo by George Platt Lynes, 1950. Used with Permission of The George Balanchine Trust and The George Platt Lynes Estate. Choreography by Jerome Robbins and George Balanchine ©The George Balanchine Trust. Jerome Robbins Dance Division, The New York Public Library for the Performing Arts.

Jurriaan Andriessen conducted the orchestra, which played the national anthems of the United States and the Netherlands before the curtain rose. Anatole Chujoy, editor of *Dance News,* applauded "Andriessen's delightful score," pronouncing it "tuneful and rhythmic and a lot of fun." The music is dynamically varied, and its slower sections, dominated by strings and woodwinds, have a poignant, melancholy beauty. The allegro movements are percussive, with a brassy, jazzily syncopated thrust that prefigures Bernstein's work in *West Side Story* later in that decade.[35]

Balanchine did not love the music, Jacques d'Amboise recalled, which is surprising, since he had chosen it himself. His distaste may have arisen from personal considerations. Around that time, Tanny was rumored to be engaged to Jurriaan Andriessen. Claire Nicolas White, a Belgian/Dutch immigrant and friend of his family, had married a grandson of the architect Stanford White. By 1950 she was living on the White estate in St. James, Long Island, where Jurriaan came for a visit. Everyone got the impression that he was deeply in love with Tanny and planning to marry her. Later, Claire heard that the engagement had been called off because Balanchine himself had interfered.[36]

Whether or not this rumor reached Tanny, she was certainly aware of another offstage manipulation by Balanchine. When she was a teenager, Lucia Chase's Ballet Theatre was considered the most glamorous company to join. At fifteen, Le Clercq had auditioned for its resident choreographer, Antony Tudor. Afterward, Tudor told her: "I know I can't take you. Balanchine said I can't take you." Rather than being upset by this news, she had felt oddly heartened. That was the moment she had first realized that Balanchine had set her apart.[37]

Was he infatuated back then? By the time she had turned twenty, he didn't bother to hide it. A photograph published in a small-town paper in early March 1950 showed him preparing to broil a steak as Tanny salted it. The caption read: "The ballerina's only diet problem is to eat as much and as often as she can. Dance director George Balanchine often cooks a steak for her." By then, his marriage to Maria Tallchief was more of a professional relationship. "For five years," she and Balanchine had "spent fourteen hours of every day rehearsing and performing." Now she wanted to have a more balanced life and perhaps children, an impossibility if she lived with him. His ballets were his babies.[38]

George Balanchine's aversion to domestic life was deep-seated. "If I had my own children," he told John Gruen, "I wouldn't be able to do it [run a company]." Stravinsky's devotion to his first wife, a chronic invalid who died of tuberculosis in 1939, baffled Balanchine when he went to visit them in Nice. Their sons looked "terribly" alike to him. "Svetik looks like Fedya and Fedya looks like his father. . . . [T]he faces are the same, and Stravinsky sees himself in them. Do you think that's interesting—looking at yourself all the time?"[39]

Balanchine craved variety, but he nevertheless exchanged marriage vows with four of his beautiful muses. He had many infatuations as well, some of them hopeless, including one with a tall, intense ballerina, Diana Adams, who joined the company in 1950 as a principal, along with her then husband, the dancer Hugh Laing (an on-and-off-again lover of Antony Tudor). She was complicated, a moody perfectionist with flawless technique who was subject to paralyzing stage fright. In spite of her nerves, Adams was also a thoughtful, intelligent, and generous person with a lovely demeanor onstage and off. She became a close friend of Le Clercq's, along with Robbins, Patricia Wilde, and Magallanes.

Jerry Robbins, especially, was always eager for fun. He went along on excursions to parks in Brooklyn, Long Island, and New Jersey. "Jerry and I went to Coney Island a couple of times and to Palisades Amusement Park," Tanny recalled. "We rode the Cyclone, the Hurricane, and the Loop the Loop. I was terrified. I sat with Diana and Jerry and was so scared I buried my face in his chest and bit him. He didn't look too thrilled when I suggested that we try it again. When we did, I screamed and bit him again."[40]

When the spring season ended, the exhausted dancers were eager for a spree. Balanchine was working in Europe, but he didn't mind lending his car. In high spirits, Tanny headed for Florida in his black Mercury convertible with Maria, Nicky, and a young student from the ballet school, Joe Frank Varcasia, whom they "all adored," according to Tallchief. Zipping along a southern highway, singing along with Frank Sinatra and Nat "King" Cole on the radio, they vowed not to work on the entire trip. They were having a fine time until a policeman stopped them for speeding. After a frantic search, Maria realized that the registration was not in the car. The officer gave them a lecture and demanded they pay a "fine" immediately in cash, then let them go. (Balanchine apologized later for neglecting to tell her that his car papers were at home.)[41]

In Daytona Beach their happy group swam, slept, sunbathed, talked, and ate. And ate. When they got back to New York, other members of the company were shocked to see them. Maria had gained fifteen pounds, and Tanny nearly as much. (Her normal weight was around 108 pounds.) Feeling guilty, both women went on crash diets before the upcoming tour, the company's first one abroad. Balanchine's ballerinas had an image to uphold. In the early years, they had not all been rail-thin, like Le Clercq or those in his Russian troupe with whom he had barely escaped starvation. In this new land of plenty, there was more variety. At first, Balanchine had liked "big beautiful American girls," according to Vera Zorina. He admired the "wonderful legs and big, strong ankles like horse" of one female dancer, but later came to favor those, like Tanny, who were "*thin* like needles."[42]

Her unusual proportions may have sparked this preference. Le Clercq made a striking impression onstage, covering space quickly with those long legs, and yet was easy for a male partner, even a small one, to lift. Balanchine, while still in Russia, had invented his own one-handed high lift, making a ballerina in arabesque appear to be floating through the air and then putting her down, on pointe. To him, the lines of Tanny's light, strong body with bones "like a bird's" were ideal for ballet. The crystallizing of this aesthetic had consequences far beyond Le Clercq's dancing life, especially for female dancers not genetically predisposed to be thin. A ballet culture of extreme thinness that has circumnavigated the globe can be traced to Balanchine's infatuation with Le Clercq, and it has persisted well into the twenty-first century. But what came naturally to her became a constant struggle for others which, in some cases, has led to severe eating disorders. "In shape for us is being hungry," a corps member of a "prominent" company said in 2016.[43]

Patricia Wilde, a strong dancer who struggled to keep her weight down during most of her Balanchine years (from 1950 until the mid-1960s), joined the company just before the five-week tour of England. Balanchine had convinced her to leave the Ballet Russe de Monte Carlo, where she was a principal dancer, and join the newly formed New York City Ballet as a principal. She proved her value on opening night by replacing Maria Tallchief, who had injured a tendon. "In those days," Wilde said, "each one of us was very important to the company. There weren't enough people to rehearse you, so you had to keep yourself in training and prepare yourself for the roles. It was very difficult. . . . There was Maria, Tanny, Diana, Melissa. . . . Everyone had a unique talent, especially Tanny. She was divine."[44]

During the two weeks before the company's first appearance at the Royal Opera house in London, Balanchine was uncharacteristically nervous. He rehearsed his principal dancers for two hours, every day, after the school was closed for the evening. Le Clercq remembered that they were "maybe two boys and three girls. No piano—he would play it when he felt like it, and otherwise it was just him snapping his fingers." It was all technique, the same steps and gestures practiced over and over. "He was young at that time, he had all his energy, and he insisted," she remembered, many years later. "No, dear. Turn out. No, dear. No. Once more. Once more. Once more. No. No. . . . Again. Again. Again. Try again. Again." They did this in silence, over and over. "That's where I really learned to dance," she said.[45]

The hours of preparation paid off. On opening night at Covent Garden, July 10, the company received fourteen curtain calls. Le Clercq (partnered by Moncíon) was singled out for the incredible grace and poignancy of her performances, especially in *Symphony in C.* Leigh Ashton of the *London Daily Mail* pronounced her "a remarkable dancer, particularly with her arms and hands." Hardly anyone since Pavlova, he wrote, could match her "fluttering quality, and Tanaquil very rightly received most applause." On August 1, he noted that she had "danced exquisitely again" with Robbins in *Bourrée Fantasque,* "the high spot of the evening."[46]

Edith Le Clercq got favorable press, too. "We nominate for a Ballet Mother's Medal Mrs. Jacques Le Clercq," *Dance News* reported a month later. In London for part of the season, Edith "never entered the Opera House except through the audience's entrance, and stayed in a different hotel from her daughter." Tanny, the article revealed, had "a very painful ingrown nail on her big toe which had to be cut open, and she was out for a few days." Edith had already returned to New York. Was this, in part, to facilitate an intimate connection between her daughter and Balanchine? It's clear, from a letter Tanny sent to her mother in early August, that Edith was aware of his intense interest.[47]

Maria Tallchief was not. In her memoir, she relates how, early in the tour, at dinners with her husband and members of the company, she had gotten the impression, from flirtatious looks, that Tanny had fallen for their ballet master, Lew Christensen. She even spoke to Balanchine about it, concerned because Lew was married, but she never pressed Tanny on the subject.[48]

Before they left London, a minor disaster occurred. Betty Cage, the company's business manager, wrote an urgent letter to Morton Baum in New York. Someone had broken into her office, stealing a cashbox, petty cash vouchers for five weeks, four passports, and payroll envelopes for the fifty-three dancers (still paid in cash then), which had been "locked up in a suitcase in a locked office." The sums involved were small, but essential.

Betty Cage, photo by Tanaquil Le Clercq, 1950s. Courtesy of NYCB Archive.

Although the tour was a critical success, it soon became apparent that it would be a financial disaster. Audiences were large in London but sparse in the provinces.[49]

Whatever Baum's response (City Center having its own financial troubles at that time), intelligent, indomitable Betty found a way to continue. She had a well-merited reputation for being capable of holding the Balanchine/Kirstein enterprise together with a shoe ribbon, working tirelessly for little pay since 1947 as the company's "labor negotiator, certified public accountant, legal expert, mother superior, confessor, psychiatrist," as Lincoln Kirstein put it. On more than one occasion during her nearly forty years on the job, she had threatened to quit, but she remained, throughout the lean times, a loyal stalwart—beloved, essential, and mysterious. Her swarthy looks and fortune-telling (using cards) sparked speculation about her ethnic origins, but Betty maintained a public silence on that subject. Edith Le Clercq had so much faith in Betty Cage that she named her co-executor of her will.[50]

Jerry Robbins was also dancing on that tour, but he only stayed a week in London. Tanny saw little of him, socializing for the most part with Lew, Maria, and Balanchine. For three weeks touring Manchester and Liverpool, she roomed with Maria. (Balanchine was away most of that time.) Just before the trip, Maria had fallen in love with a dashing young pilot she had met at a going-away party for Robbins and wasn't sure what to do about it. Leaving Balanchine seemed "unthinkable." When she finally dared to reveal her powerful, disturbing attraction, Balanchine calmly replied that he didn't want to separate, but Maria should feel free to do what she wanted. He seemed almost "too eager," Maria thought, to let her leave.[51]

He must have already been making his attraction to Tanny evident, at least to her, because she was clearly disturbed about the situation. She wrote to her mother, "Made up my mind that I can't possibly stay here alone with George—it is bad enough now, the little I see of him." On tour, she was often alone with his wife. At night, in their shared rooms, "I poured out my heart to her," Maria wrote in her memoir, "wondering whether or not I was still in love with George and if I should leave him."[52]

According to Maria, Tanny just listened. After the company returned to New York, the Balanchines met privately before announcing their separation to the press. They decided that the fact that Balanchine did not desire children would give "grounds for annulment," Maria wrote. As a young dancer at her peak, she was not in a hurry to have children, but since no-fault divorces had not yet become standard, putting out this story "seemed reasonable and we went ahead with it." Maria pursued her new relationship, and they continued to work together in the dance studio. He was choreographing a new ballet for her, *Sylvia: Pas De Deux*.[53]

One evening after a rehearsal, she spotted Balanchine walking with Le Clercq on Madison Avenue, near the school. She rushed to catch up to them, until she realized with a shock that something had changed. "George was staring at her in the same way he used to look at me. . . . He was in love with her!" Maria was only momentarily upset: "I sympathized with her, wondering if she had any idea of the problems that went along with being romantically involved with George."[54]

By the time Le Clercq was ready to talk about that summer, many decades had passed. "When we came back, they got separated," she said to Holly Brubach. "Maria got an apartment. And I started seriously going with George. After a year, they got an annulment, because Maria wanted to have babies. (She was Catholic.) In one of the newspapers, I remember, there was a picture of Maria and George with the headline 'No Papooses.'" That was a crude reference to Maria's Osage heritage and the now widespread tale that she wanted a child and Balanchine didn't. Not that it was a complete fiction. In Maria's words: "His attitude was that anyone could have babies. Only a few people were able to dance."[55]

Balanchine's courtship of Le Clercq must have been a sudden one. It's obvious that she had not been preparing to drop Jurriaan for him when she had extended an invitation to the Andriessen family to see a performance of *Jones Beach* in London, where they could meet her and Edith. Saying goodbye to Tanny, Jurriaan may have felt that his Rockefeller grant was a decidedly mixed blessing. Under its terms, he had to remain in New York.

His mother did not advance his case. She had replied, in a letter to Tanny, that her husband was too busy to cross the Channel and they were both staying home, but their daughter, Cilia, would be in Surrey, staying with Lady Jeans, a family friend, and would be coming to see "Jurriaan's ballet." Mrs. Andriessen extended a warm invitation to Edith to stay with them in Holland. She and Jurriaan's father were pleased that their son and Tanny were "so fond of each other," but also "glad to hear that you, after all, did not marry just quickly, as 'marrying just quickly' of course never is all right. It must have its time to grow and be prepared. The thing is too severe to be in haste with it. Naturely [sic] we wish you to marry in the Catholic Church and hope you will understand that. You have to start on a Christian base. It is just because we like you both to be happy that we are so sincere about it."[56]

After the company returned to New York, rumors about Le Clercq and Balanchine circulated throughout the school and company. They had not gone to great lengths to conceal their relationship, even though he was still legally married to Tallchief.

Fifty years later, Davie Lerner recalled having been asked by Pat McBride to hand-deliver a note to her friend, Tanny, who was living with her mother a few blocks from the school. Davie was about to leave the dance studio with the note, when he heard Pat say, as if thinking aloud: "She'd better watch out. She's playing with fire."[57]

Balanchine was indeed on fire. He continued what he had started before the London appearance, teaching his principal dancers himself, every day. "Before that, we had just warmed up," Tanny recalled. "But from then on,

George Balanchine returning to New York City from England with Tanaquil Le Clercq, photo by Fred Melton, 1950. BALANCHINE is a Trademark of The George Balanchine Trust. Courtesy of Christopher Melton. Jerome Robbins Dance Division, The New York Public Library for the Performing Arts.

we had company class on the stage. An hour and a half, no piano, just him beating time. And that was hell. But boy, he gets you that way, forcing you to concentrate on the noise your feet make when you land. . . . Once you take his classes, it ruins you for everyone else's."[58]

He gave sessions for small groups of favored dancers. "As scientists will test out their theories and hypotheses in experiments, Balanchine used these private lessons to test new ideas on technique," Jacques d'Amboise wrote in his memoir. Some principal dancers tried to avoid his classes, because he made them do the same steps over and over, to the point of exhaustion. But Tanny felt that nobody else had ever taught her to move so well. Balanchine would walk around and say: "Um, you don't have to do it if you don't want to. If you're old or sick or tired or you don't like." Nobody dared to stop, although the dancers often got tired before he did. Once he gave an entire class on ways to run onstage.[59]

Una Kai, who danced with City Ballet from 1948 to 1960, confirmed that this was a long-standing practice. "We did twenty different versions of the same kind of step, without the chance to relax a bit by using other muscles. . . . You had to live through the pain; a lot of dancers didn't want to do that."[60]

Some quit. Barbara Milberg dared to confront Mr. B during a two-hour class, citing the five-minute break per hour required by the union. Balanchine, who resented the disruptions that union rules entailed, answered her with an old Russian proverb: *You will get all the rest you want—in your grave.*[61]

As early as 1935, Lincoln Kirstein had noted in his diary what he called Balanchine's "playful sadism." He once observed a rehearsal where "Balanchine got into one of those repetitive sadistic things he sometimes can't pull himself out of. Made them repeat the same step for an hour . . . [said] if they were tired they could go home, and abruptly left himself."[62]

Paradoxically shy and imperious, distant and impassioned, the two words most often used to describe Balanchine were *gentleman* and *genius*. He was given to saying, almost boastfully, that all his wives had left him, but in truth he had a way of absenting himself, when his interest in another grew. Allegra Kent had noticed that "there was a time limit to Mr. B.'s love. . . . The ages of his wives stayed roughly the same while Mr. B. grew older." His divorces left no visible trace of bitterness. As Tamara Geva said: "There's no ugliness in a relationship with him. George has no hate in him." The extraordinary lack of rancor on the part of any of his ex-wives has led many to speculate about a lack of passion in Balanchine's sexual life.[63]

Maria is the only wife who was explicit on the subject. "Passion and romance didn't play a big role in our married life," she wrote in her memoir. He was "a warm, affectionate, loving husband," she maintained, but "despite his reputation as a much-married man obsessed with ballerinas, George was no Don Juan. . . . George saved all his energy for work. He made sure we slept in twin beds, perhaps to conserve his energy."[64]

Of course, Balanchine would not have responded to each wife in exactly the same way. Maria was a formidable woman, her will as powerful as her dancing. Tanny was a little afraid of her in those years, according to Lincoln Kirstein. As late as 1955, he wrote to Morton Baum in a letter pleading for tension-reducing concessions to the ballet company, "With Balanchine, you have the real question of Tanny and her fear of Maria, etc."[65]

"Maria was always first, imperious," Jacques d'Amboise said. "Everybody was intimidated by Maria Tallchief. She was grand and demanding." Five years before he had said those words, d'Amboise had put a more positive emphasis on her grandeur: "She was grand in the grandest way." One example he recalled later: Tallchief, after she could afford luxuries, would "come to ballet class in a mink coat, drag it on the floor and drop it where she was going to hold on to the barre."[66]

In his low-key, less theatrical way, Balanchine was also demanding, not an ideal husband for Tallchief. Her last marriage lasted. Balanchine, a perennial seeker, moved on. "When Zorina left him," Jacques d'Amboise wrote in his memoir, "Balanchine was brokenhearted; when Maria left, he was relieved." Maria, Balanchine confided to a male dancer in the company, years later, was a wonderful woman, but she "was like tiger, and after awhile you get restless and tense living with tiger all the time. Then I found Tanny—she was like flower."[67]

9

---∞---

Between Balanchine and Robbins,
La Valse and *The Cage*

Early in 1951, Tanaquil Le Clercq premiered what became her signature role in a new Balanchine ballet, *La Valse*. She's a young woman, dressed in a creamy white gown, who meets a stranger (Magallanes) at a ball.

The couple performs a hesitant, fractured waltz—approaching, then retreating from each other, even dancing back-to-back—until he swirls her around to music that sounds uplifting, yet broken, holding together even as it falls apart. The piece by the same title, composed by Maurice Ravel just after World War I, conveys the sense of an old order crumbling. "We are dancing on the edge of a volcano," the composer wrote in his notes for the work, quoting an early nineteenth-century politician, Narcisse-Achille de Salvandy.[1]

Ravel wanted to evoke "the mad whirl of some fantastic and fateful carousel" in a ballroom of the Viennese court. Finding this piece too short for the ballet he had envisioned, Balanchine preceded the final scene of the great ball with Ravel's *Valse nobles et sentimentales,* eight short waltzes that convey a pleasure-seeking discontent, a restless abandon. The ballet begins with an overture, the first waltz. The second waltz is danced by three women wearing pale gowns with underskirts that flash diabolical reds, oranges, and violets. The trio (likened by the critic Walter Terry to "three Fates in the guise of courtesans") performs a conspiratorial *pas de trois,* their hands flipping back and forth on their wrists like playing cards.[2]

Couples and the unpaired skitter across the stage, as if blown by erratic gusts, and then, at the start of the eighth waltz, the innocent young woman (Le Clercq) enters, announced by mellow wind instruments. With dramatic, angular movements of her arms, she conveys a strangely knowing innocence,

Tanaquil Le Clercq and Nicholas Magallanes, *La Valse,* photo by Walter E. Owen, 1951. Choreography by George Balanchine ©The George Balanchine Trust. Jerome Robbins Dance Division, The New York Public Library for the Performing Arts.

exulting in her own elegance. Flutes, oboes, and clarinets punctuate the restrained exuberance of her *pas de deux* (with Magallanes) that is slow and tentative at first. They cross arms in one way, then discover new ways to link limbs, as if practicing a mysterious rite while simultaneously inventing it. How to move through a world where the old rules no longer apply? Propelled by the relentless rhythm of the waltz, Le Clercq dances with and past her partner, gaining confidence with every whirl and lift, her white dress billowing high above his head. But a sinister figure (Moncíon) emerges from the shadows.

He personifies Death, although the role is not identified by that name in the program. (Balanchine "definitely asked me if I wanted to be Death," Francisco Moncíon recalled.) In the last waltz ("La Valse"), Death offers her a black necklace, black gloves, a bouquet of black flowers, and a see-through black robe to wear over her white gown. She admires herself in the cracked mirror he holds, but then, horrified by her own image, she throws the flowers to the floor. It's too late. In the grip of Death, she is whirled around, faster and faster, on a runaway carousel that never slows until he suddenly drops her lifeless body and runs off. She has been danced to death.[3]

Her suitor reappears and, lifting the corpse, carries it upstage, where others quickly surround him. Soon he is at the turning center of a macabre mass of frenzied dancers, whirling faster and faster around the lifeless, white form, hoisted high overhead, until the music comes to a crashing, abrupt stop. To enhance the chilling effect of this moment, Le Clercq chose makeup that made her look paler than the other women on stage.[4]

Critics raved. Lillian Moore wrote of her performance, "Fleet, fragile, touchingly young, incredibly lovely, she brought it a haunting quality which lifted it into the realm of poetry." B. H. Haggin applauded "the personality that irradiated her face and made it the dramatic mask of a great actress." Moncíon said that no other dancer matched "the way she reached forward and seemed to grab the empty air." She had practically torn the necklace from his hands.[5]

In several interviews, Le Clercq described rehearsals of the ballet. "'Put on the necklace and look in the mirror,' Balanchine told me. Well, there are lots of ways of putting on a necklace and looking at yourself in a mirror." Getting her hands and arms into the long gloves in one smooth move was near impossible, at first, so they used a trick. "I couldn't put my hand in it, so we wired the top. That way . . . it's open, so you know where it is and you can really go in. . . . As you pull it on, you pinch the wire . . . so that it fits."[6]

Tanaquil Le Clercq and Francisco Moncíon, *La Valse,* photo by Walter E. Owen, ca. 1951. Choreography by George Balanchine ©The George Balanchine Trust. Jerome Robbins Dance Division, The New York Public Library for the Performing Arts.

WALTER E. OWEN
NEW YORK

In the silent, black-and-white films with added music that show parts of her performance, she throws her head back and, with quick, deliberate gestures, thrusts her right hand, then the left, into the gloves Death holds out for her. "I had my way of doing it, almost as if you welcomed death. Somebody else could do it another way. He [Balanchine] gave you the leeway to do it with a little personality. Which some people might find surprising, because he's so often accused of eliminating the personality." Mary Ellen Moylan, a ballerina a few years older than Le Clercq, said, with wry humor, "If Balanchine liked what you thought he did, then he would let it stay."[7]

Edwin Denby commended that controlled depiction of wild abandon. When Le Clercq threw back her head and plunged her hands in the gloves, "diving to destruction," she made it look as if "she never even looked at the glove, but that's really impossible. So she must have been able to look at the glove without any emphasis and then put her whole emphasis on diving into it."[8]

Even in the briefest films of her performance, Le Clercq's radiance illuminates the screen. Balanchine made good use of the dramatic sweep of her long body, her mysterious allure and consummate elegance. When she begins her *pas de deux* with Magallanes, her long arms assume odd angles, as if speaking an ancient, quasi-Egyptian language. When she throws her head back, her incredibly sinuous back bends with it. She seems to have extra vertebrae.

The first time Allegra Kent saw *La Valse*, she was fourteen and Le Clercq, twenty-one. "Her quality of movement was at once fluid, abrupt, and sophisticated," Allegra wrote. "I was transfixed by her dramatic power onstage. . . . After that performance, Tanny became one of my idols." Around the same time, another teenager, Judith "Gigi" Chazin, the daughter of the professor who had hired Jacques Le Clercq at Queens College, saw Le Clercq dancing in several ballets. Decades later, Judith (by then the dance scholar Chazin-Bennahum) recalled the way Le Clercq had looked onstage. "She was luminous, startling, like a gazelle." Her presence and movements were so unbelievably delicate that "she seemed not human." After the performance, Gigi went backstage to meet her idol, bringing a rose as a gift. Tanny gave the young ballet student a radiant smile. "You must work very hard," she advised. "It will be difficult, but you will be the happiest person in the world."[9]

Le Clercq loved her role in *La Valse*, finding the ballet's ambiance "lovely . . . like going to a party." Watching from the wings, waiting for her entrance, made her want to join the waltzing dancers. "I felt that my character put on the jewelry, looked at herself in the mirror and really liked it, was rather eager to plunge into the gloves, then got the coat and thought how fabulous, and began to waltz away—almost mindlessly."[10]

This suspension of analytical thought was essential when dancing, she said. "My mind is really a blank. I do not dare to think of what steps come next, because they come too fast; the muscles have to learn them during rehearsal and remember them for me. Sometimes, during a waiting passage, I try to think of the next movement and become panicky because I can't; the moment my music cue sounds, the muscles respond at once and I am all right."[11]

Balanchine had worked closely with his costume designer, fussing over every detail and sparing no expense to make his latest muse shine. Karinska, who had generously donated time and materials to the company from its inception, now charged hefty sums for her exquisite costumes, often encrusted with jewels. (She bought costly fabrics in Paris, where she had designed costumes for ballet and theater companies in the 1930s.) After a smooth dress rehearsal, just before the opening, Balanchine said, "is fine, but we need chandelier." Lincoln Kirstein told him that they didn't have time or money for such a thing. "Yes, chandelier," Balanchine repeated in a dreamy voice, "real crystal." Ever eager to fulfill Balanchine's wishes, Kirstein dashed out.[12]

Maria had watched the rehearsal, too. She gave Tanny a suggestion that the younger dancer took to heart, "Do more." Thirty years later, Le Clercq was still grateful to Tallchief for telling her that she needed to make more of how she handled the flowers and put on the gloves. Most dancers were "too busy with themselves," Le Clercq said. But Maria Tallchief cared about Balanchine's ballets as much as she did.[13]

Lincoln Kirstein had done more, too; when the curtain rose, there was an enormous Waterford crystal chandelier hanging from the center of the stage. (He had dashed off to a store on Fifty-Seventh Street and bought it.) The stagehands managed to wire the chandelier in time for the first performance. To Kirstein, nothing was too good for George Balanchine, and for Balanchine, at that moment, nothing was too good for Tanaquil Le Clercq. "The ballet is a purely female thing; it is a woman, a garden of beautiful flowers, and man is the gardener," he famously said. "Woman can do without man in the ballet, but man cannot have any ballet company without woman . . . the goddess, the poetess, the muse." (Those words were spoken in 1965, when he had another, younger muse in mind, Suzanne Farrell.)[14]

Long after Le Clercq was paralyzed, *La Valse* haunted Balanchine, especially the ending where her limp body was held aloft in the center of the stage, as the swirl of dancers spun her around, clockwise, in a mad, deathly whirl. Five years after the premiere, she did dance until she collapsed, and came close to dying from polio. Balanchine always felt guilty about having cast her as the doomed girl in this ballet, now perhaps forever associated in his mind (according to the scholar Elizabeth Kendall) with a solo he had helped his friend Lidia Ivanovna make for herself to music by Sibelius, "Valse Triste," a dance "about being trapped and fighting with death."[15]

Le Clercq was too down-to-earth to share his fatalistic superstitions, as is evident from a letter she sent from Warm Springs, Georgia, during her convalescence. After all, one can imagine her reasoning, many classic ballets end with at least one death, a theme in all the arts since their inception. Hadn't he cast her as the star of *Cinderella* in 1949, a ballet with a happy ending? It was his first venture for television, for a CBS series *Through the Crystal Ball,* set to music by his beloved Pyotr Ilyich Tchaikovsky, an homage to Le Clercq as well as the composer, who had never completed the score for an envisioned *Cinderella* ballet for the Bolshoi. (Balanchine used excerpts from Tchaikovsky's Symphonies no. 1 and 2 and the adagio from his Symphony no. 3.)[16]

Tanny, one of the first dancers to ever appear on the small screen, had been introduced to the American public at age ten in the same year as television, 1939, although few people saw the show on NBC. By 1940, there were only two thousand TV sets in the entire country, no rival to movies. Even earlier, at age nine, Tanny had been screen-tested for a film called *Zaza,* starring Claudette Colbert. Paramount Pictures offered her an eight-year contract, but her mother wouldn't consider it. Dancing came first.[17]

TV appearances that enhanced Le Clercq's profile as a ballerina were another matter. She performed in the first color telecast on June 25, 1951, "Miss CBS Color," dancing in *La Valse* with other members of the New York City Ballet, but few people saw her. There were about ten million TV sets in the country by then, but only twenty-five were equipped to view the program, a publicity stunt for the network and the ballet company that *Life* magazine featured in a story that month.[18]

Now that she was becoming better-known, Le Clercq was even more in demand as a model for top designers. On television, wholesome, well-fed actresses playing mothers were selling washing machines and other appliances to the burgeoning middle class during the postwar years. But in the pages of high-end fashion magazines that catered to wealthier tastes, European chic was reasserting itself in American fashion. They all wanted Le Clercq.

As long as outside activities didn't take too much time away from ballet, neither Balanchine nor her mother objected. Edith had continued to be a regular at rehearsals, performances, and even on tour. It's not clear precisely what year she and Jacques Le Clercq separated, although Powell's diary indicates that the final rift occurred shortly after he returned from the war. By 1953, Jacques may have already been living with the recent widow Marjorie "Midge" Limroth, who became his second wife in 1956. And yet, as late as 1950, Tanny was still helping Edith to maintain the fiction that she came "from a happy congenial home and family of which she is very proud."[19]

Although her daughter was twenty-one when she started going out with Balanchine, Edith chaperoned her first dates with him. Soon Tanny had moved out of her mother's apartment and into her own tiny place at 154 East Sixty-First Street. Most unmarried women did not live openly with male friends then. But it is clear from her letters that she was already spending a lot of time with Balanchine, in and out of a ballet studio, complicating things for Robbins. He wanted her for a leading role, the Novice, in his new ballet, *The Cage,* set to a strident piece by Stravinsky, Concerto in D for String Orchestra.

The story was a daring one, especially for ballet: A female insect emerges from her chrysalis (a kind of white bridal veil) and kills a male intruder by strangling him (her knees pressed to his neck like a vise), until he falls and she rolls the corpse over with one foot. She mates with another male, letting him lead her in an ecstatic *pas de deux* until she gets a signal from her queen. After using her powerful legs and feet to subdue him, too, she can't resist lying down on his prone body, her limbs twitching in an agonized ecstasy. But she soon dispatches this mate as well and is embraced by the tribe. And yet she seems oddly innocent, ruled by instincts she can't understand.

All males are intruders in this close-knit female world. It is a variation on the included/excluded theme that Robbins had developed in *The Guests.* (Robbins always said that he was inspired by act 2 of *Giselle,* in which the Wilis drive Hilarion to death.) In 1955, he admitted that Tanaquil Le Clercq had, in part, inspired *The Cage.* "I am very touched by the people I work with," he said in an interview, "and I am very sensitive to Le Clercq's dancing. In those days, her movement had a quality that made me think of a young animal coming into its own, like a gauche young colt, soon to become a graceful thoroughbred. There was a kind of aura about her, the spirit of the adolescent emerging into the sensitive young woman."[20]

Before choreographing the ballet, he had asked her to marry him, but she'd already chosen George Balanchine. Perhaps Robbins worked out his pain (at what he had perceived as a stinging rejection) in this ballet about lethal, insect-like females. He had wanted Tanny for the role of the innocent creature who becomes a ruthless killer, but Balanchine said he couldn't spare her, although he usually gave Robbins whatever he wanted. Throughout the early 1950s, Mr. B went so far as to insist that she should *not* take this part. Le Clercq had been reluctant to do it herself and perhaps had asked Balanchine to intercede for her, to avoid hurting her friend's feelings. (There is evidence of that in a letter she sent to Robbins later.)[21]

She did attend rehearsals of *The Cage* in the spring of 1951, as an understudy-alternate for the Novice, danced by Nora Kaye (born Nora Koreff), on whom Robbins made the role. Kaye, known for the dramatic intensity of her dancing (especially in Tudor ballets) was an outspoken New Yorker, witty and intellectually omnivorous, who shared Jerry's Russian-Jewish origins. She had worked with him since their Ballet Theatre years and defected from that company to join Balanchine's that year, which also marked the start of her brief engagement to Jerry. (An occasional lover of Nora's, he had proposed to her soon after Tanny turned him down.) Robbins's first title for his new ballet had been *The Amazons,* which he initially envisioned as a female tribe. But when he happened to see a book on spiders, *The Cage* emerged from his imagination and angst. He realized, "I did not have to confine myself to human beings moving in a way that we know is human. . . . Sometimes the arms, hands, and fingers became pincers, antennae, feelers."[22]

The ballet begins with the dancer-insects thrusting out their arched hands-pincers, throwing back their heads, and opening their mouths in a silent, grotesque grimace. "It is like a scream of triumph," Robbins said. The gesture is reminiscent of the way Le Clercq thrust her head back when slipping her hands into the gloves in *La Valse.* Jerry had just seen that ballet, which premiered in February. Insect movements also inspired the bent arms and splayed fingers of his unusual *port de bras.* He used legs (often bent and oddly angled, too) in similar ways.[23]

The set featured ropes that could be loosened and tightened to dramatic effect, resembling a giant web. According to Barbara Bocher, a corps member who was terrified by Robbins's "thunderbolt changes of mood," the ferocity displayed onstage echoed what happened in the rehearsal room. He insisted that the dancers in the corps had to "look as monstrous and grotesque as possible," not pretty. They rehearsed on pointe while he kept changing his mind, hours of new variations that required "repeated stabbing of our toes into the floor, harder and harder, it was never forceful enough." Whenever their movements weren't sufficiently ugly, everyone was subjected to his "ear-splitting rage." A recurrent mantra, shouted mainly at his corps dancers (no matter what the ballet), was so often repeated that it soon lost its charge: "You look like shit, you dance like shit, you are all shit!" But it had the power to shock Barbara, barely sixteen years old. At the end of an excruciating rehearsal, she put her leg up on the *barre* to stretch and noticed, "five spots of dark red blood where each of my toes had bled through the pink satin pointe slippers."[24]

Years later, Robbins said: "I had to work hard with the corps initially, but once they understood and felt physically a quality I was after, they went ahead like wildfire. Stravinsky's score is stinging; it really pulls your guts out of you." The ballet had a similar effect on audiences. On opening night, June 14, 1951, Robbins's own mother walked out. He didn't see all the performances himself. *The Cage* had failed to fulfill his vision, even though Anatole Chujoy proclaimed the work "the most important premiere of the season."[25]

Soon after the opening, the choreographer left for Europe. His long absence triggered many letters from Le Clercq. In September she shared a strange dream. "I dreamt last night that you had returned," she wrote. "It was frightening. I think you cryed on a sofa— it was all mixed up, but seemed so vivid— STOP ANALYZING IT RIGHT THIS MINUTE."[26]

Robbins stayed away for months, longer than anyone in the company expected, in spite of letters from Lincoln Kirstein urging him to put his insecurities aside (while acknowledging that they fueled his genius) and accept the obligations his talents demanded. Balanchine was putting together a new work, *Tyl Ulenspiegel*, with a role for Robbins, and someone had to do something for Tallchief, who was "in nobody's mind at the moment, she has not really had anything for two years, with FIREBIRD. In Balanchine's present state of wedded bliss, he is not likely to give a present to the other girl." (It was almost-wedded bliss. A legal marriage to Le Clercq was still on hold.) Kirstein expressed a longing to see Tanny in *The Cage*, "if I don't get our eyes scratched out." Balanchine, who was in Hollywood that July, "feted by the Goldwyns," along with Le Clercq, her mother, and Magallanes, had apparently opposed the idea. (She didn't perform the part until 1954.)[27]

Perhaps the reluctance came from Tanny. Before she left New York that summer, she wrote to Jerry: "I watched the Cage from the wings and it made me squirm— I think I take it all to personally it's like an insult, or nasty re-

WALTER E. OWEN
NEW YORK

Nora Kaye and Nicholas Magallanes, *The Cage,* choreography by Jerome Robbins, photo by Walter E. Owen, ca. 1951. Jerome Robbins Dance Division, The New York Public Library for the Performing Arts.

mark made to me— I don't know it, and I don't want to bother Nora about it, and I wouldn't be good. . . . Please don't be mad, I can practically *see* you shaking your head over all this now—"[28]

After she returned to New York, she saw *The Cage* again and now thought it "marvelous," she wrote to him on Queens College stationery. (Her father had lent her his place, bigger than hers, while he was away at Yaddo, a colony for artists and writers.) She could not understand the critical reaction to the ballet, why everyone said, "it's repulsive, strange terrifying but it's the best thing Jerry's done." As for herself, she assured him, "I loved it."[29]

Robbins worried that the "love" and "communion" in the *pas de deux* between the Novice and her mate (Magallanes) had not come across. "I don't see love in *The Cage* at all," Tanny answered. "It isn't there, so why do you expect it? It seems to me she just 'uses' Nicky [Magallanes] then kills him. . . . You don't kill when you are in love— *only* kill *with* love— I think it's fine the way it is." Whatever did she mean? Was she thinking of the obliteration of self in a love affair?[30]

The Cage was not the first ballet in which a female had performed the ritual killing of a male onstage. Le Clercq had done it as the leader of the Bacchantes in *Orpheus,* exiting the stage afterward with what the critic David Vaughan, archivist of the Merce Cunningham company, later described as a memorably "obscene strut." Balanchine privately expressed his irritation that Robbins's new ballet had imitated his own work in some measure. He advised a dancer who dared to voice her revulsion for *The Cage* to close her eyes and just listen to the music. And yet he was filled with (albeit disgruntled) admiration, telling Jacques d'Amboise that Jerry's ballet "about insects eating men" was "not something I would do, but it's great." Balanchine had long been familiar with the Stravinsky concerto but he'd never figured out how to do anything with it. "After Robbins did *Cage,*" d'Amboise recalled him saying, "I decided not to try."[31]

Once Jacques had asked Balanchine why Robbins chose to work at the company, when he was already famous and making more money elsewhere. Mr. B had sniffed and answered, "He wants to see what makes Balanchine Balanchine, so he can steal from Balanchine." The rivalry between these men, personal and professional, was too intense, perhaps, for a close friendship, but their connection was strong and mutually beneficial. Each admired the other's talents. Balanchine and Kirstein called Robbins the greatest native-born American choreographer. They said it to flatter and cajole him, at times, but they meant it. "You are the only choreographer that the country has produced who has the equivalent authority as Balanchine and you will have to replace him when he is absent, incapacitate [*sic*], or dead," Kirstein wrote to Robbins. "I realize the responsibility but our talents do not entirely belong to us, nor do we choose them."[32]

Balanchine considered Robbins the master of a language of American gestures that he would never be able to speak as fluently. Whenever dancers complained that they couldn't work with Jerry because of his temperamental and demanding ways, Mr. B assured them that being cast by him would be good for their careers. He answered one grumbler with the words, "You know, dear, he will teach you how not to treat people."[33]

Balanchine knew that Robbins's ballets attracted bigger audiences, so he kept *The Cage* in the company's repertoire, where it remains. The first time the ballet was performed in Europe, it was briefly banned in Lausanne, Switzerland, but a court in The Hague ruled against those who had tried to ban it in Holland for "shameless" and "pornographic" content. The French and Italian critics were far more positive. Thanks in part, perhaps, to the initially negative publicity, the ballet became wildly popular and is still performed by companies around the world.[34]

Le Clercq made her New York debut as the Novice in October 1954, after Kaye returned to Ballet Theatre, although she had performed the part earlier that year on the U.S. tour. Critics lauded her dancing, but some denigrated her interpretation. "She lacks the almost vicious intensity with which Nora Kaye attacked the role," Lillian Moore wrote, finding her "coiffure, a 'ponytail' with straggling ends . . . most distracting."[35]

On the European tour of 1955, Nicole Hirsch of *France-Soir* missed the "somewhat unwholesome" personality which had infused the choreography with anxiety whenever Kaye danced. But Christine de Rivoyre, a prominent French journalist/novelist, did not agree. In the pages of *Le Monde,* she pronounced Le Clercq "excellent" as the Novice, noting the "unsettling mystery" of this "creature without weight, with eyes like precious stones, angular arms, arabesques that always seemed about to break, being so stretched out, as extreme as her thin body."[36]

Robert Barnett, a company soloist then, recalled that all the principal women in *The Cage* wore wigs, but Tanny "took her hair and braided it and used egg whites to stiffen it like tentacles on her head. It was completely her idea." A hint of antennae? She performed the role as long as she danced, to growing acclaim.[37]

When the Novice first emerges, she moves on tentative, oddly placed, and

Tanaquil Le Clercq as the Novice, *The Cage,* choreography by Jerome Robbins, photo by Walter E. Owen, 1955. Jerome Robbins Dance Division, The New York Public Library for the Performing Arts.

angled feet, as if testing her legs, the *young animal coming into its own* that Robbins had imagined. By her last performances of the ballet, she had infused the *pas de deux* with something akin to the "love" that he had wanted. The critic Clifford Gessler wrote in the *Oakland Tribune* in 1955, that unlike Kaye, Le Clercq had introduced "something like human feeling in a drama otherwise singularly devoid of it."[38]

Cakewalk and Convalescence

Four months after *La Valse* premiered, Le Clercq appeared in *Cakewalk,* the first ballet choreographed by a woman (Ruthanna Boris) for Balanchine's company. Boris had been a student in the original School of American Ballet class of 1934 and had also worked with Balanchine at the Ballet Russe de Monte Carlo, where she became a principal dancer. Invited by Mr. B to join his company, she had chosen to complete a 1950 tour first, not wanting to break her contract. Upon her return, he told her, coldly, that he no longer had room for her at the New York City Ballet. "If Anna Pavlova would come back from the grave I have no place," he said. Kirstein assured Boris that Balanchine was only being vindictive because his feelings were hurt. He advised her to choreograph a dance for the company with a role for herself in it, and Balanchine agreed to let her try.[1]

Boris found inspiration in some leftover costumes from Lew Christensen's ballet *Blackface,* stored in a warehouse. She decided to use them for a comical work without a story, based on the music and dance styles of an old-fashioned minstrel show, but leaving out the blackface and demeaning comedy. In preparation, Boris took lessons from an eighty-year-old woman who had been a cakewalk dancer. *Cakewalk,* set in the antebellum South, used music by Louis Moreau Gottschalk, a nineteenth-century composer/pianist from New Orleans who had fused folk tunes with marching band music, the waltz, and lyrical, virtuosic piano works. The dancers entered doing the *grands battements* in front, with legs as high as possible, that gave the dance its name. A painted backdrop by Robert Drew of a Mississippi River steamboat, in addition to some of his original costumes, had been recycled from *Blackface.*[2]

After years of dancing in Balanchine's demanding ballets, Le Clercq was having a ball. She and her shorter partner, Beatrice Tompkins, danced the roles of the two Ends. In standard minstrel shows, the endmen told jokes and performed comic songs. Boris translated their routines into steps full of tricky shifts from pointe to flat feet. The Ends had the best parts in this long, repetitive ballet. They did a comical duet with hopping turns, shoulder shrugs, sideways-leaning steps with kicks in sync, fluttering fingers, and a knock-kneed, hand-switching, bent-over Charleston. Boris had gotten additional comic mileage out of the height difference between Tanny and Bea Tompkins (one of the shortest members of the company).[3]

To George Balanchine, this was silly stuff. Ruthanna Boris was wasting his treasure, Tanaquil, on a ballet that he deemed unworthy of her gifts. After glimpsing an early rehearsal for *Cakewalk,* most likely through the peephole in the studio door, he told Boris that he did not want Tanny to "dance like that." Without giving her time to reply, he said (as Boris recalled): "It is not good for her to make funny! Soon she must dance Odette; now she must prepare. She likes too much funny! She makes funny every day, after the class. You must find someone else for your ballet!" Boris asked him to please wait until she had finished the dance. She would show it to him at a final rehearsal. Reluctantly, he agreed.[4]

To be prepared by Balanchine to alternate with Maria Tallchief in the lead role in *Swan Lake* was a huge honor, but it was no lure for Le Clercq. Almost every ballerina in the world dreamed of being the Swan Queen, but not her. "She had her own ideas about dancing—about everything really," Tallchief observed, "and relished roles that showed her in a more unconventional light."[5]

"There he goes," Tanny complained to Ruthanna Boris, "trying to ruin my life again!" She was determined to do *Cakewalk* no matter what: "I don't care what he says! I love it!"[6]

One afternoon, Boris went into a studio to do a practice *barre* at lunchtime, an hour when she expected it to be empty. Le Clercq was stretched out on her stomach on the floor, reading. She waved hello with one foot but kept on reading. She read a great deal for her own pleasure when she was young, including essays by Gide and the novels of Henry James.[7]

Mr. B opened the studio door. He exclaimed something that sounded like *Aha!* Then lowering his voice, he addressed her with irritation. "Tanny! You read but pirouettes need practice. Please, close book, go to small studio, practice pirouettes. Not enough strong yet!" Tanny did not budge. Eyes fixed on her book, she said in a loud, angry voice, "Practice! Practice! Practice! Always my body! What about my mind?" Balanchine clutched his head and shook it from side to side. Boris caught his eye and gave him a grinning, pantomimed, *What can you do?* He marched out, exasperated.[8]

Tanny continued reading. When she finally got up, she stretched and did some ballet moves, as if warming up, still holding her book under her right arm. After a series of turns in an improvised dance brought her to the door, she did an arabesque with her head facing Boris, waved goodbye with her book, and left the room. Had she dared to defy Balanchine because he was so infatuated that she knew he would not push her too far? In any case, her resistance worked. When Boris was finally ready to show her ballet in three parts to Balanchine, he watched it all and said, "You make good dance, interesting classical ballet American dance. Is okay." Hearing that, Tanny took off running in a big circle around the studio, shaking her hands with exuberance.[9]

Years later, Boris recalled the pleasure of working with her, "a sweet, attentive, diligent pupil" with a body that covered space "like a young tornado, whirling like a dervish. Tanny loved to move—she played with the space around her as if it were a living thing; indeed, space that she filled with her improvised bouncing, leaping, and running came alive around her as she passed through it."[10]

Although the public received *Cakewalk* with enthusiasm and Le Clercq was pronounced "excellent" in it by Walter Terry, who noted the "long and loud applause" for "this fine bit of Americana" in his review, Tanny indicated, in more than one letter to Jerry, that she did not think of it as a great ballet. Neither did Balanchine, who agreed with Terry that it was too long. He made cuts in *Cakewalk* on European tours without consulting Boris, to her irritation. And she never did become a member of his company, although she choreographed and/or performed in other works for it and his dancers.[11]

Cakewalk was not Boris's first contretemps with Balanchine. Since 1940, when she was dancing with the Metropolitan Opera Ballet, she had been a member of the American Guild of Musical Artists (AGMA), the union representing ballet dancers and opera singers. Later, she served on the union's board. At first Balanchine was skeptical about unions for dancers, and they had argued about the issue. "What kind of artist will you be?" he had asked her. "Do you want to count the pirouettes by the dollar?" She had answered, "Why not? Then maybe we will do more pirouettes."[12]

Making Balanchine see the advantages of unions for anyone other than manual laborers took longer than winning his approval for *Cakewalk*. He hated the interruptions for the rehearsal breaks that union rules required. But Kirstein, always on the side of labor even though he was a manager, must have been more persuasive than Boris. Ballet Society was listed as an AGMA sig-

Publicity photo of Tanaquil Le Clercq (*on floor*), with, *left to right:* Mary Ellen Moylan, Maria Tallchief, Marie-Jeanne, and Ruthanna Boris (*on ladder*), photo by Larry Colwell, 1951. Courtesy of NYCB Archive.

natory from the 1947–48 season on. After it was renamed the New York City Ballet, the company signed a "Basic Agreement" with the union "for the 1949 and/or 1950 season." Balanchine even served on the committee that planned AGMA's annual Christmas party, a successful fundraiser for the union that was held at the Met on January 1, 1950. "My Muse must come to me on union time," he famously said.[13]

Many years later, he apologized for his prior stubbornness. "Ruthanna, do you remember? You said union was good. I said union was bad. You were right. I was wrong. Union makes my work easy; it tells us what we must do, what we must pay, takes care that dancers know what they should have. This saves us time; it saves us money; it makes us partners with our dancers, not enemy to them—and teaches dancers to take care of themselves. So, please, here is my apology."[14]

He had a hard time understanding why money mattered so much to others, an attitude Tanny shared. Writing to Jerry Robbins from her hospital bed in Copenhagen, she had thanked him for the flowers, gifts, and letters he had sent and expressed the hope that his latest Broadway show "makes tons of money— You must explain to me some day why you need so much money." Balanchine's lack of angst is more surprising than Le Clercq's, a Depression-era child who hadn't experienced deprivation and had never struggled to survive as a dancer.[15]

In the summer of 1951, the company was on a long layoff, with no tours. In July, Le Clercq sent a postcard of the California coast, just south of Big Sur, to Robbins, who was on his way to Greece. "Is the sky really so blue?" she asked, "and is the air like no other?" The card had a black-and-white vertiginous view of Lucia Lodge and Highway No. 1. "Our drive here is fabulous—sea on the left, cliffs on the right— Passed San Simeon." Hearst's Castle brought to mind the film based on his life, *Citizen Kane,* "very spooky— fog coming in and a storm starting— love, Tansy" She wrote nothing about her mother or Magallanes, who had been with them in Hollywood the week before.[16]

Returning to New York in the heat of early August, she tried to open a window in Balanchine's apartment (residential air-conditioning being a rarity then) and cut her wrist and thumb. "I almost fainted twice (real coward)," she informed Robbins, who was in Italy. Tanny recuperated at Natasha Molostwoff's beach house on Fire Island, that long, skinny sandbar off the South Shore of Long Island. "Really dread the thought of working," she confided in another letter to Robbins a few weeks later. "The body just ain't willing."[17]

Molostwoff, a Russian-speaking exile a year older than Balanchine, had come to the United States from Azerbaijan as a girl. First hired as a secretary, she became an assistant to the director of the School of American Ballet, Eugenie Ouroussow, and assumed that position in 1976, when Ms. Ouroussow died. Warm and intelligent, Natasha had known Tanny and Edith, to whom she was also close, since Tanny's first day at the school. With Natasha, who was part of the ballet world but not a dancer vying for Balanchine's attention, Tanny could relax.[18]

The fall season began on September 4, so rehearsals started early, on August 13. Le Clercq stayed at her mother's place on Madison Avenue, near the dance studio, although she seemed to have retained the use of her father's place as well. They had a sort of "salon." Edith "gets the food all ready and when rehearsals are over everyone comes over— It's fun," she told Jerry. On August 28, she wrote a long, gossipy letter to him. "George and I are definitely not married. . . . Maria and Nicky aren't carrying on. She likes that flyer that was at your going away party." Tallchief did marry the dashing young pilot, Elmourza Natirboff, a handsome Circassian with "the manners of a Russian aristocrat." But their tumultuous marriage in 1952, soon after she received an annulment from Balanchine, lasted less than two years. Her marriage to a Chicago businessman, Henry Paschen, endured. Elise Paschen, their only child, became a distinguished poet.[19]

Although she admired Maria enormously, Tanny was intimidated by her. "Diana is doing Barocco with Maria," she told Jerry in that same long letter, "and said the same things I did when I danced Mozart with her. You just feel very inadicuate suddenly and as if a steam roller ran over you." The letter continued with the first indication that she might not be up to dancing by September: "George just won't do Apollo untill I can. He is so stubborn sometimes. I've told him it doesn't make any difference to me, only La Valse does." She signed the letter: "Love Pussy Piston and her snapping gams."[20]

She had grown increasingly impatient for Jerry to return. "I wish you would come back," she wrote. "You *have* to some time you know? So why not soon." He was in Italy by the time she moved back into her own place. "Daddy came back from Yaddo," she reported, "so I'm in my *apartement*. I think it is the dirtiest, grittiest apt in N.Y. I clean and next day— filth." (The French spelling of *apartment* may have been for comic effect.) Her father, she informed Jerry, "is a member of the poetry society." She confessed that she had also been a member until "I laughed to hard, and couldn't go back again."[21]

Just before the opening of the fall season, she sprained her ankle. The X-ray showed "a little bone disconnected," she told Jerry. "Got all in a flurry but they finally said it was an *old* injury— Probably one of those times I kicked you in *Bourrée.*" The doctor had ordered her to stay off the foot for a week, so Maria had taken over one of her signature roles, *La Valse.* "I don't know why I get such a feeling of ownership," she complained. "It just would be nice to have some one thing that is yours come what may—how selfish can I get."[22]

Near the end of September, Monción wrote to Robbins that "Tanny's mishap" was putting a heavier load on other ballerinas in the company who were not up to the task: "Maria plays *Valse* like a bewildered girl, instead of the decadent, greedy characterization which makes Tanny's version so effective."[23]

Her recovery was so slow that it seemed unlikely she would perform during that brief season of less than three weeks. Balanchine postponed a revival of *Apollon Musagète* (now called *Apollo, Leader of the Muses*), his seminal work from 1928, because she was not up to dancing the role of Polyhymnia, the Greek muse of sacred poetry and song, dance, and pantomime, originated by Felia Doubrovska. Set to a Stravinsky score for stringed instruments, the ballet included a fast variation for Polyhymnia, full of whipping turns and arms, seesaws from arabesque to grand battement, and abrupt changes of direction, a dance she had to perform, much of the time, with a finger held to her lips. Her part also required the jazzy prancing to syncopated rhythms, rather like a 1920s music-hall hoofer, that she excelled at.

Balanchine's *Apollo* originally began with the god's birth, followed by visits from the three muses, his half sisters (Calliope, muse of poetry, and Terpsichore, muse of dance, being the other two), and ended with his ascent to Mount Parnassus. The work, his first collaboration with Stravinsky, is the earliest Balanchine ballet still in his company's repertoire. He looked back on it as "the turning point of my life. In its discipline and restraint, in its sustained oneness of tone and feeling, the score was a revelation. It seemed to tell me that I could dare not to use everything, that I, too, could eliminate." He kept eliminating elements every time he revived the work, a process he described as "reducing what seemed to be multiple possibilities to the one which is inevitable." (His deletion of the birth scene that opened the original ballet is still lamented by many who remember it, but that scene has been retained by other companies.)[24]

A planned revival of Balanchine's *Concerto Barocco* did open on time. Choreographed in 1941 and frequently performed since then, this early abstract ballet is widely considered the perfect embodiment of its music, J. S. Bach's Double Violin Concerto in D Minor. After she recovered from her injury, Tanny was one of the two principal women (along with Diana Adams) who

André Eglevsky in *Apollo* with the three Muses, *left to right:* Diana Adams as Calliope, Maria Tallchief as Terpsichore, and Tanaquil Le Clercq as Polyhymnia, photo by George Platt Lynes, 1951. Used with Permission of The George Balanchine Trust and The George Platt Lynes Estate. Choreography by George Balanchine ©The George Balanchine Trust. Jerome Robbins Dance Division, The New York Public Library for the Performing Arts.

regularly soloed in this masterpiece, performed since 1951 in simple practice clothes. Their long legs and arms could have conducted the orchestra, rising and falling in rhythm with the musical lines. A ballet with a *pas de deux* of heavenly lifts and deep backbends, its complex choreographic patterns mirror the score with a breathtaking precision that sometimes has a jazzy, fugal syncopation. Near the end of the second movement, the *Largo ma non tanto,* the lone male dancer holds his partner at an angle, like a broom, to sweep the floor with the tips of her pointe shoes, a lift that in its upward sweep and daring is as rapturous as the high ones.

The dancers in *Concerto Barocco* are the ever-moving parts of one musical machine, the eight corps members doing essentially the same challenging steps as the soloists and for even longer, dancing without pause. Near the end of the twenty-minute ballet, the corps begins a series of rapid hops on pointe, followed by the soloists, a step requiring extremely strong ankles and feet. When the ballet opened at City Center on September 13, 1951, Tanny could only watch; her ankle was still too weak. But she had been busy, preparing for the November opening of an exhibit of her photos at the New York Public Library's Music Library, on East Fifty-Eighth Street, "so I am enlarging like crazy," she wrote to Jerry.[25]

Dance News published a short piece on the exhibit by Walter E. Owen, a photographer who called her work "topnotch." She preferred natural light, she told him, and her favorite part was watching an image slowly appear in

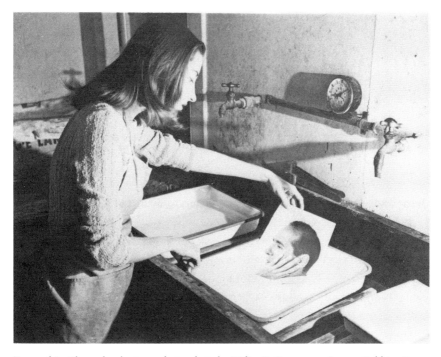

Tanaquil Le Clercq developing a photo, photo by Walter E. Owen, 1951. Jerome Robbins Dance Division, The New York Public Library for the Performing Arts.

Tanaquil Le Clercq holding Ciro-Flex camera, photo by Walter E. Owen, ca. 1953. Jerome Robbins Dance Division, The New York Public Library for the Performing Arts.

the developer solution. He photographed her doing just that, bent over a tray of developer as an image of Jerry Robbins appeared.[26]

Le Clercq had picked up the photography bug from Robbins and, like him, developed, enlarged, and printed her own pictures. She had started out using a cumbersome Ciro-Flex before receiving, as a gift from Balanchine, a lighter-weight, more expensive Leica. He also had technical knowledge about capturing dance on film, evident in a reference to what was most likely a freezeframe, now lost, enclosed in a 1952 letter to Le Clercq: "1/400th [of a second] with an F.8 lens opening."[27]

She preferred to take shots when her subjects were "completely relaxed," she told Don Langer, a photographer and teacher who wrote an article about her first show. Among her best are her photos of Robbins and Balanchine.[28]

Langer's article for the *New York Herald Tribune* was a snapshot of Le Clercq in action, photographing dancers from the City Center wings during the Seventh Waltz of *La Valse,* then handing her Leica to a stagehand to make her entrance during the Eighth. To photograph dancers in motion, she told him, you must "wait for a natural pause in movement." (Three years later, she disclosed to the readers of her fan club zine, *TANNY,* that she favored still shots to taking pictures of dancers onstage.) Langer praised her ability to build mood and tell a story "with a minimum of detail" but felt that she would

Jerome Robbins, photo by Tanaquil Le Clercq, 1950s. Courtesy of NYCB Archive.

George Balanchine, photo by Tanaquil Le Clercq, 1950s. BALANCHINE is a Trademark of The George Balanchine Trust. Courtesy of NYCB Archive.

need more printing experience for her prints to convey the "much wider tonal quality" of her negatives.[29]

Nevertheless, the general public and other photographers admired her work. Le Clercq received letters of inquiry about a "new-found technique" displayed in some photos overlaid with an "intricate and symmetrical pattern of light streaks." She had been trying to develop a roll of film in her darkened kitchen when her cat pushed open the door, letting in light. All letters on the subject of these unusual effects were answered the same way: "To make pictures such as these, first get a curious cat."[30]

Le Clercq had continued to receive glowing tributes to her dancing, too, even during her period of convalescence. Thanks to Edith's connections to a "special correspondent" for the *St. Louis Post-Dispatch,* a long profile had appeared in that paper in September, "Adding Exotic Beauty to a Ballet." It mentioned the first color telecast of *La Valse* and a photo spread in the May 1951 *Vogue* that had featured Le Clercq. Her "exotic beauty and fluid grace" was deemed "a direct inheritance from her mother, Edith Whittemore Le Clercq . . . one of the most talented St. Louis debutantes of her day" and, lest anyone had forgotten, the "premiere danseuse of St. Louis's Junior League."[31]

Tanny described her training: "You work, and then you collapse." Her schedule included two practice periods of ninety minutes each. "I study visually," she revealed, "although each person has a method of her own. I don't find it helpful to read about dancers or the dance, and generally speaking, I don't care to see dancing on the stage. Not unless it approaches perfection."[32]

Perfection in her eyes was and remained Balanchine's work. He was discreetly dubbed "her tutor and perhaps her closest friend." When she had started, he said, Tanny "looked like a cute little dancing mosquito." And then his tone turned rhapsodic: "She was formed the way a dancer should be formed, long of limb and fine of bone. . . . At 16 you don't know. You wait and you watch her, and you make her work. You know that she has the build and the intelligence and the fire. You teach her to have faith, and to believe in her work, for without it she would be a mechanical doll. And always you watch, and then one day you know, and you thank God."[33]

It is the only serious note in this article. Tanny, readers of the *St. Louis Post-Dispatch* were told, is a dark-haired, green-eyed voracious consumer of books who "reads in taxis, planes or dressing rooms," a habit that provoked complaints from her companions on a recent trip. What's more, "She enjoys swimming, but is so inept that she can barely remain afloat. . . . She doesn't particularly enjoy eating, and she doesn't enjoy drinking." What else wouldn't she do? "Under no circumstances would she marry a dancer."[34]

"And why would anyone else want to marry me?" she had asked, rhetorically. "I can't cook and I can't sew, and I've never trimmed a hat in all my life." The picture of marriage Tanny presents here seems far removed from her actual life, which was emancipated and rather bohemian by the standards of her mother's relatives. Only about one in three American women of working age were in the labor force by 1950, and even fewer upper-class women. Le Clercq was clearly conscious of her audience for this interview, comprised of women much like her mother, homemakers who knew how to cook, sew, and trim a hat. Hats were an everyday item for fashionable women like Edith, well into the 1950s, who would trim them by adding details (flowers, feathers, ribbons, etc.) to match their outfits. Their closet shelves held piles of round hat boxes. (After the 1956 opening of the hit film *My Fair Lady,* fancy hats for women reached a peak of popularity, but the relaxed youth culture of the 1960s soon made them obsolete.)[35]

Tanny's flippant remarks were taken seriously by the special correspondent, who concluded that her subject was a waif in need of a protector: "She looks lonely and she looks lost and young and vulnerable." If Le Clercq looked lost, it may have been because she was still unable to dance. And Robbins was constantly on her mind. She was fed up with his malingering, as she saw it. He had been gallivanting all over Europe and Israel that summer, mixing work and play, while she was laid up. "My ankle is absolutely no better— This is 5 weeks," she informed him. "I can't point and can't get up on toe and it's swollen all the time— also that Mortons to (my other foot) is hurting like mad. It's a nerve that gets pinched between bones." This gloomy period of inactivity brought to mind another time she had been unhappy, during the summer of 1949. She confessed that on her trip with Betty "the unhappiest time I spent was in Rome— " She had loved Italy, "Adored Florence best— Venice—but Rome kind of made me hot and heavy and 'depressed—'"[36]

By October, she got word that Jerry was sick and not coming home. Tanny suspected that was just an excuse for lingering in Europe. In a scathing letter, she ripped into him: "I think you stink. If you are sick why don't you come back? . . . If you can't dance you could at least come back and help. . . . As far as I can see you put on a *few*— three ballets—then rush off to Europe, to make money. . . . You are a wonderful dancer . . . you never dance—The best young choreographer and never choreograph—What the hell goes on? I'm sorry if this makes you so mad you won't write to me, I wish you would just explain— I'm understanding up to a point— Love Tan"[37]

The best older choreographer, they both knew, was George Balanchine, who had been preparing a new ballet for Jerry, she revealed, not knowing that Kirstein had already told him. (It was the title role in *Tyl Ulenspiegel.*) It did not take much reading between the lines for Robbins to get the wounding message that she felt he was betraying the company by staying away.

"George is your ideal, good," he wrote back. "But don't be a little girl about it and expect everyone else to be like him. He is my ideal too. I adore him as a person and he is my God as an artist. . . . [Y]our feelings around him must affect your feelings to me."[38]

Robbins had private troubles that he hadn't told her about, although he had shared them with Kirstein. Anticipating that others in the company would be furious at him for not returning, Jerry had told himself, as he wrote her, "Tanny will understand that it isn't caprice." Now *he* didn't understand *her.* "Was it because of George that you were so angry with me . . . or was it you, because of you. And where do I stand anywhere, anyway, with you."[39]

"I knew we would get around to the who stands where? and with who," she answered. "I just love you, to talk to, go around with, play games, laugh like hell etc. However I'm in love with George— maybe it's a case of, he got here first— Maybe not— I don't know— anyway, I'm staying with him— Can't we be friends? like they say in the movies— Please write— See you soon? Love Tan."[40]

Whether or not Le Clercq's letter was the main trigger, Robbins returned to New York in late October brimming with ideas. Soon he was working on a new ballet, *The Pied Piper,* with a terrific part for her. She didn't know that Jerry had stayed away because of his fears of being called to testify before the House Un-American Activities Committee (HUAC). Early in 1951, Ed Sullivan, the host of the most popular variety show on television, *The Toast of the Town,* had booked Jerry Robbins for an Easter appearance. But hearing rumors about his private life and Communist ties, Sullivan had abruptly canceled the appearance.

Sullivan was an unlikely TV host, a balding, middle-aged man utterly lacking charisma. He had an unctuous and shifty Uriah Heepish manner, no doubt on full display when he offered Robbins this deal: If he would give up the names of fellow Communists in the entertainment field, Sullivan would issue an innocuous excuse for the cancellation. If Jerry didn't, he threated to expose his homosexuality and political sympathies in his syndicated newspaper column. Like many people in New York theatrical circles then, as the dance scholar Lynn Garafola wrote, "Robbins knew many Communists and Communist sympathizers. He had lent his name to many left-wing causes and taken part in performances sponsored by organizations denounced in the late 1940s as Communist 'fronts.'" But he claimed not to know any Communists, although several were his close friends and associates. (Others were sympathizers like Nora Kaye and Ruthanna Boris, who participated in "The Bright Face of Peace," a world youth festival in Prague in 1947.)[41]

Sullivan, an unofficial bloodhound for HUAC, wasn't buying this. Terrified of public exposure and the loss of his livelihood, yet afraid to name names, Robbins fled the country. In the 1950s, homosexuality was a crime in England and the United States, punishable by prison time. Mass firings of homosexuals in the U.S. government had coincided, not accidentally, with the Communist witch hunt by right-wing members of Congress. In 1947, a group of producers, directors, and screenwriters (known as the "Hollywood Ten") refused to answer HUAC's questions and had been jailed for contempt of Congress. Upon their release from terms of up to a year, nearly all were blacklisted by the studios. (Some, like Dalton Trumbo, managed to keep writing for the movies under pseudonyms.) Now Senator McCarthy and his feared committee were going after big names on Broadway, in order to gain maximum publicity. Robbins had choreographed a 1951 hit musical, *The King and I,* soon to become a film. He was a big catch for HUAC and its henchmen, of which Sullivan was one of the most notorious.[42]

Since he had refused to give Sullivan what he wanted, Jerry Robbins was outed as a Communist sympathizer on the front page of the *Philadelphia Inquirer,* prompting his departure. (His friends kept the story out of the New York papers.) Letters piled up in Paris from his lawyer, pressing Jerry to come home and make a deal. (Le Clercq's letter may have been the last straw. He had returned to New York less than two weeks after receiving it.) After mounting pressure from the government and his lawyer, in May 1953 Robbins submitted to FBI interrogation. He named eight people, who soon lost their jobs. They, along with many others, never forgave him, nor could he forgive himself. His own sister and a favorite cousin didn't speak to him for years.[43]

Le Clercq surely had heard something about this, but until 1956 there's not a hint of it in her letters to Robbins. In late fall, soon after his return, she was strong enough to appear in a revival of a 1936 ballet by Antony Tudor, *Lilac Garden,* with new costumes by Karinska and décor by Horace Armistead. Her part, full of what critic Robert Sabin described as "exciting lifts," required as much acting as dancing. Every step and gesture conveyed powerful emotion. *Lilac Garden* is considered the first "psychological" ballet, a masterpiece still performed today. It was set to a moody piece by Ernest Chausson, Poem for Violin and Orchestra, Opus 25. The dramatic lighting by Jean Rosenthal further underlined the ballet's themes of unrequited love and stifled sexuality. The elegant costumes and set, a formal Edwardian-era garden party, seemed too opulent to Tudor. His original ballet was set in a "slightly decayed garden," decidedly middle-class, where a plot hinging on a marriage of convenience made sense.[44]

Hugh Laing, Nora Kaye, Brooks Jackson, and Tanaquil Le Clercq, *Lilac Garden,* photo by Roger Wood, 1952. Arenapal. Jerome Robbins Dance Division, The New York Public Library for the Performing Arts.

It is the eve of the wedding of a young woman, Caroline (Nora Kaye), to "The Man She Must Marry" for purely material gain. (In 1936, as well as at the November 30, 1951, revival at City Center, Tudor danced the latter role himself.) Also present at the party is "An Episode in His Past" (Le Clercq), who has a series of fleeting, angst-ridden encounters with her ex, the prospective bridegroom. She adored her costume, a long, fluid dress of Italian silk, and found the ballet "wonderful to dance" although she found the steps "uncomfortable" because "exactly where you don't want to go—*that's* where you go." Tudor did copious coaching, but unlike Balanchine, it was not about the steps, she said, but a "running commentary" on character motivation.[45]

Robert Sabin described Tudor's work as an "art of tension and release." To further heighten the tension, another party guest is the man Caroline still loves, "The Lover" (Hugh Laing). In the end, Caroline leaves the party with the man she doesn't love, holding the lilacs "The Lover" has given her. (At the original opening, Tudor had sprayed the theater with lilac scent.) "The Lover" is left alone on the stage.[46]

A Reluctant Swan and a Dragonfly

By November, Le Clercq was back in rehearsals for the winter (1951–52) season, preparing multiple roles. She was to make her debut in Balanchine's *Swan Lake* and, a few weeks later, to dance in a new Robbins ballet, *The Pied Piper,* which she compared to "one of Jerry's Broadway shows: flashy, happy-go-lucky, and clever." Balanchine had acquiesced to Baum's desire for a classic ballet to bring in crowds because the New York City Ballet needed money. He set one condition, to have the décor designed by Cecil Beaton.[1]

At that time most Western companies performed a one-act version of *Swan Lake.* (The Sadler's Wells Royal Ballet, with its full-length version, was a major exception.) Balanchine's one-act ballet was inspired by Lev Ivanov's choreography for acts 2 and 4 of the Petipa-Ivanov production. He used the music from act 4 but also included the valediction of Odette. Keeping most of Ivanov's choreography for the Swan Queen intact, Balanchine had largely rechoreographed the ensemble dances.

He had also heightened the drama, enhanced the role of the corps de ballet, and instructed the orchestra to play Tchaikovsky's score at a quick tempo. Balanchine had no interest in the original ballet, with its complicated narrative, and he made light of its mythic overtones. "How can you take the story of *Swan Lake* seriously?" he said. "It's time for a young prince to marry, he falls in love with a girl-swan, and naturally nothing good comes of it. It's nonsense!"[2]

Swan Lake premiered in 1951 with Maria Tallchief in the lead role. Cecil Beaton had designed the exquisite costumes, too, and his sets were inspired by German Renaissance engravings: a forest scene rendered in white ink on black backgrounds. Tallchief described the rehearsals: "It was one of the most difficult things I ever did. . . . I could see what he [Balanchine] wanted, but then I couldn't do it." The problem, she felt, was conveying the right mood in gestures, while keeping up the fast pace, rather than anything purely technical.[3]

"For my taste, the real Odette is more cold, more unobtainable, not dramatic," Balanchine said. His ideal Odette, like his ideal woman, was elusive, one who lured all the more by being resistant.[4]

Tanny had first performed as a swan at the King-Coit School, but she was considerably taller now. "I'm not a swan, I'm a crane," she protested to Balanchine, but she reluctantly yielded to his vision. Barbara Walczak, a solo-

Maria Tallchief, *Swan Lake,* ca. 1952, *BALLETS RUSSES, 2005.* Choreography by George Balanchine ©The George Balanchine Trust ©Zeitgeist Films/Permission of Everett Collection. .

ist in the company then, recalled how Balanchine demonstrated the Swan Queen's steps in a manner that was "incredibly beautiful." He kept asking Le Clercq and Diana Adams (who alternated with Tallchief in the role) to be "larger, wilder, more creaturelike." His instructions were insistent and relentless: "Don't put your heels down—it makes too much noise. Run faster. You're not turned out enough." Even though "like a gnat" he would "annoy and annoy you," Le Clercq said, he was "the only one I would trust absolutely 100 percent. If you think you've done something very well, and he says, 'Dear, it was very nice but you didn't move. It's English style. It's small. It looks very pretty, but you're meant to travel, cover space'—you'd remember that."[5]

He got her to go further than she thought she could, although she never felt comfortable in a role that made all the ballerinas who had inherited it tense. They had to perform complex steps on pointe, nonstop, while doing movements of the head, neck, and arms that risked a loss of balance. There was always the chance of a bad misstep or even a fall caused by miscalculation or a slippery stage. A sudden gust of wind could do it, when the company performed outdoors. In the celebrated adagio of the ballet, Odette must balance upon the tip of a toe shoe while her bent leg flutters beside the straight one with a tremulous, doomed poignancy.

Le Clercq may have been all the more intimidated because Tallchief had a reputation for being immune to stage fright. There was the oft-repeated story (which Maria denied in her memoir) that before going onstage for the first time in *Firebird,* she had been relaxed enough to bake an apple pie. "I would never bake an apple pie before I danced," Tanny said. "I would be lying on my bed, and then getting up and eating steak, and then taking a little powdered dextrose for quick energy." It was a common remedy the dancers carried with them on tour. This simple sugar, made from corn, gave them a fast burst of power, but it has little nutritional value. If too much is consumed, it can raise blood sugar to dangerous levels. Possible side effects include dehydration, shortness of breath, unexplained fatigue, nausea, and confusion. Just before going onstage, Tanny disclosed, "we cross ourselves, knock on wood, spit (nobody knows why; just an old ballet tradition), and leap out into the lights."[6]

On February 27, 1952, Le Clercq made her debut as Odette. She didn't realize how frightened she was until she put on her costume. Then she started crying so uncontrollably that the opening-night curtain was held for a half hour. "At last, still sobbing and trembling, she reached the wings and was pushed onstage. As she danced, she rained tears on her partner."[7]

She was afraid to look at the newspapers the next day, but John Martin's review in the *New York Times* was a rave: "Last night Tanaquil Le Clercq danced her first 'Swan Lake.' It is small wonder she was frightened, but she can breathe freely, for this morning she is definitely a ballerina. This is a very young Swan Queen, but no less royal because she is timid and fearful." It was "probably the most important moment in her career," according to Chujoy. He felt that one was not truly a ballerina without doing a major role in a classical ballet.[8]

It did not get much easier for her. Jacques d'Amboise recalled how, when she was scheduled to do *Swan Lake,* Mr. B would stand in the wings of the theater, shove her onstage, and "she'd stumble on for her entrance." Once, he pushed her so hard, she fell. Just to see that she was scheduled for *Swan Lake* made her so queasy that she would often vomit. It was her "least favorite role," Robert Barnett recalled.[9]

"I didn't feel I was ready for it," she said, thirty years later. "But George had nobody else at that time; Melissa [Hayden] would have been the logical one, but he didn't want to use her. Okay. So he shoved me into it, and I felt totally incompetent. I danced it off and on, not often, not often enough to ever feel comfy in it. I always felt, 'I shouldn't be here.'" Years later, she described her reluctance in words that echoed Maria Tallchief's: "It's a goal that you never reach . . . to dance like your image of you dancing. You have an idea of how you should look and how it should be done—and you never can do it, ever."[10]

Balanchine was not in New York for her second performance in March 1952, but in affectionate letters addressed to Miss Tanaquil Le Clercq, aka "pc" (for pussycat) and "My Baby Darling," he asked her how it had gone. He was in Milan, staging his *Ballet Imperial* for the ballet company of La Scala. At the first rehearsal, he wrote her, the tallest girls ("not very tall") looked to him like "ladys [*sic*] of the evening in the morning. . . . They all can sort of crawl bravely on their toes. . . . But my first impression is probably wrong. In a few weeks, this all will be beautiful."[11]

In a subsequent letter dated March 11, he announced that the ballet was done, "except for good dancing. I miss you Darling." He lamented that he was not receiving her "famus every day letters, even evry next day, or even two days apart." He signed off with the charming cat/mouse pictographs that appear in multiple letters to her.[12]

Le Clercq was near the end of an exhausting New York season, during which she had been suffering with a cold, when this letter arrived at her apartment on East Sixty-First Street, probably crossing one of hers, now lost. Although she had not achieved her ideal vision of the Swan Queen, her performances in the role continued to win plaudits from audiences and critics.

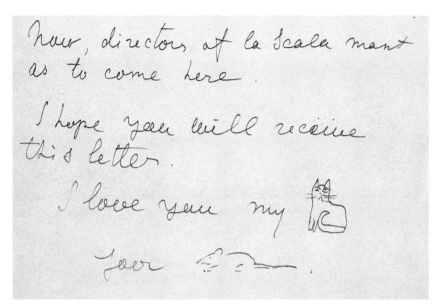

Signature by George Balanchine, letter to Tanaquil Le Clercq, 1952, Harvard Theatre Collection, Houghton Library, Harvard University, courtesy of the George Balanchine Trust. BALANCHINE is a Trademark of The George Balanchine Trust.

It was like a couture garment that she filled to perfection but couldn't wait to take off. *Caracole,* however, a thirty-minute ballet Balanchine had set to Mozart's Divertimento no. 15 in B-Flat Major, was pure pleasure. Le Clercq, dressed in a fluffy tutu with puffed sleeves, her head adorned with a tall, plumed headdress like a show horse, was partnered by Magallanes in the critically celebrated andante section.

Caracole is a term used in horsemanship to describe a half turn to the right or left. Was Balanchine's choreography for this ballet for five ballerinas and three male principals inspired by the precise prancing of Viennese horses? Even though the costumes (by Christian Bérard, originally for Balanchine's *Mozartiana,* 1933) were recycled, those bobbing white feathers (which the men also wore) seemed to suggest it. Maria Tallchief wrote in her memoir that the feathers "went waving all over the place every time we moved." Although Edwin Denby didn't like the costumes, he called the ballet, which premiered in February 1952, a "heavenly piece" that made its dancers look "effortlessly fantastic." It took considerable effort to achieve that effect.[13]

Caracole did not win favor with most London critics when the company

Tanaquil Le Clercq, Diana Adams, and André Eglevsky, *Caracole*, photo by Fred Fehl, 1952. Choreography by George Balanchine ©The George Balanchine Trust. ©The New York Public Library for the Performing Arts.

took it on tour in the summer of 1952. The precision of its choreography, the almost note-for-note rendering of Mozart's music, was compared to "drilling," mechanical and lacking in emotion. (Four years later, Balanchine used the same music and most of the steps to make a nearly identical work without the cumbersome costumes, *Divertimento no. 15*.)[14]

Caracole garnered more favorable reviews in continental Europe, along with *Swan Lake* and *The Pied Piper*, throughout the five-month 1952 tour, which almost didn't happen. Angry ballet enthusiasts had written letters to the board of City Center, protesting a scheduled series of performances in fascist Spain, then under the rule of the dictator General Francisco Franco.

Balanchine refused to cancel. The company *had* to tour that year, just to break even. In spite of abundant artistic success in 1951, by the year's end, it still had a deficit of twenty thousand dollars, even after canceling the fall season to save money. Some principal dancers supplemented their income by doing TV guest appearances, which paid handsome fees. Ruthanna Boris choreographed a CBS-TV adaptation of Rumer Godden's play *A Candle for St. Jude,* which aired on February 4, 1952. Le Clercq had a lead role, in which she did a *pas de deux* with Marc Platt, a former member of the Ballet Russe de Monte Carlo who had danced in *Oklahoma!* and other Broadway and Hollywood musicals. He told Boris that working with Le Clercq was "one of the most enjoyable professional experiences in my life. Tanny was so sweet, so patient, such a hard worker! We had so many good laughs together. She wasn't temperamental, the way some can be. I loved dancing with her."[15]

Hers was a major speaking part in the show, in which she played a young, ambitious dancer with decidedly modern ideas about her art. Her melodious, aristocratic alto conveyed imperious conviction in every line. Whether dancing, modeling, or acting, her grace and assurance charmed the critics. In the ballet company, they had a new nickname for her, one taken from football: "Triple Threat LeClercq."[16]

Given New York City Ballet's perilous economic situation then, Balanchine was eager for a new work from Jerry Robbins, whose ballets helped to fill City Center. On February 14, 1952, the company premiered *Ballade,* set to Debussy's Six Epigraphes Antiques and his flute solo, Syrinx. Robbins, inspired by Picasso paintings of circus performers, had created a wistful, poetic ballet on an unusual theme: what happened to the roles uninhabited by dancers? "There's that Petrouchka costume lying on a rack somewhere, or there's the role in limbo." He elaborated, decades later, "It's only when someone gets into that role that the role comes to life—exists again—and then when that person stops, the role collapses."[17]

The balloon man in the ballet represents the choreographer. He hands out balloons to deflated characters who are slumped over, as a light snow falls on them, until his bright gifts bring each one out of hibernation, back to life. When he takes back his balloons, the dancing figures collapse again, all except Le Clercq's androgynous character, Pierrot. She deliberately lets go of the string of her balloon before the man can reclaim it. He "gives her a dirty look and walks off. Curtain," as a *Daily News* critic described the ending.[18]

Robbins explained that Le Clercq's character "can't collapse because she has let go of the force that gives her life—or sleep. She's in a state of nowhere, really, while everybody else is in hibernation." Baffled critics were also in a state of nowhere, with no idea what the ballet meant. In her biography of Robbins, Deborah Jowitt sheds some light: "Tanaquil Le Clercq, dressed as Pierrot, rebelled at the realization that she lived only through the power of the balloon and let hers go. When the man retrieved his balloons, only she remained awake, unable to stir her comrades—facing an independent but lonely future." Was Robbins subconsciously expressing his feelings about her having favored one particular balloon man (Balanchine) over him? Walter Terry, kinder than others, pronounced the ballet "enormously poignant, enchanting. Sweet and tender and nostalgic, but what does it recall? Nothing very specific, admittedly."[19]

"Why did it have to mean anything?" Tanny said in an interview many years later. "Jerry established a mood and it worked." The mood he had established in the audience was more disgruntled than charmed. "It had a wonderful feeling when you did it," Barnett maintained, "but it just didn't go out toward the audience. It was too intimate."[20]

After an intermission, *Ballade* provided some unforeseen comedy. The next ballet on the program was Balanchine's *Pas de Trois,* with Maria Tallchief, André Eglevsky, and Melissa Hayden. Right in the middle of Eglevsky's *double tours,* Tanny's balloon came down and the three dancers "were kept busy dodging same to thunderous applause." Henceforth, the stage manager kept a BB gun on hand to shoot down the balloon before the curtain rose again.[21]

The Pied Piper, which Robbins had set to Aaron Copland's Concerto for Clarinet and String Orchestra with Harp and Piano, was far more successful with the public. After the premiere on December 4, 1951, it became a staple of the repertoire. The original piper was the great clarinetist Benny Goodman, for whom Copland had composed the piece in 1948. Goodman appeared onstage at the opening performance, perched on a stool to one side and accompanied by the orchestra in the pit. The set (if you could call it that) had a deliberately undressed look, with just a ladder and some flats leaning against the back wall of City Center.

As the piper played, his notes lured the dancers out like the rats in the old German tale "The Pied Piper of Hamelin." They scampered onstage in twos and threes, dressed in practice clothes, dancing as if possessed. Even their attempts to resist the piper were cleverly used in the dance. They *had* to move to his tune, which pushed and pulled them around the stage before they all collapsed, their twitching limbs still prodded by the music. "What did

I do?" Tanny said in an interview. "Well, I chewed gum and did a jazzy little dance. It was easy—and no toe shoes! We even got paid for providing our own 'costumes.'"[22]

In the liveliest part of the ballet, Le Clercq and Robbins danced a wild jitterbug with all the dancers onstage. Walter Terry described this section: "They do the Charleston, they lie on the floor in a vast vibrating mass, they freeze . . . pretend to resist or they yield crazily to a screaming command of the clarinet, to an irresistible rhythmic pattern . . . to the tickle of a single pointed note." The audience was tickled, too. *The Pied Piper* was a crowd-pleasing, laugh-filled lark with staying power. It got more applause on opening night in Paris, during the summer tour of 1952, than Balanchine's *Orpheus,* even though Stravinsky himself was conducting his own score. Nevertheless, it is now, along with *Ballade,* one of Robbins's *lost* ballets.[23]

Rehearsals with Robbins were never a lark. Early on, he had seen potential in Barbara Bocher, who had joined the company in 1949, at fourteen, garnering a lot of press attention as its youngest soloist during the company's first appearance in London the next summer. Robbins gave her solo roles in several ballets, including *The Pied Piper,* but they came at a price: he subjected Barbara to a barrage of backstage lectures, telling her that it was time she broke free of her mother, advice he probably had never dared to give Tanny. (In a memoir, Bocher blamed her departure from the company later on Robbins and, to a lesser degree, on Balanchine's failure to protect her from him.)[24]

The lighthearted mood of *The Pied Piper* gave no hint of this backstory. European audiences loved the playful Americanness of the ballet, with Le Clercq in a ponytail, cracking gum and bopping around the stage. Denby wrote that she was the only dancer in *Piper* who "does the style right, and looks witty and graceful and adolescent." The way that Tanny kept her wrist loose, but not floppy, reminded him of wonderful dancers he had seen at the Savoy in Harlem in the 1930s. Perhaps she had picked that style up in her classes at Dunham's school.[25]

At the end of *The Pied Piper,* a magnesium flash under the clarinetist's stool was followed by a blackout. When the lights came back on, the piper had vanished. But some clarinetists refused to remain onstage for the explosion. (The dancers began making bets on who would chicken out.) At the New York premiere, Benny Goodman had to be coaxed to remain seated until the end. It was not an unreasonable fear. The explosive flash powders in theatrical use then were unpredictably sensitive to variations in temperature and humidity. Margaret Hamilton, the Wicked Witch of the West in *The Wizard of Oz,* had been hospitalized after suffering second and third-degree burns from an explosion on set.[26]

On the 1952 European tour, after a fight with the music director, Leon Barzin, a clarinetist in Paris rebelled. His substitute, afraid of the explosion, would only perform in the refuge of the orchestra pit. Balanchine was pleased to sit on the stool onstage and mime the part, "& boy, no wonder he stopped dancing," Robbins sniped in a letter to Bobby Fizdale. "As Tanny said turning pale while watching him, 'what a ham.' It may make a difference in their relationship." It did not. Balanchine liked doing this part so much that he added fresh bits to his performances, night after night.[27]

Some company members balked at performing in Franco's Spain, although few would have dared to tell George Balanchine. A lofty, patrician figure, he ruled the company, sitting "on his own throne," as Jacques d'Amboise put it. And yet he often followed Kirstein's egalitarian inclinations. When European journalists asked him to name the stars of his company, he answered: "We don't have stars. All my dancers are stars." By 1958, New York City Ballet was listing its dancers alphabetically in programs and on posters.[28]

Le Clercq's letters home show no concern over the armed soldiers everywhere in Spain, although others on the tour expressed uneasiness about them. She judged the country by the reception the ballet company received. In Barcelona, at the beautiful, grand old Liceu Theater (later partially destroyed by fire), "They threw bunches of flowers at us," she reported to friends. Pigeons were released, flying up to the highest balcony, while the audience stood and clapped for at least five minutes. They were showered with gifts—Spanish lace *mantillas* for the women and cuff links for the men.[29]

She even liked the raked stage of the Liceu, similar to others in European theaters. It had been built on an angle, sloping upward from the front of the stage to the back, away from the audience, where it was highest. This steep angle gave her a chance to "really jump," she recalled. "It's hard getting uphill but coming down you're a goddess." Barcelona was *divine,* she wrote to Bobby Fizdale during that part of the tour, but not the bullfight she had witnessed, the poor bull "so weakened it seems very ill-matched."[30]

Jerry Robbins, touring with the company as a dancer for the first time in years, was shocked by his reduced status. At thirty-three, he felt he should no longer have to perform onstage. "This is silly," he remembered saying to himself. "What am I doing out here trying to look like a boy?" He felt like the odd man out throughout that tour. But the company was too small to spare anyone.[31]

Posters bearing the Balanchine name in large type, often set off by a box, were another irritation. Robbins, notoriously touchy about billing, was annoyed about the great man's name "plastered all over the affiches & no one else's." (Later, Jerry insisted upon and got a box around his own name, on posters, programs, and theater marquees.) In a letter from Lausanne to Bobby Fizdale, he gloated that *Pied Piper* had been "the rage of the first season in Paris," with *The Cage* "a close second." Jealousy over Tanny's impending marriage may have contributed to his irritation. He decided to stop dancing after the tour was over.[32]

Betty Cage was also irritated on that tour, but not with Balanchine. "The sort of thing that Nora does," she wrote to Kirstein, "is new to this company. The private press-agenting [*sic*] that goes on with her, the cocktails with all the right people, the interviews which she and Jerry manage to give with no mention of anything but *The Cage* and themselves. There is no one else in the company who acts that way." It was upsetting some of the principal dancers, she told him, especially Maria Tallchief and Melissa Hayden. Betty did not think that Jerry Robbins was a team player who could be counted on: "One day he protests that he wants to help, the next day he says he wants to go to New York and do a show, and every day he says that no one gets any publicity except George and that the tour is solely for the purpose of adding to George's personal fame." She asked Kirstein not to make a commitment to any ballet, by anyone, with a prominent part for Nora.[33]

Le Clercq never worried about how she was billed. As late as 1956, the company press book praised her flair for comedy and drama, as well as "the natural chic that made her one of the most versatile of ballerinas," but declared that Maria Tallchief was "considered the finest classical ballerina in the United States." If this bothered Tanny, she gave no sign of it.[34]

When the principal dancers and choreographers posed for a publicity photo around a grand piano, Balanchine sat on the bench, between Tallchief and Le Clercq, his back to the former in a tableau straight out of a ballet by Tudor. He was in between marriages, too, waiting for an annulment so that he could marry Tanny.

Jerry Robbins stood in the back, as far from the three of them as possible. He was not happy about the hierarchy at City Ballet, with Balanchine on top and the best dressing rooms assigned to the favored, as he wrote Fizdale from Lausanne. It reminded him of the old Ballet Theatre days when he had struggled for recognition. Now it felt even worse to him because he desperately missed his current boyfriend (the dancer, Buzz Miller) and his relationship

PR photo by Shoor (ASMP), February 1952, on back: "Taken the evening before George Balanchine announced his intended divorce from Maria Tallchief and his future marriage to Tanaquil Le Clercq." *Right front to left, clockwise:* Tanaquil Le Clercq, George Balanchine, Maria Tallchief, Melissa Hayden, Frederick Ashton, Diana Adams, Janet Reed, Jerome Robbins, Antony Tudor, Nora Kaye. BALANCHINE is a Trademark of The George Balanchine Trust. Jerome Robbins Dance Division, The New York Public Library for the Performing Arts.

with Tanny seemed drastically altered. "I don't see much of her," he told Bobby, "as George dictates everything—even that she should not learn Nora's role in *Cage.*" Tanny had the other women in the company "in a tizzy," he claimed, because she had been "acting like queen bee, (& not very well) & George favoring her more than he ever did anyone." Her clear preference for Balanchine was making Robbins seethe with a mixture of personal and professional jealousy. He could only seem to connect with Le Clercq onstage. "We danced Bourrée tonight," he reported, "& Tanny was human for a change."[35]

On tour, Le Clercq often shared a dressing room with her friend Pat Wilde, a good sport who was always willing to fill in for anyone. She found Tanny great for "jokes and crazy silliness" but also "more intellectual than any of us and probably just plain smarter as well." Le Clercq was always reading something interesting, too, Wilde recalled in her biography, written by Joel Lobenthal with her cooperation. Shorter than Tanny, with a more compact body, Pat rarely competed with her for roles. She occasionally had what ballet dancers called "a weight problem," but Tanny, she recalled, "never seemed to need to diet. She was very hyper."[36]

The contrast between Wilde's struggle to lose weight and Le Clercq's efforts to keep hers up got press coverage. "Sometimes I think if I lost one ounce, people might not be able to see me!" Tanny declared. Dancing for hours didn't make it easier for her to gain weight. Only rest and drinking "glasses of rich cream and pure chocolate every day" during the ballet seasons seemed to work. "Before I dance, I'm too tense to swallow," she said, "and afterward I'm too tired to chew." Most dancers had the opposite problem. Even male dancers were not immune to pressure from Balanchine to be as thin as possible without being emaciated. Jacques d'Amboise heard him say to one "devastated" man, "You know dear, maybe you beginning to look too healthy." When a female dancer did an arabesque facing the audience, he insisted that her rib cage had to be visible.[37]

Whenever Patricia Wilde gained weight, Balanchine would send her off for a vacation to swim, rest, and get thin again. His ideal ballerina weighed no more than 115 pounds. He said, "Legs must be fairly long, bones small and well-formed, head rather small." Tanaquil Le Clercq fit this description perfectly. Perhaps Balanchine's obsession with thinness grew as he watched her grow to his ideal height, not too tall, since pointe shoes can add five inches. His preferences were practical, as well as aesthetic: A heavier dancer was not as easy for her partner to lift and couldn't land as quietly from a high jump as a thin one. Balanchine would reward a ballerina who had lost weight by giving her a prominent role, and then take it away if she gained weight. If she couldn't keep her weight down (and fluctuations of five to ten pounds mattered to him), she might even be dismissed from the company. (Some found refuge in Jerry Robbins's ballets, as he was less concerned about extra pounds, Bettijane Sills, a company soloist in the 1960s, wrote in her memoir.) Later, Balanchine disputed the notion that he only preferred one body type, likening his company to a pipe organ that required all pipe sizes to make music.[38]

He was both ahead of and behind his times: By the 1960s, the advent of the model Twiggy had marked a return to the "flapper" look—androgynous, slim, small-hipped, and small-breasted—that had vanished with the Roaring Twenties of Balanchine's youth. By the late twentieth century, fashion designers and photographers (mostly male) were featuring matchstick-thin child-women in their ads, and a growing drug culture made "heroin chic" popular. It was characterized by extreme thinness, a corpselike pallor, dark circles under the eyes, and blood-red lips, far more extreme than the dancers in *La Valse*.

Le Clercq was at her peak during the rise of the sex siren Marilyn Monroe in the 1950s, a time when the Hollywood ideal vacillated between the voluptuous (Monroe, Elizabeth Taylor) and the fashionably slim (Audrey Hepburn). The movie studios capitalized on Audrey's svelte looks (a mix of genes and wartime malnutrition), but they also celebrated maternal curves during the postwar baby boom with wholesome, motherly actresses like Doris Day. Balanchine's taste, more *haute couture* than populist, ran counter to the popular culture of the 1950s. The body mass indexes of Hollywood stars had a far greater range than those of the ballerinas in the New York City Ballet.

Mr. B knew what he desired and insisted on getting it. He kept a watchful eye on his harem, resenting the boyfriends and husbands of his female dancers, distractions who might lure them away from his company. Those who were dating kept the news from him, not meeting their dates near the school, although he liked gossip and welcomed personal confidences from young women. "In his own quiet way," Sills wrote, "he demanded complete allegiance."[39]

Flitting between his ballerinas, each one doused with a different perfume he had chosen, Balanchine would sniff the air and know who was in the studio that day. The competing aromas, Barbara Horgan said, could be "overpowering." During the 1952 tour, he chose a scent for Tanny at Dior. (Later, she favored Guerlain's Shalimar, a bold scent, not for the meek.) Perfume also helped to mask the smell of cigarettes. Almost everyone in the company smoked, before people realized the health risks involved. It was a way for

Tanaquil Le Clercq and Nicholas Magallanes, 1950s. Courtesy of NYCB Archive.

dancers to quell appetites and maintain their trim physiques, not that Tanny needed help in that area before paralysis.[40]

For her, smoking was calming, especially after the crisis of polio, although it was the worst thing for her lungs. Mr. B smoked "nonstop," Jacques d'Amboise wrote. He gave cartons of cigarettes as presents to company members, and, in every respect, his impact on all of them cannot be exaggerated. In many cases, it outlived their careers.[41]

"Mr. Balanchine was there with us," soloist Barbara Milberg Fisher wrote in her memoir. He was "the teacher who gave company class, the primary choreographer who rehearsed us at home and on tour. . . . Sometimes it seemed as if the company were flowing out of his veins." His young charges, totally dependent upon his opinion, worked hard to please. "He flirted constantly with the girls as he worked," Villella recalled, "and for the most part, he ignored the men."[42]

In class or at rehearsals, Le Clercq continued to call her future husband "Mr. B," as everyone in the company did. When others complained about his imperious, controlling ways, she would not hesitate to join in. Diana Adams remembered how Tanny could make Balanchine laugh with a bit of silliness, such as barking like a dog. Her often flippant style must have required some inner recalibration on his part, as he had become used to a level of respect that bordered on reverence. But his playful letters to her reveal a tender, loving romanticism.[43]

Jacques d'Amboise recalled that his teaching style was "clear, precise, and gentle in his directions, no waste of time, and no coddling." Unlike Robbins, Balanchine never berated anyone who failed to do a certain step. He would just change that part of the dance to show that dancer's strengths. "I have beautiful dancers to work with and if I had better ideas they would look even better," he said. He thought of himself as a craftsman, not a genius, preferring the title he'd had in Diaghilev's company, ballet master. Putting an entire ballet together in a few rehearsals, he expected the dancers to match his energy and ambition. "What are you saving it for?" was a repeated refrain in his classes. "Be generous. Why are you all so stingy?"[44]

Before Le Clercq, d'Amboise wrote, Balanchine's muses had all been "fast, virtuoso dancers" like Maria Tallchief. Tanny, the first one he had trained himself, was "an elegant praying mantis, but in no way predatory." No wonder that Balanchine wanted to give her wings.[45]

When they returned from the long European tour, he prepared a prenuptial gift for her, the role of the dragonfly in a new ballet, *Metamorphoses*. Le

Tanaquil Le Clercq and Todd Bolender, *Metamorphoses,* photo by Fred Fehl, 1952. Choreography by George Balanchine ©The George Balanchine Trust. ©The New York Public Library for the Performing Arts.

Clercq was partnered by Todd Bolender, playing a beetle. Todd supported her from below while dancing on his knees, not at all easy for either of them.

Metamorphoses, set to a piece composed by Hindemith in 1943, Symphonic Metamorphoses on Themes of Carl Maria Von Weber, premiered at City Center on November 25, 1952. Le Clercq had what one critic considered "the only good role in the ballet, and she danced it dazzlingly, with strong, stabbing movements of the legs, a completely controlled torso, and wonderfully expressive hands and feet."[46]

Those stabbing motions, reminiscent of *The Cage,* perfectly matched Hin-

Tanaquil Le Clercq in costume for *Metamorphoses* with George Balanchine, photo by Clifford Coffin, 1952. BALANCHINE is a Trademark of The George Balanchine Trust. Courtesy of NYCB Archive.

demith's percussive and inventive variations on his Romantic source material. Seeing Robbins's work may have spurred Balanchine to make his own insect ballet. He joked that the human body was limited and that "the centipede, with one hundred legs, could ignore three or four of them and still come up with something interesting to see." For the last movement of the ballet, Le Clercq wore a huge pair of wings (about as long as her legs) to flutter around the stage with other winged dancers, but not dancing much. A critic who praised her performance called the ballet as a whole a "lavish and muddled extravaganza." This *lost* ballet is no longer performed, and the costumes by Karinska were destroyed in a 1953 warehouse fire.[47]

Among the pile of gifts George Balanchine gave her that Christmas, he offered his hand in marriage. Having waited more than two years for his annulment from Tallchief, Le Clercq accepted right away. Balanchine was shocked at the speed of her response and reminded her of how much older he was. (She was twenty-three and he was forty-eight.) He thought she should think it over and ask her mother. Tanny told him there was no reason to ask: "I'm old enough, and yes, I'll marry you!" As she told Holly Brubach, more than four decades later: "What's to think over? I was crazy about him."[48]

The preparations for their New Year's Eve wedding must have been minimal. She had performed in a premiere the night before, *Concertino,* a short, frothy ballet that Balanchine made for Le Clercq, Diana Adams, and André Eglevsky. It was set to Concertino for Piano and Orchestra, a piece composed in 1932 by the French composer Jean Françaix. Walter Terry wrote in the *Herald Tribune:* "LeClercq and Adams appear as very elegant cancan dancers, busy with pony trots, light actions of several kinds, and even some smooth and very aristocratic *attitude* turns. Assisting them is Eglevsky, agile and foolishly gallant." At one point, the powerful Eglevsky (dressed in a formal, dark jacket and tie, but wearing matching tights, not trousers, like a faintly decadent music hall impresario), carried both ballerinas draped backward over his forearms. They steadied themselves with one arm on each of his shoulders, their heads tipped back and legs way up, pawing the air like circus horses. "It was technically difficult," Eglevsky said, "especially hard on the breathing. . . . One of the girls would kick and I would stumble on the foot up in the air, look around, and wonder what it was doing up there."[49]

This deliberately ridiculous ballet was performed with a serious air. The two women wore feathered headdresses, chokers, and short, dark, ruffled tutus that matched their bodices. Briefly, Eglevsky crouched behind them as they crossed the stage. He walked with comically bent legs while holding onto their skirts, a balletic Groucho Marx. That was a gesture that Balanchine may have gotten from Ruthanna Boris, who had one of the Ends in *Cakewalk* dancing a bent-over series of steps, while clutching the tail of the other's coat.

Le Clercq and Adams took turns performing combinations—*fouettées, entrechats,* and pirouettes—each one pausing to watch the other, as if showing off or trying to match each other. They did a complicated series of *attitudes* (like arabesques, but with the raised leg bent), swayed from side to side, and stirred the air with one free foot spiraling in corkscrew fashion, all the while maintaining balance on pointe. Diana kept a solemn face throughout, even when, with one leg way up to one side, she was finally carried offstage by Eglevsky. When he returned and lifted Tanny in the identical *grand battement à la seconde* position, her leg as high as a leg to the side could possibly go, she managed, just before he carried her off, to take a few seconds to pantomime powdering her nose and waving at the audience with prissy flickers of her wrists. The critics were moderately enthusiastic, although a British reviewer noted that "the choreographer performed the considerable feat of making three top ranking artists . . . look ridiculous. Karinska's costumes for the girls were delicious."[50]

The wedding had a far greater impact than the ballet. The ceremony was secular, performed by a friend of Tanny's family, a Long Island justice of the peace. Only Edith Le Clercq and Natasha Molostwoff attended. Balanchine had picked the date, his bride said, "so we'd start the New Year married." (He may have been advised by an accountant that he could write her off on his 1952 taxes, too.) A reception at Stravinsky's home followed.[51]

The twenty-five-year age gap did not bother her mother. Balanchine had always been attentive and courteous to Edith. Muriel Stuart, who had discovered Tanny as a child, thought that Edith had "sort of maneuvered the wedding," she told Joel Lobenthal. "Mama wanted the name; Mama wanted the prestige. Mama was this kind." Whatever the truth of that, nobody could rival Mr. B in the eyes of either woman. George Balanchine was no longer an "old fogy" to Tanny. Near the end of her life, she told Holly Brubach that she had loved the way he stood, his elegance, even his smell. The line of his jaw reminded her of the movie star Gary Cooper. Her deep love and awe are evident in the way she photographed him.[52]

Jacques d'Amboise and Pat McBride Lousada both said that Balanchine was the great love of her life. Jacques did not feel he could say the same about any of his other wives. At midnight, Stravinsky popped champagne corks to celebrate the brand-new year and marriage. As more and more Russians ar-

George Balanchine, photo by Tanaquil Le Clercq, ca. 1952–53. BALANCHINE is a Trademark of The George Balanchine Trust. Courtesy of NYCB Archive.

rived, filling the air with words Tanny couldn't understand, she leaned over and said, jokingly, to Lincoln Kirstein, as he wrote to a friend, "Oh, my God, what Have I Let Myself IN FOR?"[53]

Jerry Robbins was wounded, although the wedding had seemed inevitable during the tour. Tanny had written him, more than a year before, "Can't we be friends? like they say in the movies." Their friendship endured, although it ebbed and flowed, along with a powerful undercurrent of attraction on both sides.[54]

Women and men found Robbins attractive. His speaking voice was a deep, seductive baritone with a much warmer timbre than Balanchine's thin tenor,

George Balanchine and Tanaquil Le Clercq at their wedding reception, December 31, 1952. BAL-ANCHINE is a Trademark of The George Balanchine Trust. Courtesy of NYCB Archive.

and his personality could be just as warm and engaging. The dancer/choreographer Glen Tetley, who had danced in Robbins's short-lived company Ballets: USA, said, "Jerry changes diametrically when he walks in that stage door—because he's a sweetheart offstage." Tetley loved his "absolute precision—about everything. I've never known anyone who gave directions in such specifics. If you have lived through that, you've really passed through something. He wears you out completely."[55]

Tanaquil Le Clercq had lived through that and managed to keep her friendship with Jerry. His love and respect for her and George Balanchine were unshakeable. Robbins was already working on another role for her, the nymph in *Afternoon of a Faun,* while she was on her "honeymoon" in Milan. (Balanchine was staging opera-ballets at La Scala.)

To the female dancers in the company, the wedding had been good news. With his relentless focus on Le Clercq, there would be less pressure on the other women. "She married him for all of us," a former ballet school classmate of Tanny's told a friend. Tanny was not blind to her husband's restless nature and marital history. Although dazzled by Balanchine and deeply in love, she knew that he could turn away from a woman as quickly as from a ballet he had finished. For a young bride, she was remarkably sardonic about her long-term prospects. At her wedding reception, she remarked to Lincoln Kirstein, "If it lasts a year, it'll be worth it."[56]

12

~oOo~

Afternoon of a Faun

The marriage made headlines around the world, but daily life was far from glamorous. In the couple's ground-floor apartment at 41 East Seventy-Fifth Street, Balanchine did all the cooking, which he enjoyed, although breakfast was not his forte. She got up at 9:00 a.m., later than him, because she usually had a performance the night before. "He would fix me coffee and hand me a *zwieback*," she recalled. (A *zwieback* is a kind of dry biscuit that used to be given to teething babies.) "I was used to my mother's freshly squeezed orange juice, two four-minute eggs, two pieces of white, crustless buttered bread, four slices of crispy bacon and Ovaltine—that was breakfast, not strong coffee and a dry zwieback. But, hey, I could adapt."[1]

She went off to class and would meet him in the studio later, to rehearse whatever ballet they were working on. If they didn't have a performance that night, they might go to the movies, sitting up in the balcony, where smoking was permitted. They often watched double features, two films for the price of one. He loved science-fiction films and, most of all, Westerns, those uniquely American myths. The wide-open country, the daily struggle for survival, may have reminded him of Russia. After he dropped the silent French *s* at the end of his name and became George, an American, he had expressed his sense of belonging by putting on western shirts and string ties in imitation of his cowboy heroes. (To the end of his life he wore the silver and turquoise bracelet that an Osage relative of Maria Tallchief's had given him.)

Had it not been for Lincoln Kirstein, of course, Balanchine might have never become an American. Passionate about the arts from an early age, Kirstein had wanted to dance, but his family discouraged him, so he had focused on fine arts and writing. Once he had seen something that Balanchine's young wife never would: the great choreographer in Fokine's *L'Oiseau de feu* (Firebird) in 1926 made up for his role as the monstrous Kastchei, a Genghis

Khan figure with "gilded claws, a frightful vulture." Kirstein, a teenager then, had been impressed by "the fantastically evil way" his character "manipulated the others."[2]

Offstage as well, Balanchine knew how to manipulate. Almost always, a dancer reluctant to take on a role would be coaxed into it, not pushed as Le Clercq had been in *Swan Lake*. Some felt that Balanchine had also manipulated Kirstein, who had his own artistic ambitions, by keeping him focused mainly on the business side, where he knew Kirstein possessed talents he lacked. But he valued his advice on visual arts, too, especially in the choice of set designers. (It was Kirstein who had recommended Noguchi for *Orpheus*.) These close collaborators spoke rarely and socialized even less, although they had acquired country homes diagonally across the street from each other.

And yet, whenever the bipolar Kirstein had a mental health crisis (which became more frequent after a major one in May 1955), Balanchine would treat him with compassion and sometimes go out of his way to help. For the most part, he did so at a distance, "horrified at his [Kirstein's] operatic outbursts and messy breakdowns," according to the Kirstein biographer, Martin Duberman. Balanchine had weathered many of his partner's ups and downs, along with Kirstein's mother, who, according to Martha Graham, "used to come regularly to New York from Boston in the 1930's to make sure he was all right."[3]

Rose Kirstein had worried about her older son since the year of his birth, 1907. A botched circumcision (which entailed removing sweat glands from his groin, ostensibly to save him from septicemia) had left "physical and psychological scars," so that by adolescence, he was "given (in his own words) to fits of anxiety and despair." And yet it was Kirstein who had helped Balanchine through several severe health crises of his own in the 1930s, some related to lingering tubercular lesions and others of more mysterious origin. Balanchine suffered a series of alarming seizures in those years, possibly caused by treatments he had been taking on the advice of Lucia Davidova, his "best platonic woman friend" outside the realm of dance, as she described herself. Lucia was also close to Stravinsky. These injections "of parathyroid and adrenaline" were "known to have a convulsive effect on dogs." (Balanchine's propensity for taking dubious remedies on the advice of well-placed, wealthy, and medically naïve friends would eventually prove fatal.)[4]

In spite of these early setbacks, the school and company thrived. George Balanchine was wanted everywhere, now that his fame was worldwide. Although he focused mainly on the artistic side of the New York City Ballet, he was aware of costs, too. He continued to make dances for the theater and other companies, to help support his own, since he received no salary, just a twenty-five-dollar royalty for each performance of any of his ballets, about enough to buy a few weeks' worth of groceries for a family then. Touring was crucial to refill the company coffers.

As the wife of the genius who kept the New York City Ballet going, Le Clercq was in even greater demand as a model for fashion magazines like *Vogue* and *Glamour,* and popular "women's" magazines like *Town & Country.* In February 1953, *Cosmopolitan* published a profile of her, "Ballerina," obviously written before her marriage. Twenty-three-year-old Tanaquil is described waking up in her tiny apartment, reminded by her aching muscles that she has danced the night before. "She slips into high heels (they relax her muscles) and makes breakfast, the only meal she can cook." By eleven in the morning, she's at the school doing "a half hour of stretching and bending at the bar." Then there's solo practice and possibly a lesson and rehearsal, too. Lunch is sent up, as there's no time for a break.[5]

After rehearsal, she's free before the evening performance, and usually "goes home to take a bath and rest until around five, when she eats a light supper." Other dancers in the company during its early years have described grueling rehearsals that could last late into the night on days without performances, especially in Robbins's ballets. But Le Clercq would have avoided saying anything to a reporter that might catch the attention of union vigilantes. Today's dancers, although they have higher pay and benefits, might envy the schedule outlined in this magazine piece. By the twenty-first century, twelve-hour workdays were not uncommon during performance weeks and the company's seasons had become longer, up to fourteen weeks.[6]

The pressure on Le Clercq didn't ease up after she became Mrs. Balanchine, the quintessential Balanchine ballerina, long and thin, right down to the tip of her fine and delicate nose. One day, Allegra Kent came to class and found Tanny at the *barre* with a bandage on her face. She explained to Allegra that she had kicked her leg too high in front, doing a *grand battement,* and hit herself in the nose! Luckily, it wasn't broken. "She had karate-kicked herself," Allegra wrote in her memoir. "I was very impressed." Another time, during *Bourrée Fantasque,* Allegra remembered, "I watched her exuberant leg swing to the back and nearly knock out her partner, Todd Bolender. I heard the thud over the music. . . . Todd looked behind him, bewildered."[7]

On performance nights, Le Clercq said in an interview long after she had stopped dancing, she usually arrived at the stage entrance by 7:30 for an 8:00

Tanaquil Le Clercq, backstage at City Center, ca. 1954, © Anton Alterman/Harold Roth Photography.

p.m. curtain, with just enough time to put on her makeup and costume. She seemed to have forgotten what she had told the readers of *Good Housekeeping* in 1955, that "an hour before the curtain goes up on a performance, the stage is crowded with little groups of dancers . . . trying to get a little more out of that sometimes reluctant servant, the body." They spent "hours backstage," waiting for the stage manager's routine call, "Places, all you pretty, pretty people!"[8]

Outside the door to the corps de ballet dressing room, there was a sign, *No Mothers Allowed*. Edith, of course, could safely ignore it, being the mother of a principal dancer. She was still intensely involved in Tanny's life. The umbilical cord had stretched a bit further over the years but was never severed. For Edith, it seemed to be a lifeline. She was always on hand with needle and thread, or to make sure that her daughter ate home-cooked meals whenever Balanchine was away.

During the spring season immediately following his marriage, he made no new ballets for his company. Balanchine was in Italy, staging opera-ballets in

Milan and Florence, when Le Clercq was rehearsing what became one of her signature roles, the nymph in Jerry Robbins's *Afternoon of a Faun*. "All the ballets I ever did for the company were for Tanny," Robbins said later. "Tanny could do anything."[9]

Balanchine missed her. On May 1, he wrote to "My dear Boopsy Woopsy" from Florence, "I met you again in the beauty shop window." He may have seen a framed clipping from that *Cosmopolitan* article or a face that reminded him of hers or recalled a moment they had shared. His *Polonaise* for the Mussorgsky opera *Boris Godunov* had just premiered at La Scala April 20, and everyone had thought it the "best thing I ever did," but he felt "lonsom" without her. He asked her to "give my love to Edith and Natasha" and signed "your loving old husban G."[10]

Shortly afterward, he wrote again to say that he would be home May 12 "with our money" and hoped they could travel to California by car. A tour of the West was scheduled for July through mid-August, followed by a European tour from early September through mid-November. "Please tell Edith to consider going with us to Italy," he suggested. "To witness our triumph."[11]

Robbins's *Afternoon of a Faun* was an audacious enterprise, which might have appeared arrogant in the hands of a lesser talent. He used the symphonic poem by Claude Debussy, *Prélude à l'après-midi d'un faune,* which had inspired Nijinksy's legendary ballet for Diaghilev's Ballets Russes, set in a forest in ancient Greece. There, a faun—half man, half goat—chases a bevy of Grecian nymphs (Nijinsky's sister, Bronislava Nijinska, being one of them), their clothing and stylized movements in profile modeled on dancing figures painted on Greek urns that Nijinsky had seen in the Louvre. In a mottled leotard with a tail and a dangling ornament over his groin, Nijinsky had danced the role of the faun who pursues an enticing nymph. She leaves her long scarf behind when she runs away with the others.

The frustrated faun caresses the scarf, a surrogate woman that he carries up a rocky crag, places on the ground, and kisses. Then, at the ballet's climax (in every sense of the word) he lowers his body upon it, legs and pelvis first. Suddenly his back arches in an orgasmic spasm. This moment shocked many at the opening night in Paris on May 29, 1912. Applause mixed with boos. The next day, the director of *Le Figaro*, a leading daily, set himself against admirers of Nijinsky's new work (who included the sculptor, Auguste Rodin), by denouncing its "vile movements and erotic bestiality" in his newspaper, thereby assuring the ballet a long life.[12]

Robbins's version was set in a ballet studio with softly billowing curtains against a blue sky, a set designed by Jean Rosenthal. His nymph and faun were a girl and boy meeting by chance in a rehearsal room, but he kept the envelope of the original: The sleeping faun awakens and returns to sleep at the end. He retained, as well, the idea of the erotic, eternal longing for the unattainable found in Nijinsky's work, which has been called the first truly modern ballet.

A poem by Stéphane Mallarmé had furnished the inspiration for Debussy's *Prélude.* Nijinsky hadn't read it. Robbins must have read the Mallarmé in translation and perhaps in French as well, with Tanny's help. Mallarmé's faun contemplated only two nymphs, one virginal, the other more aware of her sensuality. Robbins had reduced these to one.[13]

Soon after the premiere on May 14, 1953, Tanny's father, who had seen Nijinsky's version in his youth, sent Robbins a letter. The professor had just given a two-hour lecture on the poem, but he found more to admire in Robbins's *Faun* than in all the works that had inspired it: "What you have understood so well is that the two nymphs of the original are one and the same." Balanchine was equally admiring. He told Jacques d'Amboise that he had never thought anybody could redo this Nijinsky classic until Jerry showed him how it could be done. Only a silent black-and-white film shot from a side angle gives a glimpse of Le Clercq's performance with her first partner, Moncíon, which Lillian Moore felt had perfectly captured the mood of sublime detachment required. But there are wonderful photos in which he looks at her as if he could see exactly what had inspired Robbins to make this dance. Moncíon is a Greek bronze come to ardent life. Le Clercq, caught in his gaze and grasp, is a delicate, white marble.[14]

She loved her role in *Faun,* especially the magical moment when she stepped through the open doorway into that otherworldly ballet studio of sheer silk walls: "I always imagined it to be a hot summer day and I was wrapped up in a roomy cocoon with Debussy's music. His music tells you how to dance the ballet, what manner to use." Rosenthal's set was a work of art, with its doorways, windows, and skylight open to two skies, the dominant one a sharp, undiluted blue and, through one window only, a starless black.[15]

At the start of the ballet, the boy is stretched out on the floor, napping. He's bare-chested, wearing only ballet shoes with white socks and black leggings. The C-sharp of a flute begins the long, opening phrase that slides down in semitones before slowly climbing up again, the panpipe of a mythic faun. The

Tanaquil Le Clercq and Francisco Moncíon, *Afternoon of a Faun,* choreography by Jerome Robbins, photo by Fred Melton, 1953. Courtesy of Christopher Melton. Jerome Robbins Dance Division, The New York Public Library for the Performing Arts.

theme is picked up by the other woodwinds and given new colors by strings, horns, and a watery-sounding harp. The boy awakens, stretches, arches his back, rises with a few swaggering steps, preening and striking poses, before he lapses into slumber again.

Le Clercq enters on her toes, her hair flowing just past her shoulders in the only video record of her full performance. At first, she has eyes only for her own image, reflected back to her in the imaginary mirror, as she practices pirouettes, arabesques, and unsupported slow turns. "Making the ballet went very smoothly," she recalled. The only part that took a lot of time was "deciding which way we should be facing until Jerry finally determined we should be looking out toward the audience, as if the mirror in the ballet studio were there." This brilliant solution heightened the seductiveness of the dance, although it took Robbins many changes of mind before he settled on it. Each dancer responded to the challenge of looking out at the audience without seeming to see it. The way that d'Amboise, her second partner, checks himself out in the imaginary mirror suggests the bravado of a working-class kid, fused with those Greek figures that had inspired Nijinsky's ballet.[16]

Le Clercq's look is more distant, dreamy and yet knowing, teasingly seductive in its remoteness, as if something is simmering inside her. Her practice session doesn't start at the *barre,* but in the middle of the studio floor. She performs simple bends, turns, and stretches as the lilting notes of the flute soar. With every unsupported turn, she seems to slip into the music without leaving a ripple—seamlessly, easing her body through the air with a measured, rhythmic control. All the while, she observes herself—every movement, every gesture. She moves, as the choreographer had instructed, "as if the air is thick as honey."[17]

And then, as if by accident, a few exuberant *développés* and pirouettes bring her to the boy, of whom she seems simultaneously aware and unaware. He wakes to her presence, startled, all his senses on alert. She retreats to the safety of the *barre,* does slow *grands pliés,* then stretches out one provocative leg to the side. She is there and yet remote, lost in her own image. We can't tell whether she is unaware of his interest as he rises to stand behind her, leaning into her scent, or simply pretending to be oblivious.

Suddenly, he lifts his prize and her arms sweep in a slow, exultant arc over their heads. And yet even as she turns, slowly, in his arms, one leg almost wrapped around his torso, they seem more intoxicated by their own bodies than by each other. When he puts her down, she bends one knee on pointe and swings it—slowly, teasingly, from side to side—opening and closing her leg like an invitation. And yet all the while, her wide, innocent-seeming eyes are hypnotically fixated on the mirror, not on her partner.

We can tell when they are looking at themselves or each other in the imaginary mirror we have become. Their concentration is that visible. Every gesture, every look, throughout this short ballet, is infused with what Jerry Robbins later called her "terrific sexuality, underneath—The possibility of that—which was much more interesting than the obviousness of it" that made him envision no one but Tanny for this role.[18]

She is at once innocent and seductive, wrapped in that consummate elegance that left her fans breathless. She incarnates the two nymphs in one. "How can you not love the ballerina you dance with?" Jacques said, decades later, on the soundtrack of the film about Le Clercq's life entitled, like the dance, *Afternoon of a Faun*.[19]

Robbins had auditioned several dancers as her first partner, his then lover, Buzz Miller, and an African American student at the School of American Ballet whom he was close to, Louis Johnson. Neither of them got the part. Later, Johnson speculated that "Balanchine didn't want to have me . . . because that ballet would have put me permanently into the company."[20]

In his biography of Robbins, Greg Lawrence writes that he "was apparently unable to get approval for casting either of them" and speculates that perhaps Louis Johnson wasn't chosen because the company was reluctant to have a Black male doing a *pas de deux* with a White woman in 1953. Given that Tanny was to be partnered in Balanchine's *Western Symphony* by Arthur Mitchell less than two years after *Faun*, that seems unlikely, although Mitchell (promoted to principal in 1956) was the only Black dancer in the company until the 1970s, apart from guest dancers, unless one counts the multiracial, Dominican-born Francisco Moncíon. Still, it's hard to imagine Balanchine ruling out any fantastic dancer based on his or her race, and he did not usually intervene in Robbins's casting decisions. Furthermore, he liked provocative pairings, at least in his own ballets. Perhaps Balanchine was feeling competitive and wanted to be the first one to break a taboo.[21]

One also has to consider that Jerry Robbins did what he always did, trying multiple dancers in the same role until he settled on a combo that satisfied him. Since he was close to Buzz and Louis, it would have been easier for him to blame the decision on Balanchine. He had tried Jacques d'Amboise, who resisted doing the part at first, because he hated the way Robbins would play one dancer off against another, hoping to squeeze something more out of each one: "He'd call for a rehearsal and you'd discover you had two or three understudies. He made you try your part with various people, switching partners all the time."[22]

Even when a dancer thought that Robbins had made his final choice, after a week or two of rehearsals, "suddenly, Jerry would say, 'You lost everything you had. You're falling apart. Get in the back. . . . ' And he would have another dancer take your part." So Jacques rebelled. He would sit on a bench and read a book during an entire rehearsal. Robbins would give an order, and d'Amboise would ignore it or answer commands with defiant questions.[23]

Le Clercq never had to worry about being replaced. He scheduled the first performance of the ballet with Frank and Tanny, the second one with Jacques and Tanny. Jacques asked Balanchine, "Do you mind if I ask Jerry not to cast me?" Somehow, he managed to avoid doing *Faun* for six months.[24]

When the company was on tour in Paris the following year, Monción wasn't with them. Jacques, just promoted to principal in 1953, did *Faun* with Tanny for the first time on the same program as *Western Symphony*. The French loudly applauded both ballets. Christine de Rivoyre found *Faun* extraordinary and pronounced Jacques d'Amboise, in the pages of *Le Monde,* a "very beautiful dancer, at once virile and sensitive." The ballet seemed to her a slow, harmonious game "of a strange delicacy," as if the dancers "were moving under water." Jacques decided that he had been wrong to resist the part for so long and he was always eager to perform it from then on.[25]

Her performance with d'Amboise is documented by a grainy video for Montreal's "L'heure du concert" series (Radio-Canada) in October 1955, available on YouTube. Rosenthal's magical set is missing, but the dancers make their own magic. Jacques d'Amboise was scrappier and more boyish in the role than Monción, less detached and austere, according to those who saw Le Clercq dance with both men, who were sixteen years apart.

Jerry Robbins said that the inspiration for his dance had come, years before, from seeing little Eddie Villella as a kid in class, "stretch his body in a very odd way, almost like he was trying to get something out of it. And I thought how animalistic." To a French interviewer, he offered a more intellectual gloss on the ballet, "meditations on the nature of the self, the essence of narcissism." The journalist did not pretend to know what Mallarmé would have thought of this interpretation, but it struck him as evidence of Robbins's own "tormented intellectualism."[26]

Robbins had transmuted the onanism of Nijinsky's ballet, which had caused a near riot in Paris, into a dancer's self-regard, which is not the same as narcissism. His *Faun* is about the ecstasy of using the body as well as possible in service to an art. It's also about reaching and retreating from connection in the midst of the solitary pursuit of an always elusive perfection, that is, it is his own life story.

The gestures of the dance mimic passion, but the dancers are eerily detached from each other. Robbins said that part of his inspiration for the ballet came from seeing two dancers practicing a love *pas de deux* in the studio, watching themselves in the mirror, while remaining oblivious of the sexual possibilities inherent in the positions their bodies assumed. Le Clercq's movements are languorous and sultry, sometimes excruciatingly slow, which made them doubly difficult, as when she descends to the floor on a single pointe in *plié* (unobtrusively supported by Jacques) with perfect control.

Years later, she recalled how they had worked on the ballet in the old studio on Madison Avenue, which had no air-conditioning: "I'd complain about the heat and tug at my tunic and he [Robbins] would say, 'Great. Keep it in.'" That tug became part of the dance. He also used the way she would lift her long hair and then let it fall. Midway through the ballet, the boy seems to caress the girl's hair without touching it, then leans in to smell it. Tanny's head moves in rhythm with his phantom touch. On shorter-haired ballerinas, these gestures didn't work as well.[27]

"When Jerry made something on you," Tanny recalled, "it was a cinch. He played to your idiosyncrasies. Every twitch. Which was so good for the morale. Unlike Balanchine's roles, which made you think that your performance wasn't good enough, that it would never be good enough." But it was not a cinch to step into a part that Robbins had designed for another. When Allegra Kent took over the role after Tanny was paralyzed, she recalled how Robbins "criticized every detail. If a tiny frown appeared, it had to go."[28]

Kent's extraordinarily pliant body was not as elongated as Le Clercq's, whose legs measured more than thirty-three inches from heel to hip. There was, quite literally, no way that Allegra could measure up to Jerry Robbins's expectations. "All the roles I did for Tanny had to be divided," he said much later. "No one could do them all the way she did. . . . She could be hilarious and she could be the most lyrical, moving dancer you've ever seen."[29]

Over the course of their long friendship, Tanny's regard for Jerry wavered, at times, and with it her valuation of his work. In later years, she made it clear to some friends that she vastly preferred Balanchine's ballets to anyone else's, although she probably never told Robbins that. (Pat McBride Lousada went so far as to say that Tanny didn't *like* his ballets.) But Balanchine's faith in Robbins never waned. Extremely competitive, especially with men, he was remarkably generous to the younger man, considering him the greatest American-born choreographer. He lent him favored dancers (though not necessarily his current muse) and encouraged him to keep making more ballets.[30]

Faun was a great one, forever part of the legacy of Tanaquil Le Clercq. Later, Jerry Robbins formally dedicated the ballet to her. On that last ill-starred European tour of 1956, she wrote to him from Salzburg, right after a performance of *Faun,* "a dream to dance. Thank you. Thank you. I feel *so* good in it. . . . We got about 7 or 8 curtain calls. . . . I wish I could buy you the whole of Salzburg—the way I feel today."[31]

In between ballet seasons and tours, the Balanchines took time out to relax, but leisurely summers weren't possible, as the company was usually on tour then. They could only manage brief getaways, often at Natasha's cottage on Fire Island. She had always been generous about sharing it with friends.

George Balanchine and Tanaquil Le Clercq on Fire Island, ca. 1953. BALANCHINE is a Trademark of The George Balanchine Trust. Courtesy of NYCB Archive.

The New York City Ballet's first tour of the American West, in the summer of 1953 (July 2–August 14), felt like a holiday to Le Clercq. She loved traveling by car, enjoying rare moments of leisure, if not complete privacy, with her husband. (Her mother, as usual, came along.) As they headed toward their first engagement, a two-day booking in Colorado (July 2–3), Tanny sent frequent letters and postcards to friends. Reading her charming letters, one realizes how young she was then, just a few months shy of her twenty-fourth birthday.[32]

One written to Bobby Fizdale is typical of her breezy style, making fun of herself and others. They were to perform on an outdoor stage in Red Rocks Park, impossible in the rain, and were staying in a rural area about eighteen miles from Denver: "We have a 5 room house on Bear Creek, one mile from Evergreen— All cooking facilities and the like— It is heaven. George cooks. Edith and I wash— There are lots of chipmunks, which I am taming with peanuts— They are really cute as hell." Her handwriting was sophisti-

Tanaquil Le Clercq to Robert Fizdale, undated letter, 1953. Jerome Robbins Dance Division, The New York Public Library for the Performing Arts.

cated, mixing cursive and printed letters in a style all her own, with frequent misspellings, dashes in place of commas, and a smattering of French words mixed in.[33]

"I hope it rains the 2nd and 3rd then we won't be able to dance— I think of it every morning when I wake up— If I concentrate enough, who knows it may come true— We go west to L. A. try and find a nice house there, and George has the Vespa— He is very dark, and plumpy you wouldn't beleive it, he can hardly walk his derrière is so plump."[34]

With only two more bookings (LA's Greek Theater, July 6–August 1, followed by San Francisco's War Memorial Opera House, August 3–14) this tour was more relaxed than most. She was not as happy about conditions on the grueling ten-week European tour later that year (covering twelve cities in three countries from September to mid-November), although it wasn't the workload that bothered her. Le Clercq was used to dancing more than one role in matinee and evening performances, but she was appalled by the inconsiderate behavior of some audience members.

From Bologna, Italy, she sent a letter to Lincoln Kirstein, who knew how to fix a problem with a phone call. Men in the audience, she alerted him, chain-smoked unfiltered cigarettes throughout an entire evening, making the cast choke, so that by the fourth ballet, "you couldn't see anyone, the haze was so thick." It must have been really bad. After all, she lived with George Balanchine, a nonstop smoker at that time. Kirstein most likely addressed the problem, as there seemed to be no further complaints from her on that issue.[35]

By the end of that tour, the dancers were exhausted. They had zigzagged across Italy on slow-moving trains, leaving Milan to go to Venice for a few days, and then returning to Milan for another engagement, in order to accommodate the schedules of various theaters and opera houses. They had hauled everything they needed, including food and wine to share on long train trips, in heavy suitcases that didn't come with wheels in those days. Balanchine tried to alleviate the discomfort, as best he could, by making sure that his company crossed the Atlantic "first class in a BOAC Stratocruiser that boasted a downstairs lounge." Everyone was on board, including "key members of the orchestra." (If the plane had crashed, it's not likely that the company would have recovered.)[36]

Before jet travel, flights on propeller planes were long, bumpy, and delayed by one or more required refueling stops. Carolyn George (later d'Amboise), then still in the corps, snapped Tanny at an airport, waiting for a change

Left to right, counterclockwise: Una Kai, Ann Crowell, Tanaquil Le Clercq, and Maria Tallchief, Stop at Goose Bay, Labrador, at end of tour, photo by Carolyn George, 1953. Courtesy of Jacques d'Amboise. Jerome Robbins Dance Division, The New York Public Library for the Performing Arts.

of planes with other exhausted company members. Le Clercq was coming home with gifts for friends and family, including a bird cage, possibly for Magallanes, an amateur ornithologist.

Tallchief's ballet teacher, Madame Nijinska, had once told Maria: "When you sleep, you must sleep like a dancer. When you stand and wait for the bus, you must wait for the bus like a dancer."[37]

Tanny and Maria were not posing. They were sleeping like dancers during a refueling stop in Goose Bay, Labrador, after an arduous tour and long flight across the Atlantic Ocean. Even asleep, they were the picture of grace.[38]

13

A Dewdrop and a Dance Hall Girl

During the decade that Tanaquil Le Clercq performed, major choreographers made more than thirty-two roles expressly for her, but George Balanchine was the only one whose working process left her awestruck. "I never could find out when he invented anything," she said. "I mean, he'd be at home, I'd be at home, he would go through the music, maybe play it once or twice, and the next day he'd have a whole thing. He'd feed it to you as fast as you could learn it."[1]

Ideas poured out of him with such speed that sometimes he didn't realize, at first, exactly what he had created. "When he finished, he would sit and ask the dancers to show him what he had done, and he would seem to be very astonished," recalled Boris Kochno (1904–1990), the Russian librettist/ballet director who had collaborated with Diaghilev and Balanchine in the 1920s and early 1930s. In 1971, Jerry Robbins wrote in his journal that watching Balanchine choreograph a ballet was "so extraordinary I want to give up."[2]

In 1954, Balanchine premiered three ballets that displayed Le Clercq's tremendous versatility as a dancer: *Western Symphony, Ivesiana,* and his version of a classic, *The Nutcracker* (using the original score by Tchaikovsky), his first evening-long story ballet for the company. City Center had just won a $100,000 grant-in-aid from the Rockefeller Foundation, and Morton Baum wanted Balanchine's company to take full advantage of it by mounting a dazzling new *Nutcracker* that would attract a broader public.

The Nutcracker had taken three years to develop. It is based on the version of E. T. A. Hoffmann's Christmas tale *The Nutcracker and the Mouse King* by Alexandre Dumas [the father], with details from the original Hoffmann novella. Balanchine kept the plot and some of the choreography of the original ballet in two acts by Lev Ivanov. He occasionally performed the character role of Herr Drosselmeyer himself, the mysterious clock- and toy maker, godfather to a little girl, Clara (Marie in the Hoffmann story), to whom he gives a Nutcracker that makes her brother (Fritz) so jealous that he breaks the toy. Clara sneaks back to the Christmas tree to cradle and protect her wounded doll and falls asleep. Drosselmeyer repairs it while she sleeps.

At midnight, the Christmas tree in Clara's grand house grows, and all the toys around it come to life. Toy soldiers battle an army of mice led by the Mouse King. The Nutcracker turns into a Prince who takes Clara through a forest of waltzing snowflakes and on to the Land of Sweets (act 2), where the Sugar Plum Fairy (Tallchief at the premiere), supported by her Cavalier (Magallanes) presents dancing sweets, swirling flowers, and a series of exotic dances by Hot Chocolate, Coffee, and Tea. To Balanchine, Clara's dream is not a dream, but "the reality that Mother didn't believe." He saw Hoffmann's tale as a defense of a child's imagination against the punitive German society of the nineteenth century.[3]

As a child, Georgi Balanchivadze had danced in the original Mariinsky version of the ballet. First, he was a mouse. Then he grew into the roles of the Nutcracker/Little Prince and the Mouse King. As a teenager, he had done the Jester's hoop dance, choreographed by Petipa's ballet master in character dancing, Alexander Shiryaev, a role Balanchine renamed Candy Cane and inserted, almost unchanged, in his own ballet. Tamara Geva said that he "was a good dancer, light and wiry" who "was given solos at the Maryinsky Theater." He had performed the hoop dance "as I've never seen it done before or since. He never touched the ground, flashing in and out of the hoop."[4]

Young Georgi had improvised some of those unusual moves himself. However, because of an old knee injury and a failed operation to repair his meniscus, he had largely given up dancing by his late twenties, preferring to focus on choreography. The bad knee did not limit his ability to show his students, in steps and gestures, exactly what he had in mind. When asked how she had developed her roles, Maria Tallchief said: "I only had to look at George. He was so beautiful, the way he demonstrated the movements."[5]

The first performances of The Nutcracker featured thirty-five children from the School of American Ballet and two of its star students, Jacques d'Amboise and Tanaquil Le Clercq. Dewdrop was a role that Balanchine had made expressly for her, a dancer light as dew landing on a petal. (It does not exist in the Ivanov ballet.) He had asked Robbins to choreograph the comical battle scene between the mice (danced by adults) and toy soldiers (danced by children), a sequence that still generates cheers and applause at every performance.[6]

On the day of the opening, February 2, 1954, a few of the costumes weren't ready, so Balanchine and Robbins went to Karinska's studio that afternoon. While they sat on the floor, stitching the ones needed for the Arabian dance (Coffee), Robbins looked at Balanchine in amazement. "How can you just sit there on the opening night of one of our major ballets . . . and be so calm?" he wondered. "Well," Balanchine placidly replied, "I think next month I'll be in a car with Tanny and we'll be driving across the country to California and we'll stop and the food'll be good and the weather'll be good. It'll be good."[7]

The Nutcracker was the most expensive ballet Mr. B had ever staged. He had insisted on a large Christmas tree that would seem to grow out as it rose, "like an umbrella." Costs climbed with the tree, to eighty thousand dollars by the time the ballet was ready, twenty-five thousand for the tree alone. As Lincoln Kirstein cheerfully proclaimed, "it took genius to acquire such a debt." But Morton Baum, in charge of City Center's budget, was upset. He had reserved only forty thousand dollars for the entire production, so he wondered whether they might do without the tree. "[The ballet] *is* the tree," Balanchine famously replied.[8]

His gamble paid off, but at first it looked like the whole extravagant venture might literally go up in smoke. Barbara Horgan recalled that the tree "was wired to light up as it rose. On opening night, you heard *pop, sizzle.* There was smoke and a smell as it rose, and we really thought it was going to catch fire. Some gasps came from the audience—actually, all of us were gasping. Somehow the tree straightened itself out. . . . [T]hat's how things were then. There was so little time that you dealt with problems as they happened. And the final result was magical."[9]

Tanaquil Le Clercq's virtuoso performance as Dewdrop, glistening amid the waltzing flowers, created a sensation. Karinska designed an exquisite costume for her: a form-fitted bodice, a jeweled crown, and a daring wisp of a tutu so tiny that it was modified for successors who didn't feel they could match her silhouette. In a sparkling swirl of pale-pink mesh studded with rhinestones, she appeared to Allegra Kent like a "slender rainbow of a girl." Her long, expressive arms punctuated every tricky pirouette, leap, *bourrée,* and traveling arabesque as she raced through the corps de ballet Flowers, doing split-legged jumps in all directions and a rapid series of *fouettés,* arms opening wide and hands strumming the air. Thirty-four years later, critic Richard Buckle recalled "a breathtaking balance" as she posed in arabesque just before one of her spectacular exits. Maria Tallchief found it hard to make her second-act entrance as the Sugar Plum Fairy after watching Le Clercq. "I

Tanaquil Le Clercq as Dewdrop, *The Nutcracker,* photo by Walter E. Owen, 1954. Choreography by George Balanchine ©The George Balanchine Trust. Jerome Robbins Dance Division, The New York Public Library for the Performing Arts.

stood in the wings shaking. I felt I couldn't go on right on after the tremendous success of her Dewdrop on opening night."[10]

One evening, a young Candy Cane dropped her hoop in the middle of the ballet. Everyone stared at the threat to the dancers on stage, Allegra Kent remembered: "The audience's focus was riveted on the large ring of wood sitting front and center, an invitation to disaster. . . . A few Flowers, ladies of the *corps,* made ineffectual stabs at displacing the object when it was underfoot. Tanny looked unconcerned. During one of her solos, when she was hovering close by, she kicked the hoop cleanly off stage with precise musical aim, not missing a beat in the choreography, and she brought the house down. A small, inscrutable smile beamed on her face for a second or two while she continued her work."[11]

The critics raved, and the run was extended for months. Now Kirstein and Baum could breathe easier about money. In the first week of February, the box office collected a record fifty-two thousand dollars, a huge amount in those days. Le Clercq performed excerpts from the ballet, along with other dancers, on the *Ed Sullivan Show* on CBS, an irony most likely not lost on Robbins. George Balanchine appeared on the cover of *Time* magazine in 1954, making him one of the most famous artists in the world. But John Martin of the *New York Times* bemoaned the success of this "inferior ballet," as he feared its popularity would undermine the "Balanchine revolution," and that henceforth the New York City Ballet productions would be more about spectacle than dance.[12]

Later that year, Tallchief took a break from the company (with Balanchine's blessing) to tour with Serge Denham's Ballet Russe at a salary of two thousand dollars per week. That was considered an extraordinary sum then, even for a dancer of her stature. During her absence, Tanny took over several of Maria's signature roles, including the Sugar Plum Fairy, although she preferred doing Dewdrop.[13]

After thousands of performances, *The Nutcracker* is still the New York City Ballet's biggest commercial success. Balanchine and Kirstein's dream had come to life, just like those dancing toys onstage. In 1954, the nonprofit company made more money than it lost—twelve thousand dollars. It was not a fortune, but profit margins continued to enable its growth. After that first season, 50 percent of the people who came to City Center to see *The Nutcracker* were seeing a ballet for the first time. The company devoted entire seasons to this one ballet, a Christmas tradition later maintained by other companies as well, which probably made John Martin groan. But he had been wrong: the ballet's success did not keep Balanchine from mounting far more avant-garde works.

Several weeks before *The Nutcracker,* Le Clercq had premiered a vastly different role in one of the strangest ballets Balanchine ever made. *Opus 34,* set to music by the Austrian American composer Arnold Schönberg, should have been dubbed *"Operation Ghastly,"* the *Daily News* reported, "since it is probably the first dance work ever inspired by compound fractures, blood transfusions, and scar tissue."[14]

Schönberg had named his twelve-tone piece, commissioned as music for an imaginary silent film in 1929, Accompaniment to a Cinematographic Scene. It was an angst-filled ten minutes that he had composed in accordance with a sequence of titles ("Threatening Danger, Fear, Catastrophe") supplied by the music publisher. (Balanchine had the orchestra play the piece twice.) Walter Terry found the ballet "utterly absorbing from start to finish" and singled out Le Clercq's "brilliant" performance in the second half. She and Herbert Bliss performed what Jacques d'Amboise called "a flopping pas de deux—a pair of medical models of veins, blood vessels, muscles, sinew, viscera, and nerve endings that had slipped off the surgery table."[15]

Monción remembered that Le Clercq "wore a long gray wig" for her role as a patient and that male dancers "dressed in black were under a huge black cloth, and she was lifted by them, so that you saw this creature rising and then being engulfed in all this black and disappearing, and then coming up again." This part inspired "considerable shocked laughter," the *Daily News* reported, "but the true balletomanes countered with loud shushing."[16]

Soloist Barbara Milberg described a moment in which Le Clercq, lifted by two men, was "held over a hospital cart and turned almost inside-out, 'operated on' in midair with those elegant legs forced open, her behind spread out toward the audience. It was obscene and appalling."[17]

Although the music was identical, the two halves of the work were like different ballets to Le Clercq. In the first half, she said, the dancers "did odd things," such as all thrusting a leg forward and shaking "their calf muscles." In the second half, "Herbie [Bliss] and I started out on stretchers, wrapped in bandages, and I had a stocking over my head so my face was all mushed. It was lots of fun." Near the end, Monción said, she "started walking in a seductive and beguiling manner downstage." Just before a curtain rose behind her, exposing a "huge klieg light," she picked up a red cloth and draped it over her shoulders (symbolizing "blood?" she wondered). The light lasted for nine seconds, according to Edwin Denby, momentarily blinding "the first ten rows" of the audience. (He felt that five seconds would have been more than enough.) People shrieked. But Denby joined others in praising the ballet. In any role, he observed, "Le Clercq's delicacy of timing can give her characters a grace in courtesy, a quick awareness, that makes them exceptionally interesting." He thought that it was her "solitary pacing that made the last minute of Opus 34 so marvelous."[18]

Life imitated art. Three weeks after the January 19 opening, she was rushed to Polyclinic Hospital for an emergency appendectomy. It was reported that Le Clercq had "suffered an attack on stage . . . but completed her performance." (Any facial grimaces would have only added to the show.) The evening of February 12, *Opus 34* was replaced by an old standby, *Filling Station*, choreographed by Lew Christensen in 1938. Tanny called Betty Cage to say, "Well, here I am on a hospital bed again. I just go from operating table to operating table."[19]

She threw off the real bandages and donned the fake ones again, finishing the season on March 21. Sometime that spring, she made her debut as the Novice in *The Cage*. At the start of the United States tour in May, a Chicago critic wrote of Le Clercq's performance in that ballet, "She is beautiful, pitiful, and in the end implacable."[20]

In September, she danced in two other Balanchine premieres. *Ivesiana*, with a score made of four separate pieces by an American composer, Charles Ives, was never a commercial success, although many, including Le Clercq, admired it. The dense, atonal music of the section called "The Unanswered Question" was accompanied by equally "haunting choreography," Jacques wrote, where Allegra Kent was borne aloft like "a sacred icon" and "passed around the waists of her bearers as if they were threading a belt through loops," the elusive muse incarnate.[21]

John Martin proclaimed the ballet "astonishingly creative and of almost hypnotic persuasiveness. It is tinged with morbidity and is couched to a large extent in a quasi-modern-dance idiom," qualities he felt might "stem from the music, which is certainly dark in mood." Le Clercq premiered a role in the lighter "In the Inn" section of the ballet, a marked contrast with the intense dissonance of the rest, musically and choreographically. She knew that she was good at the "semi-jazz" required for her *pas de deux* with Todd Bolender (who originated the role) which remained, in memory, one of her favorites.[22]

Balanchine had used her long legs in a dance of high kicks, flexed feet, and precise pointe work that yielded, at unexpected moments, to the ragdoll, boneless floppiness that had made her performance in *Jones Beach* so riveting. African American jazz dance and the work of Jack Cole, a Broadway/Hollywood choreographer, had clearly influenced Balanchine and Robbins's choreography. Shifting seamlessly between ballet and Broadway, they had absorbed more from modern dance than ever streamed from ballet studios onto Broadway stages, although Balanchine and Robbins did manage to alter the size of that imbalance. Balanchine knew and admired Cole's work, according to Jacques d'Amboise, who had taken classes in the Cole technique and could demonstrate, seated in a Harlem restaurant more than sixty years later, some of the precise head, neck, and arm movements ("isolations") that marked "a Cole dancer."[23]

Cole had added East Indian movements to his eclectic mix of jazz dancing and ballet, like Dunham, training dancers and actors to move an isolated part of the body while keeping the rest still. The Cole technique is evident in the *Ivesiana* "In the Inn" *pas de deux* where the female dancer juts her head forward and back or contracts her torso, and when the male dancer wobbles his head from side to side, while his arms assume geometric shapes, like a figure on an ancient stone frieze. This playful dance, lightly flirtatious, but not romantic, ended with the most memorable handshake that Allegra Kent had ever seen on a stage, a firm gesture of parting before each one exited stage left and right. Kent saw others do the handshake, but never, in her estimation, as well as Le Clercq and Bolender. "The moment is interesting," Kent declared. "It's against the music."[24]

On that same program, Le Clercq could really strut her stuff with Jacques d'Amboise in the last section (*Rondo*) of Balanchine's *Western Symphony*. Although they didn't get to wear the gorgeous costumes by Karinska for the opening performance, "Applause was loud and long and the bravos shattering as multiple curtain calls were demanded," reported Walter Terry. Four years later, the ballet was still a crowd-pleaser, performed every season at home and abroad, and it has remained in the New York City Ballet's repertoire. On the company website in 2018, it was described as "a rodeo of frisky fillies and lonesome cowpokes with a rousing non-stop finale that brings the curtain down." It's a hoedown with *fouettés*.[25]

The score, a pastiche of folk tunes with a ragtime swing, was composed by Hershy Kay, a successful Broadway orchestrator. In the *Rondo*, you can hear portions of "Oh, Dem Golden Slippers," a song written in the nineteenth century by James A. Bland, an African American composer. Mixing acrobatic cowboy stomping, strutting and leaping, American folk dancing, classical ballet, jazz dancing, and the sassy prancing of the music hall, Balanchine made good use of his wife's wit and flair for comedy.

Both qualities were on display again that year when he staged a *pas de deux* from *Coppélia* for her to perform with André Eglevsky on a Canadian telecast. It is a brief extract from act 2 of the three-act 1884 Petipa version (set to music by Léo Delibes) that showcases Le Clercq, in the role of Swanilda. Eglevsky is Franz, Swanilda's intended, in love with a doll, Coppélia. Swanilda takes her revenge, pretending to be this doll come to life. She lures him in for a kiss, then delivers a sharp, quick slap to his face with mechanical precision, a masterstroke of comic timing. Even as her character pretends to have no will, Le Clercq embodies willfulness.

As Eglevsky slowly turns her, she maintains a high *developpée.* With exquisite control, she imitates the jerky arms and legs of a mechanical doll, flopping over when tugged upright and abruptly flinging her arms up and open as if in response to a key turning in her back. The graceful, rhythmic swing of her arms as he moves her from side to side is a triumph of precise movement that feigns a lack of agency. When the scent of the flowers he offers brings her to life, she does rapid hops on one foot while she swings the other leg like the arm of a metronome. In the constricted space of a TV studio, she whips off a dozen *fouettés,* as well as perfect pirouettes and *entrechats.* Her performance is a tour de force from start to finish.[26]

In 1955 Le Clercq appeared as a dancing doll again in *Jeux d'Enfants,* a ballet inspired by old-fashioned toys made of wood. The music (Georges Bizet), lighting (Jean Rosenthal), and the set design and costumes (Esteban Francés) got raves, but the choreography (Balanchine, Barbara Milberg, and Francisco Monción) did not. This wooden trifle soon died.

As Nancy Reynolds wrote, "Few ballets, particularly those so splendidly mounted, have been greeted with such a dearth of enthusiasm." Elements from the ballet (music, costumes) resurfaced when Balanchine choreographed a *pas de deux* for a new one in 1975, *The Steadfast Tin Soldier,* about the love of a one-legged soldier for a paper doll. Vanquished on the field of critical opinion, it nevertheless survived much longer than its predecessor. A 2014 videorecording was included in the New York City Ballet's 2020 digital fall season.[27]

By 1955, City Center had already begun annual three-month winter ballet seasons, packed with performances of *The Nutcracker* to accommodate crowds of children and their parents. Performances for the Paris leg of the upcoming spring tour of Europe were sold out, apart from the scalpers selling tickets for

Tanaquil Le Clercq, *Jeux d'Enfants,* photo by Fred Fehl, 1955. Choreography by George Balanchine ©The George Balanchine Trust. ©The New York Public Library for the Performing Arts.

outrageous prices. But d'Amboise, a principal dancer by then, had no problem getting permission from Balanchine to take time off to appear in films, guest at other companies, and take his honeymoon trip during *Nutcracker* season. With Arthur Mitchell filling in for him, Jacques married Carolyn George, by then a soloist in the company, on January 1, 1956, the day after the Balanchines' fourth anniversary.[28]

For years afterward, the couples often celebrated their anniversaries on December 31. Tanny would usually choose the menu for these dinners, although Balanchine cooked. There were two bottles of wine on the table, and the meal was almost invariably Porterhouse steak, rare, with Dijon mustard, a salad, and new potatoes with butter and herbs. As Balanchine served the potatoes, Jacques recalled, "he delighted in operating the peppermill. 'Listen to sound. Percussion, very delicate. Like ratchet, but not so loud.'"[29]

Making a face of mock dismay when the food appeared, Tanny would say, "Oh! This again?" After dessert (typically ice cream) they played cards. Tanny refilled Jacques's wine glass, over and over, declaring that it might improve her chances of winning, even with her husband as her partner. Jacques was capable of polishing off a bottle on his own. In the studio the next day, she would playfully taunt him: "Do I detect a whiff of Bordeaux? Oh my gosh! You're sweating wine. I guess I will have to support you during our *pas de deux.*"[30]

Le Clercq's impeccable comic flair was on display in a wonderful part Robbins made for her in what has been called the funniest ballet ever: *The Concert or, The Perils of Everybody, A Charade in One Act,* which premiered in March 1956. It is at once a spoof of a classical concert and classical ballet, mixing comical mugging and dance. The ballet begins with the entrance of the pianist, who attacks the piano keys with a dust cloth, sending off powdery clouds, then scrutinizes the offstage spectators with myopic disdain. Le Clercq gave a daffy performance as an onstage audience member carried away by the music, a selection of pieces by Chopin. Her part was full of ecstatic shimmies that provoked howls of laughter, especially when, in the words of Walter Terry, she "launched herself into a whirlwind of action, with hair lashing, her face and her feet trying desperately to keep pace with the music until complete collapse struck her."[31]

This dance was like a Jules Feiffer cartoon come to life. Her music-loving character was so enthralled that she hugged the piano and didn't notice when a latecomer in need of a seat stole hers. Her bent posture remained the same, head on the piano, rump high in the air. At one point, she did an *arabesque penchée* and kept going down until she slapped the floor with both hands. Her partner deliberately whacked her on the head, she staggered and collapsed, and then he hauled her offstage. (Robbins spent a lot of time in rehearsals on ways to fall.) Was this revenge for all the times she had hit him with her foot in *Bourrée Fantasque?*[32]

Robbins didn't only highlight her comedic side. He choreographed a dreamy, poignantly poetic solo for her music-loving character. After Tanny was paralyzed, he dropped this slow mazurka from the ballet. He could not imagine another ballerina doing justice to his memory of a dance that "was so her." *The Concert* was the last ballet of his she danced.[33]

Todd Bolender premiered the role of The Bored Husband who abandons his wife and scoops up Le Clercq's character for a fling, in every sense of the word. When Bolender became ill just before a performance, Balanchine himself was the last-minute surprise replacement, wearing Todd's shirt, vest and tie, bowler hat, and knee socks held up with garters.

Tanaquil Le Clercq, George Balanchine, Richard Thomas (*kneeling on floor*), others unidentified, *The Concert,* choreography by Jerome Robbins, photo by Fred Fehl, 1956. BALANCHINE is a Trademark of The George Balanchine Trust. ©The New York Public Library for the Performing Arts.

From April 3 to April 22, 1956, the company performed at the Chicago Opera House, a longer engagement than anticipated, because of the high demand for tickets. Le Clercq found the town so "dreary," she wrote to Robbins, that she had spent hours watching movies, double features before and after each performance. Eager to start her spring planting, she left early. In 1946, Balanchine had purchased a large piece of land in Weston, Connecticut, seven and a half glorious acres, acquiring the property for a pittance ($8,500) from a wealthy benefactor, Alice DeLamar. In 1955, he bought a modest prefab Hodgson house from a company in Vermont. It was delivered, set on a foundation, and erected in a few hours. "When the workers finished that day there was still no roof," Tanny told a local reporter, "but the front door was locked and we had the key."[34]

Alice, born in 1895, had inherited ten million dollars when her father died in 1918, a staggering sum then. She had devoted her life to philanthropy, supporting the arts, artists (including her sometime lover, actress Eva Le Gallienne), and conservation. DeLamar sold off parcels of her properties for a fraction of their worth to those she liked and admired, until the area surrounding her house became a de facto arts colony. Her estate in Connecticut, Stonebrook, had an enormous pool with a private entrance through the basement of the main house. Guests in the cottages she owned nearby, as well as friends in the area, were welcome to use the pool, apart from the two hours in the middle of the day that Alice reserved for herself.[35]

On occasion, swimmers were surprised by Alice, abruptly surfacing in their midst, having swum out from the house. People gossiped that she'd had this channel built to facilitate her nude swims. Tanny and her friends occasionally swam there but more often preferred to talk, play word games, read, enjoy picnics and walks in the woods.

Balanchine planted roses, peonies, day lilies, irises, and rose-of-Sharon (Le Clercq's favorite) on the property. He relaxed by cooking, doing carpentry, and even washing and ironing clothes. These activities may have reminded him of the daily chores at the dacha where his family had grown their own vegetables. He genuinely enjoyed manual labor, including what were then called *womanly* tasks. Whether in a ballet studio or at home, he had a powerful need to keep moving, making order out of disorder.

Tamara Geva owned a place in Weston, too. Once she dropped by and found Le Clercq alone outside, weeping. Tamara asked her what was wrong. "The only thing he's interested in is work," Tanny complained. "That's what we all found out, my dear," the older woman answered with sympathy.[36]

In 1956 Le Clercq had plenty of work, including a prominent role in a Balanchine ballet, *Divertimento No. 15,* premiering at the Mozart Festival in Stratford, Connecticut on May 31. Originally, he had intended to revive *Caracole* for the festival, but then decided to refashion it, providing a new name and costumes (by Karinska) for what was essentially the same ballet to the same piece by Mozart, Divertimento no. 15 in B-flat Major, although the *Andante* section was new. Balanchine preferred to name his ballets for their scores, a way of paying homage to his primary inspiration. The ballet features five ballerinas assisted by three cavaliers, backed by an ensemble of eight women. The uneven pairing of men and women makes for surprising, ever-shifting groupings. There is no story, just elegant, fast dancing that's like watching exquisite eighteenth-century porcelain figures come to life.[37]

After the brief festival, Le Clercq wanted to skip the annual tour of Europe (August 26–November 11) and stay home. "She was exhausted," said a former corps dancer. "She begged George Balanchine for a break. Everyone knew that." But he refused to grant her wish. Balanchine may have felt that she would have plenty of time to rest, with nearly three months off before the tour began. She had already enjoyed an April vacation in Puerto Rico with Patricia Wilde and other friends, where they had performed in exchange for lodging.[38]

Her exhaustion may have had more to do with the strained state of her marriage than overwork. She didn't want to spend that summer on tour with Balanchine, but how could the company spare her? No one else could perform the variety of roles Le Clercq took on. As Robbins said, "She could be very elegant or she could be very classical or she could be wild . . . a phenomenal dancer." But she could also be so worn out that she dreamed of being incapacitated. Dancing was such hard work, she confessed in an interview, long after her career ended, that "there were evenings when I'd go to the theater and I'd want to be anyplace else. I'd think, 'Oh if a taxicab would just hit me a little bit, just a nudge. Then I could call and I'd have to be replaced for a week. It would be so sensational. Just a small nudge.'" And then, in a more serious tone, she had quickly added, "it's such a good discipline, because you're doing something that you sometimes don't want to do at all . . . inspiration doesn't come each night." Her way to cope with reluctance? "Pretend and do it. Feel it? Who cares!"[39]

An ever-loyal trouper, she agreed to make the trip. Arthur Mitchell was looking forward to partnering her on his first European tour with the company. Five years younger than Tanny, he had been a teenager in Harlem when he won a scholarship to the School of American Ballet in 1952. A jazz, tap, and modern dancer, he had received some ballet training at Dunham's school, studying with Karel Shook. Balanchine had noticed him on Broadway, but it was Lincoln Kirstein who, after seeing Mitchell perform at the High School for Performing Arts, had pleaded his case for a scholarship.[40]

Although he had to make up for a lack of rigorous ballet training early on, Mitchell worked hard with his mentor, Shook, the ballet teacher of many celebrated Black dancers, including Alvin Ailey, Carmen de Lavallade, and Geoffrey Holder. After a few years at the school, Mitchell was invited to join the corps de ballet for the 1955–56 tour at a salary of ninety dollars per week. He gladly accepted, even though he could have made more money on Broadway. The mothers of two White corps members complained. They did not want their daughters paired with a Black dancer. Mr. B promptly fired the two girls.[41]

When he made his debut as Le Clercq's partner in *Western Symphony* at City Center on November 8, 1955, Mitchell was still a member of the corps, although he was performing a principal role. Promoting him would have meant paying him more, and the company's finances were shaky. "The dance world was small then," he said. "Everyone knew everyone," and "we all had no money." He vividly recalled that first public *pas de deux.* "When I stepped onto the stage, some guy right behind the conductor cried out, 'Oh my god! They got a n . . . !'" Mitchell's laugh swallowed the offensive word, before he concluded: "And the place went crazy. The audience was catcalling, 'Give him a chance!'"[42]

The pair didn't miss a beat of their saucy dance. Now they were more than dance partners and friends. They were allies against bigotry. "Most people in the arts, really," Mitchell said, "whatever our problems are, we do love each other. And particularly with dancers because when you dance, you're so close with the individual, that comradery is there." Le Clercq and Mitchell got a standing ovation.[43]

A decade later, she wrote in her *Ballet Cook Book* (as rich in anecdotes as recipes) that Balanchine had adapted the role to Mitchell's strengths but would not modify the costume for him. "Arthur thought he should wear a brown cowboy outfit, not black as Jacques d'Amboise had previously worn in the role." Balanchine told him that he thought it was an "awful color." Mitchell gazed at his hands and said, "Well, I've always been very fond of it." Balanchine did not relent but tried to soften the offense with the words: "You know brown is not a good color for the *stage;* in life, yes."[44]

"A Negro cowboy?" Tanny continued. "If there were any doubters among the ballet's early audiences, their skepticism would one day be removed once and for all." Over a decade later, "there appeared a work of scholarship entitled *The Negro Cowboys,* fully documenting the place of the colored cow-puncher in American life and lore." (In what is now known as the pioneer era, 25 percent of all cowboys were Black, a fact most producers of Westerns ignored until the 1970s.)[45]

Fortunately, the company did not anticipate racist outbursts from European audiences. Getting ready for the tour of 1956, Le Clercq never imagined that in three months, she and Mitchell would be dancing together for the last time.

Tanaquil Le Clercq and Arthur Mitchell in costumes for *Western Symphony,* photo by Moneta Sleet Jr., ca. 1955. Choreography by George Balanchine ©The George Balanchine Trust. Johnson Publishing Company Archive. Courtesy Ford Foundation, J. Paul Getty Trust, John D. and Catherine MacArthur Foundation, Andrew W. Mellon Foundation and Smithsonian Institution.

14

"The Royal Family" on Tour

In August, as the New York City Ballet prepared for the tour, polio was making headlines on both sides of the Atlantic. Because summer was the peak season for transmission, many public swimming pools had shut down. Dancers lined up to get the new vaccine developed by Jonas Salk. When first licensed in April 1955, it had been reserved for children. A year later, when adults became eligible, the Balanchines discussed the issue. They were both ambivalent about taking the shot, not being in the target age group. Supplies of the vaccine were still limited, and only people twenty-five and younger, deemed the most vulnerable, were urged to take it.

Tanny would turn twenty-seven in October 1956. Not having studied statistics, that two-year cushion may have appeared protective to her. Getting shots before a trip was routine, so she joined the long line, but it moved too slowly, leaving room for second thoughts. She hated getting shots, which sometimes made her sick, and there had been disturbing incidents, widely reported in the press. A recently vaccinated girl in Idaho had come down with a case of paralytic polio traced to the shot. How could they tell? Her paralysis had begun in the vaccinated arm, not in her legs. More cases emerged in other states, one in nearby New Jersey. Later, all these tragic errors were traced to a bad batch of vaccine from one California laboratory where a "killed" virus had not been adequately weakened. From that one mistake, winds of rumor cleared fresh paths for the virus. Some frightened parents would not allow their children to be vaccinated.

Le Clercq had dropped below her usual 108–9 pounds that spring. She was afraid, in her weakened state, to risk starting the tour ill, even if the shot gave her only mild aches and fever. Crossing the Atlantic by propeller plane, with refueling stops in Ireland, Newfoundland, or Labrador, could take up to nineteen hours. She jumped out of the line, according to Jacques d'Amboise, who had just gotten his shot, and told him that she would get the injection after they returned: "I'll be miserable on the plane. I'll be even more miserable if I have a shot." Jacques understood. Young and strong, even he was worn down by the punishing schedule of a dancer on tour. His weight on departure might be 175 pounds, but he would return from a grueling tour, three to six months later, weighing between 155 and 160.[1]

Whenever the Balanchines went on tour together, a large suite to accommodate Edith Le Clercq was usually reserved for them. More than once, in hotels where they weren't known, the management, assuming that Balanchine was with Edith, booked them into the same room and gave Tanny the single! Barbara Horgan said that for years people at the ballet company referred to the three of them as "the royal family," presumably not in their presence.[2]

By the summer of 1956, it was not a happy family. At least once since her

Tanaquil Le Clercq, George Balanchine, and Edith Le Clercq, Venice, Italy, 1956. BALANCHINE is a Trademark of The George Balanchine Trust. Courtesy of NYCB Archive.

marriage, Le Clercq had openly demonstrated fury over "her husband's roving eye, which never abated no matter how seriously he was involved with any woman," Joel Lobenthal wrote. "One night," a dancer in the company had observed, "Balanchine put his hand on her arm as she came offstage. She threw it off, and with real enmity in her voice told him not to touch her."[3]

On that particular night, her fury had come from his closeness to a beautiful dancer, Barbara Milberg, with whom he shared a passion for music, not a romantic relationship. By 1956 Le Clercq had more cause for jealousy over his newest, youngest muse, the phenomenal Allegra Kent. Balanchine had created a memorable solo for her in *Ivesiana,* when she was seventeen. She was the lovely, pliant girl in white, born aloft by four men. An elusive muse incarnate, her feet never touched the ground. Although Allegra would not be named a principal dancer until 1957, she was called upon to fill in for Tanny after Copenhagen. Had she been willing, Allegra might have replaced her as the next Mrs. Balanchine as well. "He always wanted romantic elusiveness," Lucia Davidova said. "In his ballets the man always seeks and the woman flees. . . . He really can't catch her and . . . the minute he does, she is less important."[4]

Before the tour, Jacques d'Amboise had gotten the impression that the tension in the Balanchines' marriage was coming from his obsession with another elusive muse, Diana Adams. Some company members included Adams and Magallanes, both close to Le Clercq, as members of "the royal family." After Diana's divorce from the ballet star Hugh Laing, in 1953, "Balanchine lavished more and more attention on Diana," Jacques observed. But this was another frustrated passion. Throughout the summer of 1956, Diana was contemplating marriage to a man named Charles, a possibility she discussed with Tanny, who found her friend's hesitation over her choice unduly prolonged. As she wrote to Jerry Robbins, "you can't just work at things for ever and ever and perhaps spoil the present." Was she thinking of her own marriage as well?[5]

By the summer of 1956 "Tanny was raring to blow out!" according to Pat Wilde. She could have fulfilled an old dream and remained in Europe. In January she had written a letter to her fan club about the 1955 European tour: "We were a fantastic hit everywhere. You cannot believe what it is like. People just thanking us for coming . . . raves . . . flowers. Adulation of the kind that is given to Marilyn Monroe or Frank Sinatra over here. In Europe they treat us like royalty."[6]

Trapped on a tour that she had wanted to skip, exhausted and on the edge

Tanaquil Le Clercq and George Balanchine at Paris Opera, 1956. BALANCHINE is a Trademark of The George Balanchine Trust. AFP Photo/Intercontinentale.

of her nerves, Tanny got thinner and thinner. Now she found herself part of a new triangle. Edith's usual place was often taken by Diana that summer, Wilde observed. She found it strange that "It was always Diana, Tanny, and Mr. B." This triangle wasn't all that new. When he was a teenager, d'Amboise had often seen the three of them smoking together backstage. He had envied Balanchine's easy comradery with the two gorgeous ballerinas, chatting with Mr. B in their underwear.[7]

Wilde read this as a sign of transition, Balanchine's attention shifting away from Tanny and toward Diana, her contemporary. But she felt that Diana was helpful to Tanny, too, defusing the tension. Adams, such a nervous, intense person that Wilde preferred not to share a dressing room with her, nevertheless provided a buffer. Tanny adored Diana, as well as dancing in Balanchine's ballets, which made the situation doubly difficult. Could she bring herself to leave him and the company, now when it was doing so well? Perhaps she wouldn't have to leave, if Diana took her place. Maria was still with them, although he had made few new roles for her.[8]

Few dancers defected from the company during the 1950s, even though Balanchine never bothered to hide his preferences in order to spare the feelings of less favored ones. He liked to compare his principals and soloists to animals. Le Clercq, Tallchief, and Magallanes, he had once said, were the best kind of animals, agile monkeys. Barbara Walczak, a soloist he had cruelly dubbed a porcupine, left the company in tears by the end of the decade, after he told her that he had younger, better dancers for her solos.[9]

Walczak likened Balanchine to a chameleon. Warm and engaging at times, he could suddenly turn chilly, especially when confronted by dancers who wanted to keep doing the roles that they had come to consider their own. There was no way he would keep casting a performer he didn't want. Dancers were tools, used and discarded when he lost interest in them or found a better, younger replacement.

Barbara Walczak became a teacher, although not at the School of American Ballet. She had no desire to dance for any other company, not that there were many viable opportunities then, if a ballet dancer didn't want to try Broadway. As she averred, "everything was second best after working with Balanchine." He was unique in "the feel of his choreography on your body. The feel of having him set the steps on you—of the music, of the counts, of the kind of kinesthetic movement and quality—was addictive. It felt so wonderful. No other choreographer felt that way." Le Clercq, knowing full well the truth of this, must have been weighing her options on the tour of 1956, just as she had in the summer of 1949.[10]

No one knows for certain where on the tour she was infected with the poliovirus, but afterward there was much speculation, centering on three stories. In Venice, Peggy Guggenheim threw a party for the New York City Ballet at her palazzo on the Grand Canal. Tanny wrote to Bobby Fizdale that she had preferred the company of Peggy's Lhasa apsos, who regularly toured the canals in their mistress's private gondola, to that of her party guests. On the way to the event, Pat Wilde recalled, Tanny, "always trying to be a little daredevil," had dipped her fingers into the water and tasted it. Horrified, Pat scolded her. The canals were contaminated with fecal matter, a known route of polio transmission, and the disease can incubate for a month.[11]

Strangely, Shaun O'Brien, a dancer who had a long career in character roles, recounted a repeat performance. After food and champagne at the party, they had all piled into gondolas for the ride back. Someone wondered aloud whether the water was fresh or salty. Le Clercq said that there was one way to find out, plunged her hand in, and seemed to lick a finger. Had she really tasted foul canal water twice in one day, or was this a bit of pantomimed comedy?[12]

Whatever Tanny did or people thought they saw her do, it's far more likely that she got polio in Germany. The country had been hit by multiple outbreaks that year. She could have picked it up anywhere on their route, although everything points to Cologne and Mrs. Few, the wife of the American cultural attaché. She had come down with a severe case right after hosting a reception for the company, where she shook hands on a formal receiving line. Le Clercq met her again the following spring in Warm Springs, Georgia, when they were both in recovery.

But the canal stories gained fatalistic resonance after Betty Cage, who had a reputation for clairvoyance, revealed that Tanny had been asking her for a card reading for weeks that summer. When they got to Berlin, the stop after Venice, Betty finally gave in. She laid out the cards and read disaster in them for Le Clercq but didn't dare to say anything to her or the deeply superstitious Balanchine. Betty, credited by Barbara Milberg with "twenty-twenty insight," hoped she was wrong.[13]

Long afterward, company members referred to that tour as the summer of hell. The company's route, dictated by theater availability, sent the dancers zigzagging from Germany to France and back again. At the end of September, Diana sent Jerry a postcard from Berlin: "We are crossing borders with such rapidity we can't remember what language to try & speak— Fearless and I are developing stammers! We are doing so many matinées, not much 'hilarity' going on."[14]

"Fearless" was probably Tanny. It was cold and raining nonstop by the time she got to Munich. They were to dance in Frankfurt the next day, without a break, she wrote to Jerry, "and I don't really want to go to Frankfurt Brussels or Antwerp. . . . [T]he matinee starts at 4:00 evening at 8:00— Ugh—" Although it was early October, it already felt like winter to her. "I'm lonesome and dreary— I bore myself— hate my 'personality' Have nothing to talk about— I think we have exhausted our conversation— what do we talk about anyway— what did we ever— To quote poor you 'I'm not as depressed as I sound'— love Tanny"[15]

Most of her letters and cards to Jerry were playful and teasing, like their friendship. As Jacques d'Amboise said: "Balanchine was always Balanchine. He sat on his own throne. Jerry could giggle and laugh." When the ballerina Janet Reed had first seen Tanny and Jerry together, she had thought "they had a thing going," that "they were in love, or he was in love with her." The letters they exchanged in 1956–57, during her hospitalization in Copenhagen, allude to a memorable interlude on Fire Island in the summer of 1956, just before the European tour. Robbins had rented a cottage and Le Clercq spent time with him there. "I do think of the beach, and often," Jerry wrote her, months later, during the bleakest winter of her life. "I think of the porch with the white paint that came off and the dunes and the night. I can relive it all very easily."[16]

Hearing that he was on vacation in St. Thomas, Tanny wrote to ask him to take a walk on the beach at night for her. It seems a veiled reference to a particular walk they had taken, given added poignancy because at the time she wrote that letter, probably in a penciled scrawl, she could no longer walk. Whenever she thought of him, she wrote, "We are always on the beach . . . [and] I am not scared of you at all."[17]

Something about him had clearly frightened her before those few days on Fire Island. Gossip was rampant in the ballet world, and although Jerry guarded his private life from public scrutiny, Tanny must have heard rumors that set off alarm bells in her psyche. Still, she and Jerry had generally been candid with each other. Earlier that year, he had written to her about a talk he'd had in Italy with Bobby Fizdale during which they had both decided that the "grand passion" between them was over. "He knew I preferred to be with you— & admitted to preferring to be with you *himself.* Now there's a situation."[18]

She sent him an undated note, written in her shapely, pre-polio handwriting, probably soon after departing on tour: "Darling— I'm going to miss you like crazy— Around 930, at lunch, around 5:00 and at 11:00— Can't possibly write, or say for that matter 'thank you' the way I feel it— I'm so bad with compliments, and so good with insults. . . . Have a nice summer— it seems so long till I see you, better perhaps, all the way around/ All my love— T." Their affair—if it ever was one—was a bubble in the sea of a long, affectionate, and problematic friendship. Tanny, her closest friends and colleagues felt, had never loved anyone as much as Balanchine. But she had been strongly attracted to Jerry, decades before she declared herself "a one-man woman" to Holly Brubach. And by the summer of 1956, her marriage was falling apart.[19]

It's hard to imagine Jerome Robbins ever limiting himself to one person of any sex. Throughout his adult life, he juggled partners so frenetically that in his diary he characterized his sexual behavior as "COMPULSIVE." She was certainly aware of Jerry's bisexuality, which he didn't conceal from friends, but probably not of the mind-boggling numbers involved. Did she imagine he could be capable of a singular devotion to her, or had a growing distance from Balanchine made her hope so? Her letters do more than hint at the possibility, especially a postcard from an English art collection, the Wallace.[20]

She probably sent it during a brief excursion to London, or perhaps from Salzburg, the company's first stop. (It had not performed in London since 1952.) Balanchine usually stayed in a hotel near the Wallace Collection. Dawn Powell noted in her diary that her friend Jacques Le Clercq had called from Grosvenor on August 20, "where he was with Balanchine and Tanaquil and his new bride." This date is wrong, since the company flew out of Idlewild airport, New York, on August 21, and August 20 was the day of Jacques's marriage to a widow from Sea Girt, New Jersey, Marjorie "Midge" Limroth, witnessed at City Hall, New York, by Tanaquil and George Balanchine. Her father had known his new wife, who was engaged in sales of some kind, for at least a year. (Midge and Jacques had flown to Geneva on a holiday together in April 1955.) His Mexican divorce from Edith was not finalized until June 7, 1956.[21]

In the mid-1950s, Jacques Le Clercq had been involved with several other women, off and on. In June 1954, Dawn Powell encountered a certain "Martha" at a party in Jacques's apartment. The gathering impressed Powell as "very splendid in an old LeClercq way. In corner was gray-haired lady looking like Edith revived. Startled by what seemed a reconciliation I went over and lo, it was his great love of 20 years ago, Martha, who had put the riveting crack in his marriage—the beautiful girl who contrasted with Edith. At 45, she looks like Edith did at 45, sweetly genteeled [sic] umlaut lips, prissy pronunciation. . . . The drunken party got more raucous. 'Everything is just the same,' said Martha."[22]

Around the same time, Jacques Le Clercq had a contretemps with yet a third woman, documented in an angry letter he had received a dozen years later. The furious woman reminded him of money she had lent him in Paris in the 1950s, never repaid. He had lured her to New York in 1953 with a promise of marriage, she claimed, but shortly after her arrival, she had discovered that Jacques was already living with the woman who was to become his second wife. (This letter became part of his daughter's inheritance.) It's not clear when she had first met Midge (the former Mrs. Frederick Limroth, widowed in 1953), but Tanny informed Jerry about her stepmother in a letter from Copenhagen, getting her name wrong ("Margaret") and misspelling her nickname, too ("Midje").[23]

She'd had more pressing concerns in London, expressed on that aforementioned postcard addressed to Jerry (a glossy photo of *An Idyll* by Francesco Bianchi Ferrari). Its back was filled, edge to edge, with the tiny writing not seen in her letters after polio. Not one of those minuscule words is about her father, his new wife, or George Balanchine. "Why didn't we leave it as it was," she wrote. "You remember me saying at Denis's house what I wanted so much? If ever you feel you'd like it too, tell me please. . . . On the surface we both feel the same about our chances as an 'us'— You are afraid of the pain it might bring you. I am afraid of not fighting for what I feel will be happiness, because I couldn't live with myself if I didn't. . . . So the stage is set for Act II— Let's hope the cast hasn't gone home. Love, T"[24]

Act 1 had presumably ended with her marriage to Balanchine, which put her on Jerry's short list of people whose rejections had left a lifelong wound in him. Now, at a moment of crisis in her marriage, she had turned to him again, with such fierce determination that she seemed willing to pit herself against her mother and Balanchine. Robbins did not discourage her. A letter from Tanny was "the most perfect way to start the day," he wrote her, and "when I don't get one something seems missing." She had been writing to him almost daily since leaving New York, even on the first sunny day of the tour, "a terrific free day" that she had spent playing badminton and walking in the hills around Salzburg in bare feet. These acts of rebellion angered Balanchine and her mother, always concerned about injuries. "I didn't get mad," Tanny boasted to Jerry.[25]

Subsequent letters document a saga of calamity. Early in the tour, Tallchief, recently married to her third husband, discovered that she was pregnant. When she suffered cramps in Switzerland, the doctors recommended bed rest. Tanny, Diana, Patricia, and Melissa "Milly" Hayden pitched in to cover the gap. No principals thought twice about jumping in at the last minute to cover for anyone, even a missing member of the corps. But replacing a dancer of Tallchief's caliber was a daunting task. Le Clercq was already worn out when she assumed this extra heavy load.

She was performing nonstop, often in a state of stress. The weather was moody, too, summery in Venice, but cold by the time they arrived in Germany ten days later. Yet in spite of icy rain, toe infections, bronchitis, marital stress, and exhaustion, she danced through Austria, Switzerland, Italy, Germany, Belgium, and France. Even on so-called days off, dancers were often called upon for press appearances to publicize the tour. Le Clercq wrote to Robbins, "Di and I had our pictures taken at the Berlin Zoo— with *two* lion baby cubs. Mine growled when he was put on my lap and sort of started to 'worry' my thumb. I was extremely scared— especially since I noticed the photographer had band aids all over his fingers." In Berlin, a fifteen-year-old dance student, Karin von Aroldingen, saw performances of *Bourrée Fantasque* and *The Pied Piper*. She was struck by Tanny's "eccentric quality" and extreme thinness. Her memory of the dancer's singular presence informed von Aroldingen's choices when she was later tapped to perform Le Clercq's signature roles in *La Valse* and *The Four Temperaments*.[26]

In early October, Tanny reported sad news to Jerry: "Maria lost the baby. I guess she danced too hard." Required to rest from her ordeal, Tallchief did not return to finish the tour, which was winding down, to Le Clercq's relief. In Brussels, their stop just before Paris, she had enjoyed meeting the king, finding him far more attractive than his image on stamps. Backstage, Nicholas Magallanes took her picture. She looks lovely, but terribly drawn, even "frighteningly thin," in the recollection of a French critic. Tanaquil Le Clercq had been danced, not to death as the young girl in *La Valse,* but into a state of exhaustion. And yet even while performing multiple roles almost daily for months, she didn't skip practice sessions to go sightseeing. "Tanny was in class every day," Allegra Kent remembered. "I know. I was there also."[27]

Dancing the role of Odette still made Le Clercq anxious, but she had no choice with Tallchief gone. The dancer Richard Rapp, another friend on the tour, caught a performance she did "in Brussels with Nicky Magallanes that was the finest *Swan Lake* I've ever seen."[28]

When the company reached Paris, they heard more bad news: Igor Stravinsky had suffered a stroke in Berlin. He had revived, consumed a copious meal, and gone on to another engagement in Munich. There he had collapsed again. It was not clear whether or not he would live. In a terrible state, Balanchine had flown to Munich to be with him. Did his absence, even under those grim circumstances, alleviate some of his wife's stress? She seemed to revive in Paris, judging from her stellar performance in October, with Jacques d'Amboise as her partner, in the film of *Western Symphony,* shot in "a frigid television studio with a cement floor."[29]

Today's TV studios have sprung wood floors, but in the early days of televi-

Tanaquil Le Clercq backstage in Brussels, photograph by Nicholas Magallanes, 1956. Courtesy of NYCB Archive.

sion, scant attention was paid to flooring. Villella once broke eight toes dancing on cement. And yet Le Clercq's performance gives no hint of the terrible conditions. Watching this short color film is exhilarating and heartbreaking. Sashaying her way toward the audience on pointe with saucy, swishing movements of arms and legs, she delivers a kittenish parody of a Hollywood vamp and Wild West dance hall girl rolled into one. Her smiles are contagious, full of fun, as if there is nowhere else that she would rather be.[30]

To keep up her spirits, she wrote long, gossipy letters to Jerry Robbins almost daily. She'd had a "divine dinner" in Paris, she told him, adding, with sardonic humor, "Then Nick [Magallanes] insisted we sit at Café Flore— so we sat & sat. I got colder and colder— and he recognized no one and no one recognized him."[31]

Near the end of October, she shared some good news with Robbins: "Stravinsky is better but is recovering slowly— I wish he would go home and compose instead of conduct— After all no one can compose but surely lots of people can conduct." There were days when she wished that Edith would go home, too. That same month, she wrote: "She annoys me so much sometimes I could just scream— It's really cause we are so much alike— I see my mannerisms in her, and I hate them. . . . And yet I really deep down think she is a wonderful person."[32]

Tanny opened her heart to Jerry more readily than to most people. He respected her privacy, revealing little of an intimate nature about her, even in his personal diaries, although he saved all her letters (handwritten) and kept carbon copies of his (typed) for posterity. This well-documented relationship remains, in part, a mystery. Suffice it to say that they were close, almost feverishly so for a short time when they were both young. In her last letter to him from Cologne, the day before leaving for Copenhagen, she confessed that she was not looking forward to the New York winter season (December 18–March 3) with just two free weeks after the tour, followed by rehearsals "for three then perform 8 weeks possibly 10— All through Christmas, New Year— till the end of February— Horrors." This scenario appears rosy in light of what befell her days later.[33]

In Copenhagen, Balanchine stayed with his wife when the New York City Ballet went on to Sweden and then New York. He would not come back to full-time work for nearly a year. Suddenly, he had become a model husband, intent on restoring her mental and physical health. Guilt consumed him, not over insisting that she make the tour but not that she take the polio vaccine, nor for her heavy workload. He deeply regretted having cast her as a polio victim in the *March of Dimes* ballet and as the doomed girl in *La Valse*.

The hellish summer had ended, but not the fallout from it. Robbins wrote to Balanchine to offer help, which was gratefully accepted. He called Kirstein twice from Boston, where his new musical, *Bells are Ringing,* was in tryouts. In tears, he expressed his willingness to do anything needed, although he made it clear that he would not have time to make new works for the company, given all his theatrical commitments. Recuperating at home, Maria Tallchief heard the sad news and, as she later wrote in her memoir, "my heart broke." Guilt gnawed at her, too: "I told myself that if I hadn't become pregnant perhaps Tanny wouldn't have had to substitute for me in all those taxing roles she never wanted to dance."[34]

Most company members found out on the train to Stockholm, Sweden, hours after Betty Cage phoned Barbara Horgan around 6:00 a.m. on the day of their departure, Thursday, November 1. Afraid of sowing panic, the administration had waited until the last minute. The principal dancers, friends of Tanny's, were devastated and terrified. Being older than the corps de ballet members, many of them had not had a polio shot. Luckily, nobody else in the company was seriously afflicted. One corps member, Ann Crowell, lost the use of an arm in the middle of a performance in Stockholm, but soon recovered from what she had thought was a pulled shoulder. Years later, Jacques d'Amboise wrote, a doctor told her that she had muscle damage from a mild case of polio.[35]

After Tanny's final performance in Copenhagen that Sunday, she was too sick to perform. Balanchine, not realizing the seriousness of her illness, went to the theater on Monday to train her replacement in *Divertimento*, Yvonne Mounsey. Robert Barnett, who was off that night, was eating at the theater restaurant, right by the stage door, when Edith Le Clercq arrived, frantic. She told him that Tanny was "very sick" and she had to find Balanchine right away.[36]

The recommended massage therapist initially summoned had proved useless. Balanchine's remarkable self-confidence in his own judgment, even in areas where he lacked expertise, could be dangerous, to himself as much as to those who had faith in him. By the time a medical doctor arrived, Tanny's fever had reached 106°F. The pain was so intense that she lost consciousness. In the hospital, the Danish physicians thought she had meningitis or some other virus that was going around, so they isolated her and further delayed the appropriate treatment. They feared she would die.[37]

Vida Brown, the company's ballet mistress, shared a room with Melissa Hayden in the same hotel as the Balanchines. At 5:30 a.m., most likely on the morning of the company's departure, Balanchine knocked on their door. He looked "drawn, pale, somehow shrunken," too distraught to come in from the hallway, in the recollection of Vida more than forty years later. When he revealed the terrible diagnosis, she embraced him and they both wept. Then Hayden emerged and "flung her arms around them both," all three weeping.[38]

Tanny had been moved to another hospital in Copenhagen, Blegdam, which specialized in polio, where an iron lung helped her to breathe. This now obsolete machine, invented a year before her birth, put pressure on weakened lungs, forcing them to move and take in oxygen. She was trapped in it for a month, not knowing whether she would ever be able to breathe again on her own. It must have been terrifying, especially for someone for whom moving her body was life itself. And yet she tried to be positive, at least in retrospect, about her situation. "I thought it was cozy," she said, years later, "back to the mother's womb, I guess. It was warm, and it breathed with this hissing noise that never stopped." Once she got past the fever and the most intense pain, Tanny was removed from the iron lung, but she had to endure a respirator strapped to her chest until she was able to breathe without it. By November 15, she was no longer critically ill, but eating was a big problem. She would gag, but nothing came up. This continued into January.[39]

Letters and telegrams arrived from all over the world. President Eisenhower wrote to Lincoln Kirstein to express his concern. The queen of Denmark, who had seen Tanny dancing just a month before, came to visit her. In a letter dictated to Edith, Tanny wrote to Jerry Robbins about the flurry of advance preparations: "The window washer came to wash the windows— all unsightly instruments of torture were hidden. Edith said potted plants were put in the hallway." Tanny found the queen "so chic and nice looking, for the first five minutes I thought it wasn't the Queen at all." A famous maker of silverware, Georg Jensen, named a new silver pattern after her, Tanaquil. It was only stainless steel, she drolly told Jerry, who was sending her orchids, special-delivery letters, and packages every few days.[40]

Balanchine remained by her side, taking time only to stage one of his ballets for the Royal Danish Ballet, a thank-you to the Danish government for paying Tanny's hospital bills. He donated the royalties from two ballets to the Danish Polio Fund. "The doctors are doing miracles," he said, in a public statement. "My wife and I are able to do little in return."[41]

Edith remained in Copenhagen, in a room adjoining his at the Hotel d'Angleterre. Writing on hotel stationery in her neat, elegant hand, she told Jerry that Tanny was able to breathe on her own for short periods but was too weak to see anyone yet. "I feel full of hope then she sinks into a deep emotional depression & even George is sent out of the room— and she and I go through it together."[42]

Balanchine assured journalists that she would dance again. Decades later, Holly Brubach asked her when she had realized that she would never walk again. "I knew immediately," Le Clercq answered. Her letters to Robbins tell another story. Even before she could hold a pen to write on her own, Tanny had hopes of getting back on her feet. "I guess I will get completely well but it will take *so* long and I'm so helpless *now*," she dictated to Edith. "I want so badly to write to you myself and I try but I just can't quite make it."[43]

Edith thanked Jerry for the letters and presents he had sent, especially a heartfelt, encouraging letter that Tanny held in her hand and read over and over: "The first time she has been able to do such a thing . . . and for a half-hour she was her witty self. She is so brave it would break your heart. She gets through the days very well as doctors and nurses are doing things to her constantly and time passes but the nights— She described them to me tonight when George was out of the room (She won't let him see her cry). Nightmares of the chest respirator not working and suffocating which wake her up, then she starts thinking of the uncertainty of the future— and she is in constant pain."[44]

Jerry wrote to Tanny: "Dearest one, There is so much we can't understand that happens in life— I don't stop thinking about you." Dictating to her mother, she could not tell him all that she wished to say, so she tried to write back with her left hand. She was right-handed and her fingers worked, but that arm was too weak. Eventually, she found a way to write a few lines with her right hand, by having her mother move the paper along. Through Edith, she sent a playful, possibly coded note: "Dear Unkie Jerry— I would like an animal to sleep with . . . a softish, cuddly something— leopard, tiger, pussy cat or dog." She specified that she would like one with "a nice expression."[45]

He took the request literally. A large stuffed dog with a bunch of violets at its throat was delivered to the hospital. The early Christmas gift made Tanny extremely happy, a stand-in for Jerry himself, and she kept it on a chair by her bedside. She wondered in a letter whether he had enjoyed picking it out, not suspecting that money and instructions had been sent to a Danish friend, who had done the shopping for him. "You are helping more than any human being," Edith had written Jerry the month before. "How can we ever thank you for taking over the Company— for making it possible for George to stay."[46]

Robbins did turn up in New York, ready to lead the company as promised, even though his hit musical, *Bells Are Ringing,* had just opened on Broadway, and he had been simultaneously working on the next one, *West Side Story.* But Lincoln Kirstein had already assigned several principal dancers to take over, and a few of them were busy staging their own ballets. Jerry, miffed, did not want to steal their thunder. "Sometimes I think," he wrote to Tanny, "Lincoln's genius lies in lousing things up better than anyone else." Betty Cage (who had gotten her information from Kirstein) griped behind Robbins's back that you didn't offer to help and then go off on vacation. But Jerry *had* stayed in New York to rehearse the New York City Ballet for several weeks before the winter season, although he did not look forward to it, he wrote Tanny, "because I know I won't see you . . . can't wait until you write more yourself. I love you very much."[47]

He'd had "a hard time with Tanny's illness," Robbins said in an interview many years later. He found it hard to work with the company "as if it was the same. It just didn't— wasn't for me." As Christmas neared, he was having second thoughts about obeying orders from Tanny and others to stay in New York. The School of American Ballet was sending Natasha Molostwoff to Copenhagen. "I envy Natasha coming to see you," he wrote. "She keeps telling me to ignore your letter and to come with her anyway."[48]

Instead, he went for a much-needed vacation in the Virgin Islands. By the time Natasha arrived with the marshmallows, sweet potatoes, and bottle of bourbon that Balanchine had requested, Tanny was much better, but still a shocking sight. "She was white and slack as a piece of paper and scared to death," Natasha remembered. Balanchine cooked a turkey at a friend's house, where he prepared a Christmas feast, supplementing whatever he found locally with Natasha's provisions. But eating was still a problem, Tanny wrote to Jerry. "I gag— Nothing comes up, its like spasms— hiccups."[49]

With his usual determination, Balanchine had tried to tempt her with a taste of home. "Tanny couldn't even lift her fingers. It was horrid," Natasha recalled. In front of her friend, Tanny dared to cry. She was immensely touched by a gift from the stagehands at City Center, who had taken up a collection on her behalf. They'd raised fifty dollars, which they gave to Natasha to buy a gift. "And I doubt I ever spoke to more than ten of them. Isn't that wonderful?" Tanny wrote to Jerry. She must have gotten wind of his vacation from Natasha. In that same letter (via Edith) she mused: "I suppose you will be basking in the sun. . . . [S]ometimes I despise you— you are so free. You can go anywhere, do anything." While he was away, she would be having electric shocks to her legs after the New Year, in an attempt to "sort of awaken them." She added, with acerbic humor, "It would be funny if they electrocuted me instead." Sitting up, she told him, made her feel "like a filet of sole trying to balance on its tail." That letter was postmarked December 31, 1956, her fourth wedding anniversary.[50]

While Robbins was lying on a beach, slathered in suntan lotion, she was being constantly oiled and turned over, an experience that made her feel "like a chicken on a roto-broil," she wrote him just before Christmas. "Think of all those virgin fish you are scaring," she teased in another letter, sent in January. She reproached him for not writing often enough, although mail was slow in the Virgin Islands. It must have been a challenge to keep up with all her letters. Apart from sporadic vacations, Robbins worked nonstop, and she was not his only correspondent. His letters, fewer in number than hers, but longer, were packed with news and expressions of his love for her. No wonder she had come to depend on them.[51]

By the time Natasha returned to New York on January 7, Tanny's spirits had markedly improved. Being with an old friend who had adored her since her childhood must have helped. Natasha had brought with her some of the warmth of summer sojourns at her cottage on Fire Island.

A letter came from Jerry, the first in two weeks, Tanny pointedly wrote him. She let him know that she had attracted a new admirer among the patients, a boy of three who had gotten the idea that she was a genuine cowgirl from the Wild West. So she called him her "pardner" and asked how he liked his "grub." The good news: her eating had improved. The hospital had changed her medication, and now she was no longer gagging on every bite. The bad news: the muscles of her legs had not responded to electricity, but she was still having treatments three times a week. "I hate it— but I pray it will help." It didn't, but her upper body got stronger. By early January, she was able to write in her own hand, "I'm not even thinking anymore of complete recovery, just something." She tried to make light of her bleak future. "Do you realize that in three years I will be thirty? Thirty years old!! . . . I'll be cured, but thirty."[52]

Jerry wrote about his lessons with Stella Adler, and she replied that she had been thinking about acting, too, perhaps *A Midsummer Night's Dream*: "John Housman still tells Lincoln he wants me for Titania. I wonder if I could be up and walking and do it? Maybe I would be too scared. I have decided for a while at least not to do anything I don't *want* to do." How could she have made it through those harrowing weeks and months, if she hadn't been able to entertain fresh possibilities? "The days crawl by. . . . [I]n the beginning I thought I would go crazy— Come back to New York cured but nuts."[53]

Some nights Tanny couldn't sleep because she itched all over without being able to scratch herself. The kidney stones she passed "tickled," she wrote, as if it tickled her to be able to feel anything at all in the lower half of her body. She even made light of her bowel problems. Her dancing life had required immense discipline, but now she found a grim comedy in her lack of muscular control. Edith wrote to Jerry: "The doctor told her her bladder was infected again and they would have to do things which he hoped would not be 'too painful.'"[54]

One morning in late January, Jacques Le Clercq showed up at the hos-

Tanaquil Le Clercq, George Balanchine, and Natasha Molostwoff at Molostwoff's cottage on Fire Island, 1953. BALANCHINE is a Trademark of The George Balanchine Trust. Courtesy of NYCB Archive.

pital, alone and without advance warning. "I love him, adore him, admire him, from a distance," Tanny wrote, in her own hand, markedly firmer now. "*Never* close to. . . . Edith is jumpy and George is being a sort of good relations type. . . . G. entertains J. while E. feeds me— Then they all have dinner together except me— Almost good to be sick, to miss such an evening— I think the time your father ought to have come was in the beginning, when you *might* have died says Edith, not *now*— Get the jist?"[55]

Another day, Jacques came to the hospital "quite drunk, made no sense— He just wanted to talk about me when I was little— Anecdotes interesting no one." Tanny confessed to feeling stiff and unnatural around her father and suspected that he felt the same. She wished he had stayed away "and left me alone, he never was around when I ever really needed him— Just when *he* felt like it."[56]

They were all relieved when the professor left. "He felt lousy the whole time he was here poor man," Tanny reported. What was most likely the *delirium tremens* of acute alcoholism, she assumed was a nervous condition: "He just shakes with nerves— Really shakes and shakes. I think he looks extremely badly." She, on the other hand, was looking better than Jacques had expected. He kept saying that Tanny seemed fine to him. Balanchine replied, Edith reported to Jerry, "Yes, she is, except she can't move." Her father seemed to believe, Tanny joked, that her illness was "a plot of Edith's to keep him away."[57]

"Aunt Edith" had previously written to her "nephew" Jerry that Tanny's mood was improving: She had "actually told George & me the other day: 'I'm so happy!' That was before her father arrived." Edith added that her ex-husband was "too blind (mentally) to notice that she can't raise her arms." She thanked Robbins for his letters and presents, which Tanny adored: It made her "happy all day when something comes from you."[58]

Balanchine had put everything else aside to care for his wife, apart from his brief sessions at the Royal Danish Ballet. She viewed his newfound devotion skeptically. "George carried me to the chair," she wrote Jerry, "this is very nice as I could sit half hour now, and maybe some tonight. I'm not 'chained' to my bed— George is so pleased. I would almost say he enjoys me this way— To have someone totally dependent on one seems to agree with some people." She didn't realize that he and Edith had to take sleeping pills so they would have the strength to be there each day and put up a brave front for her.[59]

Being dependent did not suit Tanny. She wrote: "I'm better off here— Or if I go home— I will lounge around the apartement and be *completely* dependant on George, to move me, feed me etc.— That would *never* work— It's awful to be helpless— *I* hate it." She hated being at the mercy of the nurses, too, not all of whom were gentle. One, she wrote Jerry, kept washing her with her watch on "and scratches my ass. She also rubs too hard in the wrong places— It must be like sleeping with somebody for money or something."[60]

Balanchine dictated a letter to Lincoln Kirstein via Edith, to thank him for Tanny's Christmas present—Natasha. "Edith and I are trying to be cheerful. We are hoping and hoping and hoping and waiting." His façade was *too* convincing. "George is fine," Tanny wrote, "he loves this life says we see more of each other than we ever did— Says the hospital is home for him."[61]

Those bleak months were brightened by the letters from Jerry that arrived, like his presents, via special delivery. In February Tanny wrote him that she had eagerly awaited a fitting for braces, so that she would have more independence. Other patients were able to walk with a combination of braces and crutches. But this didn't work for her, no matter how much she tried. George assured her that the braces would be better in America. He was in touch with a friend, Dr. Henry Jordan, chief orthopedic surgeon at Lenox Hill Hospital, where he wanted to bring her. She was not convinced: "My braces are just fine— Fine— Only I can't move my legs. . . . I thought by the time I get all that crap on, plus two canes and two ladies, if I try very hard, something will move— Well it won't. . . . I get the strangest feeling sometime that all of this is not happening to me. . . . I'm somewhere else."[62]

It was all the more frustrating because her dependence on her husband made her feel guilty. She knew *he* would be better off in New York, but Tanny was reluctant to give up her now familiar hospital routine. When Balanchine went for a brief visit to friends in Jutland, she was in a horrible state, "so scared something might happen to him— Then I would die— He has been here every day of Nov. Dec. Jan, and I didn't want to let him go off for three days in Feb. . . . I'm so scared all the time— of everything." With Jerry, like Natasha, she did not hide her pain.[63]

From November to January she wrote him:

"I cry all the time. I can't stop feeling sorry for myself."[64]

"I keep asking—Why? Why me—Why polio."[65]

"Its funny I cry when I think of you— Regret?"[66]

Jacques d'Amboise imagined what must have gone through her head as she realized that her dancing life was ending, a moment that comes for every dancer eventually, but rarely one so young: "I'm not a dancer anymore. Who am I?" She had danced for twenty years. Her legs had been an "elongated, stretched out path to heaven." Now they hung limp as a pair of stockings. Her first look at them had been horrifying: "When I woke and saw my body my legs, feet, hips," she wrote to Jerry, "I was so shocked & repulsed."[67]

As her hands got stronger and her mental state better, she began a series of letters that she signed with an assortment of playful, creative kisses, decorated

X marks. There was an invasion of kisses, descending on parachutes, a one-sided kiss, a croquet kiss (bent over), an old-fashioned one (tied with bows), a hairy one with a beard and moustache, and one kiss. . . . . . . leading to another that took up most of a line.

He sent back his own kisses, admittedly not as witty as hers. "Our 'relationship' is odd," she wrote him, "but *I* like it— it's one of *my* favorite relationships." She underlined the word *I* twice and closed with a string of *x*'s marking the weeks until her return, "a kiss a day, while I'm away." But suddenly, the kisses stopped. When he complained about this and a letter she had signed, "Platonically," she answered, "I never sent any more kisses because I just couldn't think of any *original* ones . . . as for platonically, I don't know why, may be I just got scared of how my letters read to someone else."[68]

But as that fear subsided, new ones intruded. She wrote: "Love you— Jerry— Jerry— love you. . . . No matter how I seem or act— I'm fine, I've thought of you all the time, and I love you. . . . I'm so excited at the thought of seeing you that I don't know *what* to do. I've thought about it *so* often and now it will happen. I almost wish it wouldn't."[69]

Jerry was looking forward to "having you cut me up with your remarks when I visit you, planning surprises for you." He wanted to take her to the park and museums. Balanchine, she told Jerry, in a letter that crossed his in the mail, had similar ideas. He envisioned day trips home from Lenox Hill and excursions through Central Park. The prospect didn't thrill her: "Rather like walking a dog. . . . Perhaps you might take me sometime— or is it embarassing? People will stare I suppose— I don't *think* I want to go home. . . . Miss you very much— it's past, and it's silly but I like to close my eyes and think of the beach— and you go with it— xxxxxxT."[70]

"What makes you so nice?" she mused in March. "Funny, I had to get so sick to find out what you can be." She offered to bring him a sweater, like a Danish one with silver buttons she had sent to Jacques d'Amboise. Two days before she boarded the plane home on a stretcher, accompanied by her husband and mother, she sent "kisses I *want* to, but may not give you when I see you." Betty Cage and Edward Bigelow met them at the airport on March 14. Tanny had let Jerry know that she would call him that day. Unlike Kirstein, who had been kept out of the loop to forestall the press, Robbins could keep a secret.[71]

15

Warm Springs, Georgia

Le Clercq's private room at Lenox Hill Hospital was paid for by Lincoln Kirstein. Balanchine, Martin Duberman wrote, "had exhausted most of his own funds in Copenhagen, where Tanny had to be turned from one side to another every hour and had required three nurses." Her friends were eager to visit, but she wasn't ready to face other dancers. In November, Edith had written to Jerry, quoting Tanny: "I am so vain. I don't want anyone to see me, *ever* in a wheelchair." She accepted few visitors besides her mother, husband, Jerry, and Natasha. The first time her old friend Pat McBride saw her at the hospital, she and Tanny had "burst into tears."[1]

Jerry, who lived near the hospital, dropped by constantly with food and presents. He wheeled Tanny up to the roof, in defiance of hospital rules, and took desultorily glamorous pictures of her. She didn't even try to smile. He may have told her about the musical he was working on with the composer Leonard Bernstein, *West Side Story* (a Romeo and Juliet story about street gangs in New York), and perhaps had danced on the roof a bit, to show her what he had in mind.

She wrote him a charmingly oblique thank-you in third person for his frequent visits: "let me tell you about my friend— He comes all the time, he phones, he brings me everything, and anything. . . . I hope there is no feeling of 'duty' or 'imposing' on his part. I would hate it if there were. Also he reads out loud to me, which I adore. He says I can call any time. Which I wouldn't, but it's very nice to know."[2]

Balanchine, in public and private, remained steadfast in his belief that she would soon be back on her feet. "She wants her own body back," he told an interviewer, "or even any little bit of it that she can get back. She will work, she will do exercises endlessly. Tell Tanny to do this a hundred times"—he flexed his wrist—"and she will do it with pleasure."[3]

Tanaquil Le Clercq on the roof of Lenox Hill Hospital, photo by Jerome Robbins, March 1957. ©The Robbins Rights Trust. Jerome Robbins Dance Division, The New York Public Library for the Performing Arts.

Her doctors recommended that Tanny be taken to the Warm Springs Foundation, founded by President Franklin D. Roosevelt. Stricken with polio as a young man, he had regained some feeling in his legs by swimming in the waters of Warm Springs, Georgia, where he had established his foundation. It was hoped that the state-of-the-art therapies the place offered might speed her rehabilitation during the crucial first year. After that, there would be little hope of making further progress. She left for this retreat in April, accompanied by her husband and mother. Tanny sent Jerry a postcard with a black-and-white picture of the main building, rather like a columned plantation house. "Looks like a super duper motel doesn't it," she wrote. "First day always hard— Tests tests."[4]

She wrote to Bobby Fizdale, "It is just wonderful here, so beautiful." She admired the red brick buildings and took pleasure in having a private room, painted blue, with a window beside the bed, in spite of the fact that it was right next to the noisy spot where bedpans were emptied. The grounds and amenities were luxurious, with therapy pools and a movie theater: "First two rows are stretchers, next row wheelchairs, then seats where George and Edith sat." Although her mother's hovering got on her nerves, Tanny acknowledged that "she is a wonderful person. If we don't 'get along' sometimes, I must say the fault is all mine."[5]

Sociable by nature, Tanny was popular among the patients. She told Bobby, "The girl that gives the bed pans said, 'I never seen a new one make friends so fast.'" She made progress fast, too, with the dedication and discipline of a dancer. With physical therapy, her arms gained strength. Soon she could manage the wheelchair by herself. Others were far worse off. "There is a girl here who can't use her eyes because of polio," she wrote Jerry, "to me that would be the worst."[6]

After Edith and Balanchine returned to New York, the days seemed to crawl by. Tanny wove placemats for friends. She took up the clarinet, to strengthen her diaphragm and exercise her fingers. She wrote letters and waited for mail and phone calls. Balanchine's letters, decorated with ink or pencil drawings of cats and mice, usually closed with some variant of the refrain: "I am thinking of you all the time and love you very much." He thanked his "Darling P.C." for her "lovely letters" and told her not to "worry about your hands and rest of it because it will all be well."[7]

Alas, those lovely letters to Balanchine have been lost, but Jerry Robbins, who did not write to her as often that summer, saved everything. "Dearest Jerry," she reproached him. "I'm shattered, you don't write to me and don't call— I come expectantly into my room after 10:00 treatment . . . makes me HATE the letters I get." When he finally called, she was ecstatic. "You see what a phone call will do?" she wrote. "I feel absolutely changed. Suddenly I just love you."[8]

Sometime in May, she had met a patient named Ellen Few and recognized her as the wife of the cultural attaché who had received the company in Cologne. Now Tanny thought that perhaps she, too, had gotten polio in Germany, but she didn't blame the most likely source. Mrs. Few was "just wonderful," she wrote Jerry. "I know now how an 'older' woman can be beautiful, she is to me." She felt sorry for Mrs. Few, "kiss of death— No legs— no arms only trunk and right hand."[9]

Although she found pleasure in the company of other patients, she hated the racism and ignorance prevalent among the White members of the staff. "Can't understand how they think or act," she wrote him again. Just because she had praised Lena Horne, whom she had seen perform in San Francisco, a nurse had threatened to get the KKK after Tanny.[10]

In July, Nicholas Magallanes, Diana Adams, and Richard Rapp came for a visit. "Diana is a dream," Tanny wrote. "I love her truely." That was the month, Tanny confessed to Jerry in the same letter, that she had taken up smoking again: When Balanchine phoned to tell her that he had managed to quit for good, she'd had a cigarette in her hand the whole time they had talked.[11]

He had stopped smoking for her sake, she believed. One day in the hospital in Copenhagen when "he wanted to kiss me," Tanny recalled, "I said, 'Ooh, you don't smell good— why do you smell like that?' Not a very nice thing to say. And he said, 'Oh, I've been smoking.' He never smoked again."[12]

At first she had been too sick to smoke, but she later resumed the habit. For a long time, she had concealed her smoking from Balanchine, even getting Robbins to lie for her. Years later, she apologized in a letter: "Dear Jerry— I'm sorry I made you lie for me [about the cigarettes] will really pull myself together and stop smoking or tell George I do." She struggled with the addiction for two decades until she finally gave it up. After that, she didn't like to be around smokers, even though her mother and many of her friends still smoked.[13]

In Warm Springs, whenever she sat up, Tanny could not take a deep breath. She knew that smoking was dangerous after polio, because of the risk of a life-threatening pneumonia. Her lungs were more vulnerable now. And yet, she needed something to take the edge off her nerves when "things are so terrible, life just isn't what I thought—I always new I had been lucky so far, and that *something* would happen to mother, George or me, it just couldn't keep on, all taking, and no paying."[14]

She devoted herself to strengthening her hands and arms in occupational therapy. "I have been caught out in a fraud," she disclosed to Bobby. "I told my o.t. [occupational therapist] of course I could draw or paint, so decided to make a cat jig saw—And my cats are ludicrous— The[y] look scared, smug etc.— I've enclosed some preliminary efforts." She had drawn a series of cats, suggesting the personality quirks of each one. Her handwriting had steadily

Tanaquil Le Clercq, drawing of cats, 1957. Jerome Robbins Dance Division, The New York Public Library for the Performing Arts.

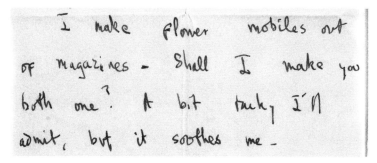

Tanaquil Le Clercq, letter to Robert Fizdale, 1957. Jerome Robbins Dance Division, The New York Public Library for the Performing Arts.

improved, but it was still an effort to write. For relaxation, she folded the pages of magazines to make "flower mobiles," she wrote. "A bit tacky, I'll admit, but it soothes me. . . . George said perhaps he will buy me a dog. I want an orange pussy. We can bring them up together."[15]

Perhaps Balanchine had been thinking that she would need company at home, after he returned full-time to the ballet studio. He was working again, but between May and November the company had no scheduled performances. And yet, when the social worker told him, during an August visit, that Tanny might be able to leave in a month, he said it was "*much* too soon. . . . Please ask them to keep my wife as long as they can," Tanny reported to Jerry. "It was very funny. HA." But the sardonic tone of her letters to friends was belied by some tender exchanges with her husband.[16]

That summer, Balanchine had been busy getting the Connecticut house and their apartment remodeled to accommodate a wheelchair. He sent a drawing of a latticework gazebo he was adding to one side of the house and asked her what colors she wanted him to paint it. "I am a haus maus maus," he wrote, "building washing squishing poison on poison ivy, preparing mousy housy for pussy wussy. With my love M." More drawings featured an industrious little "country" mouse mowing the lawn, pushing stones and a wheelbarrow, raking, tending flowers, entering a barn to milk a cow, boiling the milk, and driving a delivery truck to Georgia to deliver it to his gorgeously rendered, beloved cat. The little mouse pours milk into a bowl for her and climbs up on a table to embrace her. Tanny replied with a pictographic note: "Your [cat drawing] misses [mouse drawing] very much."[17]

In another undated letter, he reported that he was "working very hard" in Weston removing stones "that Edith brought in. I can not imagine," he wrote, "how one fragile women could bring so many stones alone. She probably could also build Keopses pira myd [Cheops's Pyramid] single handed. I'll have to take out all the stones to make some kind of order otherwise it is impossible to cut the grass."[18]

Around the same time, her father had called, dead drunk, she wrote to Jerry. He kept saying, "This is Dr. Le Clercq. I would like to speak to Mrs. Balanchine." She kept repeating, "It's me," but he didn't recognize her voice. Then a letter came from her father. He was "seeing a lawyer" about his marriage because, she informed Jerry: "He's very unhappy, his present wife is too possessive— Poor Daddy just like mother. Wouldn't you think the second time he would have known— or if he doesn't like the feeling why marry?"[19]

A few days later, Jacques Le Clercq thanked his "Darling Tan" for writing him and asked if she had enjoyed the books he'd sent. He wanted her to know that he had gone to four AA meetings and was "a new man . . . a reformed character" who hoped to go to Princeton for another degree. He was tired of living in New York while "Midge" was in New Jersey, so he had sublet his apartment, and they would find a place to share in town. On the flip side of this missive, Marjorie Limroth told her stepdaughter that she now had hope for the future of her marriage and husband, a turnaround she credited to a talk about faith and the spiritual side of life that he'd had with Balanchine in Copenhagen.[20]

Anticipating her return to their country house, Balanchine sent a charming drawing of his pussycat, seated on a cushion before a table arranged by her diligent and devoted mouse, along with a punning menu for their garden tea party: "ME-N-YOU!" It was signed, not by the mouse, but with love from the ballet master himself in a deftly rendered profile.[21]

Tanny steadily improved, mentally if not physically. She had been in an excellent mood for a whole month, she reported to Jerry. A psychiatrist, doing an evaluation, asked her, "Do you get depressed for no reason?" The question seemed ridiculous. She thought, "Well of *course*, but I also get *so* happy for no reason either— But *that* they didn't ask."[22]

Now she was able to see her situation from the outside. "I've been so wrapped up in myself I haven't realized how terrible this must be for George. . . . Legs that he can't move, can't tell me to point, straighten or bend— And no way to help." By September, after he left, she went through a gloomy spell. Bobby Fizdale wrote to Jerry (then in Philadelphia for out-of-town tryouts

Home Sweet Home drawing by George Balanchine, 1957, Harvard Theatre Collection, Houghton Library, Harvard University, courtesy of the George Balanchine Trust. BALANCHINE is a Trademark of The George Balanchine Trust.

"Me-N-You" drawing by George Balanchine, 1957, Harvard Theatre Collection, Houghton Library, Harvard U., courtesy of the George Balanchine Trust. BALANCHINE is a Trademark of The George Balanchine Trust.

of *West Side Story*), "I got terribly disturbing card from Tanny." She had not been in the mood to write much and signed her card, "Love your *ex* pen-pal." He suggested that Jerry call her up. "She wrote me several times saying 'Why doesn't Jerry write me.'"[23]

When she heard that Robbins was in Washington, D.C., for tryouts of *West Side Story,* that seemed tantalizingly close to Georgia. But he was too nervous about the New York opening of the show he had been planning for years, scheduled for September 26, 1957, to take any time off. It was his custom to go on vacation after a period of intense work, but right after the successful opening, Jerry flew to Georgia for a premature celebration of Tanny's upcoming twenty-eighth birthday, whisking her off in a rented convertible with the top down. Spreading a blanket, he arranged "a luscious picnic" with wine, she recalled, carrying her from the car. They ate, drank, laughed, and did crossword puzzles, a shared enthusiasm. Like a plant starved for sun and nourishment, she revived and bloomed in his presence.[24]

Tanaquil Le Clercq and Jerome Robbins, picnic near Warm Springs, photo by Jerome Robbins, September 1957, ©The Robbins Rights Trust.

Back at the center, she played the clarinet for him and showed him the placemats she was weaving as gifts for friends. But Jerry couldn't spare more than two days. He was working more for Broadway and Hollywood now that he was planning to leave the New York City Ballet. Without Tanny there, it was too painful to remain, surrounded by memories of their dancing partnership. Right after he left Warm Springs, she wrote him: "Dearest Jerry— This is *not* a thank-you note. I miss you, very much— The minute you left I did lots of laundry and cleaning of drawers, puffing my cigarette madly. . . . When I think of the days and evenings before me they seem unbearable, unliveable through, but then one always does— it's the one sure thing, isn't it? Til you die. I put my sunglasses away. Miss you— love, T."[25]

Her legs were still unresponsive after a year of therapy. She thought that Balanchine, in his stubborn faith, was not being realistic. He kept bringing up his own case. After nearly starving to death in Russia, he had almost lost a lung to tuberculosis in Europe. His doctors predicted he would live for only three years. Now long past that literal deadline, he still believed in miracles and prayed for his wife in the Russian Orthodox church. "You know, I am really a dead man," he had once said to Ruthanna Boris. "I was supposed to die and I didn't, and so now everything I do is second chance. That is why I enjoy every day. I don't look back. I don't look forward. Only now."[26]

"It's almost better to have polio than to be near someone who has it," Tanny wrote to Bobby. "George worries me a little. . . . He called up mentioning a friend who knew a friend and she had a piece of St. Peter or St. Paul's cape, and if you pray and wear this next to you etc. etc.— I think he still can't believe that I won't be o.k." But Edith, she reported, "has behaved remarkably well. Her only dancing daughter— and voom. I'm sure I would have gone all to pieces."[27]

She feared being forever at the mercy of her husband and mother, helpless to assert herself. "I get so impatient with George or mother," she wrote to Jerry, "whereas with you, or Di I don't." Edith was coming near the end of November to bring Tanny home, since Balanchine was busy with the ballet season. "Guess I'll get excited about it— Right now I'm not. Feel rather 'not with it' when George calls— C'est la vie."[28]

Left to her own devices, Tanny had been "behaving badly," she confessed to Jerry. She had accepted an invitation to go out with two guys and the assistant psychologist, a female, who had her own place. There, the foursome "had dinner, and a *lot* to drink and she [the psychologist] started necking with one of the guys— and one thing let to another ANYWAY the next day

I couldn't remember how I got home!" Feeling guilty, she had refused a second dinner invitation, but yielded when asked again. This dinner party had gone much like the first. In her own defense, Tanny asked Jerry: "have you ever tried talking by *one* wavering candle while two other people who have blown out *their* candle are scuffling in the dark? Well it's impossible, on top of that I like the man— Well it's all very harmless, but you know how I stew over such things. . . . It's a good thing I'm going to N.Y.C. Have a beautiful time in St. Thomas. Take a walk for me along the beach at night please." She was, perhaps, reminding him once more of a moment they had shared just the summer before. Jerry, she knew, would be taking another long overdue Caribbean vacation. *West Side Story* had proved to be a huge commercial and critical hit.[29]

Returning to New York, she discovered that Balanchine had transformed the five-room, rent-stabilized abode at the stylish Apthorp where they had been living since at least 1955. The limestone, Italian Renaissance Revival building, built between 1906 and 1908, covered the entire block between West Seventy-Eighth and Seventy-Ninth Streets, from Broadway to West End Avenue. Its regal swagger must have reminded Balanchine of imperial St. Petersburg. Designed to lure the wealthy from their mansions, the building had barrel-vaulted entranceways large enough for carriages (horsed and horseless) and an oval-shaped driveway that hugged a central courtyard with fountains and greenery. The living room windows of the Balanchines' apartment, 6A, faced Broadway, but mail was delivered to 390 West End Avenue, because Broadway was not considered a fashionable address in 1908. The original apartments had been twice as big, but the newer, smaller ones had spacious rooms, high ceilings, original moldings, and fireplaces with ornate mantelpieces.

While Tanny had been in Warm Springs, the doorways in the apartment had been widened, both bathrooms remodeled to accommodate her disability, and Balanchine had redecorated the place. He wanted their home to be as cheerful as possible, since she would be there most of the day. It had white walls relieved by artworks, two grand pianos, and a French chandelier. The chairs and sofa, discards from a theater set, were covered in blue Italian silk. They reminded Balanchine of the furniture in the old American hotels of his beloved Westerns.

Le Clercq was relieved of all domestic burdens. Balanchine did the shopping, cooking, and ironing. He had taken some time off from the ballet company to care for her, "bathing and massaging her, bending and stretching her legs, lifting her and inventing his own forms of physical therapy," in the words of Jacques d'Amboise. He was "husband, father, physician, nursemaid" to his wife, according to a frequent visitor, the violinist Nathan Milstein, who was "touched watching George taking care of Tanaquil."[30]

Stubbornly, Balanchine kept trying to get her muscles to contract. To make her stretch, he deliberately put things on a high shelf, so that she would be forced to reach for them. Barbara Horgan had witnessed her tears of frustration: "You know I can't get that cup!" But how could you say no to George Balanchine? He had always pushed her to do more than she had imagined possible, and he had been right. Now she questioned his reasoning, even though she did the exercises. He picked her up from behind, placed her feet on his feet, and practiced walking, Jacques d'Amboise recalled. Balanchine hoped that by this manipulation, her body would remember how to move on its own. This was a poignant parody of the dancing doll in *Coppelia*.[31]

He was demanding the impossible of her, only he didn't seem to know it. Natasha felt that his persistence saved his wife's sanity: "He made what he called a five-year plan for her. He said, 'This is our first five-year plan . . .' and got her to accept the situation." Later, he made a second five-year plan. Tanny accepted reality long before he did, but she went along with his plans, as always, his diligent pupil. He refused to listen to medical experts who told him that she would not walk again. Hadn't he defied the doctors who had wanted to amputate his tubercular lung forty years ago? And here he was, still thriving.[32]

During this period Balanchine tried, as best he could, to host small dinner parties and maintain an annual tradition, his legendary Easter feast in the midst of the spring season. (Some years, when he didn't have time to prepare the elaborate Russian dishes, Tanny revealed to friends, he would have them delivered from the Russian Tea Room.) When he went back to work full-time, he hired a woman to stay with her in the daytime. "Being home is hard," she wrote to Bobby. "Waiting for the maid to come feed me, I feel like a dog. Do you think in the other life I might be a person, while you will all be animals?"[33]

She called her illness "the polio," as if it were some alien creature that had taken possession of her. To maintain the muscle tone in her upper body, she worked out. "George said that everything was going to be fine, and then he didn't bother saying it anymore," she recalled. Instead, he would look out the window and point to the people on the street. "Look at all those people walking," he would say, "and they're miserable."[34]

Even so, she would have been overjoyed to be able to walk down a street like millions of ordinary people, miserable or not. For ten years, she once told Holly Brubach, she had considered killing herself, "And then I was fine." But in a 1969 *New York Times* interview, she had only admitted to suicidal thoughts in Copenhagen, when she had been trapped in the iron lung, "But once that was over, I didn't think about suicide." Talking about the iron lung to Brubach in 1998, she had made it seem reassuring, a return to the womb, perhaps because the memory of its horror was no longer as vivid as what she had described in 1969: "It was terrifying, the machine taking over your body. And they wouldn't give you anything for the pain, they want you to be conscious. And you hurt, you hurt all over."[35]

Balanchine helped her to weather the first decade of adjustment. There's ample evidence that, knowing he would not be with her forever, at times he deliberately ignored her pleas for help, to prepare her for life on her own. Like him, she knew how to live in the *now,* not wasting time looking back at what she had lost. But one day, finding her old pointe shoes in a closet, she had burst into tears.[36]

16

∘○∘

A New Reality

Tanny continued to struggle with the exercises Balanchine prepared for her, although she didn't share his faith that they would work for her lower body. She had remained his diligent pupil, for both their sakes. Balanchine used some of these exercises in *Agon,* the first dance he made after returning to work near the end of 1957. *Agon* is the Greek word for a struggle, a contest, although the dance has no mythological content. For its sensuous *pas de deux,* at times a strenuous struggle to maintain equilibrium, he had paired Arthur Mitchell and Diana Adams.

Arthur was keenly reminded of Tanny's condition when he had to manipulate Diana's feet and legs, as if he were dancing with a stuffed doll, although she had to exert considerable effort to give that illusion. (Balanchine had explicitly told him to think of his partner as a doll.) Getting the ballet ready on time was a struggle, too. As rehearsals proceeded, "Stravinsky was writing the music in California and mailing it in," Mitchell recalled. "We could only go as fast as the music was coming in."[1]

Agon, a masterpiece still widely performed, became part of a societal struggle, too. "Do you know what it took for Balanchine to put me, a Black man, on stage with a White woman?" Arthur said in 2009. "This was 1957, before civil rights. He showed me how to take her. He said, 'put your hand on top.' The skin colors were part of the choreography."[2]

During a tour of the South, Jacques d'Amboise said, "A stagehand wouldn't open the curtain because there was a black guy onstage." The lighting designer had to do it. Another stagehand refused to shine a spotlight on Mitchell. Balanchine calmly said, "just make light brighter and don't worry." He asked his own stage manager, Ronald Bates, to open the curtain.[3]

"I hope Governor Faubus is watching," Balanchine once said to Mitchell backstage. (The governor of Arkansas was a staunch defender of segregated

Arthur Mitchell and Diana Adams, *Agon,* photo by Martha Swope, 1957. Choreography by
George Balanchine ©The George Balanchine Trust. ©Billy Rose Theatre Division, The New York
Public Library for the Performing Arts.

Arthur Mitchell and Diana Adams, *Agon,* photo by Martha Swope, 1957. Choreography by George Balanchine ©The George Balanchine Trust. ©Billy Rose Theatre Division, The New York Public Library for the Performing Arts.

schools.) Although by the 1960s Balanchine was widely and justly criticized for not including more dancers of color in his company (Arthur Mitchell having remained the sole exception), no one could accuse him of not having stood up to the prevalent bigotry of the 1950s, even in the face of economic pressures.[4]

Still, the Balanchine aesthetic, born in St. Petersburg, appeared racist to some of his critics. The women in *Swan Lake* and *Serenade* were warned, as late as the company's 1961 California tour, not to get sunburned because

Balanchine wanted them "to look alabaster under the blue lights," Bettijane Sills recalled. The company had grown as it prospered, but it had not become more diverse. Some superb Black dancers (Talley Beatty, Louis Johnson, Mary Hinkson, and John Jones) guested, from the 1940s on, but they were never invited into the company. Balanchine always maintained that his preferences were personal, having nothing to do with race or even perfection.[5]

He saved his perfectionism for the kitchen. Had he not been a choreographer, Balanchine would have made a superb and exacting chef. He spent most mornings and evenings at home with Tanny, doing all the cooking. Afternoons, when Balanchine was at rehearsals, they managed with part-time help. Whenever he went out of town for work, she often chose to cope alone. Before her illness, Tanny had not liked solitude. But now she was wary of becoming Edith's dependent child again. Mixed with that may have been the worry that her mother's constant presence would irritate her husband, a not unjustified fear. There had been some grumblings. Even at the peak of her strength and beauty, Le Clercq had been unsure of his constancy.

And yet her pleasure in life returned, especially when they could get away. Her letters to friends are full of descriptions of meals and of the delight she took in the Weston garden with its glorious roses. "Simply heaven in the country," she wrote to Bobby. "I feel like I'm on a second honeymoon— Just the two of us, it's marvelous. Went to the drive in movie. . . . Technicolor Western Cynamascope frankfurters, mustard— What more can you ask?"[6]

"It's not so bad," she told Jacques d'Amboise. "It's a gift in a way." When she was dancing, she might be home on the rare Saturday she had no matinee, eating breakfast with Balanchine, when a phone call came from the theater. Balanchine would hang up and tell her that she was needed to replace an injured Swan Queen. "Do you think you could do?" It may have been her only free day that week. She would get up and go to the bathroom, feeling sick to her stomach. Balanchine used to say that he always knew when Tanny was scheduled to dance *Swan Lake* because she would start throwing up. "That's never going to happen again," she told Jacques.[7]

Francisco Moncíon once asked her if she missed dancing. "Just *Faun* and *La Valse*," she told him. "The rest of it used to make me sick." Such stage fright is extreme, but not too far from what all dancers experience, to varying degrees. Mikhail Baryshnikov spoke of "a certain terror before I go onstage." Rudolf Nureyev, asked for advice to young dancers, said: "Give up before it's too late. It's a very hard life. It's very strenuous and becomes unrewarding very soon."[8]

Balanchine had expressed relief when his dancing days ended, apart from character roles, although he was still in constant motion. In Connecticut, he puttered around the place, shirtless in the summer heat, making repairs and changes. Newly installed ramps accommodated the wheelchair, so Tanny could navigate on her own. She had turned to writing, collecting recipes for a cookbook centered on the world of ballet. Before, she could barely cook an egg. Now she marveled that Diana called *her* up for advice on food preparation.

Edith came every weekend, bringing things they didn't want. "She was trying to press something upon me or George, wouldn't take No for an answer— so I said I don't like, and don't want it here," Tanny wrote to Bobby Fizdale. "All right all right, it's *your* house"— Well doesn't that go *without* saying? Of *course* it's my, our house I don't need Edith to tell me— We will give her land where she wants. Why doesn't she save, or work, and build her *own* house— The land is free, if she *wants* her house near our future garage the electricity and water would also be free— And she can decorate it, and clean it all day long— So THERE, and don't tell me to be nice to my mother. She is over-powering, and quite selfish at times— Things should only be done *her* way? And she doesn't work or do anything for anyone (George says) except herself." Shortly after writing that letter, she wrote again to let Bobby know that she'd had a little talk with her mother and things were better. "She will spend some week-ends with her friends, and leave us ALONE."[9]

They weren't alone for long. Old and new friends came to their country retreat throughout the year, but she saw Jerry Robbins more often in the city. Whenever he returned from a working trip or vacation, he usually brought her gifts—a new lens for her camera, a book, once a dress from Italy. Their shared love of photography had endured. Now she had more time to take pictures, but it was hard for her to wield a heavy camera and near impossible to develop and print photos without help, although she still took portraits of those close to her with a new, light Olympus.

Near the end of the summer of 1958, shortly after returning from a long trip, Robbins came to a dinner party at the Apthorp. He felt, he wrote to Bobby Fizdale, "like something's happened during the summer, or else because I didn't write, or something she's come to some conclusion about. . . . I just felt not as close or as comfortable as I had been. . . . Naturally of course she's still the most wonderful, charming and most touching woman that I've ever known. George seems to be in very very good shape and has become kind of a wonderful story teller, and what is so much fun is to watch him act something out while constantly checking Tanny to see how he is going over. They seem to be more devoted than ever before . . . all to the good."[10]

By September, things seemed to have improved. "I talked to our girl Tanny today," Jerry wrote to Bobby. "It's her birthday Oct 2 and she's decided to cook for me or have someone cook for me and we'll have a joint party." The party was a disappointment, at least for Robbins. "There were others there and so she was her usual spiteful nasty self to me. It seemed more than ever. I cant [sic] tell if she has turned on me because I didnt [sic] see her in so long a time or whether it was the usual amount of drink and stimulation that brings out the worst in her all over me. Diana was there, and Nickie, Natasha, Edith and George. I couldn't get with it very much but then she didn't let me. George talks a huge streak these days, more than ever, and Tanny is hooked on cooking. . . . She looks wonderful, her hair is short and bobbed and poofed, her breasts seem very large now, and George says that she is starting to have a few very slight but evident minute abilities to feel or tense tiny muscles."[11]

Fizdale, who was on a tour, wrote back: "I think it's all because she's in love with you in a way and that is frustrating and complicated for her. You'd have to see her alone for it to be pleasant between you. . . . Try to get things on a good basis with her—it's so important to her I *know*."[12]

For Jerry's birthday, October 18, Tanny made a *pâté*. Wrapping it in newspapers, she had it delivered to his place. He ignored it. Then she got a letter from Bobby, asking her to be nicer to Jerry. "I think he should be nicer to me as he just may feel left out when you come trotting over here to *soirées*," she answered. "I am 'nice' to him— I'm just not 'slobbering' shall we say— And he hasn't thanked me for my *pâté* yet."[13]

Rather than conveying this message, the ever-diplomatic Bobby wrote to Jerry, "Got a 20 page letter from Tanny about the *pâté* she made for your birthday." In December, Jerry wrote back from London, where he had gone for the opening of *West Side Story,* "Spoke to Tanny & she was fine with me."[14]

In December 1958, *Life* magazine did a rosy story on the Balanchines at home, with photos by Gordon Parks. Balanchine, its readers learned, "spends the mornings with her before he has to rush off for rehearsals. . . . Hurrying home, he puts his work behind him and tenderly, patiently devotes himself to being the man around the house." He was photographed feeding Tanny samples from the pan as he cooked dinner, stirring a drink at a wooden bar he had made himself, presiding over a candle-lit party, standing next to her wheelchair as they listened to Bobby Fizdale play the piano, and stretched out in bed beside his wife, watching TV.[15]

Tanaquil Le Clercq and George Balanchine, photo by Gordon Parks, 1958. BALANCHINE is a Trademark of The George Balanchine Trust. The LIFE Picture Collection, Getty Images.

"Their dinner guests are most often from the fields of music and the dance," the story read. "But these days, in a home where ballet has been so important so long, the subject is never mentioned—until Tanaquil Balanchine brings herself to discuss the world that was once so brightly hers." Experimenting with different hairstyles and embroidering rugs to exercise her fingers, she tried to make the best of her situation. A reporter from *Dance News* called to request an interview about her rug-making, no doubt inspired by a photo that had appeared in *Life*. Tanny resented the intrusion. *Dance Magazine* didn't have color photos, and the rugs would not look good in black-and-white, she wrote to Bobby Fizdale.[16]

Why, she wondered, did she still have to display her life for the press? No one would be interested if she weren't a paralyzed dancer married to the great George Balanchine. So she had let out a laugh, Tanny recounted to Bobby with relish, and told the inquisitive woman that she didn't have to answer

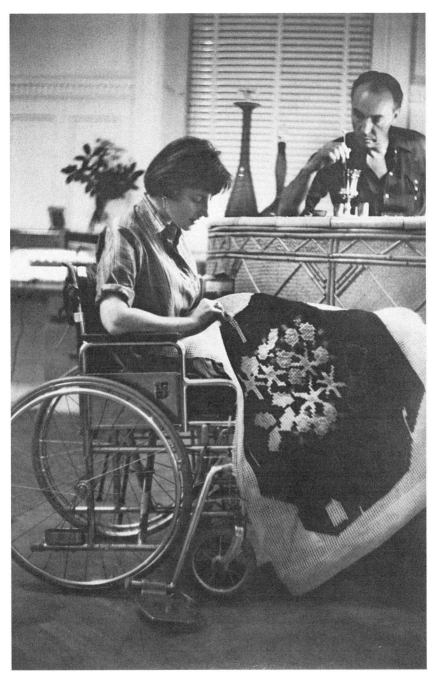

Tanaquil Le Clercq and George Balanchine, photo by Gordon Parks, 1958. BALANCHINE is a Trademark of The George Balanchine Trust. The LIFE Picture Collection, Getty Images.

questions anymore! After a shocked silence, Tanny explained that "my life was PRIVATE— my rugs for my OWN pleasure." She attributed her rude outburst, in part, to the two gin-and-tonics she'd had before the phone rang.[17]

In spite of ample coping skills, she went through a down period in the spring of 1960. Bobby Fizdale wrote to Robbins, who was in Hollywood for the filming of *West Side Story,* "Tanny says that if not for me she wouldn't even know where you are so why don't you write." Jerry didn't respond right away. The work was intense, he had fallen for his young star, Natalie Wood, and the producers were pressuring him about time and budget. (By October, unhappy with the cost overruns, they fired him.)[18]

Fizdale wrote again, a few weeks later: "Could you manage to send Tanny a postcard or call her up (without, of course, saying that I suggested it). She telephoned yesterday and for the first time in her life she just said to us that she was very depressed and had nothing to look forward to. George has been very busy with dentists, etc. and they haven't been able to go to the country very much and from what I can gather when they do go there they are surrounded by old Russian friends of George's and Tanny feels rather trapped. . . . She told me that you hadn't written and I said that you hadn't written to me either and she said Yes, but he's called you twice."[19]

Robbins answered: "I guess I haven't written Tanny because I just felt that she didn't care. Last year when I went away she didn't write at all." He promised to write and call her and must have phoned right away. In a letter written just one day after Jerry's, Bobby wrote, "I had an hour chat with Tanny today and she seems much more cheerful than she did last week." The letters flew back and forth between the three friends, registering their emotional temperatures. Her relationship with Robbins often required mediation. As with her father, sometimes it worked better from a distance.[20]

In 1962, Balanchine gave Patricia McBride (not to be confused with Tanny's childhood friend, Pat McBride Lousada) the lead role in *La Valse* and asked his wife to coach her at home. "He had no feelings that I would be upset about that," she told Holly Brubach, who asked if she *had* been upset. "Yes. Slightly, yeah," Le Clercq admitted. "On the other hand, how is she going to learn? He'd forgotten it, and she's such a sweet girl—she did a great job. So when you think of it, he's right."[21]

Patricia came to the Balanchines' apartment with Nicholas Magallanes to learn the role. Later, the pair practiced with the whole company in the studio, rehearsing the final scene where the young woman's limp body is whirled overhead while others dance around her, faster and faster, in a mad, diabolical swirl. Had George Balanchine really forgotten this dance? It's possible. His dancers retained the steps, with "muscle memory," far better than he did. Perhaps he hadn't forgotten but thought it would be good for Tanny to share her knowledge. Or he may have simply been too busy to do it himself.

With great generosity, Tanny helped a young ballerina to shine in her place. Patricia McBride was superb. But several critics wrote that as the doomed girl in *La Valse*, as well as in her other signature roles, Tanaquil Le Clercq had never been equaled. Richard Rapp agreed. He remembered Balanchine demonstrating how a dancer should "hold her hands with separate curved fingers . . . like a flower opening." You can see Le Clercq doing exactly that in the photos and silent films (with added music) of her performance in *La Valse*, "unique in my memory," Rapp declared.[22]

That same year, Tanny invited a Swarthmore College student, Anne Few, to stay with her for five days when Balanchine was out of town. (Anne was a daughter of Ellen Few, the wife of the cultural attaché in Cologne who had most likely been the source of Le Clercq's polio.) Tanny gave Anne a ticket for *A Midsummer Night's Dream* but probably didn't go herself. Afterward, she threw a caviar party for Anne, inviting Arthur, Nicky, Diana, and a few other friends. She was pleased to have the manual dexterity to toast the bread and spread the caviar herself, she wrote to Bobby Fizdale, as fast as her guests could gobble it up. They stayed up until 2:00 a.m. Anne was still sleeping when Tanny arose, at 8:00 a.m., for her physical therapy session—"Do you think perhaps one gets *more* perky as one ages," she mused to Fizdale. Le Clercq was only thirty-three.[23]

Losing hope that she would ever dance or walk again, Balanchine renewed his focus on Diana Adams, a reluctant muse who had remained enticing to him. From 1959 to 1964, he created a dozen new ballets for her. But because of injuries and pregnancies, one resulting in a miscarriage, she did not dance at the premieres of many of them. He poured out his anguish to Lucia Davidova. According to her, he had already confessed to his wife: "Tanny, if I go on with my marriage, I think I'll stop creating. I know the stimulus. In order to continue working I have to follow my love." It's not hard to imagine her pain at hearing those words, news made all the worse by her ongoing struggle to cope with a body that no longer seemed to belong to her. She did not accompany her husband on the company's first tour of the Soviet Union in 1962. He wrote to her throughout the trip, sending letters and telegrams signed with love.[24]

She reinvented herself, writing two books in quick succession, letting her hair grow longer and dying it blond. It had started to gray early, as she had written to Jerry from the hospital in Denmark, one more cruel injustice, "too mean. . . . I shall be walking sure, but I'll be old, grey haired with spectacles." But even that bleak picture had proved too optimistic a forecast.[25]

The company arrived in the Soviet Union in October, during the Cuban Missile Crisis, but the dancers knew nothing about it until they were told to avoid the American embassy in Moscow. (Demonstrators were throwing glass bottles of ink at the walls around it.) Balanchine seemed more distressed by the slow annihilation of the city of his birth than about the prospect of World War III. He refused to call St. Petersburg by its Soviet name, Leningrad. He longed for the city of his youth and the Tsar's Imperial Theater, where the glittering dancers onstage were matched by the stylish audiences. Everything looked drab to him. Nothing was as he remembered. He had already decided to skip the Kiev portion of the tour (November 11–18) in order to get to New York by November 9. "Will tell you all about when I come, impossible to describe," he wrote to Tanny. In a postscript, he likened the experience to a science fiction film they had seen, *Invasion of the Body Snatchers*.[26]

Frustrated by Diana, alienated from the world he had left behind, Balanchine had grown increasingly depressed. When Tanny heard that he was cracking up and had to come home, she called Lincoln Kirstein to say that she didn't want to see him. Kirstein insisted that Balanchine *had* to get away. The New York City Ballet had received prolonged ovations on the tour, but Balanchine was losing weight and not sleeping. His hotel phone rang at odd hours, and the radio would turn on suddenly. Local authorities seemed to be harassing him, surveilling him, or both at once.[27]

After a week of recuperation at home, he joined the company in Tbilisi, the capital of Georgia, a place he had never seen. En route, he sent a telegram from Vienna, with love to Tanny and an "EXTRA SCRACH" for their adored cat, Mourka. They were his nuclear family now. His parents and sister were dead. (Tamara had escaped the blockade of Leningrad, thanks to family connections, only to die in a train bombarded by the Germans near the sea of Azov.)[28]

A crowd greeted Balanchine with flowers and kisses at the Tbilisi Airport. For decades he had sent letters, food, and clothing to his family but had not seen his closest relatives since leaving the Soviet Union. His only living full sibling, Andrei Balanchivadze, had become a renowned Soviet composer. Their reunion was a warm one until, after a full day that included a visit to their father's grave and a convivial dinner at Andrei's home in Tbilisi, they had listened for hours to recording after recording of Andrei's recent compositions. Natasha Molostwoff, who had accompanied Balanchine, waited with increasing anxiety for him to say a few kind words. Head in hands, he could not pretend to like his brother's music. Finally, brushing off the slight with a joke, Andrei turned off the phonograph. As children, Andrei's daughter said years later in a filmed interview, the brothers had played four-hand piano, but according to Andrei, the more gregarious of the two, he had overpowered his reserved older brother whenever they quarreled. Andrei had told his children that Georgi was "not of this world," in contrast to his own "down to earth" self.[29]

Balanchine was relieved to return home to Tanny and the cat, who was, perhaps, his most unusual muse, apart from the elephants. He had been the first teacher to show Tanny how to land from a jump on the ball of her foot like a cat, not making a sound. Now he would rush home after rehearsals to exercise her and Mourka, building their strength and agility. The result was Le Clercq's first book, *Mourka: The Autobiography of a Cat,* published in 1964. "I have let Tanaquil Le Clercq write it down," the author slyly wrote in the voice of the cat, "and we have permitted Martha Swope to take dozens of pictures of me doing fabulous things."[30]

Swope, an advanced dance student at the School of American Ballet who had become a photographer of actors and dancers, had started her professional career by taking pictures of *West Side Story* rehearsals in 1957. Soon after, she became the first official photographer for Balanchine's company. The night Martha got an unexpected call from Tanny, Jeanne Thomas Fuchs, Martha's ballet school classmate and a close friend, was visiting. "You won't believe this," Martha said when she got off the phone. "That was Tanny. She wants me to take pictures of their cat."[31]

The two were wild with excitement, having worshiped their idol from afar. Since Copenhagen, only her closest friends had seen her. It was the book about Mourka, Jeanne felt, that helped Tanny to "come out of her shell . . . but it took a long time." Martha Swope's cover photo for the American edition, reproduced in *Life* magazine, showed Balanchine crouching under the big, white-and-ginger-colored cat, captured in midleap, paws fully extended. He claimed that the cat was a natural dancer. (Russ Tallchief, a nephew of Maria's, said that he had heard that Balanchine had trained Mourka by throwing the cat up in the air.)[32]

The cat was a "domestic shorthair," Le Clercq told a reporter from the *Newark Evening News.* Looking around dramatically, as if to make sure Mourka

George Balanchine with Mourka, photo by Martha Swope, 1964. BALANCHINE is a Trademark of The George Balanchine Trust. ©Billy Rose Theatre Division, The New York Public Library for the Performing Arts. Mourka signature by Tanaquil Le Clercq.

wasn't listening, she confided, in a lower tone, "He's an alley cat, but he doesn't like to be called that." Born of poor, but honest parents, she wrote in the book, Mourka was the product of a broken home. Managing to overcome his disadvantaged youth, he became a ballet star thanks to his own hard work and a chance meeting in a New York City back street with George Balanchine, who gave him a scholarship to his school. Mr. B found his *entre chats* and *pas de chats* outstanding. (The French word for cat is *chat*.) "I am the perfect example," Mourka declared, "of how any cat can get ahead if he is brilliant, witty, and hard working."[33]

Mr. B joked that cats were better suited to the dance than humans. At last, he said, he had found a body worth choreographing for. The cat would twist as he leaped, spinning in air. After months of hard work, they were finally ready to face an audience. Mourka performed for Stravinsky at a Christmas party in the Balanchines' apartment and their guests recollected that it was "the only time they had ever seen Balanchine nervous before a performance."[34]

Mourka cleared the *barre,* as Tanny might have put it in her punning prose. Martha Swope, who had become a good friend of Tanny's by then, had taken ravishing photos of the cat "training" with members of the company for the book. Dancers posed with Mourka, as well as their own cats. Suzanne Farrell's cat, Bottom, played the role of Mourka's love interest. Suzanne (born Roberta Sue Ficker) had acquired Bottom on the advice of Balanchine, who thought that having a cat would help the teenager learn how to caress an animal for her role as Titania, the fairy queen in love with a donkey, in his first original two-act story ballet, *A Midsummer Night's Dream.*

Mourka is the generic name for a female cat in Russian, so to name a male cat Mourka is rather like calling a female dog *Rover* in English. When he spoke of his Mourka, Balanchine often used the pronoun *she,* as if translating from the Russian. "You cannot teach pussycat what *you* want," he said, "but you will make her do what *she* wants. . . . I just start to play and she start to jump and I developed that jump and she started to go backwards. . . . She loved it! . . . I didn't train her. She trained me."[35]

Curious members of the press used an ostensible interest in the feline phenomenon as a way to learn more about his owners. Elegantly dressed and groomed, her shoulder-length hair dyed blond, Le Clercq was determined to show the curious that she was doing just fine. She confessed to one, with disarming frankness, that she was "a television addict, just like the children everyone complains about who never read anymore. I don't either." Tanny liked to keep her tone light and mischievous when talking to the press, very much in the manner of her husband. "I don't think of myself as a writer at all," she said. "I just did glorified captions." She shared with Balanchine a bubble-puncturing, saucy irreverence and delight in deflating expectations, refusing to fit the image of a dancer tragically confined to a wheelchair. "After all," she said, "I had ten years. It isn't as if I had never had a chance to make a career." As she told one reporter, "It's really nice to be able to sit in the audience and not dance."[36]

Dance Magazine sent the critic Robert Sabin, who wanted to "interview" the cat. Mourka leaped onto the table for a serving of cream in a saucer. As Le Clercq answered questions, she tossed paper balls for the cat to retrieve. Sabin marveled at "her body in as immaculate trim as if she were still dancing" and how "she gets around the apartment so gracefully and easily that one literally forgets that her lower body is immobilized in a metal chair. . . . George Balanchine is a lucky man," he enthused.[37]

More reporters came to see Mourka, but the cat would "only jump for George," Tanny revealed. With self-deprecating humor, she added that the cat book had been easy to write. "I sat at the typewriter until I felt like a cat. . . . Now I'm me and writing about dancers and it's harder." She was preparing profiles of the more than ninety contributors to her upcoming cookbook.[38]

Ballet was an art for the young, she said, a month before her thirty-fifth birthday. "I think the critics are sometimes a little late in recognizing the true qualities of young dancers . . . while their work is at its best, alive and wonderful, and overpraise them when they are past their prime." Was she thinking of those who had persisted in labeling her "coltish" when she had already reached her peak? As late as 1954, while praising her "enormous talent," Walter Terry had written that Le Clercq was "well on the way to ballerina status" if she could only tame her comic gifts and a "coltishness" that he had seen creeping into her Swan Queen.[39]

A dancer's career is short, she declared in 1964, so that "by the time you've gotten your technique, you're going downhill already. . . . At thirty-something, you don't look the way you did when you were twenty-four. . . . [I]t's one of those awful things that by the time you can say 'I've arrived,' you're starting to diminish." Several stars of the New York City Ballet retired soon after *Mourka* was published. Tanaquil Le Clercq was no longer the only one who had confronted a question posed by Jacques d'Amboise, decades later: "I'm not a dancer anymore. Who am I?" But she was the only one who, while still a young woman, had to navigate, in a wheelchair, a society that had barely begun to consider the needs of people with disabilities.[40]

Tanaquil Le Clercq with Mourka, photo by Martha Swope, 1964. BALANCHINE is a Trademark of The George Balanchine Trust. ©Billy Rose Theatre Division, The New York Public Library for the Performing Arts.

Once her legs had conquered space with ease. Now they were a useless weight she had to pick up, with only one reliable arm, to place on her bed at night. This was the daily reality of a woman who, to paraphrase Ruthanna Boris, had been like a *tornado*, always *bouncing, leaping and running*, making the space around her come alive by the way she moved through it.

Testing Times

By the time Balanchine returned to work, Le Clercq had mastered life in a wheelchair. He would leave the door unlocked when he went out so that she wouldn't have the bother of opening it. She had a cast of loyal helpers, known to the doormen who screened her callers. Edward Bigelow "never turns me down," she told Jacques d'Amboise. Bigelow drove her to shopping malls in New Jersey, far easier to navigate than the multilevel stores in Manhattan, where she chose clothing easy to put on and off. Polio had slowed her circulation, making her more susceptible to cold, so she wore warm knee socks and skirts that covered her knees. Jackets worked better than coats, which would bunch up in a wheelchair. (Her mother would snip and stitch the clothing, making adjustments.)[1]

Natasha Molostwoff was Tanny's go-to person for making unpleasant calls, such as complaining about a failed delivery, because "she has the meanest phone voice!" she told Jacques. Although he had a thriving career, a wife, and (by 1964) four children, "When Tanny needed someone to take her to a party," he wrote, "I would sometimes get summoned. 'Jacques, come pick me up, George is busy.' My function? To help her into her chair, to the elevator, and out of the building. 'Now go get a cab,' she'd order." With Jacques, whom she had known since her teens, Tanny could be bossy, in a playful, big-sister way, but her tone was matter-of-fact, he recalled, never angry or commanding.[2]

Once she had adjusted to Balanchine being away in the daytime, a crisis in the spring of 1963 brought him back to her. Weeks before the opening of a new ballet based on Stravinsky's Movements for Piano and Orchestra (and with the same title), Diana Adams, by then married to Ronald Bates, revealed that she was pregnant. She had orders from doctors not to dance, as she had already suffered one miscarriage. Despondent, Balanchine told Lucia Davidova, "Somebody just put their hand on my head and is holding me under

Jacques d'Amboise, George Balanchine, and Diana Adams, rehearsal of *Movements for Piano and Orchestra,* photo by Martha Swope, 1963. BALANCHINE is a Trademark of The George Balanchine Trust. ©Billy Rose Theatre Division, The New York Public Library for the Performing Arts.

the water." Threatening to cancel the ballet, he stayed in his apartment and refused to take phone calls. Tanny was in a tough position. Did she handle the calls for him and console him for the loss of his current muse, who had replaced her in several roles? Whether or not she made light of the situation whenever she spoke to Diana, Tanny must have realized that for Balanchine, it was a major blow. He felt personally affronted by Diana's pregnancy, as if she had done this to thwart *his* plans.[3]

Jacques, Diana's partner in the dance, volunteered to rehearse with her seventeen-year-old understudy, Suzanne Farrell. Reluctantly, Balanchine agreed to give her a try. Diana Adams, working as a scout for the company in 1960, thanks to an infusion of Ford Foundation money that stipulated national outreach, had found Suzanne, then fourteen, in Ohio and suggested that she might try for a place at the School of American Ballet. "She was naturally quite graceful," Diana recollected, "uncommonly so."[4]

Balanchine had occasionally given Suzanne corrections in class but had paid little attention to Diana's understudy in rehearsals. But Suzanne, who had joined the company in 1961, had been watching intently. Jacques helped her to master the duet as Diana, lying on a couch in her apartment, used hand movements to demonstrate the steps. When Balanchine saw Suzanne in rehearsal, he was overjoyed. "God took away Diana, but sent me Suzanne!"[5]

As Diana said, "Whatever Balanchine thought was possible, she thought was possible.... [W]atching him teach her was like seeing an engineer tuning and revving up a fantastic new machine. The intensity of her concentration was almost terrifying to watch." Jealousy is unavoidable in the ballet world, but it is especially acute when dancers, still in their twenties and thirties, are supplanted by an inexperienced teenager. After 1963, Allegra Kent noted, Balanchine created most of his new works for Suzanne: "They seemed to need only each other, and the rest of the company be damned."[6]

Balanchine's romantic life was inextricably bound to the ballet. As Vida Brown observed, "I really don't feel that sex was a major part of Balanchine's makeup.... His idea of sensuousness was movement." Close friends of his contradicted this widely shared impression. Balanchine had numerous flirtations and girlfriends, in between and sometimes during his marriages, Nathan Milstein noted, and was "very sensual—but he always sought permanent relationships with women, not quick liaisons."[7]

Balanchine had been with his last wife far longer than the others, helping her through an ordeal that anyone would find horrendous, and especially a dancer. But he was a man who thrived on a rapture that only a young ballerina could give him. Like a lepidopterist, he vaunted over obstacles in pursuit of the beautiful and rare, and yet once he possessed the prize, he soon required another. Natasha had observed this restless quality in him in friendship, too. "Distant Balanchine was not, but knowable, I'm not sure," she said. "He would lose interest in a particular group of friends and move completely to another. He needed change."[8]

Tanny agreed. "I think the reason George and I were fourteen years together was the polio," she said to Holly Brubach, long after their divorce. She was referring not to the length of their legal marriage (sixteen years and a month) but to the years that they had lived together. "I really think he was honorable. Well, why else would he stay?" She didn't think that his love for her explained it. "You see people married for so long. Sometimes it works, but then sometimes it doesn't," she added, with the unflinching honesty Jerry Robbins adored. "If you switch people, say, you get a whole different life. I think it renewed him; it gave him air."[9]

Living with Tanny but longing for Suzanne, Balanchine became emotionally distraught. He had fainting spells and blackouts in the 1960s, possibly caused by panic attacks. His desires fought with his deep concern for his wife. This agony of indecision dragged on for years, until his behavior became public knowledge, especially among the people Le Clercq frequented, something that must have made her private pain all the more acute. She was no longer hiding from old friends and by the 1960s had decided that she wanted to see a ballet again. Barbara Horgan, who had been helpful in countless ways since her return from Copenhagen, arranged for a car to take them. After watching Sara Leland make her debut in *La Valse,* Tanny gave her a critique. "At first, I hated to see anyone else dance my roles," she admitted to the readers of the *New York Times* in 1969, "but then the ballets were different and so were the dancers, and I found myself not minding."[10]

Going to the ballet with some regularity now, she couldn't miss Balanchine's adulation of Suzanne, clear from the way he featured her onstage. "Saying George was interested in her is putting it mildly," Maria Tallchief wrote. "He was obsessed. Never had I seen him so taken with anyone." And yet Tanny displayed great generosity to Suzanne in the summer of 1963, when the company was performing in Washington, D.C. She and Diana invited the teenager to play cards with them in their hotel rooms. "I think they both knew all too well how lonely and isolating it can be to have been singled out in a ballet company, and they were very kind to me," Suzanne wrote in her memoir. Tanny sent a beautiful bouquet of flowers with congratulations on

Suzanne's opening performance in *Movements for Piano and Orchestra,* playfully signing the accompanying note, "Love, Igor," but Suzanne didn't get the reference to Stravinsky. Afraid that she had attracted a dangerous admirer, she showed the note to Edward Bigelow, who recognized the handwriting. Suzanne was thrilled to learn the truth. "I admired her enormously," she wrote, "and would have liked to be her friend."[11]

Enraptured by Suzanne and encouraged by the support of Nelson Rockefeller and his brothers (who had raised nearly $200 million to build a new arts complex at Lincoln Center, on Manhattan's Upper West Side), by 1964 Balanchine was in a frenzy of activity. The State Theater at Lincoln Center was designed expressly for his ballet company, its stage built to his specifications. The entire complex of buildings—with the ballet, opera, and symphony buildings grouped around an open space with a fountain in the middle—was modeled on Michelangelo's Campidoglio in Rome. This enormous public square was supposed to facilitate the sharing of resources—musicians, sets, costumes, and ideas. In reality, it engendered more competition for dancers and choreographers between the New York City Ballet and its longtime rival, American Ballet Theatre (the renamed Ballet Theatre), performing in the opera house.

Although his marriage was crumbling, Balanchine's company had never stood on a stronger foundation, literally. Thanks to a Ford Foundation grant that totaled over $7.7 million (some of it earmarked, like a previous grant, for the promotion of ballet around the country, but roughly three-fourths of it going to Balanchine's company), the dancers signed their first full-year contracts in 1964, and Balanchine collected his first salary, $10,000 per year as artistic director of the company and $9,000 as head of the ballet school. For sixteen years, he had worked for no salary, living comfortably off the $12,000–$15,000 per year earned from royalties (at twenty-five dollars per performance), and he preferred to continue that way. But the foundation had insisted he accept a salary as a condition of their grant. They did not want to trust their money to a volunteer.[12]

There were howls of outrage, particularly in the modern dance community, about all the money going to Balanchine's ventures when other companies, far more diverse (racially and in terms of body types accepted), had to scrounge. Although known for its "color conscious" grantmaking, the Ford Foundation grants to institutions, which included historically Black colleges, regional theaters, and dance companies, included no stipulations that they had to become more diverse.

Jerry Robbins did not join the naysayers. After viewing a gala premiere in the new theater, which included a performance of *Agon,* he wrote to Richard Buckle, "I don't think six million dollars is enough reward for such genius."[13]

Balanchine's newfound affluence made his domestic life easier, at least in practical ways. He could afford to hire more helpers, although he still prepared dinner nearly every evening. His wife often joined him in the kitchen, eager to learn how to cook. She was collecting recipes from friends and associates in the dance world for what became *The Ballet Cook Book.* Since it was hard for her to approach the stove in a wheelchair, she learned by helping with prep work. Jacques d'Amboise contributed more than thirty recipes to her book. George Balanchine provided twenty-seven, including horseradish ice cream and a laborious dessert that took more time to assemble than he had spent making some of his ballets. Not happy with the recipe tester chosen by Le Clercq's publisher, Balanchine wanted to hire a dancer with culinary talent.

Martha Swope told Tanny about her friend, Jeanne Thomas Fuchs, a dance student who could cook. The fact that she could dance, too, Balanchine felt, would make it easier for her to understand this book full of ballet stories and photos. Jeanne was nervous the first time she came to the apartment because, as she said more than fifty years later, "I was so in awe of her." But Tanny was "terrific," unpretentious and relaxed, and they became close friends.[14]

Since Jeanne was a small person, Balanchine taught her his own back-saving way of lifting Tanny, a simple, intimate piece of choreography. You had to "wrap your knees like a vise around her knees and she would put her arms around your neck and then you would just shift her weight sideways . . . from the chair to the car," Jeanne recalled. To get Tanny back into the chair, she performed the whole process in reverse. The doormen at the Apthorp allowed the Balanchines' dented Volvo station wagon (kept in its underground garage) the privilege of entering the courtyard so that Jeanne didn't have to perform these maneuvers on Broadway.[15]

Her mission was to test Balanchine's recipes prior to publication, no one else's. Working all day in his kitchen, she re-created the dishes until he was satisfied, making tons of sauerkraut. (He had fond memories of his mother's homemade varieties, stored in barrels for the winter.) Balanchine would come home from work, taste everything, and if something didn't meet his approval (which happened more often than not), Jeanne would prepare it the next day to his specifications. He was "very kind and pleasant always," she said, but "an aloof kind of person . . . poised and controlled . . . not dramatic at all." After long days in the studio, he needed calm.[16]

Edith, who lived nearby on West End Avenue, popped in all the time, eager to be useful, bringing snacks and sweets. Tanny didn't complain about her mother, or anyone else for that matter, but Jeanne noticed that she was not as relaxed when Edith was there, although she still relied on her mother's aesthetic in matters of fashion and décor. The apartment was full of artworks, including an exquisite drawing of Vera Zorina ("Brigitta" to Tanny and all Zorina's friends) by Tchelitchew, an Audubon print of an eagle, and a painting by Magritte, *Les Intermittences du coeur* (The fickleness of the heart), its

Edith Le Clercq, ca. 1920. Courtesy of NYCB Archive.

title taken from the fourth section of Proust's novel. Jeanne's favorite was the Tchelitchew, "beautiful and mysterious," which Tanny also admired. She never showed any jealousy of Balanchine's previous wives.[17]

In a prominent place hung a portrait of Edith, painted in her youth, that Jeanne found "absolutely stunning." Tanny also kept an undated, exotic photo of her mother, signed with a Chinese stamp and characters. Like her daughter, Edith had been a stylish, glamorous young woman.

Tanaquil Le Clercq, ca. 1953. Courtesy of NYCB Archive.

Now in her seventies, she sought ways to make herself useful. Since her written French was better than Tanny's, she would help her with any French correspondence. Jeanne (whose mother was French) could appreciate this talent as much as Tanny did, but she was always aware of a tension between mother and daughter. Edith seemed "a very exacting kind of woman" to Jeanne, "not overtly affectionate."[18]

Tanny, who was not sentimental about family, or anything else, once said to Jeanne: "I look at my mother's face and I know that that's what's going to happen to me. I'm going to end up with that small mouth" and "those lines below her nose and around her lips." Edith, Jeanne noticed, was always pursing her lips, as if trying to pronounce a German vowel, a nervous habit that Dawn Powell had captured ("sweetly genteeled umlaut lips") in her diary.[19]

Frustration may have fueled her nervousness. Edith made it obvious that she would have loved to be part of the recipe testing, but Tanny fiercely guarded her independence, something her old friend Pat McBride had also observed. "She [Tanny] was rough with her [Edith]," Pat said, "but I could see she had to be."[20]

Jeanne spent days alone with Tanny in the apartment, working on the book from midmorning into early evening, stopping only for lunch breaks. After the recipe testing was finished, she continued to help on the project, doing library research and making phone calls, including some personal ones. Tanny hated those routine "How are you?" calls, even from well-meaning friends. The two women relaxed by playing word games. Le Clercq regularly solved the Double Crostics in the *Saturday Review of Literature* and the crossword puzzles in the Sunday *New York Times*. Several years later, the *Times* published puzzles that she had created. She mailed one to Jerry Robbins, with apologies for not being able to fit in his birth name, Rabinowitz, this time. (That was just as well, as she had spelled it "Rabinovitch.")[21]

When she had first started working at the apartment, Jeanne did not notice any tension between the Balanchines, but she almost never spent an evening with them, since she had two school-aged children. Once she had been invited for a weekend in Saratoga Springs, the upstate summer home of the New York City Ballet, and had a marvelous time. Balanchine was already at work there when Bigelow drove her and Tanny to their cottage. Balanchine didn't dine with them but came home late each night, after evening performances, in time for a short exchange with everyone before bedtime.[22]

Back in New York, the Balanchines invited friends to dinners where they served dishes from her forthcoming book. The ballerina who had once written to Jerry Robbins that she would prefer to "starve rather than lift a finger to cook for myself" had acquired culinary skills. But Balanchine's obsession with Suzanne had put a great strain on their marriage. Martha Swope saw the signs. She had been invited to dinner occasionally before, but suddenly, she told Jeanne, she was invited all the time. "There's something really going on," Martha said. "I think I'm just there as a buffer between them."[23]

Balanchine was following a familiar pattern. As Leon Barzin, the founding musical director of City Ballet, said: "I think his marriages were all based on finding persons who could satisfy him as dancers. The best, of course, was Tanaquil Le Clercq. . . . She danced to music, not to counts." Robbins had made a similar observation about her. He had found it hard to rehearse with the company now that she was gone because "the counts in the faces of the girls in the corps drive me crazy."[24]

Unlike Robbins, Balanchine never wasted much time mourning what he had lost. As Suzanne developed and grew, he made most of his new works for her. He even "offered Suzanne an ultimate gift, the power to choose which ballets would be on the program and who would dance them," d'Amboise attested. The company was in turmoil. In 1965, Maria Tallchief left. She was quoted, in *Newsweek* magazine, saying words that seemed to punctuate her abrupt departure: "I don't mind being listed alphabetically, but I do mind being treated alphabetically."[25]

In her memoir, Maria deconstructed this now famous remark. She had made it years before, in 1958, after returning to the company from a long absence. It was an answer to Walter Terry, who had asked what she thought of a change in the way ballerinas were listed on programs and posters. She had said that she really didn't care how she was billed, so long as she was dancing. "I still had the first dressing room. . . . I still did the first performances of all my ballets. Nothing of consequence had changed in the slightest."[26]

The drastic changes came during the mid-1960s, a period that company members later called "the Suzanne years." Patricia Wilde retired early, in her thirties, and other ballerinas quit, too. He had given Suzanne roles they thought they deserved, even those that had always been theirs. It was a faint echo of what had happened when he had been besotted with Le Clercq, creating new works with her in mind, but Tanny had always resisted taking over the powerhouse roles, like Odette in *Swan Lake*, in which other ballerinas in the company shone. Not Suzanne. "There wasn't anything she wouldn't risk for Balanchine," Diana Adams said.[27]

Years later, Adams expressed to Balanchine her amazement at the range of roles he had made for Farrell. "Well you see, dear," Balanchine said, "Suzanne never resisted." Not in the studio, at least. Adams said, "no one has ever, ever worked in his class like she did." Others might resist what appeared to be an impossible combination or step. Tanny and Diana had done it often. ("We would argue with Balanchine," Adams recalled.) Suzanne's faith was absolute; whatever Balanchine asked of her as a dancer seemed possible.[28]

Nearly every morning he would walk to the apartment Suzanne shared with her mother, not far from the Apthorp, to accompany his latest muse to the Empire Coffee Shop, across from Lincoln Center, for breakfast. Since the two almost always arrived at the studio together, many dancers assumed (falsely, according to Suzanne's memoir and people who knew them well) that they were having an affair in the mundane sense of the word. It was an affair of the heart to be sure, on both sides, that defied all labels, one that can be traced in the ballets he made for her. Mutual adoration and a love of dance were its molten, malleable core.

Even male dancers were disturbed by Balanchine's behavior. It affected their training too, because everything revolved around Suzanne and her unique abilities. No jumps would be given in a dance class if Suzanne had a bad knee that day. Patricia Neary, for whom Balanchine had made major roles, dared to confront him. "I have a right to love," he told her. Neary eventually left, too, joining the Geneva Ballet in 1968. But few older dancers even considered other companies, after Balanchine.[29]

Allegra Kent was particularly upset by the gala benefit preview of a new Balanchine ballet, *Don Quixote,* on May 27, 1965, because she found it so cruel to Le Clercq. A three-act ballet based on the novel by Cervantes, it had a score commissioned from Balanchine's friend Nicolas Nabokov, a cast of more than a hundred, a live horse and a donkey, and elaborate sets that included huge, turning windmills and a mechanical giant that inflated to a height of twenty feet.

Suzanne was cast as the object of the obsessive love of the impoverished, addled Spanish nobleman, Don Quixote, who takes a simple farm girl for a noblewoman he calls Dulcinea. He did not assign her an understudy, as he wanted no one else as his Dulcinea.

Balanchine performed as the old Don on the preview night, a character he had described for the dancer he had cast in the role, Richard Rapp, as "an old man, but . . . young in feeling and vigorous in movement." He told the press that it would be his last performance, but it wasn't; Balanchine would pop out now and then for surprise guest appearances. "I'm doing this to make money for the ballet," he said, at the gala opening. "It's as simple as that." Top tickets cost one hundred dollars apiece (about eight hundred dollars today). Some critics found his performance touching, although there were no official reviews of the preview. The evening, a financial success, netted $94,300 for the New York City Ballet fund.[30]

Tanny could not have missed all the publicity before the gala. Photos taken at rehearsals appeared in mass-circulation magazines, with her husband kissing Suzanne on the forehead in a manner that did not seem fatherly. The press copy was full of sly insinuations. In an article in the *Saturday Evening Post,* Le Clercq's innocent remark about Balanchine's love of TV Westerns ("He likes a lot of action.") afforded a journalist a perfect segue to an action-packed studio rehearsal with Suzanne: "This year, Balanchine is getting more action than ever." A quote from Alexandra Danilova ("He marries his materials. . . . [I]t is more interesting to take a young maiden and create a woman") is followed, a paragraph down, by the declaration that Suzanne is his "current favorite." But what some in the press ignored was the absolute dedication to their art of Balanchine and Farrell, separated by more than forty years but united in their vision.[31]

Jeanne was at the preview of *Don Quixote,* sitting up in the balcony with Martha Swope, where the tickets were only five dollars. Watching the performance, she felt very sorry for both Balanchines. "He exposed himself to the whole world," she said, "an old man hopelessly in love with a very young woman." Suzanne was nineteen, and he was sixty-one. Balanchine, still a consummate performer, had dared to emphasize the pathetic frailty of the Don by stumbling and falling to his knees. Suzanne embraced him, helped him to his feet, danced around him, leaned against him in arabesque, as he stumbled some more, eliciting, again and again, the rapturous solicitude of his partner. Focused on making his muse appear as lovely as possible, Balanchine showed no fear of looking ridiculous.[32]

The theater was packed with celebrities of the arts, commerce, politics, and philanthropy, including two sisters of the late John F. Kennedy, Jerry Robbins, Leonard Bernstein, Le Clercq, and all of Balanchine's ex-wives. From her wheelchair, Tanny watched Suzanne, as Dulcinea, do a pantomime of washing the old Don's feet and drying them with her hair. He gazed at her adoringly. To many dancers in his company, he seemed as delusional as the old Don. "How could Tanny bear this?" Allegra Kent wondered.[33]

Suzanne, who had rehearsed with Richard Rapp, had been as surprised as anyone that Balanchine, at the last minute, had decided to perform the

George Balanchine and Suzanne Farrell in costumes for *Don Quixote,* photo by Martha Swope, 1965. BALANCHINE is a Trademark of The George Balanchine Trust. ©Billy Rose Theatre Division, The New York Public Library for the Performing Arts.

title role. Particularly hard to watch was the *pas de deux* where, barely danc- ing, the Don followed his Dulcinea around the stage. As Suzanne said in her memoir, "the spontaneity and vulnerability in evidence that night were all too real." And yet, long afterward, she remembered that evening as "the most wonderful night of my life." After the gala preview, she and Balanchine made an appearance at the champagne reception, "and then the two of us slipped away to have doughnuts and coffee."[34]

Did Le Clercq sit through the rest of the party on the huge promenade of the State Theater? Somehow, the Balanchines patched things up, celebrating their fourteenth anniversary in 1966 with a lavish New Year's Eve party. There was "a case of champagne" and an "excellent buffet," Jeanne recalled. Pierre Vladimirov and his wife, Felia Doubrovska, their neighbors in the Apthorp, were part of a large group that enjoyed singing along to live piano music.[35]

A Book Launches, a Marriage Ends

Months after that anniversary, on April 13, 1967, Balanchine premiered a new ballet, *Jewels,* said to have been inspired by his visit to the jeweler Van Cleef and Arpels. Its three sections—"Emeralds," "Rubies," and "Diamonds"— were set to music by Fauré, Stravinsky, and Tchaikovsky, respectively. "Diamonds" was widely viewed in the company as a pre-engagement present to Suzanne, but it is also a love letter to the Mariinsky dancers who had dazzled Balanchine as a boy. Suzanne, in glittering white and partnered by Jacques d'Amboise, won applause for her lyrical grace and off-center balances and turns on pointe in *attitude* and arabesque.

The last-straw moment for the Balanchine marriage occurred on April 17, 1967, the premiere of the first feature-length ballet film made in the United States, according to its producer, Columbia Pictures. Balanchine had adapted *A Midsummer Night's Dream* for the screen, with Suzanne Farrell as Titania, Edward Villella as Oberon, and Arthur Mitchell as Puck. Other principal dancers had smaller solo parts. Balanchine was credited as one of two directors of the film, shot on a sound stage in Manhattan, which featured many close-ups of Suzanne's face. "One day, she appeared wearing a small necklace, a delicate little pearl on a gold chain, given to her by Mr. B. She wore it in the film. It was all the talk," Bettijane Sills noted in her memoir.[1]

An hour before the 9:00 p.m. screening, a champagne reception on the promenade of the theater, sponsored by the mayor of New York, John Lindsay, and his wife, was to be held. Balanchine planned to have Suzanne sit with him and the mayor. Tanny gave him an ultimatum: if she were not invited to sit at his table that evening, she would not be home when he returned. He replied that he was taking Suzanne to the gala and walked out without another word. Le Clercq called his office and left a message that she would be moving to the Mayflower Hotel. Not getting the message, Balanchine reserved a room for himself at the Empire Hotel. Neither of them went home that night.[2]

George Balanchine with Suzanne Farrell at *A Midsummer Night's Dream* film premiere, photo by Martha Swope, 1967. BALANCHINE is a Trademark of The George Balanchine Trust. ©Billy Rose Theatre Division, The New York Public Library for the Performing Arts.

"Balanchine and Suzanne Farrell sat as guests of honor at Mayor Lindsay's table," Natasha Molostwoff remembered. She was at an adjacent table with John Taras and Edith Le Clercq, who had been drinking at the party. Edith said: "I'm going to go over and ask him, 'Where is your wife, Mr. Balanchine? Why isn't she here with you?'" Natasha answered: "If you do that, your daughter will never forgive you. I'm your friend." Edith replied, bitterly, "You're no friend." Taras took her arm, steered her to O'Neal's restaurant across the street, and then brought her home. "I think Tanny and Balanchine's separation was a bigger blow to Edith than to Tanny," Natasha averred. (Even close friends rarely referred to him as George.)[3]

Wilson McNeil Lowry, vice president of the Ford Foundation and the man who spearheaded its support for dance, had vivid memories of the gala: "Suzanne Farrell had bought her first evening gown for the occasion. George Balanchine wore her on his arm like an emblem. When he caught sight of me in the throng, he said with a proud, even over-excited manner: 'Miss Farrell, this is a Ford. Mr. Lowry, this is a Cadillac.'"[4]

That night, Jeanne, at home with her husband and children, got a phone call from Tanny at the Mayflower. "Please come," she said. "I left George." Jeanne and Martha rushed over and the three friends had dinner together. "I can't stand it anymore," Jeanne remembered Tanny saying. "It's Suzanne, Suzanne, Suzanne. . . . I've put up with all I can."[5]

Martha and Jeanne insisted that she *had* to go back to the Apthorp. The whole apartment was equipped for her disability, everything wheelchair accessible. The bathtub had a mechanism to lower her into it. The second bathroom had a wider than normal entrance. Eventually, they were persuasive, and Edward Bigelow brought Tanny home the next day. He probably helped to move Balanchine's possessions out into the hall, among them the wooden bar and, perhaps stuffed into it, the letters written to Tanny, later discovered in Balanchine's office by Barbara Horgan. The building's crew took everything down to the cellar, ready to discard with the trash.[6]

Someone (probably Bigelow) alerted Balanchine, and he rushed over to reclaim his possessions. Later, he arranged for the transport to his new (smaller) apartment of one of their two Steinway grand pianos. He left the other Steinway for Tanny, along with their rent-stabilized apartment and the house in Weston. They signed an agreement not to make further claims upon each other. Once things calmed down, he visited from time to time. "He never forgot to send her something beautiful for Christmas or her birthday," Natasha said. "He provided for her."[7]

The Ballet Cook Book, a thick tome (427 pages), appeared that year, 1967, although the official publication date was 1966. Tanny's short biographies of each contributor are as close as she ever came to writing a memoir. She listed her contributors alphabetically, by then a New York City Ballet tradition. Among all the ingredients that went into her book, there is not a drop of bitterness, just delicious recipes and a sly wit that seamlessly fuses dancing with cooking. Many of the flattering photos of contributors had been taken by Tanny, who specialized in portraits. Her written profiles of dancers are also unfailingly generous. She rose above her personal trauma, even in the midst of it, to praise Suzanne's dedication, devotion, and discipline, and then added another *D,* Dulcinea, for "Suzanne's shimmering performance of that lead role in *Don Quixote.*"[8]

Eager to promote her new book, she made herself available for interviews again. Just as in the book about Mourka, her byline was Tanaquil Le Clercq. (She had told her publisher that she didn't want to trade on Balanchine's name.) Jacques d'Amboise, Allegra Kent, and Melissa Hayden, all contributors, assisted at her 1967 book signing at Bloomingdale's, a chic department store.[9]

Jacques d'Amboise, Melissa Hayden, and Tanaquil Le Clercq at book signing at Bloomingdale's, photo by Martha Swope, 1967 ©Billy Rose Theatre Division, The New York Public Library for the Performing Arts.

Allegra had taken over many of Tanny's signature roles, and it was well known that Mr. B had once been obsessed with her. And yet the former ballerina, dancing with her nimble pen, wrote with unmitigated admiration of Allegra's "incredible body" that "appears to be made of rubber-taffy." She wittily compared Allegra's ability to "roll herself up" to the filled, rolled pastry that she had contributed to the book.[10]

After this successful book launch, Tanny took a celebratory trip to France with Martha. It was June 1967, just a few months after the dramatic separation from Balanchine. Nevertheless, in May he had sent a letter to his bank in Switzerland, authorizing his wife to withdraw funds for her trip. Balanchine was still, on most occasions, a consummate gentleman.[11]

In Paris, Tanny and Martha met up with Angelo Torricini (a decorator friend who had worked on the Apthorp apartment), his sister Claude, an artist, and her husband. Martha shot a home movie of Tanny with her friends at an outdoor café close to the Tuileries Gardens, a sequence that appears in the film *Afternoon of a Faun*. Chic and butterfly bright in blues and reds, Le Clercq exudes a glamorous insouciance as she plays with her big sunglasses framed in zebra stripes. Snagging a blue handkerchief from a man's breast pocket, she does a little wavy dance with it. A waiter offers her a larger partner, a red checked napkin, which she briefly considers, then laughingly declines. Her eyes and hands keep dancing.[12]

As her friend Pat McBride wrote: "Her wit and strength never left her, nor did she indulge in self-pity. It was always a treat to be in her vivacious company." Le Clercq could make you forget the wheelchair. But you could not forget to be present. "She refused to tolerate the sort of half-conscious, automatic responses with which so many people cruise through social situations; you learned to pay attention, or you were banished," Holly Brubach observed. "This may seem harsh. In fact, it was extremely benevolent, because it woke you up to the exquisite texture of everyday life."[13]

Whatever his faults, Jerry Robbins was always wide awake, even in his dreams, and certainly not given to cruising through life on automatic pilot. As George Balanchine receded from Le Clercq's life, Robbins was resuming a more prominent place, at least in her thoughts. She let him know (via a postcard) that she and Martha had stayed for a few days in a four-hundred-year-old house Karinska owned in Domrémy, the birthplace of Jeanne d'Arc (Joan of Arc), "2 doors away from the church and Jeanne's birthplace." She would be wrapping up this "Dreamy trip" in London, most likely with a visit to Pat McBride, now married to a distinguished solicitor/artist/art pa-

Allegra Kent and Edward Villella, *Bugaku,* photo by Bert Stern, 1963. Choreography by George Balanchine ©The George Balanchine Trust. Conde Nast Collection/Getty Images.

Martha Swope and Tanaquil Le Clercq in garden, Domrémy, 1967. Photo by Martha Swope, 1967 ©Billy Rose Theatre Division, The New York Public Library for the Performing Arts.

tron, Anthony Lousada, who would be knighted in 1975, making her Lady Lousada.[14]

That fall, Tanny held an elaborate dinner party at her apartment to celebrate Jerry's forty-ninth birthday on October 11, 1967. It drew notice in the press. The formal-looking invitations featured a list of dishes and wines (loosely translated into French) she had named for some of his ballet and theater hits, over a dozen of them. Here's a sample:

> *Saumon Gipsy* (*Gypsy Salmon.* Jerry had choreographed the musical *Gypsy,* a word Tanny applied to him, as is evident in an interview she gave later, as well as from their letters.)
>
> *Pommes de Terre, papa, pauvre papa, maman t'as mis dans un placard et je me sens si triste* (Potatoes *Oh Dad, Poor Dad, Mamma's Hung You in the Closet and I'm Feelin' So Sad,* the title of the first play by Arthur Kopit (winner of a Drama Desk Award, 1962) that he had directed. She left out the hanging part.)

The wine list included:

Chateau Age d'Angoisse (Chateau Age of Anxiety)
Chateau Baron Peter Pan (Chateau Baron Peter Pan. Robbins directed
  the musical.)
Chateau Apres Midi d'un Faun (Chateau Afternoon of a Faun.)[15]

Robbins invited her to stay at a house he had rented for years in the hamlet of Snedens Landing (now called Palisades) on the western bank of the Hudson River, across from Dobbs Ferry, just north of the New York/New Jersey divide. She was not fond of the house, which had been built piecemeal. Staircases joined its sections, a challenge for anyone in a wheelchair, although with Bobby Fizdale and Arthur Gold in a nearby house, there were always helping hands.

Le Clercq had visited many times, but this time she felt different, her neediness too obvious to disguise. The subtle sexuality that Jerry had found so alluring when choreographing *Faun* (and three years later, perhaps, on the beach at Fire Island) had been compromised by polio. Tanny once told Jeanne that she had tried to make love with her husband "three times" after her illness, but it had proved "impossible." She had never said exactly why, and Jeanne didn't press her, "but imagine," Jeanne mused, "if you can't move."[16]

Tanny responded to Jerry's invitation with the acute honesty that he had always treasured. "If what you say is true about not relying on someone for your happiness," she wrote, "it seems to me I'm doing just that— with you. Like out of the frying pan and into the fire. And if you say you're a friend helping a friend that's OK on your side, but I don't feel quite the same about you as I do say about Bobby or Arthur who are friends— So thank you for the country invitation but I can't come."[17]

Soon after writing that heartbreaking letter, she changed her mind and went to Snedens anyway. Afterward, she sent her host a note with a blank check dated November 3, 1967: "Dearest Jerry— Thanks ever so much for the lovely time at Sneden's also for shopping for me— Enclosed is check to cover it—love T." That may have been a dig at his notorious cheapness in small matters. (He saved her uncashed check and note.)[18]

Not long afterward, Tanny met someone with whom she seems to have enjoyed an extended relationship. She would occasionally refer to this man, who had a Middle Eastern name, perhaps "Omar," according to her friend Abraham "Abe" Abdallah, one of the few people in whom she had confided. Abe, who had met her later, vaguely recalled Tanny saying that this man had built the stone fireplace in her Weston home but was no longer part of her life. It's an image out of a romantic novel: a man with capable hands lifting stones to assure her a warm hearth.[19]

Jeanne also heard about this man from Tanny. She thought that he was from North Africa and called "Ali." She was certain that he was a good friend of Angelo Torricini's and younger than Le Clercq. "Well, it's somebody to get into bed with," Tanny had said in her matter-of-fact way. Jeanne was not surprised that she'd had a lover, "for the touching and the intimacy that she obviously craved." After the affair ended, Tanny never expressed to Jeanne a longing to try again with anyone else. "The bar was pretty high," Jeanne felt, after marriage to Balanchine.[20]

In early 1969 Balanchine flew to Mexico to obtain a quick divorce. Knowing that Suzanne was an observant Catholic, he had not only promised to marry her but had even suggested that they have a child together (an offer that he had never made to anyone else). Suzanne, interested in being the best dancer she could possibly be, not a mother, was clearly frightened by the prospect of marriage to Balanchine. As she said in her memoir, "Our interaction was physical, but its expression was dance." Marriage may have "given George what he thought he wanted. But I could not see what it would have given our work that we didn't already have. . . . I could love him best onstage where I was at my best."[21]

"He called me when we got divorced, crying," Tanny told Holly, nearly thirty years later. "By then I didn't care as much, thank God. 'I'm sorry, I'm sorry,' he said. It was maybe the second time I've known him to cry." Jacques d'Amboise thought Tanny was "heroic" to accept what looked to others like a shocking abandonment. His wife, Carolyn, spoke for many members of the dance world when she asked her husband, "Who would have ever believed that we could lose respect for Balanchine?"[22]

Le Clercq defended her ex-husband and, according to her friend Randall "Randy" Bourscheidt, never responded to any comments on Balanchine's private or public life. But in the midst of the ordeal, she may not have been as accommodating. Abe, who had met her soon after the divorce, learned from those who had weathered the prior period with her that she had "fought very hard to stay married."[23]

Although their marriage had been drastically altered by Balanchine's need for constant change and by her illness, she must have found it hard, at nearly forty, to imagine a life without him. He had formed her from the age of eleven, not only as a dancer. This deep attachment influenced many of her

Tanaquil Le Clercq in wheelchair, Weston ca. 1970. Courtesy of NYCB Archive.

choices for the rest of her life. It had marked him, too. He assumed the grave weight of responsibility for her, a load he would never completely shed.

Right after his trip to Mexico, Balanchine left for Hamburg, Germany, to stage Glinka's opera, *Ruslan and Ludmilla*. While he was away, Suzanne, twenty-three by then, married Paul Mejia, a company soloist two years her junior and the son of Romana Kryzanowska. Their relationship had been an open secret, possibly the catalyst for Balanchine's seeking a quick divorce, but Suzanne's marriage, in a hastily arranged ceremony on February 21, 1969, came as a shock to him all the same.

He threatened not to return to New York. Edward Bigelow, Lincoln Kirstein, and Barbara Horgan flew to Germany, in turn, to bring him to his senses. Horgan had enraged him further by attending the wedding, but she managed to persuade him to come back. Suzanne did not learn about his divorce until she returned from her honeymoon, although his intentions must have been clear to her. When Balanchine came back in April, he was cool and vindictive, asking her to coach a young soloist in a role that had been hers. But the major turning point came on May 8, the annual Spring Gala Benefit. A principal role Paul had danced in *Symphony in C* just that Saturday had been given to another dancer. Suzanne sent a note to the administration: if Paul did not dance that night, they would both resign.[24]

Balanchine substituted another ballet, *Stars and Stripes,* and fired both Mejias. He even had them barred from the State Theater practice rooms. They guested for various companies (although many others were afraid to make offers, for fear of enraging Balanchine) and tried to eke out a living. Late in 1970, they joined Maurice Béjart's Ballet du XXe Siècle in Brussels. Although not a stylistic fit, Béjart's company gave the couple a professional home.[25]

Years later, Balanchine apologized for his behavior to several people, including Suzanne. But on November 20, 1972, in a public interview with John Gruen, he displayed undisguised enmity toward Paul Mejia, painting him as a manipulator who had seduced Suzanne to feed his own ambitions. "[H]e threatened me," Balanchine claimed. "He said he would leave with her if I didn't give him roles. . . . Why should I have given him leading roles? I have Edward Villella, I have Jacques d'Amboise."[26]

It was Farrell, not Mejia, who had chosen to deliver what she later said was never intended as an ultimatum. Nearly everyone listening to the interview knew that. Balanchine and Gruen were conversing on a stage at the New School, with Tanaquil Le Clercq, Jerome Robbins, Alexandra Danilova, Felia Doubrovska, Muriel Stuart, and many more members of the ballet community in the audience. Balanchine could not have missed Le Clercq's presence; she had gotten a huge ovation when she was wheeled in. It must have pained her to see him publicly defend his vituperative pettiness.

"For a female dancer marriage means the end of her individuality. Men don't lose this individuality," Balanchine had insisted. "I say dancers should have romances, love affairs, but not marriages." Gruen asked him, pointedly, why he had only married ballerinas, since he didn't approve of them marrying. "I may have made lots of mistakes," Balanchine admitted. "When you are young, you don't think. Now I feel I should not have married any of them. The point is, I am a cloud in pants," he added, stealing a line from Mayakovsky that he had repeated so often, it had almost become his own. "I am a workingman—a gardener. . . . I am a servant—when I was married, I served." What did Tanny make of this thoughtlessly cruel answer? Nearly everyone in that audience knew that Balanchine had been besotted with Suzanne, not in his youth, but just a few years before.[27]

His pain may have been all the greater because he had encouraged the highly musical Mejia (a student at the School of American Ballet since age eleven) to choreograph. The two of them had played four-hand piano, even though Balanchine was handicapped after losing the tip of a finger in a lawn mower accident in 1964. He was the one, perhaps, who had first brought the couple together, since he habitually invited a third person (for the sake of appearances) whenever he courted a young woman. Mejia was not the first or last dancer that Balanchine treated badly out of jealousy or spite, although it's doubtful that anyone else ever elicited such virulence. "She [Suzanne] calls me and says, 'We want to come back,'" Balanchine confided to his audience, "And I say, 'You are still we? How about you?'" He blamed Farrell's departure on her fascination with Mejia, as if the young man were an evil hypnotist.[28]

Neither Suzanne nor Paul blamed Balanchine. Mejia was particularly magnanimous since, as he said years later, "For me, ballet dancing was finished." He became a choreographer and was the artistic director of the Fort Worth Dallas Ballet from 1987 to 98, where he applied all that he had learned from Balanchine's classes. "I understand his feelings completely," Mejia declared, "and I am not bitter at all at what he did. . . . He must have suffered greatly, doubly, because it was me, whom he adored. I know that he loved me, even in the later years when we talked a little bit again, even though he did not want me around." Given how intensely Balanchine worked, how thin the line between his personal and professional lives, continuing to rehearse with Suzanne at that time would have been impossible for him. It's hard to imagine how he could have kept working at all.[29]

But today his abuse of power has come in for unsparing scrutiny. Others may have behaved worse, some of his critics have written, but that doesn't excuse Balanchine's behavior. He hurt more people than Farrell and Mejia. Her departure was a huge loss for his company. As the dance scholar Laura Jacobs wrote: "When she was onstage, the elements were earth, water, air, and

Farrell. Here was classical dancing of unprecedented transparency. And it was Made in America."[30]

His vision cleared, in time, but for years following his divorce Balanchine was lonely and depressed. He remained attached to Tanny and the home that they had made together, feeling responsible for both. In June 1969, Kirstein wrote to Robbins: "Balanchine spent the week in Weston, mowing Tanny's lawn, painting her house, and resting from the inevitable let down after the euphoria launched by Suzanne's exit. . . . Everyone hopes that Balanchine will now go back to Tanny but the truth is she knows it would only be until Gelsey [Kirkland] or X. Y. or Z are mature enough to move him. Oh dear."[31]

That summer, Mourka vanished. Frantic, Tanny reached Balanchine by phone. He was in Saratoga for the summer season, but he dropped everything and drove to Weston, nearly two hundred miles away. He did not return to Saratoga until, days later, he had found the cat.[32]

Farrell stayed away for five years, until Balanchine agreed to take her back. (He never extended an invitation to Mejia.) Seeing her dance in Europe, Jacques had reported to Mr. B that she was better than ever. Then he helped her draft a letter: "As wonderful as it is to see your ballets," she wrote Balanchine, "it is even more wonderful to dance them." Balanchine asked Le Clercq whether he should allow Suzanne to rejoin the company. She told him that he should. "I think she was terrific," she told Holly, "and when she left there was a gap. There were nice dancers but not of her caliber, and I think he needed her." When Farrell returned in 1975, she filled a big hole left by the defection of a principal dancer, Gelsey Kirkland, to American Ballet Theatre. Delia Peters, a member of the corps known for her wit, quipped, "Suzanne's coming back is the best thing that's happened to us since she left."[33]

Jeanne, who was not a fan of Suzanne's footwork, once criticized her performance after accompanying Tanny to the theater. (Although Farrell's combination of grace, daring, and musicality was incomparable, she was not an allegro dancer, like Tallchief.) "No, no, she's really good," Tanny said. "I see what George sees in her." That remark made Jeanne admire Tanny all the more. "She could detach herself from her own personal hurt," Jeanne said. "She had a generosity of spirit that is unusual." Le Clercq knew that she had made an indelible impression on the world, thanks to George Balanchine, and "she never forgot what she owed to him."[34]

Her lifelong loyalty to Balanchine extended to his political party, Republican, even after it veered to the right of the GOP of his patron, Nelson Rockefeller. Tanny was an odd sort of Republican, one with a socialist bent who believed that money should flow to those who needed it most. After she came into money in the 1980s (some from her mother but far more thanks to Balanchine), no matter how her friends might protest, she would insist that "the person with the most money should pay the bill." In this way, too, she was not that different from Balanchine. As Nathan Milstein wrote: "He was a very conservatively oriented man but with a broad view, not dogmatic at all. He believed that the state should help the poor and should sponsor culture."[35]

The Ballet Cook Book is cleverly and subtly political. In the midst of a discourse on falling soufflés, Le Clercq takes on the Daughters of the American Revolution, a group notorious for refusing to allow the celebrated African American contralto Marian Anderson to appear at its theater in 1939: "The first time I fell, hard, all the way down, the company was appearing at Constitution Hall in Washington D.C. Though the stage was extremely slick, we had been expressly forbidden to use any rosin on it for fear of ruining the D.A.R.'s floor. It was in the finale of the last ballet that I fell with a resounding thud, right in the middle of the stage, and spun around once on my tutu-pants, then reeling, struggled back to my feet. 'Just imagine,' I was later comforted, 'the last time Margot Fonteyn danced here she fell down in the exact same spot.' Toward the Daughters of the American Revolution I have never felt kindly since."[36]

Tanny's attitude toward those who considered themselves more American than other, more recent citizens, is succinctly summed up in the first line of her profile of Robert Joffrey, the founder of the Joffrey Ballet: "His father is an Afghan, his mother an Italian, which makes Robert Joffrey (real name Abdullah Jaffa Anver Bey Khan) a one hundred per cent American, born in Seattle."[37]

She was far from a conservative, and yet defecting to the Democratic Party in the 1960s, while it still counted segregationists like George Wallace in its ranks, may not have seemed a viable alternative to her. Since Martha Swope was a lifelong Democrat whose vote canceled out hers, the two friends made a pact to always spend election days together, rather than voting. By this conscious act of omission, Tanny could still remain true to Balanchine, the "leader of her thinking and her heart," according to Martha, "her whole life."[38]

19

────────── ⚬◯⚬ ──────────

The Dance Theatre of Harlem Years

Occasionally, Le Clercq would privately coach a dancer in a role that she had performed. Pat McBride Lousada was sure that she would have loved to teach at the School of American Ballet, had Balanchine been able to endure having his former wife wheeling around his theater, a daily reminder of loss. "The person who saved her was Arthur Mitchell," Pat said. Although at thirty-five he was still in demand as a performer, the assassination of Dr. Martin Luther King Jr. had spurred Mitchell to create a ballet company for the community he had come from. In 1969 he founded Dance Theatre of Harlem (DTH) with his friend and mentor Karel Shook, a renowned ballet master and choreographer. Shook, who had spent most of the 1960s with the Dutch National Ballet, answered Mitchell's summons and returned to New York City. Balanchine and Kirstein served on their original board of directors.[1]

As early as 1966, Mitchell had been giving ballet classes at the Harlem School of the Arts. The following year, Le Clercq became part of his mission to recruit and train students, not necessarily all African American, who would establish classical ballet as part of the vibrant culture of Harlem. "Tanny, you have all this in your head," he told her one night at a restaurant on the Upper West Side. It was time, he felt, to share it. She hesitated, at first. He understood why it was a tough decision for her, physically and emotionally. It was still hard for her to be around other dancers, even outside a studio. But after thinking about it for a few days, she had agreed. The offer, coming as her marriage unraveled, was a lifebuoy. Le Clercq had been at the center of the ballet world when Mitchell entered it; thanks to him, she still had a place there.[2]

From her students' memories, still warm more than forty years later, one can catch glimpses of her at work during the decade she taught, 1967–77. She started in early fall, on Tuesday and Thursday afternoons in the basement

Karel Shook (*left*) with Arthur Mitchell in new studio under renovation, photo by Marbeth, 1971. Courtesy of Dance Theatre of Harlem.

of the St. James Presbyterian Church on West 141st Street, next door to the Harlem School of the Arts (founded in the early 1960s by soprano Dorothy Maynor, whose husband was the pastor of the church). Ballet classes cost fifty cents per week, just a token, but Arthur Mitchell felt that if students paid nothing, they would not take their lessons seriously. Adding his own funds to donations from wealthy patrons, within a few years he had created a company and was able to buy and start renovation work on its permanent home, a two-story former garage with a basement.

Le Clercq's first class included a fourteen-year-old, Yvonne Delaney Mitchell (no relation to Arthur), who recalled that day as though five decades had not passed: "One day, this beautiful lady in a wheelchair was rolled in." The chair had to be carried downstairs to the basement studio, as did Tanny, who was seated before the students arrived. Elegant in a skirt and blouse, her shoulder-length blond hair pulled back, she sat up straight. Mr. Mitchell (as the students called him) introduced her to everyone, and then she demonstrated the steps, literally by hand, while counting out the beats. Le Clercq was "very soft spoken and focused on every single student," Yvonne said, not just the most promising. Her teaching style was gentle, like that of her idol Felia Doubrovska. Students had to pay close attention not to miss anything. Yvonne did not realize then that one of Le Clercq's arms was much weaker than the other until, decades later, she saw the documentary *Afternoon of a Faun.* "Her one good hand was so swift, graceful and precise."[3]

She could move both hands and arms, but her right arm had suffered more from polio, so that arm had to be supported by the left hand and arm. The damaged muscles in the area from her elbow to her shoulder would tighten up, unpredictably, making the right arm stiff at times. If she picked up a full glass or cup with her right hand, she would immediately transfer it to her left. Many students didn't notice, because both hands were agile.[4]

Guided by decades of experience, her fingers danced to music that she often had to make with her own voice, because the school could not afford the luxury of an accompanist every day. She would hum a tune, emphasizing the beats that she gave extra punctuation with her snapping fingers, as Balanchine did, and reinforced her hand signals with verbal instructions. Her pointe classes were "some of the most wonderful" in the memory of Virginia Johnson (a DTH principal dancer), because Le Clercq "had to explain in detail what she wanted."[5]

Classes began at the *barre,* where the students exercised more than thirty minutes (but less than forty-five) before moving to the center of the room

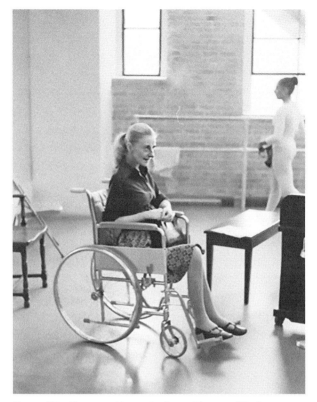

Tanaquil Le Clercq teaching at the Dance Theatre of Harlem, 1970s. Courtesy of Dance Theatre of Harlem.

for another fifteen minutes of exercises, turns, and positions, finishing the ninety-minute class with combinations of steps across the floor. Even beginning students had no trouble learning her balletic sign language. Putting her hands together in a wide *V,* she indicated that the students were to assume the first position. She told them how many *demi-pliés* she wanted them to do by moving her arms like softly flapping wings several times. For *grand plié,* her hands came together in her lap, and then one arm stretched out to assume second position as the students came back up.

Her fingers spoke eloquently, too. She would flutter them for *petits* and *grands battements.* Her thumb represented a foot, and the fleshy part of the hand at the base of her thumb stood for the heel of the foot. By rotating her hand, she could demonstrate the exact degree of turnout required. If she wanted a foot to wrap around an ankle, for example, she would wrap one hand with the other in exactly that way. "She commanded the room," Yvonne said. "Her physical body was in the chair, but her spirit was still moving."[6]

Asked about her teaching by a reporter for the *New York Times*, Le Clercq explained that she would use "an advanced student to demonstrate the movements." On the day the article was published, February 28, 1969, a lifelong Harlem resident, Desmond W. Margetson, was moved to write her a letter to express his gratitude that she was teaching in his community. Margetson, a gifted artist and engineer, had sketched her at the ballet school in the late 1940s and still recalled "the memorable pleasure of having a conversation with you. . . . You knocked me out! It was obvious then that you had 'soul.'" By teaching in Harlem, Le Clercq had joined a growing Black Arts movement (born from the Harlem Renaissance) that fused the arts with social activism. By teaching from a wheelchair, she had become a pioneer of disability rights, too, along with Arthur Mitchell.[7]

Thanks to a Ford Foundation grant, by July 1970 the school was able to offer a full summer program. Le Clercq taught classes three days a week in the basement of its new location, the Church of the Master on 122nd Street and Morningside Avenue. (Mitchell and Maynor had quarreled about the use of the grant money and parted company, so for a short time he had borrowed a West Nineteenth Street studio from Glen Tetley until he found the church.) Inside the brick-walled space of his school's new sanctuary, an Americanized European art form thrived.[8]

Outside, Harlem and communities beyond it were going through tumultuous times. Integrationists were confronted by segregationists and separatists. Even before the assassination of Dr. King in 1968, advocates of Black Power had dethroned venerated icons of the civil rights movement, such as James Farmer, the founder of the Congress of Racial Equality (CORE), who resigned under pressure from Black nationalist forces within his organization. Dr. King himself had been vilified by militants with the epithet "Uncle Tom" shortly before his death, along with other integrationist leaders, now celebrated—Bayard Rustin, A. Philip Randolph, and Thurgood Marshall. Balanchine honored Dr. King's memory with a new work, *Requiem Canticles,* with music by Stravinsky, performed by Arthur Mitchell and Suzanne Farrell, along with an ensemble cast bearing lighted candelabras. At the end of the moving work, given a single performance in 1968, "the audience departed in silence." But by 1970, anger prevailed. Right after Balanchine's elegant new theater at Lincoln Center had been emptied by three bomb scares, militant

Black Panthers spray-painted "FUCK THE RICH FUCK THE PIGS FUCK THE RICH FUCK THE PIGS" on its marble exterior.[9]

In this heated atmosphere, not only radicals in Harlem questioned why Arthur Mitchell wanted to train Black dancers to do ballet, a European art form. "Everyone said I was absolutely insane," he recalled. But he managed to duck the crossfire. His dedicated teachers and students focused on their mission, to train superb dancers of all colors and thereby change the image of classical ballet. Mitchell and Le Clercq, the pioneering pair who had challenged prejudice and preconceptions with a *pas de deux* at City Center in 1955, conveyed their commitment by actions, not rhetoric. They knew that ballet technique would provide a strong foundation for their students, no matter where their dancing careers took them. Tanny had about fifteen students per class, including young men, and she attended to the needs of each one, nodding encouragement to all. They came from many countries—the Caribbean, Brazil, Europe, and beyond.[10]

Martial Roumain, born in Haiti, had studied African-style modern dance, but Le Clercq was his first ballet teacher. He had started with her in 1967, when he was awarded a scholarship at age fifteen, late for a ballet dancer. Tanny's kind and gracious way of teaching endeared her to him: "She gave you the loving attention that you needed to grow." Martial had flat feet and needed extra help getting them to arch properly when he stood on half-pointe in *relevé*. Tanny worked with him on stretching his metatarsals, the five long bones in the midsection of the foot. She had him kneel with a pillow under his feet, and then sit back on his heels, applying a gentle pressure. He found her a "fantastic" teacher.[11]

The discipline instilled by Le Clercq, Mitchell, and other teachers at the school affected every aspect of their students' lives. Martial Roumain became a choreographer and educator, in addition to his distinguished career as a dancer with companies founded by Eleo Pomare and Alvin Ailey. He danced in hit Broadway shows, including *West Side Story* and *Bubbling Brown Sugar,* and did some acting, too. More than fifty years after studying with Le Clercq, he was still coaching dance students around the world. Other students who didn't remain professional dancers went on to have exemplary careers. Marcia Sells, who danced in the company from 1976 to 1979, became an attorney and the dean of students at Harvard Law School. She remembered the astonishing agility of Le Clercq, who could "zip across the room and correct your turnout. She could be anywhere in a flash."[12]

The dancer Theara Ward, who began her studies with Le Clercq at age thirteen, recalled how her teacher "came in that studio like a whirlwind and you knew you had to be on your A plus game." Ward danced her first principal role with DTH at age seventeen, in the *pas de deux* of *Agon*. She won critical acclaim for roles in other Balanchine ballets (including *The Four Temperaments* and *Serenade*) and had an eclectic career in musical theater, teaching, and arts administration. Tanaquil Le Clercq, she said, had taught her about "speed, clarity, stamina and articulating your feet," lessons that provided a strong foundation for Theara's achievements. "Dance Theatre of Harlem was a family," she declared, "and Tanny was a member of our family." Many decades later, whether they were still dancing or not, Le Clercq's students lit up at the mention of her name. They had nothing but praise for their former teacher, who had communicated far more to them than steps. "She loved us," Ward said.[13]

Balanchine provided exercises to help her students, came to the school to coach, and gave DTH the rights to perform his work without paying royalties. Le Clercq consulted with him "every Tuesday," and they had remained "good friends," according to Vera Stravinsky, the composer's widow. In August 1970, DTH premiered its first Balanchine ballet, *Concerto Barocco,* at Jacob's Pillow. Anna Kisselgoff wrote in the *New York Times,* "No young company has made such progress in so short a time." On May 6, 1971, Balanchine featured twenty-one dancers from his company and twenty-three from DTH in *Concerto for Jazz Band and Orchestra* (co-choreographed with Arthur Mitchell) at a spring gala in Lincoln Center. The ballet, performed only once and in practice clothes, had lighting designed by Ronald Bates. The eponymous score by Rolf Lieberman had seven movements, including a "blues," a "boogie woogie," and a "mambo" for the entire cast.[14]

"Balanchine had a lot of jazz in his soul," said Lydia Abarca, a principal dancer with DTH who loved dancing in Balanchine's "jazzy ballets," like *Agon* and *Bugaku.* Growing up in Harlem, she had studied at Harlem School of the Arts before obtaining a full scholarship to Juilliard. After continuing her studies at the Harkness School, Lydia became a star of ballet and Broadway, touring with DTH domestically and in Europe until 1977, when she left to perform in films.[15]

Tanny was instrumental in helping to establish Arthur's company. He considered several of his leading ballerinas to be "products" of her hard work: Lydia Abarca, Virginia Johnson (who became artistic director of DTH), and Theara Ward. Sarita Allen, who took ballet classes at the DTH school, became a leading dancer with the Alvin Ailey company. Most students found Arthur incredibly demanding, but to Virginia Johnson, who had been told by ballet

George Balanchine and Arthur Mitchell, rehearsal for *Concerto for Jazz Band and Orchestra*, photo by Martha Swope, 1971. BALANCHINE is a Trademark of The George Balanchine Trust. ©Billy Rose Theatre Division, The New York Public Library for the Performing Arts.

teachers that a Black girl could not realistically hope to be a ballerina, his high expectations felt like benedictions. He wanted to change the image of Black people in society, not just on stage. It wasn't enough for the students to carry themselves well in the studio and during performances; he expected that level of self-awareness from them everywhere they went.[16]

Mitchell insisted on elegance in the way each one presented him or herself to the world, much like Balanchine did, through their appearance, words, and actions. That did not mean that he preferred ironed hair to an afro, upper-class diction to colloquial speech, or a Europeanized beauty or mode of dress to an African one. One could sport an afro and a dashiki, speak in any dialect one had mastered, so long as one did so beautifully. Choreographers of color made masterpieces for his company, such as Geoffrey Holder's 1974 work *Dougla,* a Caribbean wedding dance, born in Trinidad, that melds African and East Indian dance steps and gestures to make a classic, original work of shimmering power. "We were pioneers and we were militant about it," Virginia Johnson said. Theirs was an inclusive militancy. "Arthur Mitchell created this space for a lot of people who had been told, 'You can't do this.'" He showed them that "they didn't have to be defined by somebody else's perception of them."[17]

Black Power, to these dancers, meant that there was nothing they couldn't attempt. It was a time of boundary-breaking in all the performing arts: In Argentina, Astor Piazzolla, a son of Italian immigrants, was making a glorious fusion of Argentine tango and American jazz. André Watts, a classical pianist born in Germany to an African American army officer and a Hungarian pianist, had been electrifying the world since his teens. Leontyne Price was singing traditionally "White" roles at the Metropolitan Opera. And in Harlem, Virginia Johnson was soon to perform the *Shout!* solo set to a soul-stirring rhythm-and-blues song by the Isley Brothers, "Get into Something," in Louis Johnson's groundbreaking work *Forces of Rhythm*. With a score that mixed classical and contemporary music, Johnson's work revealed his mastery of multiple dance styles—ballet, modern, jazz, and ethnic dance. As Virginia Johnson said, "He could bring together all those different languages in one work to say, 'Yes, it belongs to us.'"[18]

Johnson never forgot how moved she had been to discover Tanaquil Le Clercq in the dance studio, this "beautiful dancer, full of ideas," seated in a wheelchair. Tanny pushed her students beyond their comfort zones, to go a little faster, a little farther, "because she wanted to get you forward onto your legs. She wanted to get you into the movement. But she had a way of describing it that you *had* to try it. It was a test. It was a fun thing."[19]

Her lessons didn't stop in the studio. Every student in the school was assigned a ballet mom and dad to look out for them. Tanny wasn't one of those, given her disability, but she took a keen interest in all the students in the school, not just her own. Many students were on full or partial scholarships, so Arthur Mitchell had arranged for some of them to be her drivers as a way of earning their lessons. Since she knew that most had financial hardships, Le Clercq would lend her apartment to students when she went out of town or even hand over the keys for an entire summer when she was in Connecticut.[20]

Michael Stewart, a scholarship student, started driving Tanny in her Volvo wagon in 1974, at age twenty, after he finished college. By then, the school occupied spacious quarters in a refurbished garage at 466 West 152nd Street, between St. Nicholas and Amsterdam Avenues, a long block now officially named, by the City of New York, Dance Theatre of Harlem Way. The new building, like all the others, lacked an elevator. Michael would carry Tanny inside and seat

Virginia Johnson in costume for "Shout!" solo from *Forces of Rhythm* by Louis Johnson, photo by Martha Swope, 1973 ©Billy Rose Theatre Division, The New York Public Library for the Performing Arts.

her on a chair, bring the wheelchair upstairs, then go back down and carry her up the stairs in his arms. "We called it 'our pas de deux,'" he said.[21]

Although she taught afternoons, Michael would pick her up in the morning because he had a dance class at eleven. She was happy to make a full day of it, socializing with people in the school's office until it was time for her class at 1:00 p.m. Tanny was almost always in her wheelchair, ready to go, by the time Michael arrived at the Apthorp, where they sometimes breakfasted. On the way uptown and back, they would smoke in her car. He took her ninety-minute class twice a week and found her a "very giving" and "easy to follow" teacher, much more pleasant than Arthur Mitchell, who had a more "regimented" approach.[22]

Once Michael arrived to find her in a disheveled state, clearly not well. She telephoned Peter Martins, a former star of the Royal Danish Ballet who had joined Balanchine's company as a principal in 1969. Martins agreed to teach her class that day, and henceforth he was the person she would call first whenever she felt too ill to teach, which happened rarely.[23]

Her students benefited from Le Clercq's connections, not only those with celebrated dancers. Marcia Sells recalled that she went out of her way to make sure that Marcia ordered her first pair of custom-made pointe shoes from the shoemaker at Capezio whom she considered the best. She then invited Marcia and her mother to the Apthorp apartment so that she could teach Marcia how to break them in properly.[24]

Traditionally, ballet shoes and tights were designed to blend into Caucasian skin, in order to give the desired long, unbroken line from the top of the thigh to the tip of the toe. In the early years of the school, all students wore traditional "ballet" pink shoes, light pink "nude" tights, and black leotards. That's all they could find. Arthur Mitchell addressed this injustice. By 1972, Dance Theatre of Harlem had pioneered new colors for ballet shoes and tights—olives, tans, and browns—to match the varied skin tones of its students. Availability was a problem, so students painted or dyed their own tights and shoes. Some applied pancake makeup with a brush to their shoes to achieve the desired effect, a laborious process that consumed from two to six hours. (It wasn't until 2016 that a few companies introduced shoes and tights for darker skin tones.)[25]

By the 1970s, the dearth of dancers of color in ballet companies was getting more press. Clive Barnes, perhaps the most influential theater and dance critic in New York then, questioned in the *New York Times* why there were so few Black dancers in major companies. A furious Balanchine told John

Gruen, "I would like to see a lot of Black people writing his (Barnes') articles." He added that it would be against the State Theater's rules to let Mitchell's dancers perform as guest artists with his company because they were "not unionized."[26]

Kirstein sent an angry, defensive letter to Deborah Jowitt (dance critic of the *Village Voice*) in the hope that her editor would print it. He and Balanchine had helped Arthur Mitchell to establish his company, Kirstein declared, and they weren't about to lure the best dancers away from DTH, undermining Mitchell's efforts. Nor would they choose less accomplished dancers in order to make "an undignified token proclamation." He looked forward to a time "when an all-black company is as much an anomaly as an all-white one." Jowitt found this letter too "hot to the touch" to publish. The *Village Voice* was not about to take on the *Times*.[27]

Balanchine answered his critics: "You must understand that Negro blood or Russian blood or Japanese blood doesn't mean a thing to me. I don't take people because they are Black or White. I take exquisite people." He said that he wouldn't hesitate to take any "beautiful, fantastic virtuoso" of any color. And yet, in the same short interview, he later averred: "I don't want to see two Japanese girls, small, in my Swan Lake. . . . It's not done for them." For the same reason, he added, he wouldn't use blond girls as geishas. "Impossible."[28]

Years before he made these remarks, Allegra Kent, a small ballerina, had appeared (in Karinska's filmy suggestion of a kimono and Edo coiffure) in his Japanese-themed ballet *Bugaku* ("dance-music"), which had been inspired by Gagaku musicians and dancers. Balanchine had set the work, which had a "highly erotic" *pas de deux,* to music by Toshiro Mayuzumi. It was performed on Western instruments, including the dancers. There was not a single Asian cast member and only one African American, Arthur Mitchell, who appeared in the second cast, partnering Mimi Paul. Mitchell remained the sole Black dancer in Balanchine's company until 1971.[29]

What was Le Clercq's attitude during this controversy? It's hard to tell. She tended to stay out of the fray, but whenever Balanchine was attacked, she would invariably take his side. Shortly before the end of her marriage, for example, Robbins wrote to ask for an explanation of her coolness in recent years. She replied in a letter written, she admitted, when "drunk, drunk, drunk, on 1¾ of a bottle of wine," that she wanted him to know, first of all, that in Copenhagen, "I'd wait for the Air Mail, Special Delivery letters from you that came in the afternoon." She did not understand why he needed explanations for her behavior now, but she was willing to supply them: After a dinner party at Robbins's place in the early 1960s, her husband had complained of feeling frustrated by word games that were "too fast, and American" for him. So she had "resolved not to let it happen again." Around that same time, she had told Jerry of troubles Balanchine was having (presumably in rehearsals) with the dancer John Jones. Jerry's answer, "Serves him [Balanchine] right," made her feel "sick all over— seemed so nasty." The letter closed with two kisses (*XX*) after a startling revelation that may have been closer to the truth: Hearing of Jerry's recent troubles with his lover, "Pete," she'd been "happy, in 7th heaven— I really guess I don't understand anything, or any of you— it's just too much for me. . . . I do miss, miss, miss you." It's a confession of deep-seated disappointment. Old hopes, quickened to life, had gone cold.[30]

John Jones, a superb dancer of uncommon versatility, had been an occasional guest artist with Balanchine's company. He had done the Nijinsky version of *Faun* (as restaged by Antony Tudor), performed with Katherine Dunham, and later joined the Joffrey Ballet and DTH. At the end of 1960, Balanchine offered him a major role in a new ballet, *Modern Jazz: Variants,* with music by the Modern Jazz Quartet, pairing Jones with Hayden and Mitchell with Adams, perhaps for the visual symmetry (Jones was Black). Balanchine's initial idea had been to hire "a corps de ballet of six black women" for the new ballet, but Arthur Mitchell told him that "not enough black women excelled in ballet at the professional level." This was an odd response, given the high level of the African American dancers training then in Philadelphia, Washington, D.C., and elsewhere.[31]

Why did Jones clash with Balanchine? Le Clercq's letter gives no clue, but perhaps he had dared to say what several critics wrote after the premiere of *Modern Jazz: Variants* in January 1961, that this new work was ballet with an overlay of Broadway, but not truly jazzy. John Jones was never given a New York City Ballet contract, although he did a memorable *Faun* with the fifteen-year-old Kay Mazzo in 1961, performing with Jerome Robbins's more racially diverse company, Ballets: USA.[32]

Some people attributed to racism the fact that Balanchine never invited Jones to join his company, although that was not a charge that Arthur Mitchell ever leveled at his mentor. After Mitchell joined the company, Balanchine wanted to make "modern ballets" for him and Glory Van Scott (a Black dancer/actress Balanchine had worked with when choreographing the musical *House of Flowers* in 1954, until he was replaced by Herbert Ross), but she had declined. As Lynn Garafola wrote, "Broadway proved far more receptive to African American talent than ballet, and unlike modern dance companies, paid dancers a living wage." Balanchine cast Mitchell as a hunter in the so-called "white ballet," *Swan Lake,* and ignored warnings from the board of his company that there would be "reprisals" if Mitchell opened his ballet, *Stars and Stripes.*[33]

Arthur Mitchell was once asked what had made him join Balanchine's company, when he could have had an easier time (and made more money) as a Broadway dancer. "I like living on the edge," he had said. Balanchine taught him "that I could be off-center and still be centered." It was a lesson that Le Clercq transmitted to her students. Fingers flying, she showed them how to go beyond what they had thought possible, faster and farther, to cover the stage as she had done. "You can teach somebody steps," she said, "you can teach them how to hold their head, but what you cannot teach is whatever it is that makes a person step onstage and look interesting. That's absolutely innate . . . it is unteachable. You have to have the technique because the technique frees you to get on to dancing. But people get all caught up in the technique and they think that's it. It's not at all."[34]

While Le Clercq was still coaching ballet students, the father she had admired "from a distance" died in Lenox Hill Hospital, succumbing to liver cancer on September 3, 1972, at the age of seventy-four. As a professor, Jacques Le Clercq had been appreciated for his erudition and richly anecdotal lectures in impeccable French. But his absences were frequent, especially in his later years, shadowed by illness and alcoholism.[35]

His family interactions had been equally erratic, rife with attempts to connect with his daughter. There was love there, even mutual adoration, although they never quite knew what to say to each other. Whenever she had taken his phone calls, Tanny would sound a bit uneasy, not the lighthearted person she generally was with her friends. And yet in his last months, she had made frequent visits to his bedside, spending hours at the hospital, and they became closer.[36]

In an obituary published in the *New York Times,* Jacques Le Clercq's second wife, Marjorie "Midge" Limroth, was not even mentioned. Tanaquil Le Clercq was listed as her father's sole heir, although Edith had evidence of other intentions. His lawyer had sent her a letter in 1961: "After our conference the other day, he called me, and insisted you be left ½ the residue of the estate, equally with Tanny. Says you were a marvelous wife to him for 20 years, etc etc. So you see, he does recognize that you are a little jewel."[37]

Perhaps Edith found some comfort in this letter. And she might have smiled to learn that her ex-husband's friend, the composer Vittorio Rieti, liked to tell a story about the time Jacques upset his mistress (Midge, Martha, or another?) by repeatedly calling her "Edith." Whatever her father's intentions toward Edith, the fifty/fifty will must have been supplanted by a later one. Midge could not have been pleased with either. But long after Jacques was gone, she kept in touch with his daughter, who was always polite to her on the phone. Some of Tanny's friends never even knew that she'd had a stepmother.[38]

Tanny gave Jeanne, who had become a scholar of French and comparative literature, her father's twenty-volume *Grand Larousse* dictionary, filled with his meticulous notes, and a portrait of Jean Giono signed by the writer to his friend and translator Jacques Le Clercq. By the time of her father's death, Tanny had made new friends who were only tangentially connected to the dance world. A young crowd, it included a number of intelligent, attractive, mostly gay and bisexual men, balletomanes who became devoted to her, especially Aidan Mooney, Abraham Abdallah, and Randall Bourscheidt. "They were fun," Jeanne said. Wheeling her around town and through the underground parking service entrance of Balanchine's not yet fully wheelchair-accessible State Theater, this trio never needed his system for lifting her. They could easily carry her in and out of taxicabs. (She still had enough upper-body strength then to get herself from bed to wheelchair and back.)[39]

Aidan, a researcher at *Newsweek,* was the first to enter her life. A close friend of Jerry's, he was the key to all the others. One day in the early 1970s, Aidan had asked Abe, a colleague in the research department, to do an errand that he didn't have time for himself, dropping off some cloth that Tanny needed for a skirt. Abe immediately felt a warm connection with her. It was the same with Randall Bourscheidt, an arts administrator, the one she got to know last. Tall, blond, and blue-eyed Randy, an elegant, erudite man with impeccable manners, became a frequent escort after 1973. She would introduce him with the joke, "he's my pusher," then common slang for a drug dealer. At the State Theater, they would invariably run into Aidan, gaining fame there for his insightful opinions, as well as the military-style beret and leather jacket he wore to almost every performance. His sartorial and verbal flamboyance "eventually put him at odds with Tanny, who maybe in that area was somewhat conventional," Abe believed.[40]

Too much intensity put her off. She had absorbed her mother's sense of decorum (and perhaps Arthur Mitchell's as well), once telling Abe that Aidan's distinctive way of dressing was "outlandish" and "ridiculous." She could only take so much of Jerry's neuroticism, too. Even Diana sometimes made her uncomfortable, Abe felt, because she "was willing to discuss things more deeply than frankly any of our group at the time did. It was an unwritten rule that one didn't delve."[41]

When Jerry Robbins first met Abe in the early 1970s, he was immediately captivated by his looks, which reminded him of Attic Greek statues. (Curly-haired Abe came from a Maronite Christian, Lebanese family.) Jerry had documented this observation by pasting front and side views of one of these statues (called, in Greek, *kouroi*) in his journal. From the side, the long-nosed elegant figure resembles Tanny, but the front view, broad-shouldered, is decidedly male. Abe (whose nose, like Tanny's, was long and thin) seemed "instantly familiar" to Jerry.[42]

At a low point in his life in the summer of 1975, he listed Abe's name (right after Tanny's) on a short list titled "A series of rejections," the ones that still stung. It had barely been a year since his relation to Abe had become less intense, although they were still friends, but there were already two more names (both male) on the list of five. Number one was not a person, but the word "critically," perhaps a reference to the critics of his early work. If so, Robbins had a strange way of mixing the personal and professional, given that he ended this diary entry with the words "all I love & count on." He could be "a bit dramatic," Abe felt, in the way he interpreted his interactions with others, who "mostly adored" him and supported his moods.[43]

In fact, Tanny and Abe never deserted Jerry, remaining part of his extensive family of friends for life, with some major fallings out on her part. And yet, missing Jerry Robbins was a constant refrain in her letters. "I *miss* you—in my 'fickle' way," she had written to him in 1971. She complained about not knowing where to write to him and told him to get an answering machine so that she could be sure he would get her messages. (He generally had far more demands on his time than she did.) But as she got older and more susceptible to cold, she distanced herself geographically, spending less time in New York.[44]

Eager to escape the mournful chill of the winter following her father's death, Tanny flew to Miami, where she had been invited to judge a dance competition. Abe happened to be there and she stayed a few weeks with him and his mother "in a rather ratty part of town," he recalled. "We ate at IHOP and McDonald's. . . . Not exactly deluxe, but she had a side to her that kind of liked kitsch." She was pleased that two boys she selected for scholarships became valuable corps members of Balanchine's company.[45]

Le Clercq traveled a great deal in her teaching years, once alone to Paris in the late 1960s, although few places there were wheelchair-accessible then. It was easy to get around, she said, because she spoke French. Wherever she went, she was rarely alone for long. Pat Lousada would receive her in England. The designer Oscar de la Renta lent his villa by the sea in Punta Cana, Dominican Republic, to Jerry, Tanny, and their friends. She frolicked in Puerto Rico, a guest of Burt Martinson, of Martinson's Coffee Company, who owned a large estate in the rain forest area of El Yunque. (A friend of Lincoln Kirstein's, he had funded several ballet productions.)

In the summer of 1973, Tanny, Aidan, and Randy accepted Jerry's invitation to be his guests at the Festival of Two Worlds in Spoleto, Italy, where Robbins had been coming since 1958. Randy had taken her to dinner parties at Jerry's townhouse on East Eighty-First Street a number of times and had dined with her at restaurants near the Apthorp, but he wasn't a close friend yet. He suspected that he had been invited on the trip because they needed another pair of strong arms to help maneuver Tanny's wheelchair over cobblestones and steps. An avid balletomane since his student years at Columbia, thanks to his friendship with Aidan, Randy would become New York City's deputy commissioner for cultural affairs not long after he met Tanny. To make sure that they would get along on the trip, he made a trip to Weston with Aidan, who discreetly left them alone to talk. As with Abe, she had put him at ease immediately.[46]

Jerry provided plane tickets for the group, which joined him in Spoleto on June 27, 1973. For his three-day *Celebration: The Art of the Pas de Deux,* he had lined up five pairs of guest stars, representing distinct "schools" of ballet from five nations, although most couples no longer lived in their countries of origin. Thrilled to be sharing this place he loved with Tanny, who had not been to Italy since the tour of 1956, Jerry showed her the main square of the town, Piazza Duomo, which he likened to "being inside your favorite painting." In a short home movie made that week, Le Clercq is at an outdoor café, covering and uncovering her face with a newspaper in a playful game of peekaboo with the camera.[47]

But her happy adventure came to an abrupt end on Sunday, July 1. As Randy recalled, he, Aidan, and Tanny attended a short, noontime piano recital in the gorgeously renovated seventeenth-century Teatro Caio Melisso. The small, packed theater was the oldest in Spoleto. When people began to file out at the end, Randy saw that Aidan, who had been helping him to handle Tanny's chair, was stuck up front, prevented from advancing by the crowd. The wheelchair was blocking the main exit, so Randy decided that he could manage alone down the three small steps into the lobby, "not realizing that centuries of wear had made them both curved and extremely slick." He pushed the handles down to lift the front wheels of the chair, and then gently advanced. But as the rear wheels rolled down the top step, they slipped. At the same time, Randy remembered, the "rubber-soled shoes" he wore "didn't give me enough traction. To my horror, I slid and Tanny's chair tipped forward."[48]

She landed on the marble lobby floor. Randy, horrified, surveyed her crumpled form. "Get me the fuck off the floor!" she told her dazed friend. He carefully lifted her back into the chair. Then they went to lunch in the piazza with Aidan, where Tanny ordered a whiskey, not her usual drink. "This is killing me!" she revealed. Although some nerves had been damaged by polio, she told him, "Trust me. I can feel this." As Randy learned from her Italian doctors, if you don't use your limbs, not only the muscles go, but also the "bones atrophy and become very brittle." They are easily broken.[49]

After bedrest had done nothing to stop the swelling of Tanny's leg, they took her to the hospital. Jerry summoned "a huge truck used to haul stage scenery." Stagehands "lifted Tanny gently into the open bed, tied down the chair." Looking down at the stricken group below, her head just visible over the back of the truck, she quipped, "If only Edith could see me now." They followed the truck by car to the hospital, where she was treated by an "adorable, Italian doctor" with a flair for comedy, Randy recalled. "I don't think we'll need to amputate," the doctor joked. "Jerry practically fainted," Randy said, but Tanny stayed cool. She was "much tougher than Jerry."[50]

Jerry wrote in his diary that he was in such a state when he saw the long hairline fracture of her tibia on the X-ray, that he almost passed out from "more than dismay or alarm—but maybe thru the pain of my love for her." His agitation was so great that at first the medical staff attended to him, not her, Tanny reported, with wry humor, in a letter to Bobby Fizdale. Later, she told Abe that she had rather enjoyed her sojourn at the small, Italian hospital. The doctor, perhaps noting her sense of style, offered her a choice of colors for the cast. Hers, a girlish pink, went from ankle to mid-thigh. Arrangements were made for her flight home via a well-connected friend of Jerry's, Camilla McGrath, who called a CEO at TWA. Randy offered to fly back with her, but she gave him a good-humored smile and said, "Oh no, darling, that's all right." He got the clear message that he had done *quite enough* already. Aidan would accompany her.[51]

They all piled into a minibus to take her to the airport in Rome, playing

Geography on the way. Jerry was pleased with the "sweet Italian porter" who helped them board the plane with Tanny, but he took an instant dislike to the American stewardess and captain, whom he deemed not sufficiently sensitive to her condition. "Pulled a big scene—& left frustrated," he wrote in his diary. Abe, waiting to meet the plane in New York, learned that a mechanical problem had necessitated a quick return to Rome, prolonging the ordeal.[52]

In mid-July, Fizdale wrote to Robbins: "Tanny returned—her usual gallant self—says her trip to Italy was wonderful and she's glad she went, leg or no leg. . . . The doctor here said the cast was perfect and it comes off on August 1."[53]

As soon as Randy got back to New York, he called to see how she was feeling and whether she was amenable to a visit. She told him to come right up. When he opened the unlocked door of apartment #6A, he found her in her usual spot, sitting at the kitchen table by the window that overlooked the courtyard, her books, papers, magazines, and telephone close at hand. "I'll never be able to apologize enough," he began. "Oh hon, it's all right," he recalled her saying, with a mischievous twinkle in her eyes. "Some things make or break a friendship." After that, Randy said, "We became much closer than we had been three or four weeks earlier."[54]

She was teaching again that fall. DTH had started to attract an appreciative audience abroad, thanks to the globe-trotting Princess Margaret, a big supporter. In the fall of 1974, the company performed in the Royal Variety show, a charitable event, at the London Palladium. It was a full evening, televised by the BBC, that also featured celebrated music hall entertainers, including Josephine Baker and Perry Como. Le Clercq watched it from a box just above the royal one.[55]

By the summer of 1977, many DTH students and company members had taken a leave to appear in the filmed version of the musical *The Wiz*. Le Clercq decided to stop teaching. The company was having financial troubles (as were the city and country), and a lot of dancers had been laid off, so it seemed like the moment to go. State Department funds for touring American dance companies had slowed, as well as grants, in part because conservative members of Congress had denounced the Ford Foundation's "anti-capitalist" agenda and threatened its tax-exempt status. Mitchell briefly partnered with Columbia University's School of the Arts and weathered the downturn.[56]

Le Clercq did not return to teach, but she stayed in touch with former students who had become her friends. In the spring of 1980, Michael Stewart, by then a dance teacher, began teaching an exercise class at the Exercise Exchange near the Apthorp. Whenever he dropped by to see Tanny, she

Tanaquil Le Clercq (*upper right box*), with Dance Theatre of Harlem company manager Richard A. Gonsalves. *Royal box below them:* Lord Snowdon and Queen Mother (*to his left*) and unidentified persons, Royal Variety Show, London Palladium, photo by Marbeth, 1974. Courtesy Dance Theatre of Harlem.

showed keen interest in his work by "thinking through some of the exercise sequences" with him and making suggestions, as he recalled decades later. "I would give her some mild stretching simulated positions like *passé* or *coupé*. She would be on the floor lying on her back and I would lift one leg and extend it up and put it in *passé* and stretch it just a bit. Then switch to the other leg." Although Tanny wore the flat, t-strap shoes she favored, not ballet shoes, and could not move her legs and feet on her own, Michael said, "I would also help her point her toes by manipulating her feet. . . . We both loved ballet—our common language." He thought "she felt she was helping me, but it also helped her feel a bit like a dancer again."[57]

Theara Ward and Fabian Barnes, *The Four Temperaments*, photo by Martha Swope, ca. 1981. Choreography by George Balanchine ©The George Balanchine Trust. ©Billy Rose Theatre Division, The New York Public Library for the Performing Arts.

They often went to movies and ballets together. She had particularly enjoyed the music in the 1983 film *Staying Alive,* he recalled. If she couldn't go to a particular ballet on the date that he was free to see it, she would get tickets for him via her friends at the New York City Ballet, who went out of their way for her until the end of her life. Tanny was "a lovely person who took an interest in me," Michael said, "and I just wish I could have spent more time with her."[58]

In 1981, Theara Ward made her *Agon* debut, partnered by Mel Tomlinson, during DTH's premiere summer season at the Royal Opera House, London. It was the first time a majority Black ballet company had appeared in that theater. The acclaimed engagement included performances of several other Balanchine ballets: *Serenade, Concerto Barocco,* and *The Four Temperaments.*

20

———— ∞ ————

"A Breath, a Memory, Then Gone"

Freed from teaching, Tanny could spend summers that stretched into fall at her house in Weston, where Edith was a frequent visitor, now that Balanchine was not there to complain about her. Every day, as the sun got lower in the sky, Edith would glance at her watch and say, "Well, it's five o'clock somewhere."[1]

Her daily drink before dinner (sometimes way before) was a sacred rite, often followed by another. In Warm Springs, a "dry county," Le Clercq had written to Robbins in 1957, her mother and Balanchine had gotten a "frantic look" in their eyes until they had sent a driver to Atlanta for a bottle. Whether at home or out, Tanny maintained the family tradition of a cocktail hour. Westport, with its upscale shops and restaurants, was five miles away, but her favorite watering hole was in Weston, an old inn called The Three Bears.[2]

Alice DeLamar's pool was open to friends at prescribed hours. Randy would pick Tanny up and carry her down the pool steps (she didn't weigh much). The first time he let go of her, Randy was astonished to see that she was able to move her legs a bit and even swim, although not fast. She had a swim vest that kept her afloat, but getting in and out of the pool seemed too much of a bother after a while, and she stopped going. Perhaps she had felt self-conscious about Alice's guests (including Hollywood royalty) seeing the withered limbs that had repulsed her in Copenhagen. But she made regular appearances poolside with her guests. To ship them off to Alice's seemed impolite, an abuse of her neighbor's generosity.[3]

By the end of the 1970s, many of Le Clercq's friends had acquired second homes in the Hamptons, on the East End of Long Island, which had been attracting artists since the nineteenth century. Balanchine had a condo in Southampton, and Jerry Robbins purchased a small cottage on Dune Road in nearby Bridgehampton in 1979, not far from Robert Fizdale and Arthur Gold,

Tanaquil Le Clercq with Robert Fizdale, early to mid-1950s. Courtesy of NYCB Archive.

who lived in Water Mill. Whenever Tanny went east, accompanied by Randy, Abe, or another good friend, she usually stayed with Bobby and Arthur, warm and generous hosts with whom she had remained close since 1949.

Like parts of Fire Island, where Tanny had spent weekends at Natasha's cottage in the dunes, the Hamptons were fast gaining a reputation as a gay paradise. Fire Island had been a besieged paradise in the 1950s and 1960s, with open harassment by the local police. As Aidan's partner, Bill Earle, recalled, "to a degree hard to convey to the young, the disdain for, disparagement of, and even disgust with, men who had sex with men was very real in the bad old days and had real world consequences."[4]

In the Fire Island discos in the largely gay communities of Cherry Grove and the more upscale Fire Island Pines, "every group of dancing men had to include at least one woman. A disco employee sat on top of a ladder and beamed a flashlight at a group of guys who weren't observing the rule." In a club in the tonier Hamptons, the police enforced the same rule. A line-dance of men always included a woman.[5]

All her life, Tanny had been appalled by discrimination against anyone for any reason. Even in the midst of her ordeal in Copenhagen, she had been moved to write Jerry: "Jacques wrote me distressing news— our lovely little French producer M Noel Govin, inventor of the Goviniscope was discovered on Mt Royal with a boy, & so they have kicked him out of the t.v. station— *so* mean we all had such fun there in Montreal." Mr. Gauvin, a producer at CBC-TV, had invented a kind of upside-down periscope on wheels, wedded to a camera, that had been named for him. Attached to this device, the camera lens, aided by a series of mirrors, could "film the floor level and pan upwards," closely and smoothly following the dancers. We can thank Gauvin for the only complete filmed record of Tanny's performance in *Faun,* captured in a TV studio in 1955. Le Clercq and d'Amboise assumed that the producers had secured permission from Robbins, who became so irate when he learned about this film, made without his approval, that he had threatened to sue CBC. After 1956, however, he was grateful to have that grainy video.[6]

By the mid-1980s, Tanny was no longer as close to Jerry as she had been, although their social circles still overlapped. They often saw each other at the ballet, where Robbins had been making brilliant new works for the company since his return in the crisis year, 1969. Randy could not point to any one incident that might explain the way she had slowly distanced herself: "A cooling off more than a falling out. . . . I never quite understood why . . . it pleased her less to spend time with him."[7]

Jerry Robbins's moody volatility had always dismayed her. He could express a longing for closeness and then become remote and hard to reach, "maddening," as Pat Lousada put it, "because it was always what suited him. . . . Sometimes he was in her life and then he wasn't." And Tanny was often irritated by the painstaking way he would divvy up a restaurant check that he could easily have paid. Perhaps he had inherited this habit from his father, who had never gotten over his losses during the Depression. "I do think he'd stop breathing," Jerry wrote in his diary, "if he felt the air cost money."[8]

During the mid- to late 1970s, Jerry and Tanny were often out on the town, half of a foursome with Abe and Randy, Aidan and Bill, or Abe and his girlfriend of several years, the dancer Deborah Koolish. James "Jimmy" Lyles, who had met Tanny through Randy at that time, developed an enduring friendship with her, as did his dog, an adorable King Charles Spaniel. James lived near the Apthorp and soon joined the list of reliable friends she could

Tanaquil Le Clercq and Jerome Robbins, 1977. Jerome Robbins Dance Division, The New York Public Library for the Performing Arts.

call upon. In 1978, Robbins, a millionaire in the days when they were far less common, once invited Tanny and her friends to a New Year's Eve party in a Brooklyn Heights restaurant. Although the food was a gift, Tanny discovered that guests were expected to buy their own drinks. She muttered to Abe that given Jerry's wealth, he could have offered an open bar. When asked to give a toast, she raised her glass and called out, "Free wine in seventy-nine!" But she had known Robbins far too long to break with him over trifles. In person or on the phone, they could still make each other "laugh like hell," as she had written to him nearly thirty years before.[9]

Jeanne thought that it was Jerry's greediness when it came to credits and money that had most repelled her. He had been stung by the letter-contract he'd signed with Ballet Theatre in 1944, which had granted him a royalty of only ten dollars per performance for his big hit *Fancy Free*. Robbins had vowed then that nobody would ever take advantage of him again. This put him at odds with Tanny at times. Although their long friendship had been full of seismic shifts, the fractures in it had always healed. They both knew what it was like to establish yourself in the deep shadow of George Balanchine, their century's colossal choreographic genius. That shadow came between them one last time.[10]

In 1982, Tanny remained in Connecticut longer than usual. Sometime in November, she got word that Balanchine had been admitted to St. Luke's-Roosevelt Hospital, near Lincoln Center. Nobody knew exactly what was wrong with him. He had recovered from a heart attack and major surgery but now was having trouble seeing, hearing, and keeping his balance. Robbins wrote to Bobby Fizdale that it was "unfair that Nature, having no regard for the soul, genius & contributions of that man, wreaks a swift & rather specially horrible natural destruction on his body, uncaring of the *who* which is contained within it." It was "like Tanny's illness, unjust."[11]

In spite of the bad news, she remained in Weston past Thanksgiving. Jerry joined her there in October to celebrate her birthday, reporting to Bobby: "we had an outdoor picnic. Fun & beautiful." That fall had been unusually warm. Two months later, he wrote Bobby and Arthur that Tanny was coming back: "She's been in the country 6 months now!" On the day in early December when he wrote this letter, Jerry's beloved secretary, Edith Weissman, died. He had held her hand until the end. But already he was cheering himself up by planning a welcome-home party for Tanny, expected in four days. As he wrote their mutual friends Bobby and Arthur, "it will be good to see her."[12]

It was not a happy homecoming. Tanny went to see Balanchine several times at the hospital, where he had been admitted in November 1982. Once

Randy took her. He wheeled her into the hospital room, had a short exchange with Balanchine, and left them alone. He could see what a powerful moment that was for them both.[13]

She absorbed Balanchine's final ordeal like a major affront to herself. One day, on the way out of his hospital room with Jacques and Carrie d'Amboise, Tanny expressed her anguish at seeing her former husband so weakened by a mysterious, as yet unnamed disease. "It's so unfair," she declared, Jacques wrote in his memoir. "He survived a lung operation, giving up smoking, cutting down on drink, a triple bypass, and now this! *THIS* is to finish him—defeat him? I feel so betrayed. George is losing the ability to see, hear, and communicate."[14]

Balanchine died on April 30, 1983, at age seventy-nine, of a rare brain-wasting disorder, Creutzfeldt-Jakob disease, although that diagnosis was not known until later. His illness may have come from injections of nutrients from sheep placentas he had received at a clinic in Switzerland. A number of famous men, including Charlie Chaplin, Winston Churchill, and the songwriter Cole Porter, had been treated in this celebrated clinic, hoping to be rejuvenated.

Close to the end, there were few people Balanchine still recognized. Tanny was one of them. During one visit, he fell asleep holding her hand. His last words to her on the phone, she wrote to Pat Lousada, "I love you," echoed her words to him.[15]

She came to the Russian Orthodox church on the Upper East Side of Manhattan for his funeral on May 3, 1983. It was standing room only, literally, and the crowd spilled outside. The church had no pews or cushions. Le Clercq sat in her wheelchair, surrounded. The space was so packed with mourners, "A few people fainted standing, unable to fall."[16]

Nancy Lassalle provided a limousine for her, as well as flowers for the funeral. With Jacques, Carolyn, their son Christopher, and her friend Randy, Tanny rode out to the cemetery in Sag Harbor, on the East End of Long Island, a trip of two and a half hours. All of Balanchine's ex-wives (apart from Vera Zorina, who was in Europe) gathered by the gravesite, along with current and former members of Balanchine's company. They filed past his open grave, dropping white roses (symbols of innocence and humility he had given to favored ballerinas) on his coffin. Jacques wheeled Tanny to the edge of the hole in the ground so that they could add their flowers. To him, her hands looked like the claws of an eagle, gripping the chair's arms. "The very bones in Tanny's face seemed to tighten," Jacques recalled. "Get me out of here," she said, after her flowers fell on the coffin. They were expected to go to a reception at Bobby and Arthur's home nearby, but Tanny could not face anyone, even her closest friends. She told Jacques that she was leaving for New York. "I've got to get out!"[17]

Jacques pushed her chair toward the limo and tried to follow her instructions. But seeing her on the verge of collapse made him feel paralyzed himself. "Don't forget to lock the wheelchair before you try to lift me out. Now, pick me up carefully. Don't bang my head against the edge of the door," she instructed, in a rapid fusillade of words. "I'd been her partner for years," Jacques wrote. "I used to tell her what to do. I would fling her in the air, catch her, spin her, and always be in total control. At that moment, I was terrified and could barely move."[18]

"Okay, next, make sure my back is placed tight against the seat," Tanny ordered him. Her tone was matter-of-fact and direct, Jacques recalled, not imperious. The only way she could make a fast getaway was with her voice: "Push that switch to fold the chair up, you can put it in the front seat next to the driver. Then you can go, get out!" Tanny had managed to pull herself together for the ceremony and to add her flowers to the pile on the coffin. Now that the curtain had fallen, she could not bear to remain another minute.[19]

Suzanne Farrell passed the returning limo on her way out east. She had not been invited to the private funeral, but Edward Bigelow drove her there in his old car. They arrived after all the other mourners had left. Suzanne had just enough time to drop some soil and a white rose on Balanchine's coffin before the gravediggers filled in the gaping hole.[20]

Ballet is an ephemeral art, embedded in the mortal human body. Balanchine once said that his ballets, like butterflies, lived for a season, "A breath, a memory, then gone." He had not realized their material, lasting value or even imagined a life for them without him. "Nothing is forever," he had said. "There will be another kind of dancing." But as he grew increasingly frail, he was urged to make a formal will. What he decided to leave Le Clercq (in a will signed on May 25, 1978) changed her life. His bequest guaranteed her financial security to the end of her days, a remarkable testament to their enduring bond and his desire to protect her, which had remained strong even when he could barely command his own body.[21]

He left her the balance in his checking account, the royalties from a book he had coauthored with Francis Mason, *101 Stories of the Great Ballets,* and the American rights to nearly ninety ballets choreographed from 1927 to 1976, including *The Nutcracker,* far more than he gave to anyone else. (She had

George Balanchine and Jerome Robbins, photo by Martha Swope, 1970. BALANCHINE is a Trademark of The George Balanchine Trust. ©Billy Rose Theatre Division, The New York Public Library for the Performing Arts.

never performed in the majority of these ballets.) He had willed to her the house in Weston, as well as the valuable painting by Magritte. She already had the right to remain in her apartment. Tanny could have lived very well on the royalties from the ballets, but Balanchine wanted to make sure that she would be more than comfortable. "I always worried," he had said, "if I would die, what would happen to her." The fate of the school and company he had co-founded evidently didn't trouble him. He left nothing explicitly to the School of American Ballet and the New York City Ballet and never formally named his successors, leaving room for a battle.[22]

After the funeral, Tanny wrote to Jerry, thanking him for sending her a book about cats: "With all you have had on your mind, these last three days, to think of something like that . . . that I could return from the cemetary . . . and be calmed and comforted by your gift. God bless you— love Tanny." The blessings soon diminished. Word must have gotten back to her that in the months leading to Balanchine's death, Robbins had put a lot of strain on the company, even threatening "to take all his ballets out of the repertoire and go to the press" if his demands weren't met. After months of negotiation, he had worked out a deal with Peter Martins, who, according to Barbara Horgan, had been Balanchine's chosen successor. As Martins's co-ballet-master-in-chief, Robbins would earn $100,000 a year "plus royalties of between $150 and $350 per performance for each of his ballets in the repertory."[23]

This was far more than Balanchine had ever demanded or earned. To Tanny, for whom his legacy was primary, squabbling over terms while the great man lingered on his deathbed must have been deeply repugnant. It could well explain the cooling off that her friends noted around this time. Divorce had never altered her devotion to Balanchine. "Although their marriage had ended," Randy Bourscheidt, said, "this enormous respect, gilded with love, that she had for George Balanchine, was never diminished."[24]

21

∘⊗∘

The Final Chapter

A yearlong fiftieth anniversary celebration of the School of American Ballet had begun in early 1983 with a performance by the New York City Ballet at the State Theater. Betty Nichols and Pat Lousada came from Europe. Many former and current dancers went to see Balanchine at Roosevelt Hospital, before and after events scheduled for February 6–8, which included performances, class visits, and a cocktail party at Le Clercq's apartment from 6:00 to 8:00 p.m. on February 7. Jeanne Thomas Fuchs attended many of the events, including the reception to open the exhibition *First a School . . .* at the New York Public Library at Lincoln Center, where Kirstein made a touching speech about Balanchine. On January 19, 1984, at a gala fundraiser for the school, students of all ages performed with company dancers on the State Theater stage.[1]

Le Clercq was attending ballet performances regularly now, sometimes accompanied by April Stevens, a daughter of Pat Lousada's sister, Carla. April had often gone to Weston as a child with her family, but she grew closer to Tanny in 1983, after transferring to the New School in her junior year. Now April was living in an apartment, close to the Apthorp, that Edward Bigelow (Carla's fiancé) had loaned to her. That proximity fostered a bond that both women came to cherish. April popped in with groceries, the paper, and Tanny's favorite coffee from an Upper West Side emporium, Zabar's. They shopped, perused fashion catalogues, went to movies, restaurants, and the ballet. Tanny told Carla that she had come to think of April as "the daughter she never had."[2]

At a nearby Italian restaurant where they often dined, one of the waiters would show his appreciation by giving Le Clercq flowers. But although people might treat her like a goddess, she was the same unassuming person in public and private. Abe, who relished her hilarious, spot-on imitations of pretentious people they knew, thought of Tanny as a "reverse snob," even though she radiated "a certain upper-class aura" that "put people on their best behavior." This was "inevitable," he said, "given her background and look." And yet "she prided herself on not being snobby to the point where it was almost an affectation."[3]

April had never met anyone who lived in the moment so happily. "Everything interested her and made her laugh. . . . She made what was in front of her what she was interested in, in the most wonderful way." Just as in her dancing days, she would dress up to go out and kept herself trim by constantly dieting and exercising. Every day at 7:00 a.m. she watched the same exercise show on TV, lifting light weights as she sat in her wheelchair. She had to stay slim, she said, in order to spare the backs of those who lifted her into and out of the chair and taxicabs. And looking good was still extremely important to her.[4]

Watching a ballet while seated next to the wheelchair at the end of a row of the rear orchestra, April was always aware of Tanny's deep engagement, especially during the dances she had performed, when she would count quietly under her breath and move her hands. When April wheeled her out to the promenade during intermissions, they would immediately be surrounded by people. Jerry Robbins often approached her chair with an expression that radiated unmistakable affection. And yet, "He was one of the people who drove her out of her mind," April said, "things about his character." But he was not someone she wanted to cut out altogether, which had happened to a few others. "She would get mad at people . . . when they didn't do the right thing . . . and in rare circumstances, she did banish people."[5]

Her love for animals, however, was unconditional. She almost always had a cat but needed a period of mourning before replacing one with another. Willy was her last cat, an Abyssinian with green eyes. Delivered to her as a kitten, he had scooted under the couch and cowered there all day. Late that night, Tanny called April, weeping. "The cat won't come out and I'm just beside myself."[6]

April had rarely heard her in such a state, not since the time she had gotten emotional on a Balanchine anniversary and couldn't keep from crying about his death. Although April was married and living farther uptown by then, she grabbed a cab and rushed over. Scooping up the kitten, she placed him beside Tanny in bed. After that night, Willy would come to her when she called. He had been frightened by the wheelchair.[7]

By the time Willy came into her life, Tanny had no immediate family left. On July 4, 1985, Edith Le Clercq died, at the age of eighty-nine. Her daughter had provided the best around-the-clock homecare for her until the end, Abe recalled, and had sat by her bedside, holding her hand. In Edith's last years, he had occasionally chanced upon her sitting on a bench on the Broadway meridian, not far from her West End apartment. Thin and elegantly dressed, often in black and with a cigarette in her hand, she looked to him like someone from another world. "I never knew my daughter very well," Edith had confessed to Joel Lobenthal in 1981, "because I always had her packed off to dancing school." Although Tanny had "never complained" to her about her plight, Edith thought that "it must dig very deeply into her that she cannot even cross the room on her own."[8]

In her mother's last decade, Tanny had expressed concern to Randy about Edith's deterioration, what she "lovingly" referred to as "vagueness," he recalled, perhaps a touch of dementia. Edith's lawyer had confided a fear that his client "did not realize that she'd inherited a fairly substantial amount of money" from her relatives. She left it all to her only child, an estate of nearly a third of a million dollars, augmented by funds from the trust that Edith had inherited from her father. She must have lived modestly. Her personal property did not even fetch one thousand dollars.[9]

With her inheritance, Tanny purchased a rather "rundown" property, as Abe described it, just down the road from her house in Weston and across from the former DeLamar estate. (Alice had died in 1983.) The new acquisition included a barn divided into three apartments suitable for renting out, an old forge, and a tiny "dollhouse" cottage. Abe had cautioned her not to take on the place, as it needed a substantial amount of work, but he came to think that "it was a good idea in the end. She was able to keep her friends nearby." Charging minimal rents, she now spent summers in a colony of people whose company she valued, adjacent to a large "conservation parcel" with "a small stream which during the spring was a real torrent."[10]

She enjoyed transforming her environment and still had enough upper-body strength to do a lot of her own gardening, cleaning, and polishing with an almost fanatical relish, bending and stretching from her wheelchair. Scrupulous about keeping closets and drawers in her apartment and house organized, she sorted sheets and towels by color, with help from hired hands or friends. Most of her Weston properties were not winterized, but a few tenants stayed year-round in the barn, so there was usually someone nearby. James "Jim" Newhouse, her maintenance man and gardener, lived in one of the apartments with his wife. Una Bates, a local woman who cooked and did errands for Le Clercq, also had an apartment. Tanny had a soft spot for Una, who was given to sudden disappearances. (Years later, her daughter confirmed Tanny's suspicion that Una had been a heavy drinker for most of her life.) Nevertheless, Una could be counted on to make a weekly soufflé that everyone enjoyed and had a "daffy charm" that Abe found "inimitable."[11]

Randy occupied "the forge," a two-story wooden building, and Holly, the "dollhouse" cottage. On weekdays, when most of her friends worked, Tanny spent the bulk of her time alone, apart from a handful of helpers who came and went. She wheeled herself out on the patio to do crosswords, observe the antics of birds, squirrels, rabbits, and wild turkeys, and to read. (Betty Cage kept replenishing her stock of murder mysteries.) If a storm came, she wheeled herself back inside. Friends worried about her isolation, although Lincoln Kirstein's place was diagonally across the street. "Once she fell in the bedroom and she was there till Jim came by to do work and look in on her," Abe recalled. The frightening incident didn't change her behavior one bit.[12]

Near the close of 1986, Barbara Horgan told Tanny that twelve of her ballets would be danced in the spring. Le Clercq proposed a lump sum, per season, of three hundred dollars, not realizing that the Balanchine royalties would steadily grow from less than $100,000 a year to far more than she (or he) had ever imagined. A wealthy patron on the New York City Ballet's board once offered a million dollars for the rights to her ballets, for the benefit of the dance company. Le Clercq said that they were not for sale and kept them to the end of her life, although she did ask Horgan, Balanchine's executor and the administrator of the Balanchine Trust, to represent her.[13]

As her royalties piled up, she saw no reason to keep it all for herself. She gave away her rights for free to struggling ballet companies. Every year, she donated fifty thousand dollars to Meals on Wheels, a largesse that her accountant, executor, and friend Norma Pane questioned. Were it not for Balanchine, Tanny argued, *she* would have needed a food service for the housebound poor. "Stop trying to stop me," she said. Norma was so moved by her generosity that she made her own annual donations to Meals on Wheels, in honor of Le Clercq.[14]

Giving had always been a great pleasure for Tanny. According to Norma, she gave away more than $150,000 per year, at least a fifth of her annual income, in large gifts (not loans) to friends and employees, not counting all the dinners she insisted on paying for. She treated friends to her favorite drink, good French champagne, as soon as she could afford it. (Once she had asked Norma to bid on a painting for her at an auction house and then wrapped it up for Norma.) And yet she was a shrewd businesswoman who gradually became rich in property and stocks. That would have been a big surprise to Edith Le Clercq, who had written in her will, "as my daughter, TANAQUIL, is not experienced in managing money or in investments, I strongly urge, but do not direct, that she engage The Bank of New York to take custody of the property which she receives directly from me under this Will and to manage the same."[15]

Given Le Clercq's propensity for largesse, what happened between her and her close friend Diana Adams is inexplicable. Sometime in the late 1980s, Abe recalled, Tanny had invited him, along with Diana and Randy, to Weston for either Christmas or New Year's Eve. Diana had flown in from California, where she was living then, to discover that Tanny was unprepared for their visit, apart from drinks. Perhaps she hadn't been feeling well, or some promised help (Una?) had failed to turn up. The four of them sat around, drinking, until Diana, exasperated, berated Tanny for giving no thought to guests who had made an effort to visit her. This was a shock because Diana, "a lovely person who radiated warmth," in Abe's words, was not prone to anger. Tanny, not used to being taken to task by anyone, was hurt. Diana's accusation must have hit her "in a vulnerable place," Abe felt. He never saw them together again. Later, Abe regretted the curious passivity of their group, that no one had thought to pick up the phone to see if any last-minute provisions could have been found on a holiday. The rift might have mended, in time, but Diana lived far away, and she died in 1993.[16]

Long after the onset of paralysis, Tanny had had recurring dreams of being at the theater and realizing that she had forgotten her pointe shoes. Later, she was walking in her dreams, but not dancing. She never dreamed of being in her wheelchair, a small, elegant one. When this model was no longer being made, she hated having to use another chair, no matter how comfortable, while waiting for her favored one to be repaired. From childhood on, she had always been conscious of how she presented herself to the world.[17]

The importance she attached to her appearance may have undermined her health. She once told Jeanne that in Warm Springs the doctors had wanted to fit her with braces and crutches, but "she got hysterical" at the idea. She preferred to be in a wheelchair. Tanny "wasn't going to be clunking around with all this stuff on her body," Jeanne said. But "sitting down all the time obviously causes problems." Dysmotility of the intestines is common in polio survivors. Jeanne felt that "never getting up, never standing up" affected her circulation, heart, and lungs, as well as her digestive organs. And yet Tanny "never ever complained" and "never seemed angry or bitter."[18]

As she aged, she became an increasingly private person, more reluctant to share her innermost thoughts. But she was never shy about telling friends what they meant to her. When Bobby Fizdale's partner, Arthur Gold, was seriously ill, Robbins wrote to let her know. She sent flowers and a long letter in which she thanked Arthur for showing her such a good time on her first trip to Paris, soon after Jerry introduced them in 1949, and for "the shows you took me to after George and I got divorced, the New Year's Eves, you two really made the divorce not seem so bad, you filled my life with shows, dinners, new people, I appreciate that you were so thoughtful, that you knocked yourselves out. . . . *Thank* you, *Love* you. . . . For YEARS and YEARS of kindness and thoughtfulness and for your friendship."[19]

Robbins, mourning the loss of several friends in the 1990s, tried, repeatedly, to maintain his formerly close connection to her. By then their friendship was in a major cooling-off period, which dismayed people close to them both. Although Tanny had many gay friends, it is strange that her letters make no mention of the ravages of AIDS. And yet she had spent considerable time with Jerry's former boyfriend, the photographer Jesse Gerstein, who had died from the disease in 1991. In spite of Jesse's having left him, Jerry had cared for the younger man until the end. Among the dozens of condolences and get-well wishes that he had saved after Jesse's death and his own hospitalization in the winter of 1995–96, when the mitral valve of his heart was replaced, there is not one from Tanny. The reasons for this rift were never clear to their mutual friends. "She was extremely discreet," Randy said, "the last person on the planet to go on about people who annoyed her. . . . [S]he preferred to remove herself, rather than to confront the person."[20]

They still exchanged sporadic birthday cards, notes, and valentines, hers all saved by Robbins. But in the early 1990s, she hurt him deeply. He had choreographed the battle scene between the Nutcracker and the Mouse King. Nancy Lassalle had given him a credit line for that work in *Choreography by George Balanchine: A Catalogue of Works*, coedited with Leslie George Katz and Harvey Simmonds. Now a film of *The Nutcracker* was being prepared, and Robbins had asked the Balanchine Trust for that line in the film credits, too.

Le Clercq, who owned the U.S. performing rights to the ballet, refused. "Over my dead body," she told Barbara Horgan. Why this slight to an old friend? "At that point, it seems to me that she was not going to let anybody get credit for that ballet but Balanchine," Jeanne said. This was one area where Tanny could still wield power. Abe remembered a conversation around that time when she had enumerated some of the honors that Robbins had received: five Tony awards, two Academy Awards, the Kennedy Center Honors, a National Medal of Arts, honorary doctorates, and the 1990 three-week Robbins festival. Why, she wondered, did one more credit line matter so much to him?[21]

Deeply wounded by her refusal, Jerry Robbins did not cut her off. Even when he could barely cope with all the demands on his time and nerves, he still longed for a connection about which she seemed more and more ambivalent. Unlike her, he had always been emotionally fragile.

But she was physically fragile. In the midst of the rights struggle, Tanny suffered a life-threatening abdominal abscess. Rushed into surgery, she was left with a colostomy. Jerry showed up, uninvited and unannounced, in her hospital room. She turned her head away and would not speak to him. Some months later, while still in recovery, she sent him a conciliatory note: "I'm not seeing anyone until this is over. . . . I know you'll understand when I say I want to keep all my energy for ME." His phone calls and letters to her stopped, for about a year.[22]

Her life had altered with the surgery, but not drastically. She could have had the colostomy reversed at any time, Abe felt, but chose not to. Jeanne remembered her saying that she'd had no guarantee from the surgeons that they would be able to reconnect her successfully, so why would she put herself through all that? It may have been easier to empty the colostomy bag than to get herself from bed to wheelchair to bathroom and back several times a day.[23]

A few years later, in 1993, Robbins wrote to ask her to co-coach dancers with him for the upcoming eight-week Balanchine Celebration scheduled to start in May. Among the seventy-three ballets chosen for this ambitious, international festival, with dancers from the Paris Opera Ballet and the Kirov, was a revival of *Bourrée Fantasque*. He wanted to watch the rehearsal with her so they could advise the dancers together. "Instead of coming in at different times, it would be easier for the dancers [*sic*] energies and our memories," he suggested. "For George and the ballet, couldn't we manage it for just a couple of hours. What do you say? love— Jerry"[24]

By then she was suffering from an increased susceptibility to cold that came with acute pain in her bones (consequences of polio). No longer able to spend winters in New York, she had recently purchased a home in Florida, where she was spending half the year, minus the day or two needed to maintain her New York residency so that she could keep her apartment. She paid $1,200 a month for the large two-bedroom, two-bath unit in the Apthorp, a landmark building that in 1978 had been added to the National Register of Historic Places.[25]

Le Clercq found her new home when visiting Abe's sister, who lived on Lake Butler in Windermere, Florida, near Orlando. Tanny's 1,200-square-foot house, right next door, had a sunken patio in the front with a ramp for her wheelchair. Built in the 1930s, Abe found it "wonderful . . . all on one floor with windows opening onto an Audubon protected island that was home to herons, eagles." Old friends visited, and hired helpers took care of her home and garden, filled bird feeders, and prepared meals. In most other respects, she managed alone. "Amazing. She had a great will," Abe said.[26]

He accompanied her to New York in the spring of 1993, for the Balanchine Celebration. Una Kai, who staged *Bourée Fantasque,* consulted Le Clercq and Robbins. Tanny also coached *Divertimento,* a ballet that Balanchine had never bothered to revive, claiming he had forgotten the steps, even though by 1952 it had become a repertoire staple. Perhaps he felt that it had been a jumping-off point for him to do even jazzier works that fused Broadway and ballet. Like the score by Alexei Haieff, *Divertimento* mixed jazzy bounce and sinuous adagio.[27]

Tallchief had also come to coach. She had taken over the principal role of the Ballerina from Mary Ellen Moylan soon after the 1947 premiere. Because of the sparse performances of Ballet Society, Moylan had performed it only once, in spite of critical acclaim, an experience she later likened to "a feast taken away after the first taste." She undoubtedly would have performed the role again had she not returned to Ballet Russe de Monte Carlo in 1947. Although Le Clercq usually danced the solo part she had premiered, she had performed the Ballerina role in 1952 at least twice in London, when Maria was indisposed, and it had been one of her favorites. Gone were the days when Tanny had felt intimidated by Maria. Veterans who had shared close quarters, members of that exclusive club, the ex-wives of Balanchine, they seemed happy whenever they ran into each other. After her third marriage, "Maria mellowed a lot," Jacques d'Amboise said.[28]

Abe, who accompanied Tanny to the coaching sessions, remembered how Maria had outraged many of the dancers. She would hover over Tanny at events and loudly tell her what was wrong about the performance and what 'George' would have thought." At the first performance, she was overheard saying to a friend, "It's a pity dancers can't *bourrée* anymore," which caused a bit of a commotion. Tanny coached gently, just as she had at Dance Theatre of Harlem, and sent flowers to the principal dancers. She didn't disagree with Maria's point of view, just the bluntness with which she had delivered her opinions. Privately, Tanny told Abe that Maria's way of dancing was no longer

From left: Tanaquil Le Clercq, Carolyn and Jacques d'Amboise, and Maria Tallchief, ca. 1993. Jerome Robbins Dance Division, The New York Public Library for the Performing Arts.

being coached at the company. And yet, even though many steps had been changed in all the ballets (often by Balanchine himself), she still found them moving. Once, after watching a performance of several Balanchine ballets, she said to Randy, "Isn't it amazing how brilliant all these works are?" Her opinion had not changed since 1955, when she had told the readers of *Good Housekeeping* that she agreed with those who considered Balanchine the best choreographer in the world. (So did Robbins, to his own chagrin.) And yet she recognized that the New York City Ballet was no longer Balanchine's company. Like him, she lived for now.[29]

The rift with Jerry Robbins mended. They had ceased celebrating their birthdays together after she moved to Florida, but he would often call and write. In 1993 she sent him "A very belated" birthday card, written in a shaky hand, that featured three views of a Cheshire cat fading away. She wrote, "Where did you disappear?" and then answered her own question, "Paris."

She thanked him "*very* much" for phoning on her birthday. The note was signed with a hand-drawn heart shape and "Tan." The notes with "Love" and *XX*'s, full of gardening advice, resumed.[30]

Robbins still saw her in his dreams. In 1994, he recorded one in his journal where she appeared in a crowded, Parisian flower market. As he ran away from a menacing salesman who was pressing him to buy something, Jerry heard Tanny softly calling his name. He turned to see her, tall and slim, "a small straw hat perched on top of her head—a quiet look on her face—framed within all the wispy trailing plants. . . . Her regard was all acceptance—forgiveness. I said Tanny—& walked over to her, put my arm around her, & kissed her on the lips. She was young—(& older) slim, sad, clear eyed & oh so touching. I looked at her again. Became conscious of other figures standing around me. . . . I kissed her fervently again it was home."[31]

Shortly before his death in 1998, Tanny sent Jerry a photo of her cat, Willy, in front of her small white house on the lake, surrounded by trees and Spanish moss. She enclosed a note: "It was great talking to you. . . . I'm looking at the lake, will do the crossword, then later catch 'Bullworth.' . . . All very quiet, but I like it that way." When he died of a massive stroke in July 1998, Amanda Vaill noted in her biography of Robbins, there was only one "small round photograph" on his bedside table, "of Tanny—not in her dancing days, but in still-beautiful middle age, with shoulder-length blond hair and laugh lines around her slanting, dark-browed eyes.[32]

Jerry Robbins was a "genius gypsy," Le Clercq said, in an article full of tender remembrance published just after his death. She shared memories of the early years, when they had been closest, and wrote, with great affection, of how much the letters and presents he had sent when she was hospitalized in Copenhagen had meant to her. In her emotional bank balance, he had made enormous deposits early on, and his friends had remained hers. Their loyalty to Tanny mirrored his own.[33]

On November 24, 1998, the New York City Ballet honored Tanaquil Le Clercq with a gala tribute on the opening night of the fiftieth anniversary season, a "black tie" affair. Although Le Clercq rarely came north in cold weather anymore, she had reluctantly agreed to appear. It was a chance to see many former dancers. Some had founded their own companies across the nation. The seeds Kirstein and Balanchine planted on American soil had scattered and taken root, not only in Harlem, four miles uptown from Lincoln Center, but from coast to coast.

Peter Martins, the sole artistic director of the company since 1990, came down from the stage to personally present Tanny with a bouquet. The audience rose to give her a standing ovation. Seated in her wheelchair, she nodded and smiled, acknowledging the thunderous applause. After projected film clips and photos conveyed highlights of her career, she watched young dancers perform some of her signature roles. A touching summary of her achievements as a dancer came from an interview with Jerome Robbins, videotaped just before his death. When a spotlight picked her out in the audience, she had pointed heavenward and said, "George."[34]

Former and current dancers filed onstage to honor her after the performances, including Arthur Mitchell, Jacques and Carolyn d'Amboise, Allegra Kent, Patricia McBride, Suzanne Farrell, Mikhail Baryshnikov, Maria Tallchief, and Tanny's childhood friend Pat McBride Lousada. Big placards had been posted, so dancers of the 1940s through 1980s could line up and find those of their own era. Jacques d'Amboise, who had danced far longer than most, went from one group to the other. "Among those of the first three decades," he noted, "a quarter of them had joint replacements; by far, the majority were hips."[35]

Gold confetti rained down on the retired dancers and those still in the company. Balloons dropped as the orchestra played "Happy Birthday." The New York City Ballet had reached the age of fifty in style. Le Clercq was sixty-nine. She had already outlived her friends Robert Fizdale and Arthur Gold, and several dancers who had died of lung cancer, including Moncion and Adams, both at age sixty-six, and Magallanes, at fifty-four. Others had been too weak or ill to make the trip. Afterward, a select group gathered for supper on the promenade. Pat Lousada recalled that Tanny "loved every minute of that evening and was the last guest to leave."[36]

Two years later, in the spring of 2000, Abe drove her to Cape Cod, at Nancy Lassalle's invitation. They shared lobsters, laughter, and the seascapes Tanny knew so well from the summers of her youth. Until then, Abe hadn't felt that the quality of Tanny's life had altered enormously since the day he had met her, almost thirty years before: "She'd get the occasional cold, but essentially she seemed to enjoy herself and get around." But after that last trip, her health went rapidly downhill. Her muscles were so weakened in the end, Nancy said, that she "could not get in and out of bed alone."[37]

She spent the rest of that summer in Weston. Abe drove her car up in early autumn. He had helped her close up the house many times, but that year felt like a final goodbye. When he visited her at the Apthorp later, she was in bed and not feeling well. He went to Florida without her that winter, planning to come back when she was up to making the trip.[38]

It was an unusually cold December, and her condition worsened. She was rushed to New York Hospital, and Randy went to see her. Tanny was struggling for breath, but he assumed that she would rally, as she had done after other health crises. Saying goodbye, Randy never imagined that he would not see her again.[39]

When Norma entered Tanny's hospital room, she saw that the doctors had put a respirator on her face. She was struggling to say something, but her words were muffled. Norma screamed at the doctors to take the respirator off, but they wouldn't. Tanaquil Le Clercq died of pneumonia on December 31, 2000, exactly forty-eight years since her New Year's Eve marriage to George Balanchine. She had lived far longer than her doctors predicted, seventy-one years.[40]

Near the end of *Afternoon of a Faun,* the boy (Moncíon, in early performances) leans over to kiss the girl (Le Clercq) on the cheek. Doris Hering captured this moment perfectly in a July 1953 piece for *Dance Magazine* in which she described the pair "sitting in that ever-alert manner of dancers and wild creatures."[41]

What follows can be seen on the 1955 video with Jacques d'Amboise as her partner. She does not appear to react to that kiss at first, but then, ever so slowly, as in a dream, brings her right hand up, cupped to her cheek, and holds its warmth. She closes her eyes, and then opens them wide again, slowly turning her head in his direction, as if seeing him for the first time. Then, standing up, she turns away from him to us again, watching herself in the mirror of our eyes. Tanaquil Le Clercq takes slow steps backward, like a sleepwalker receding from us, from him, lost in a reverie made even more poignant by the faded video. At the end, just before she moves offstage, she lowers her hand, releasing that now cooling kiss.[42]

Tanaquil Le Clercq and Francisco Monción, *Afternoon of a Faun,* choreography by Jerome Robbins, photo by Fred Melton, 1953. Courtesy of Christopher Melton. Jerome Robbins Dance Division, The New York Public Library for the Performing Arts.

Epilogue

Tanaquil Le Clercq had been in a wheelchair for forty-four years, far longer than she had danced. She had inspired two choreographic geniuses at the peak of their powers and hers, only to be robbed of it all by polio. Her misfortune was "epic," as Jacques d'Amboise said.[1]

This "thoroughbred racehorse of a dancer," whose legs "operated with the razor effect of X-Acto blades," as dance critic Tobi Tobias wrote in *New York Magazine,* had lost the use of them just before the polio epidemic ended. And yet she had managed to have a full life. People with severe polio weren't expected to live past middle age, but Tanny's strength of will and capacity for joy had kept her going. "Dear Tanny," Jacques wrote, "bravery and humor sat with you in your wheelchair."[2]

Binary solar systems, those with two stars, are not rare in our galaxy. But to have two titans of choreography, Balanchine and Robbins, blazing fresh trails for the same dance company is unique. Le Clercq inspired them to make great works that are still performed all over the world. George Balanchine changed ballet forever, and she did it with him. Her quick wit, sublime lightness, and long limbs, stretching his imagination, helped him to discover where American ballet might go. "Without dancers I cannot do anything." he had said. Years later, he went a step further: "My dancers, you might say, *are* my choreography, at the moment of performance."[3]

As Susan Sontag wrote: "The relation of dancer to choreographer is not just that of executant to auteur—which, however creative, however inspired the performer, is still a subservient relation. Though a performer in this sense, too, the dancer is also more. There is a mystery of incarnation in dance that has no analogue in the other performing arts."[4]

In a 1953 interview, Le Clercq said: "Every once in a while, you ask yourself, is it worth it going through all this, the work, the practice, having no other life but this? And, of course, the answer is no. Then, one night you give a nice performance; you come close to what you want to be and you feel so wonderful. And you know then that of course it *is* worth it."[5]

What she managed to do after paralysis is just as impressive. Tanny became an adored teacher over the course of a decade with the Dance Theatre of Harlem. From a wheelchair, she kept alive the dances she loved. Keeping her body fit while writing two books, she supervised the renovations of her properties and brightened lives with many acts of generosity. What sustained her to the end, even more than her exquisite artistry, was her talent for friendship.

"Exceptional dancers, in my experience, are also exceptional people, people with an attitude toward life, a kind of quest, and an internal quality," Mikhail Baryshnikov once said. "They know who they are, and they show this to you willingly." Jerome Robbins was once asked by his friend Fran Lebowitz, the writer and public wit, to name the greatest dancers he had ever known, male and female. Without the slightest hesitation, he chose Mikhail Baryshnikov and Tanaquil Le Clercq.[6]

On many Sundays, Randy had taken Tanny to the historic Episcopal church on West Eighty-Seventh Street, Saint Ignatius of Antioch. Now he arranged for a high Episcopal memorial service with incense and altar boys that, to Abe, "did not seem like Tanny at all." Randy Bourscheidt and James Lyles addressed the crowd. James said that she was "one of the best friends I've ever had. Also, one of the best teachers I've ever had. The lesson she taught best was life and how to live it." Randy spoke of her "unbroken spirit" and of the children from homeless shelters she had brought to see *The Nutcracker* as her guests, giving them orchestra seats, snacks, and making sure that each child was photographed with a Snowflake from the cast, individually, to have a personal souvenir. She had "no regrets, no nostalgia," he said.[7]

To put away all regrets, if in fact she had managed to do so, must have required enormous effort and discipline. Nourished by her passionate interest in the world, for decades Tanny had continued to travel, coach, socialize, visit museums, and watch films and performances. The natural world remained a deep source of pleasure. She tended to her garden, her beloved cats, avian visitors, and, most of all, the people she cared about.[8]

Her will mirrored Balanchine's, in that there was no bequest to the School of American Ballet or to the New York City Ballet. All the same, Peter Martins chose to honor her at the State Theater on May 20, 2001, where company dancers performed the "Waltz of the Flowers" from *The Nutcracker* and the second movement of *Symphony in C.* Several of her friends spoke, and there was a reception on the promenade.

The Magritte Balanchine had given her, fittingly, was donated to the Wadsworth Athenaeum Museum of Art in Hartford, the institution that had funded his first trip to America. Just about everything else she had of value went to seven heirs, not all her closest friends: Abraham Abdallah, Una Bates, Carla Bigelow, Holly Brubach, James Lyles, April Stevens Neubauer, and James Newhouse (the largest shares went to Abe, Carla, and Una).[9]

Her properties and belongings were sold, but Tanny had stipulated that friends could purchase anything they wished from her apartment, all funds to benefit the estate. Before the place was emptied out, Joel Lobenthal had seen the apartment as she had left it, having been given the job of itemizing boxes of photos for the memorial. He had been "impressed with the almost total absence of aids for the disabled. There on Le Clercq's piano was a snapshot of her with Balanchine, the exact photo I had given to Edith when I sat behind her at a NYCB performance in 1982, six months after I'd interviewed her." Next to that photo was the one of Balanchine and Jurriaan Andriessen, sitting side by side at the keyboard.[10]

Tanaquil Le Clercq's most valuable assets, by far, were the ballet rights she had inherited. The George Balanchine Trust administers the royalties from those rights for her heirs, who cannot pass them on to their descendants. Each individual's rights revert to the Trust. Some people were surprised to find themselves on her list of heirs and wondered why others, closer to her, were not. The most baffling omission was that of Randall Bourscheidt, which disturbed most of their mutual friends. Few were as close to her in the end. Randy had taken her last cat, Willy (sedated for the trip), back and forth on the plane many times. He had dined with her two or three times a week for nearly thirty years. She had planned to rectify the omission, according to one of her two executors, Norma Pane, who heard Tanny say more than once that she had to call her lawyer and amend the will to include Randy. Her final illness must have come as a shock to Tanny, as it had been to all her friends.

Her feelings—about Jerry Robbins, her will, her final struggle for life and breath—remain a mystery. "I don't think that Tanny ever exposed her inner thoughts to anyone in the latter part of her life," Abe observed. "If pressed she might have given an answer, but she was closed off in that way. . . . [S]he was surrounded by loving friends but no one I think came close to being intimate. . . . Although I knew her for a long time, I think by the time of our meeting she had given up on a lot of things."[11]

Never much of a churchgoer when she was young, she had written to Jerry Robbins, from Copenhagen, that she might have been better able to deal with her illness if she could manage to believe in something, but "somehow I don't." But in her later years, she slept with a small, well-worn black and silver crucifix under her pillow and went to church with Randy. "Her acceptance of her illness," he said, "was connected with some deeply private feeling about the most fundamentally important things in life and I think there was a spiritual dimension to the way she thought about that."[12]

Since the ground was frozen in the small churchyard in Weston, the funeral home preserved her body until the thaw. In the spring, Tanny's friends, along with members and supporters of the ballet company, gathered in Weston for the burial. Edith's ashes, which Tanny had kept in a closet in Weston, were interred nearby—close, but not too close, as she had been in life. Then everyone was invited for a luncheon at Le Clercq's favorite local restaurant, The Three Bears Inn, a traditional establishment (with six fireplaces) on the site of a former stagecoach stop.[13]

Mourners filled the old inn from wall to wall, sharing memories of the woman who had captivated and intrigued them onstage and off. Generous, lovable, and loving, Tanaquil Le Clercq could, without warning, turn the spigot of her attention from warm to icy cold to off. Full of contradictions that she had been hard-pressed to explain, even to herself, she could be exacting and forgiving, demanding and easygoing, imperious and humble. But onstage, no matter how she had felt at any given moment, she had consistently enchanted.

In a tribute published in the *New York Observer,* "Farewell to a Sublime Dancer," the distinguished critic, author, and editor Robert Gottlieb wrote, "No one who saw her will ever forget her jaunty sexiness in *Western Symphony,* her thrilling virtuosity and clarity as Dewdrop, her savagery as the leader of the Bacchantes in *Orpheus.*" In all these ballets, as well as in her signature roles in *La Valse, Afternoon of a Faun,* and *Symphony in C,* he declared, "she has been successfully replaced but never surpassed."[14]

It is wonderful to catch glimpses of Le Clercq on film, to see her performing the roles she made her own. Even among the greatest ballerinas who have ever lived, she stands out, an unearthly, yet wittily down-to-earth creature made of air, nerve, and muscle, transcending gravity on the tips of her toes. With a seemingly effortless grace that is mesmerizing, she goes beyond what we might expect a body to do, as if she is supported by music alone. As Ruth-anna Boris wrote, she was a ballerina who "gave her spirit, her essence, the soul of her being to her dancing, to her roles, to her audience."[15]

It is the same buoyant spirit that helped her weather the years she spent in a wheelchair. "People say I'm brave. I'm not," she once said to Martha Swope. "You have two choices. You can be happy or you can not be happy. And I'd rather be happy." As her old friend Pat Lousada said: "I admired her dancing enormously, but I admired her courage in facing her illness even more. . . . It was always a treat to be in her vivacious company, as I and her many other devoted friends will testify."[16]

"Soufflés fall and so do dancers," Tanny wrote in *The Ballet Cook Book,* "and both survive: the main thing is to forget it. Time heals all wounds: this does happen to be true." After comically detailing multiple attempts to produce the "perfect" cup of coffee, she concluded: "There is no recipe. There is no formula. This is a plaint about life."[17]

Tanaquil Le Clercq, *La Valse,* photo by Walter E. Owen, 1951. Choreography by George Balanchine ©The George Balanchine Trust. Jerome Robbins Dance Division, The New York Public Library for the Performing Arts.

Acknowledgments

This book would not have been published in its present form without the help of the following persons and institutions. I warmly acknowledge:

Ellen Sorrin, Barbara Horgan, and the Balanchine Trust for the Balanchine quotes, letters, drawings, and photos (BALANCHINE is a Trademark of the George Balanchine Trust); Christopher Pennington and the Robbins Rights Trust, for Robbins's writings, letters, and photos; Erin Hestvik, archivist, and Kina Poon, manager, media relations, NYCB, for help in the acquisition of rare photos and letters from Le Clercq's personal papers.

Nancy Reynolds and Lynn Garafola, distinguished dance scholars, for their generous, expert guidance; Joel Lobenthal, dance scholar and historian, for tips, stories, abundant laughs, and the sharing of his writings and rare source material. Extra thanks to all three for catching errors, large and small.

Judith "Gigi" Chazin-Bennahum and Jay Rogoff, dance scholars, and Jane Goldberg, tap dancer, author, and friend, who led me to an ideal home for this work; Ruth Doering and Esther Magruder Brooks, for eyewitness accounts of the Ballet Society years; Janice Adelson, Robert Barnett, and Barbara Walczak, former NYCB dancers, for input on 1950s productions. Extra thanks to Gigi for reading an early draft, sharing her memories of Le Clercq and her family, and her warm encouragement.

The University Press of Florida staff: acquisitions editor Meredith Babb, who took a chance on a newcomer to dance writing and shepherded the work through its initial phases; Rachel Welton, assistant editor, for painstaking, cheerful attention to details; Stephanye Hunter, editor, who seamlessly took over when Meredith retired; Susan Murray, meticulous copy editor; Marthe Walters, assiduous project editor; Robyn Taylor, accomplished book designer; Mindy Aloff, dance editor for acquisitions, for abundant enthusiasm, expert corrections, suggestions, and for bringing the marvelous Balanchine letters to my attention.

The staff of the Jerome Robbins Dance Division at the New York Public Library of the Performing Arts: Arlene Yu, collection manager and Phil Karg, supervising librarian, for extraordinary service before and during the COVID-19 pandemic; Linda Murray, curator; Tanisha Jones, assistant curator; Jennifer Eberhardt, special collections librarian; Erik Stolarski, reference librarian; Daisy Pommer, librarian and original documentations producer; Cassie Mey, oral history producer and archivist; Alice Standin, reference/photographs assistant; Tom Lisanti, permissions; Maurice Klapwald, NYPL research services. This superbly competent, hardworking team can find anything, even under quarantine.

Jacques d'Amboise (1934–2021), for priceless memories and captivating storytelling; Tracy Straus, who introduced us; Emily Reid, his assistant, who facilitated our communication; Arthur Mitchell (1934–2018), for insights on working with Le Clercq and Balanchine.

Le Clercq's former students Virginia Johnson, Yvonne Delaney Mitchell, Martial Roumain, Marcia Sells, Michael E. Stewart, and Theara Ward, for their marvelous accounts of the Dance Theatre of Harlem's birth and Le Clercq's classes, with special thanks to Theara Ward for providing her photo with Fabian Barnes, and to Virginia Johnson for permission to use photos and quotes; Lauren Redniss, artist and author, for permission to quote from her NYCB installation and for connecting me with Michael E. Stewart. Thanks to Julia Mitchell for demonstrating steps as her mother displayed Le Clercq's hand signals.

Le Clercq's friends Abraham Abdallah, Randall Bourscheidt, Jeanne Thomas Fuchs, Nancy Lassalle (1928–2021), April Stevens Neubauer, and Norma Pane (1937–2020), for stories I could not have heard anywhere else. I am grateful to Nancy for personally taking me to the NYCB Archive and to Holly Brubach for permission to quote from her article, "Remembering Tanaquil Le Clercq."

Peter Kayafas and Leah Samuels, Ballet Society/Eakins Press Foundation, and scholar Robert Greskovic, for help finding photo rights holders; Dale Stinchcomb, assistant curator, Harvard Theatre Collection, for providing copies of the Balanchine letters; Jennifer B. Lee, curator, Performing Arts Collections, Butler Library, Columbia University, for locating images; Cathy Strack and Carol J. Craig, authors, for insights on Romana Kryzanowska.

Stephanie White (dancer, former teacher at Rosella Hightower International Dance School, Cannes) and Laura Smeak (dancer, former *directrice* of the Geneva Conservatory) for giving an early draft of my manuscript their expert attention and enthusiastic support.

Bank Street Writers Lab and LICWI, for valuable critiques at the start of this project, when I thought I was writing a work for young adults; Victoria Wilson, Knopf, for telling me that I had written a book for adults and what I needed to do next; Nancy Buirski, filmmaker, for timely advice.

The Setauket Writing Group: Anita Edwards, Jan La Roche, Geraldine Morrison, Judith Saccucci, Marisela Staller, Claire Nicolas White, and Ludmila Melchior Yahil, for years of insightful comments, encouragement, and meticulous critiques.

Friends and family members: Selene Castrovilla, Lynn Daniels, Chantal Emmerman, Tatiana Gordon, Doina Harrison, Kenny Mann, and Star Sandow, reliable sounding boards; Dr. Richard Righthand, aka Dr. Sherlock Holmes, tracker of rare documents.

Chester Higgins, photographer; Aaron Bryant, curator, National Museum of African American History and Culture, Smithsonian; Douglas Remley, rights and reproductions specialist; Vickie Wilson, Getty consultant, for steering me to the holders of uncatalogued photographs of Moneta Sleet Jr.; Angela Matteo, for facilitating communication with Christopher Melton; L. Rebecca Johnson Melvin, manuscripts librarian and curator, University of Delaware Library, for help locating the Bissinger photo.

Julia Gruen, for permission to quote from John Gruen's interviews with Balanchine; Marina Eglevsky, for permission to view the film *Concertino;* Ken Tabachnick, executive director, Merce Cunningham Trust, for the Cunningham quotes; Bentley Roton for permission to quote from the interview with Francisco Monción; Martin Zelner, Esq., Le Clercq's attorney, for helpful suggestions; Chester Rothstein, Esq., for pro bono advice on intellectual property law.

Letter of Johanna Justina Andriessen, courtesy of Monica Andriessen Germino; Letter of Robert L. Chapman, courtesy of Douglass S. Chapman; Letters of Robert Fizdale, Courtesy of Richard B. Fizdale; Letter of Desmond W. Margetson, courtesy of Pastor Neil Margetson. Professor Nicholas Jenkins, executor of the Kirstein estate, for quotes from Lincoln Kirstein; McKenzie Lemhouse and Edward Blessing, South Caroliniana Library, for "Memoirs of a Dowager" by Marie R. Siegling; Deborah Jowitt's interview with Jerome Robbins on July 11, 1995, for the Kennedy Center Honors oral history archives, courtesy of the John F. Kennedy Center for the Performing Arts.

Notes

Abbreviations

AG	Arthur Gold
BR	*Ballet Review*
ELC	Edith Le Clercq
GB	George Balanchine
HLH	Letters to Tanaquil Le Clercq, Balanchine, G., MS Thr 411.1, Houghton Library, Harvard University
JLC	Jacques Le Clercq
JR	Jerome Robbins
JRDD	Jerome Robbins Dance Division, The New York Public Library for the Performing Arts
JRPP	Jerome Robbins Personal Papers, Jerome Robbins Dance Division
LK	Lincoln Kirstein
NYCB	The New York City Ballet
NYPL	The New York Public Library
P&FP	Tanaquil Le Clercq, Personal and Family Papers, The New York City Ballet Archives
RF	Robert Fizdale
RF&AG	Letters to Robert Fizdale and Arthur Gold, Jerome Robbins Dance Division
SAB	The School of American Ballet
TLC	Tanaquil Le Clercq (spelled LeClercq by some family members and journalists)

Note: Underlining in letters is rendered in italics. "Black" and "White" are capitalized when referring to persons, following the consensus of the National Association of Black Journalists (https://www.washingtonpost.com/opinions/2020/07/22/why-white-should-be-capitalized/).

Le Clercq's letters contain French spellings of English words and misspellings in both languages. Balanchine's letters also have frequent misspellings. To avoid a blizzard of [*sic*] marks, there will be only one at the first instance. Henceforth, the reader should assume that their frequent misspellings are not typos. Errors in letters by others are marked with [*sic*].

Chapter 1. Her Last Tour

1. This section is informed by d'Amboise, *I Was a Dancer;* Fisher, *In Balanchine's Company;* Lobenthal, *Wilde Times;* and Lobenthal's book review, reprinted by *Politico,* February 29, 2012, https://www.politico.com/states/new-york/albany/story/2012/02/muse-of-many-faces-ballerina-tanaquil-le-clercqs-life-and-times-before-and-after-balanchine-remembered-and-now-novelized-067223.

2. Barbara Walczak, *Balanchine, His Teaching and Classes,* video recording, 1996, Jerome Robbins Dance Division (hereafter JRDD), New York Public Library for the Performing Arts.

3. Tanaquil Le Clercq to Robert Fizdale, undated, 1956, Letters to Robert Fizdale and Arthur Gold (hereafter RF&AG), JRDD. Some dates have been surmised from internal references. The ten week European tour started in late August 1956, with stops in Salzburg, Vienna, Zurich, Venice, Berlin, Munich, Frankfurt, Brussels, Antwerp, Paris, Cologne, Copenhagen, and Stockholm. Her letter, misfiled in a folder labeled "1952–53," references Salzburg and the opera that began at 7:30 p.m. on August 24, 1956, https://archive.salzburgerfestspiele.at/archive_detail/programid/364/id/0/j/1956.

4. "Vienna Press Likes New York Ballet" (trans. from *Neuer Kurier* article), *Central New Jersey Daily Home News* (New Brunswick), August 27, 1956, 7. (The other dancers noted: Maria Tallchief and André Eglevsky.) Tanaquil Le Clerq (hereafter TLC) to Robert Fizdale (hereafter RF), undated, September 1956, RF&AG. This letter, misfiled in the "1952–53" folder, references Venice, Zurich, and Maria's pregnancy, an itinerary and events exclusive to 1956. Maria had been put on bed rest September 1956, in Zurich, preceding the Venice engagement in late September.

5. TLC to Jerome Robbins (hereafter JR), undated, postmarked October 1956, Jerome Robbins Personal Papers (hereafter JRPP), JRDD.

6. TLC to JR, undated, postmarked October 1956, Munich, JRPP.

7. TLC to JR, undated, probably August 1956, JRPP.

8. TLC to JR, undated, October 1956, JRPP.

9. Morton Baum Papers, JRDD. Eglevsky and Tallchief were the highest-paid dancers. Maria earned more than anyone else on the tour, approximately five hundred dollars per week. For years she had worked for a fifth of that amount.

10. Reynolds, *Repertory in Review,* 163.

11. Denby, *Dance Writings and Poetry,* 252.

12. *Western Symphony,* USIA film produced in Paris, October 1956, retired by USIA, 1977 (ARC Identifier: 50284), now available on YouTube, https://www.youtube.com/watch?v=lIJmiAaR_90.

13. d'Amboise, *I Was a Dancer,* 178; TLC to JR, undated, 1957, JRPP (see text preceding note 9, chapter 15, for more on "Mrs. Few," sometimes spelled "Phew" in her letters). Balanchine was flattered that Jacques named his firstborn son George, d'Amboise said in an interview with the author on July 31, 2020. In fact, the boy had been given Carolyn George d'Amboise's maiden name.

14. TLC to JR, undated, October 1956, JRPP; Lobenthal, *Wilde Times,* 193.

15. TLC to JR, postmarked Westport, April 27, 1956, JRPP. Of the haircut, she wrote, "it looks awful and my hair curls the wrong way."

16. Peter Conway, "Interview with Francisco Monción," April–May 1979, transcript, 313, JRDD.

17. Reynolds, *Repertory in Review,* 113, quoting De Zoate, *Ballet,* September-October 1950.

18. Arthur Mitchell, in the film *Afternoon of a Faun,* dir. Nancy Buirski (Kino Lorber, 2014); Mason, *I Remember Balanchine,* 248.

19. Barbara Horgan, in the film *Afternoon of a Faun*. Doctors no longer prescribe the drug to reduce anxiety (its main effect). It is addictive and a danger to health, especially with alcohol.

20. Brief extract of this scene: *New York City Ballet* (hereafter NYCB), streaming video file, black-and-white, reel 1, JRDD.

21. Jowitt, *Jerome Robbins,* 161; Lillian Moore, "The Roles That Are Tanny's," *Tanny: The Tanaquil Le Clercq Fan Club Semi-Annual Journal,* no. 4 (June 1958): 6, JRDD.

22. *Bourrée Fantasque* (wide shot), streaming video file, NYCB in performance at State Theater, New York, May 13, 1993, JRDD.

23. Lobenthal, *Wilde Times,* 193; Holly Brubach, "Muse Interrupted," *New York Times, T Magazine,* November 22, 1998, 64.

24. Brubach, "Muse Interrupted," 64.

25. There are differing versions of the timeline of her illness. This one, further elaborated in chapter 14, is based on eyewitness accounts and the Copenhagen program. TLC to JR, undated, postmark January 2, 1957, JRPP. (TLC to JR, undated, postmarked Copenhagen, December 31, 1956, also attests to her state of mind: "I get tons of mail— and *Match* is doing an article and all I wish is that this had *never* happened.")

Chapter 2. Starting Out "Like a Real Ballerina . . ."

1. Dr. Fredrika D. Borchard, "Adding Exotic Beauty to a Ballet," *St. Louis Post-Dispatch,* September 11, 1951, 45; Louise Ainsworth, "The Cat's Meow," *Weston (CT) Town Crier,* September 27, 1964, 13; TLC, "Practically Anybody Can Become a Ballet Dancer," *Good Housekeeping,* August 1955, 168.

2. Borchard, "Adding Exotic Beauty to a Ballet," 45; Donald Spoto, *Jacqueline Bouvier Kennedy Onassis: A Life* (New York: St. Martin's, 2000), 52.

3. Frederick Whittemore's profession is noted in the death notice of his wife, in the *St. Louis Star-Times,* January 12, 1944. Until 1920, Edith Whittemore was listed as an active member of the St. Louis Junior League, living at 10 Hortense Place. For Goldman details, see https://stltourguide.wordpress.com/2010/10/01/c-w-e-north/

4. The *St. Louis Star and Times,* March 1, 1919, 5, reported that her parents visited Edith in New York City, where she was on an extended visit with relatives. Undated letter, probably written in 1918, Tanaquil Le Clercq, Personal and Family Papers, New York (hereafter P&FP): Dearest Dad— Of course I know how you feel now about my doing war work outside of St. Louis but if you will only come East and see what is going on . . . and although I dont [sic] want a uniform I would like to be working and doing my share . . . Much love— Edith

5. https://www.findagrave.com/memorial/137168991/frederick-churchill-whittemore; *The Book of St. Louisans,* ed. John W. Leonard (St. Louis: St. Louis Republic, 1906), 608. By 1939, Elenore's address in St. Louis was 4535 Lindell Boulevard, an elegant apartment building in the city's fashionable Central West End.

6. Edith Virginia Young, "Society News," *St. Louis Star,* January 27, 1927, 13.

7. Young, "Society News," June 26, 1928, 15.

8. Marie R. Siegling, "Memoirs of a Dowager, 20 Dec. 1908," 12–13, 22, Siegling Family Papers, South Caroliniana Library, University of South Carolina, Columbia. The name LeClercq was acquired by Dr. LeClercq's grandfather, a German officer named Schuman, quartered in Commines, France, who had added it to his own and renounced Protestantism to convince the mayor of the town to give him the hand of his daughter.

9. Siegling, "Memoirs of a Dowager, 20 Dec. 1908," 7–8, 11–12, 13–18.

10. Siegling, "Memoirs of a Dowager, 20 Dec. 1908," 29; https://chordsoforgottenmelodies.word-press.com and https://thecowboyandthecountess.wordpress.com/tag/cudellas-waide/.

11. https://chordsoforgottenmelodies.wordpress.com and https://thecowboyandthecountess.word-press.com/tag/cudellas-waide/.

12. Ibid.

13. Siegling, "Memoirs of a Dowager, 20 Dec. 1908," 22; Paul Tanaquil [Jacques Le Clercq (hereafter JLC)], *Sotto Voce: A Poet's Pack* (New Haven, CT: Yale University Press, 1923). *Chevalier* title is in the dedication.

14. https://www.findagrave.com/memorial/106565068/margaret-leclercq_kilduff.

15. Passenger ship manifest, May 20, 1933, https://www.myheritage.com/research/record-10512-19325069/tanaquil-le-clercq-in-ellis-island-other-new-york-passenger-lists; TLC, *The Ballet Cook Book*, 217.

16. TLC, *The Ballet Cook Book*, 217; Borchard, "Adding Exotic Beauty to a Ballet," 45; "Guggenheim Fund Makes 85 Grants," *New York Times*, March 24, 1930, 30; Daniel Starch, "The Income of the American Family," Library, College of Agriculture, University of Wisconsin, Madison, 1930, https://babel.hathitrust.org/cgi/pt?id=wu.89043221407&view=1up&seq=17.

17. Edith Le Clerq (hereafter ELC) to JLC, undated, December 1930, P&FP.

18. *Certificat d'etudes de sci po Droit*, 22 *decembre*, 1931 (Certificate in political sciences and law, December 22, 1931), P&FP; JLC received a French doctorate for the thesis *L'Inspiration Biblique dans l'oeuvre poetique d'Alfred de Vigny* (Biblical sources of inspiration in the poetic works of Alfred de Vigny), December 23, 1937.

19. *Columbia Spectator*, February 29, 1940, 4.

20. https://chordsoforgottenmelodies.wordpress.com. Posted in "uncategorized," December 21, 2014.

21. Ellen Rodman, "Edith King and Dorothy Coit and the King-Coit School and Children's Theatre" (Ph.D. thesis, School of Education, Health, Nursing and Arts Professions, New York University, 1980), 29.

22. Ibid., 46.

23. Ibid., 74.

24. Ibid., 56, 61. The text of the play was adapted from a legend in the *Mahabharata* recounting the thwarted love of a king, Nala, skilled at horsemanship and culinary arts (but with a weakness for gambling), and a princess, Damayanti, who remains faithful as evil forces work to part them.

25. Ibid., 123.

26. Ibid., 55, 62 (tuition detail); 60 (ELC quote).

27. Ibid., 40.

28. Martha Ullman West, "Afternoon of a Faun, Interrupted," *Oregon Arts Watch*, July 16, 2014, https://www.orartswatch.org/afternoon-a-a-faun-interrupted/.

29. John Anderson, *New York Evening Journal*, 1934, quoted by Nancy Lassalle in "Remembering Tanaquil Le Clercq," *Ballet Review* (hereafter BR), Summer 2001, 41; Ruth Gilbert L. Doering, interview by the author, August 19, 2020.

30. Singer, *First Position*, 76.

31. Zeller, *Shapes of American Ballet*, 93–97.

32. Rodman, "Edith King and Dorothy Coit," 58.

33. Barbara Newman, "Tanaquil Le Clercq Talks about Dancing," *BR*, Fall 1982, 52.

34. Zeller, *Shapes of American Ballet*, 137; "Viennese Theme for Smart Party in New York," *St. Louis Post-Dispatch*, March 26, 1939, 58; TLC, "Practically Anybody Can Become a Ballet Dancer," 168.

35. A "special correspondent" (perhaps ELC), posting from New York: "Former St. Louisans in New York Attend Charity May Day Fete," *St. Louis Post-Dispatch*, May 19, 1940, 3G.

36. Susan Ware, ed., *Notable American Women: A Biographical Dictionary Completing the*

Twentieth Century (Cambridge, MA: Belknap Press of Harvard University Press, 2004), 114; Alan M. Kriegsman, "The ABT's 40-Year Chase for Glory," *Washington Post,* March 30, 1980, https://www.washingtonpost.com/archive/lifestyle/1980/03/30/the-abts-40-year-chase-for-glory/bc95a387-2e75-4199-8c6c-f5f448eb871a/.

37. Gruen, *The Private World of Ballet,* 85. (The name Maryinsky is often spelled Mariinsky today.)

38. TLC, "Practically Anybody Can Become a Ballet Dancer," 169.

39. TLC to ELC, note, 1937, P&FP.

40. Powell, *The Diaries of Dawn Powell 1931–1965,* entry for January 12, 1927, 11.

41. Ibid., entry for April 14, 1935, 100; ibid., entry for June 3, 1954, 339.

42. Walter Owen, "Tanaquil Le Clercq," *Dance Magazine,* March 1950, 51.

43. Rodman, "Edith King and Dorothy Coit," 89; Joel Lobenthal, "Dryads of West 55th Street," *Ballerina: Fashion's Modern Muse,* 166.

44. Powell, *The Diaries of Dawn Powell,* entry for March 31, 1940, 174–75.

45. Frances Conant Richards, "New Yorkers Take Varied Spring Trips," *St. Louis Post-Dispatch,* March 31, 1940, 2G; Gruen, *The Private World of Ballet,* 42.

46. Jennifer Dunning, "Muriel Stuart, 90, Dancer for Pavlova and Ballet Teacher," obituary, *New York Times,* January 30, 1991; Charles Engell France, "Interview with Tanaquil Le Clercq," 1974, JRDD.

47. Taper, *Balanchine: A Biography,* 205.

48. Joel Lobenthal, "Tanaquil Le Clercq," *BR,* Fall 1984, 74.

49. Holly Brubach, "Muse, Interrupted," *New York Times, T Magazine,* November 22, 1998, 62.

50. "Five Little Girls Win Ballet Scholarships," *New York Times,* October 7, 1940, "Amusements" sec., 20.

51. Holly Brubach, "Muse, Interrupted," *New York Times, T Magazine,* November 22, 1998, 62.

52. TLC, "Practically Anybody Can Become a Ballet Dancer," 169.

Chapter 3. Two Paths Converge

1. TLC, "Practically Anybody Can Become a Ballet Dancer," *Good Housekeeping,* August 1955, 170.

2. Source for Kyra Blanc's strictness, Esther Brooks (formerly Magruder), TLC classmate, interview by the author, August 28, 2018.

3. Kendall, *Balanchine and the Lost Muse,* 23.

4. Taper, *Balanchine: A Biography,* 28.

5. Kendall, *Balanchine and the Lost Muse,* 28, 36.

6. Taper, *Balanchine: A Biography,* 34–35; Kendall, *Balanchine and the Lost Muse,* 39.

7. Taper, *Balanchine: A Biography,* 34–35. Taper spells her name "Preobrashenskaya"; "Preobrajenska" is the Western spelling.

8. Kendall, *Balanchine and the Lost Muse,* 39. Balanchine never mentioned his brother's presence, so perhaps Andrei heard this story afterward (see 249n56). A letter from Meliton to the school, August 13, 1913, petitioned for Georgi's admission. If not written after his audition, this may have been the family's backup plan all along (ibid., 249n55).

9. Ibid., 45.

10. Gruen, *The Private World of Ballet,* 280; Kendall, *Balanchine and the Lost Muse,* 23; d'Amboise, *I Was a Dancer,* 42. (At the fiftieth anniversary celebration of the publication of Tanaquil Le Clercq's *Ballet Cook Book,* Guggenheim Museum, November 6, 2017, d'Amboise said that he thought Balanchine possibly had Tourette's syndrome. In an interview by the author, July 31, 2020, he added that the symptoms lessened with age.)

11. Kendall, *Balanchine and the Lost Muse,* 49–50.

12. Ibid., 138–40.

13. Ibid., 92–99.

14. Ibid., 108–12.

15. Ibid., 131; Taper, *Balanchine: A Biography,* 46–47.

16. Pat McBride Lousada, "Remembering Tanaquil Le Clercq," *BR,* Summer 2001, 50.

17. Taper, *Balanchine: A Biography,* 67–68; Kendall, *Balanchine and the Lost Muse,* 213. (Balanchine had a younger, artist/set designer friend with the same name but a different patronymic, Vladimir Vladimirovich Dmitriev.)

18. Kendall, *Balanchine and the Lost Muse,* 181–82.

19. Ibid., 161.

20. Ibid., 182.

21. Taper, *Balanchine: A Biography,* 70; Kendall, *Balanchine and the Lost Muse,* 214–29.

22. Kendall, *Balanchine and the Lost Muse,* 214–29.

23. Ibid.

24. Ibid.

25. Ibid., 10.

26. Geva, *Split Seconds,* 328.

27. Taper, *Balanchine: A Biography,* 85.

28. Ibid., 98, 100. Other accounts include Buckle, *George Balanchine: Ballet* Master; Danilova and Brubach, *Choura;* Gottlieb, *George Balanchine: The Ballet Maker;* and Kendall, *Balanchine and the Lost Muse.*

29. Taper, *Balanchine: A Biography,* 127.

30. Ibid., 151–52; Laurie Johnston, "School of American Ballet, at 50, as Rigorous as Ever," *New York Times,* January 20, 1984, B1.

31. Anna Kisselgoff, "Dance View: A 'Forgotten' Figure in U.S. Ballet History," *New York Times,* January 15, 1984, sec. 2, p. 8.

32. Zorina, *Zorina,* 169.

33. Ibid., 292.

34. TLC, "Practically Anybody Can Become a Ballet Dancer," 170.

35. TLC to ELC, undated, summer 1942, P&FP.

36. TLC, "Practically Anybody Can Become a Ballet Dancer," 53.

37. Taper, *Balanchine: A Biography,* 239.

38. Davie Lerner, "Remembering Tanaquil Le Clercq," *BR,* Summer 2001, 44.

39. Randall Bourscheidt, in the film *Afternoon of a Faun,* dir. Nancy Buirski (Kino Lorber, 2014).

40. Barbara Newman, "Tanaquil Le Clercq Talks about Dancing," *BR,* Fall 1982, 75. (*Cou-de-pied,* literally, *neck of the foot,* refers to a position where the free foot wraps around the supporting foot, toes touching near the ankle bone, either in front or behind it.)

41. Holly Brubach, "Muse, Interrupted," *New York Times, T Magazine,* November 22, 1998, 62.

42. d'Amboise, *I Was a Dancer,* 40.

43. Ibid.; Rodman, *Edith King and Dorothy Coit,* 60.

44. Newman, "Tanaquil Le Clercq Talks about Dancing," 74.

45. Richards, "Eastern Resorts Attract Former St. Louisans Living in New York," *St. Louis Post-Dispatch,* July 15, 1945, pt. 5, p. 1.

46. JLC to ELC, February 21, 1946; JLC to ELC and TLC, January 26–February 24, 1946; JLC to TLC, February 21, 1946, P&FP.

47. Robert L. Chapman to *New York Times Magazine,* December 20, 1998, sec. 6, p. 20.

Chapter 4. A "Coltish" Muse

1. Taper, *Balanchine: A Biography,* 241.

2. This quote, widely attributed to George Balanchine, is on the website for *Balanchine—Master*

of the Dance, dir. Merrill Brockway (New York: PBS, 2004), https://www.pbs.org/wnet/americanmasters/george-balanchine-master-of-the-dance/529/. Barbara Newman, "Tanaquil Le Clercq Talks about Dancing," *BR,* Fall 1982, 54.

3. Judith Chazin-Bennahum, interview by the author, August 28, 2018.

4. ELC, Last Will and Testament, June 21, 1971, New York Surrogate's Court.

5. Newman, "Tanaquil Le Clercq Talks about Dancing," 54.

6. Patricia McBride Lousada, in the film *Afternoon of a Faun,* dir. Nancy Buirski (Kino Lorber, 2014).

7. Mason, *I Remember Balanchine,* 369; Suzanne Massie, "Mr. B: 'God Creates, I Assemble,'" *Saturday Evening Post,* October 23, 1965, 100. Arlene Croce wrote in "Balanchine Said," *New Yorker,* January 19, 2009, that this is "an adaptation of a saying attributed to Glinka, 'Nations create music, composers only arrange it'" (https://www.newyorker.com/magazine/2009/01/26/balanchine-said).

8. Fisher, *In Balanchine's Company,* 17.

9. Lousada, in the film *Afternoon of a Faun.*

10. Denby, *Dance Writings,* 340.

11. Charles Engell France, "Interview with Tanaquil Le Clercq," 1974, JRDD; Reynolds, *Repertory in Review,* 87.

12. Joel Lobenthal, "Tanaquil Le Clercq," *BR,* Fall 1984, 75.

13. Pat McBride Lousada, "Remembering Tanaquil Le Clercq," *BR,* Summer 2001, 50.

14. April Stevens Neubauer, interview by the author, August 19, 2018; Lousada, in the film *Afternoon of a Faun.*

15. Lousada, "Remembering Tanaquil Le Clercq," 49–50.

16. Lousada, in the film *Afternoon of a Faun.*

17. Frances Conant Richards, "Eastern Resorts Attract Former St. Louisans Living in New York," *St. Louis Post-Dispatch,* July 15, 1945, pt. 5, p. 1.

18. Nancy Norman Lassalle, interview by the author, April 10, 2018.

19. Nancy Lassalle, "Remembering Tanaquil Le Clercq," *BR,* Summer 2001, 41.

20. Although Balanchine said the piece was commissioned in 1940, scholars have tracked it to 1938 (see Elizabeth Sawyer, "In the Teeth of the Evidence," *Dance Now,* no. 4 [Winter 2002–3]: 31–42).

21. Teachout, *All in the Dances,* 82; Duberman, *The Worlds of Lincoln Kirstein,* 411, 670, note 3; Garafola, *Dance for a City,* 6.

22. Abraham "Abe" Abdallah, email to the author, July 18, 2018. Balanchine may have gotten the idea of a split-legged leap from his classmate Lidia Ivanova, who had pioneered the daring move in Petrograd (see Kendall, *Balanchine and the Lost Muse,* 196–98).

23. David Vaughan, "Tanaquil Le Clercq," *The Guardian* (London), January 4, 2001, 20; Mason, *I Remember Balanchine,* 221.

24. *Four Temperaments* (motion picture), 16mm, silent, rehearsal at High School of Needle Trades, 1946, streaming video, JRDD; Merrill Brockway, *Choreography by Balanchine* (PBS program for Dance in America series, telecast 1977), copyrights 1978–79, Educational Broadcasting Corporation, New York; DVD by Nonesuch Records, Inc., New York, 2004.

25. Holly Brubach, "Muse, Interrupted," *New York Times, T Magazine,* November 22, 1998, 62.

26. France, "Interview with Tanaquil Le Clercq"; Duberman, *The Worlds of Lincoln Kirstein,* 411; *Four Temperaments* (motion picture), JRDD.

27. Brubach, "Muse, Interrupted," 62.

28. Ibid.

29. On George Balanchine (hereafter GB) conducting, see Igor Stravinsky, *Stravinsky, Selected Correspondence,* vol. 2, ed. Robert Craft (New York: Knopf, 1984), 270; NYCB program of February 9, 2020 (date of premiere).

30. Reynolds, *Repertory in Review,* 78.

31. Ibid., 77.

32. Ibid., 78–79.

33. "Interview with Merce Cunningham," by David Vaughan, June 13 and 16, 1978, 2 streaming audio files, JRDD.

34. France, "Interview with Tanaquil Le Clercq."

35. Details on 1947 production of *The Seasons* courtesy of Merce Cunningham Trust, Merce Cunningham Dance Foundation records, Series IV: Repertory Production Files, Seasons Dance Capsule, 1947, JRDD.

36. John Martin, "Ballet Society Offers Two Premieres," *New York Times*, May 19, 1947; France, "Interview with Tanaquil Le Clercq."

37. "Interview with Merce Cunningham," by Vaughan, June 13 and 16, 1978.

38. Ballet Society Souvenir Program, 1946–47, JRDD.

Chapter 5. The Ballet Society Years

1. Ruth Gilbert L. Doering, interview by the author, August 19, 2020. As Ruth Gilbert, she was a company member from 1948 to 1950 and took classes with Balanchine.

2. Taper, *Balanchine: A Biography,* 204.

3. Duberman, *The Worlds of Lincoln Kirstein*, 411; Taper, *Balanchine: A Biography,* 204; Lynn Garafola, "Lincoln Kirstein, Modern Dance, and the Left: The Genesis of an American Ballet," *Dance Research* 23, no. 1 (January 2008): 24.

4. Roger Copeland, "Backlash Against Balanchine," *Choreography and Dance* 3, pt. 3 (1993): 7; Jay Rogoff, "Heaven and Earth in Balanchine's Philosophy," *Hopkins Review* 7, no. 3 (Summer 2014): 402.

5. d'Amboise, *I Was a Dancer,* 208.

6. Buckle, *George Balanchine: Ballet Master,* 172; Esther Magruder Brooks (stage names Nicole Makovsky, Nicole Marais), email to the author, August 1, 2020. By the time Nelson Rockefeller (a friend of Kirstein's) ran for office in NY, Esther had left the company.

7. Brooks, email to the author, August 1, 2020; Marina Harss, "When City Center Was Balanchine's House," *New York Times*, October 28, 2018, "Arts" sec., 22.

8. Tallchief, *Maria Tallchief,* 134; "A Place to Dance: New York City Center," panel discussion moderated by Linda Murray, curator, Bruno Walter Auditorium, November 29, 2018, JRDD.

9. Harss, "When City Center Was Balanchine's," 22.

10. "A Place to Dance: New York City Center," panel discussion.

11. Garafola, *Dance for a City,* 6; d'Amboise, *I Was a Dancer,* 88–89.

12. Villella, *Prodigal Son,* 25; 24.

13. Brooks, interview by the author, August 28, 2018.

14. Ibid. Esther married Peter C. Brooks IV in 1950. Returning to his native New England, she founded the Cambridge School of Ballet in 1953, where she taught until 1969.

15. Geva, *Split Seconds,* 272; LK, *Ballet News,* May 1982, 16.

16. Cathy Strack and Carol J. Craig, *Love All Around: The Biography of Romana Kryzanowska* (self-published, January 2019), 146–49; Rosalind Gray Davis, "Romana Kryzanowska: Pilates Living Legend," https://animopilates.com/romana-kryzanowska. For more on Paul Mejia, see chapter 18.

17. Barbara Newman, "Tanaquil Le Clercq Talks about Dancing," *BR*, Fall 1982,70.

18. Gruen, *The Private World of Ballet,* 282.

19. Dee Das, *Katherine Dunham: Dance and the African Diaspora,* 105; Thomas DeFrantz, "Interview with Walter Nicks," ca. 2001, audio livestream recording, disc 2, JRDD; Jacques d'Amboise, interview by the author, June 14, 2018; Mason, *I Remember Balanchine,* 396.

20. Dee Das, *Katherine Dunham: Dance and the African Diaspora,* 106, 109, 120.

21. Ibid., 110.

22. Ibid., 107; Dee Das, email to the author, July 15, 2020 (second-position *plié* with contraction).

23. Reynolds, *Repertory in Review,* 87.

24. Peter Conway, "Interview with Francisco Monción," April–May 1979, transcript, 189, JRDD.

25. Reynolds, *Repertory in Review,* 88; France, Charles Engell France, "Interview with Tanaquil Le Clercq," 1974, JRDD.

26. TLC, *The Ballet Cook Book,* 338.

27. Mason, *I Remember Balanchine,* 179.

28. Zorina, *Zorina,* 169; Joel Lobenthal, interview by the author, June 21, 2020. In addition to Maria Tallchief and TLC, he said, Patricia McBride and Suzanne Farrell were also not naturally turned out, unlike Marie-Jeanne, Mary Ellen Moylan, and Patricia Wilde.

29. Tallchief, *Maria Tallchief,* 81; Robert Sabin, "Bright Victory," *Dance Magazine,* April 1964, 39.

30. Vida Brown, in an interview conducted by Joel Lobenthal (October 23, 2013), said that Maria was an expert seamstress who made many of her own clothes; Tallchief, *Maria Tallchief,* 81; Doering, interview by the author, August 19, 2020.

31. GB, "Mr. B. Talks about Ballet," *Life* magazine, June 11, 1965, 102.

32. Tracy, *Balanchine's Ballerinas,* 122.

33. JR, "Notes," February 7, 1983, Jerome Robbins Personal Papers (hereafter JRPP).

34. Reynolds, *Repertory in Review,* 82; Schorer, *Suki Schorer on Balanchine Technique,* 407.

35. Tallchief, *Maria Tallchief,* 81–82; Tracy, *Balanchine's Ballerinas,* 104.

36. Newman, "Tanaquil Le Clercq Talks about Dancing," 70, 66–67.

37. Ibid., 55.

38. Newman, "Tanaquil Le Clercq Talks about Dancing," 65–66.

39. Bruce Duffie, transcript, "Conversation Piece: Prima Ballerina Maria Tallchief," recorded September 19, 1994, http://www.bruceduffie.com/tallchief2.html.

40. d'Amboise, *I Was a Dancer,* 172–73; Gruen, *The Private World of Ballet,* 64.

41. Tallchief, *Maria Tallchief,* 51–52.

42. Phillip Bloom to Miss Eleanor Lambert, March 16, 1950, Morton Baum Papers, JRDD.

43. Alexander Dubé, "Balanchine, His Teaching and Classes," video recording, 1996, JRDD; "Blue Notes of a Ballerina," *Ithaca Journal,* March 2, 1950, 23.

44. "Union Wages and Hours: Building Trades, July 1, 1947," *Bulletin No. 930, United States Department of Labor, Bureau of Labor Statistics* (New York State School of Industrial and Labor Relations, Cornell University, July 25, 1951); Bocher, *The Cage,* 136 (salaries through 1950); Garafola, *Legacies of Twentieth-Century Dance,* 354 (late 1950s). For more on Kirstein's politics, see Garafola, "Lincoln Kirstein, Modern Dance, and the Left: The Genesis of an American Ballet," *Dance Research* 23, no. 1 (Summer 2005): 18–35; George Balanchine to William O'Dwyer, Morton Baum Papers, JRDD.

45. d'Amboise, interview by the author, July 31, 2020. (He said the corps had expected more on that tour, around sixty dollars per week.)

46. Tallchief, *Maria Tallchief,* 320; Lobenthal, "Dryads of West 55th Street," 167.

47. TLC, "Practically Anybody Can Become a Ballet Dancer," *Good Housekeeping,* August 1955, 169.

48. Judith Chazin-Bennahum, interview by the author, August 29, 2018.

49. TLC, "Practically Anybody Can Become a Ballet Dancer," 169.

50. Bocher, *The Cage,* 230; Nancy Reynolds, interview by the author, April 9, 2018.

51. TLC, "Practically Anybody Can Become a Ballet Dancer," 169.

52. Newman, "Tanaquil Le Clercq Talks about Dancing," 69–70.

Chapter 6. Birth of the New York City Ballet

1. Kent, *Once a Dancer,* 75.

2. Morton Baum to Lincoln Kirstein, November 23, 1948, Morton Baum Papers, JRDD.

3. Barbara Newman, "Tanaquil Le Clercq Talks about Dancing," *BR,* Fall 1982, 66.

4. Holly Brubach, "Muse, Interrupted," *New York Times, T Magazine,* November 22, 1998, 62.

5. Ibid., 66.

6. Raffaele Bedarida, "Magnifico in New York: Corrado Cagli, Migrating Artists, and the Mirage of Italy," lecture, Bruno Walter Auditorium, New York Public Library, April 8, 2019.

7. Lorenzo de' Medici, *Trionfo di Bacco e Arianna:* "Quant'è bella giovinezza/che si fugge tuttavia!/ Chi vuole esser lieto, sia:/di doman non c'è certezza" (translation by the author).

8. Reynolds, *Repertory in Review,* 83.

9. Jacques d'Amboise, interview by the author, June 14, 2018.

10. Reynolds, *Repertory in Review,* 84. The description of Rieti's music is the author's, based on excerpts by Cantori New York, in conjunction with "Magnifico in New York," April 8, 2019.

11. Franco Carlo Ricci, *Vittorio Rieti* (Rome: Edizioni Scientifiche Italiane, 1987), 255.

12. Reynolds, *Repertory in Review,* 79.

13. Brubach, "Muse, Interrupted," 63.

14. Taper, *Balanchine: A Biography,* 292; Charles Engell France, "Interview with Tanaquil Le Clercq," 1974, JRDD.

15. Susan Kraft, "Interview with Ruth Gilbert Lawrence," sound recording, November 24, 1998, JRDD; Nancy Lassalle, email to the author, August 20, 2020. See movie trailer at :40, https://www. youtube.com/watch?v=PdEaicb-pag&list=RDVSBFBls-Xx0&index=9.

16. Tallchief, *Maria Tallchief,* 91; France, "Interview with Tanaquil Le Clercq."

17. JR, interview by Martha Duffy, November 29, 1988, JRDD.

18. Ibid.

19. TLC, "Jerome Robbins," with Rick Whitaker, *BR,* Summer 1998, 13.

20. Martin, "Ballet by Robbins Called Smash Hit," *New York Times,* April 19, 1944, Amusements, 27.

21. TLC, "Jerome Robbins," 13.

22. JR, interview by Martha Duffy, November 29, 1988, JRDD.

23. Ibid.; Reynolds, *Repertory in Review,* 94.

24. TLC, "Jerome Robbins," 13.

25. France, "Interview with Tanaquil Le Clercq."

26. Reynolds, *Repertory in Review,* 94; d'Amboise, *I Was a Dancer,* 337.

27. Homans, *Apollo's Angels,* 478.

28. Dan Piepenbring, "Fleur's Flair," *Paris Review,* January 20, 2015, https://www.theparisreview. org/blog/2015/01/20/fleurs-flair/.

Chapter 7. Summer in Europe

1. Nathan Milstein, "My Friend, George Balanchine II," copyright by Nathan Milstein and Solomon Volkov, *BR,* Winter 1990–91, 88.

2. Duberman, *The Worlds of Lincoln Kirstein,* 217, 352.

3. Jacques d'Amboise, interview by the author, June 14, 2018.

4. Reynolds, *Repertory in Review,* 79 (*Zodiac*); 81 (*Blackface*).

5. Joel Lobenthal, "A Conversation with Betty Nichols," recorded in February 1983, reprinted in *BR,* Fall 2013, 56, 58.

6. Ibid., 59.

7. Pat McBride Lousada, "Remembering Tanaquil Le Clercq," *BR,* Summer 2001, 52.

8. Ibid.

9. Ibid.

10. Ibid.

11. Lobenthal, "A Conversation with Betty Nichols," 59.

12. Preger-Simon, *Dancing with Merce Cunningham,* 62.

13. Ibid., 27, 30.

14. Lousada, "Remembering Tanaquil Le Clercq," 53.

15. Ibid.; Lobenthal, "A Conversation with Betty Nichols," 60; Lousada, "Remembering Tanaquil Le Clercq, 52, 50.

16. Lousada, "Remembering Tanaquil Le Clercq, 54.

17. Ibid., 53.

18. TLC to ELC, undated, late July or early August 1949, P&FP.

19. TLC to JLC, undated, August 1949, P&FP. The envelope is missing, but had the letter been written to the only other Jacques she knew well (d'Amboise), it would not have ended up in her possession.

20. TLC to JR, undated, probably (contextual evidence) July 1951, JRPP.

21. Jacques d'Amboise, interview by the author, June 14, 2018; Joel Lobenthal, interview by the author, June 21, 2020; Fisher, *In Balanchine's Company,* 119.

22. TLC to ELC, postmarked August 11, 1949, P&FP.

23. Lousada, "Remembering Tanaquil Le Clercq," 52.

24. Preger-Simon, *Dancing with Merce Cunningham,* 175; Jean Dalrymple, press briefing for NYCB for November 4, 1949, Morton Baum Papers, JRDD.

25. Lincoln Kirstein (hereafter LK) to ELC, November 8, 1946, P&FP.

26. Dominick Dunne, "The Rockefeller and the Ballet Boys," *Vanity Fair,* September 15, 2008, https://www.vanityfair.com/magazine/1987/02/dunne198702. (Claire N. White, a friend of John de Cuevas, confirmed to the author, in March 2020, that his father's title was considered a joke.) TLC to ELC, "Thursday," September 1949.

27. TLC to ELC, "Thursday," September 1949.

28. Ibid.

29. Lousada, "Remembering Tanaquil Le Clercq," 54, 53.

30. Lobenthal, "A Conversation with Betty Nichols," 60.

31. Ibid.

32. Ibid. Nichols married Jacques Schibler in 1951. She was living with her family in Lausanne in 1983, the year she came to New York for the start of a year-long commemoration of the fiftieth anniversary of the founding of the School of American Ballet and was interviewed by Joel Lobenthal. TLC hosted at least one of the celebratory parties (see chapter 20).

Chapter 8. A "Balanchine Ballerina"

1. See Duberman, *The Worlds of Lincoln Kirstein,* 448, for the amount Baum paid Hurok. In her memoir, Maria Tallchief says $4,500. Richard Buckle says $2,500.

2. Barbara Newman, "Tanaquil Le Clercq Talks about Dancing," *BR,* Fall 1982, 70.

3. TLC, *The Ballet Cook Book,* 321.

4. TLC, "Jerome Robbins," with Rick Whitaker, *BR,* Summer 1998, 13; Reynolds, *Repertory in Review,* 101; John Martin, "New Ballet Given by City Company," *New York Times,* December 2, 1949, 35.

5. Tallchief, *Maria Tallchief,* 133; TLC, "Jerome Robbins," 13.

6. TLC, "Jerome Robbins," 18; JR to TLC, March 6, 1957, JRPP.

7. TLC, *The Ballet Cook Book,* 131; Jeanne Thomas Fuchs, interview by the author, September 14, 2018.

8. Barbara Walczak, "Doubrovska's Class," *BR,* Fall 2015, 53; Gruen, *The Private World of Ballet,* 28.

9. *Felia Doubrovska Remembered—From Diaghilev's Ballets Russes to Balanchine's School of American Ballet,* produced and directed by Virginia Brooks, 2008.

10. Ibid.

11. Walter Terry, "The Ballet: Triumphant Quartet Jerome Robbins," *New York Herald Tribune,* February 27, 1950, 9.

12. Charles Engell France, "Interview with Tanaquil Le Clercq," 1974, JRDD.

13. Reynolds, *Repertory in Review*, 110; Newman, "Tanaquil Le Clercq Talks about Dancing," 63. For more on the poem in relation to the ballet, see Wendy Lesser, *Jerome Robbins: A Life in Dance* (New Haven, CT: Yale University Press, 2018), 30–32.

14. Jowitt, *Jerome Robbins: His Life, His Theater, His Dance*, 165.

15. Reynolds, *Repertory in Review*, 109; Terry, "The Ballet: Triumphant Quartet Jerome Robbins," 9; Reynolds, *Repertory in Review*, 110.

16. Reynolds, *Repertory in Review*, 110.

17. TLC, *The Ballet Cook Book*, 320; TLC, "Jerome Robbins," 13; Homans, *Apollo's Angels: A History of Ballet*, 506; Duffy, "Interview with Jerome Robbins," November 29, 1988, transcript, 20, JRDD.

18. James Mitchell, in the film *Jerome Robbins: Something to Dance About*, produced and directed by Judy Kinberg (New York: WNET, 2009).

19. Newman, "Tanaquil Le Clercq Talks about Dancing," 71; TLC, "Jerome Robbins," 13.

20. Davie Lerner, "Remembering Tanaquil Le Clercq," *BR*, Summer 2001, 45.

21. Reynolds, *Repertory in Review*, 108; Terry, "The Ballet: Triumphant Quartet Jerome Robbins," 9.

22. Jeanne Thomas Fuchs, email to the author, October 2, 2018; "London Welcomes New York City Ballet," special to the *New York Times* (unsigned), July 10, 1950, Tanaquil Le Clercq, Scrapbooks: Clippings (microfilm), 1950–1965, JRDD (hereafter TLC Scrapbooks); Paul Holt, "Ballet Also Comes from America," *Daily Herald* (London), (date missing), TLC Scrapbooks.

23. Reynolds, *Repertory in Review*, 112.

24. TLC, *The Ballet Cook Book*, 38.

25. France, "Interview with Tanaquil Le Clercq," JRDD; Newman, "Tanaquil Le Clercq Talks about Dancing," 72.

26. Reynolds, *Repertory in Review*, 112.

27. Ibid., 111; Lynn Garafola, "The African-American Presence in Postwar American Ballet," talk delivered at the University of Santa Barbara, April 29, 2019, 7.

28. Garafola, "The African-American Presence in Postwar American Ballet," 7.

29. Zorina, *Zorina*, 250.

30. Reynolds, *Repertory in Review*, 115.

31. Jurriaan Andriessen, archived interview with the composer, recorded for "American Art Festival Week" August 1950, broadcast on WNYC, September 17, 1950.

32. TLC, "Jerome Robbins," 13; TLC to JR, January 22, 1957, JRPP.

33. Lobenthal, "Tanaquil Le Clercq," *BR*, Fall 1984, 79; Jowitt, *Jerome Robbins: His Life, His Theater, His Dance*, 170.

34. France, "Interview with Tanaquil Le Clercq," JRDD; Reynolds, *Repertory in Review*, 114.

35. Chujoy, *The New York City Ballet*, 243, 244.

36. d'Amboise, interview by the author, January 8, 2018; Claire Nicolas White, interviews by the author, 2018–19. White (1925–2020) met Balanchine at Rieti's Harlem apartment. She had gone to the Lycée with Rieti's son, Fabio (the painter), and later introduced her uncle, Aldous Huxley, to Stravinsky. She wrote opera libretti for Rieti, and he set her poems to music. At ninety-three, Claire said to the author, a friend, "I was like a child compared to those people."

37. France, "Interview with Tanaquil Le Clercq," JRDD.

38. "Blue Notes of a Ballerina," *Ithaca Journal*, March 2, 1950, 23; Tallchief, *Maria Tallchief*, 123.

39. Gruen, "Interview with George Balanchine," sound recording, March 5, 1971, JRDD; Volkov, *Balanchine's Tchaikovsky*, 101.

40. TLC, "Jerome Robbins," 18.

41. Tallchief, *Maria Tallchief*, 137–39.

42. Ibid.; Zorina, *Zorina*, 174.

43. Holly Brubach, "Muse, Interrupted," *New York Times, T Magazine*, November 22, 1998, 60;

Deirdre Kelly, "The Cult of Thin," June 30, 2016, https://www.dancemagazine.com/the-cult-of-thin-2307026233.html.

44. Gruen, *The Private World of Ballet,* 95. For Maria's injury, see *Dance News,* August 1950, 6.

45. Newman, "Tanaquil Le Clercq Talks about Dancing," 75.

46. Leigh Ashton, "Tanaquil Fluttered," *London Daily Mail,* July 19, 1950; unsigned review of *Bourrée,* August 1, 1950, *Dance News,* August 1950, 6. Both in TLC Scrapbooks.

47. Percy Flage, "Attitudes & Arabesques," *Dance News,* September 1950, TLC Scrapbooks. The letter (TLC to ELC, August 9, 1950) is quoted later in this chapter (see note 52 below).

48. Tallchief, *Maria Tallchief,* 147.

49. Betty Cage to Morton Baum, August 19, 1950, Morton Baum Papers, JRDD; Garafola, *Dance for a City—Fifty Years of the New York City Ballet,* 16 (number of dancers, tour of 1950).

50. Kirstein, *Thirty Years: New York City Ballet,* 153.

51. Tallchief, *Maria Tallchief,* 143–44.

52. TLC to ELC, August 9, 1950, P&FP; Tallchief, *Maria Tallchief,* 148.

53. Tallchief, *Maria Tallchief,* 149.

54. Ibid., 148–49.

55. Brubach, "Muse, Interrupted," 63; Tallchief, *Maria Tallchief,* 141.

56. J. J. (Johanna Justina) Andriessen to TLC, July 12, 1950, P&FP. Lady Jeans (born Susanne Hock in Austria), an organist and musicologist, received her title as the wife of the astronomer and mathematician Sir James Jeans.

57. Lerner, "Remembering Tanaquil Le Clercq," 46.

58. Brubach, "Muse, Interrupted," 63.

59. d'Amboise, *I Was a Dancer,* 137; Mason, *I Remember Balanchine,* 579.

60. Mason, *I Remember Balanchine,* 279.

61. Fisher, *In Balanchine's Company,* 40. Her translation of the proverb is slightly different from the Russian original.

62. Duberman, *The Worlds of Lincoln Kirstein,* 268.

63. Kent, *Once a Dancer,* 77; Michael Walsh, "The Joy of Pure Movement, George Balanchine: 1904–1983," *Time* magazine, May 9, 1983, 93.

64. Tallchief, *Maria Tallchief,* 89.

65. LK to Morton Baum, June 22, 1955, Morton Baum Papers, JRDD.

66. d'Amboise, interview by the author, June 14, 2018; Jack Anderson, "Maria Tallchief, a Dazzling Ballerina and Muse for Balanchine, Dies at 88," *New York Times,* April 13, 2013, A22; d'Amboise, interview by the author, July 31, 2020.

67. d'Amboise, *I Was a Dancer,* 269; Teachout, *All in the Dances,* 101.

Chapter 9. Between Balanchine and Robbins, *La Valse* and *The Cage*

1. Reynolds, *Repertory in Review,* 118.

2. Liner notes, *New York City Ballet in Paris,* DVD (BelAir Classiques, 2016); Reynolds, *Repertory in Review,* 118.

3. Reynolds, *Repertory in Review,* 119.

4. Lobenthal, *Wilde Times,* 125.

5. Taper, *Balanchine: A Biography,* 240; Haggin, *Discovering Balanchine,* 31; Peter Conway, "Interview with Francisco Monción," April–May 1979, transcript, 305–6, JRDD.

6. Holly Brubach, "Muse, Interrupted," *New York Times, T Magazine,* November 22, 1998, 63; Barbara Newman, "Tanaquil Le Clercq Talks about Dancing," *BR,* Fall 1982, 67.

7. Nancy Buirski shows an extract from *La Valse* in her film, *Afternoon of a Faun,* taken from a streaming video of a 1951 film in the Victor Jessen Collection, JRDD. Le Clercq's performance,

captured by Carol Lynn at Jacob's Pillow in August 1951, can be viewed on YouTube at https://www.youtube.com/watch?v=gCO3HlH6_c4; Brubach, "Muse, Interrupted," 63; Tracy, *Balanchine's Ballerinas*, 88.

8. Don McDonagh, Arlene Croce, and George Dorris, "A Conversation with Edwin Denby: Parts 1 and 2," *BR* 2 no. 5 (1969): 3–4.

9. Allegra Kent, "Tanaquil Le Clercq, A Great American Ballerina," *Dance Magazine*, April 2001, 62; Judith Chazin-Bennahum, interview by the author, August 29, 2018.

10. Reynolds, *Repertory in Review*, 118–19.

11. TLC, "Practically Anybody Can Become a Ballet Dancer," *Good Housekeeping*, August 1955, 55.

12. Bocher, *The Cage*, 119.

13. Newman, "Tanaquil Le Clercq Talks about Dancing," 67.

14. "Mr. B Talks about Ballet," *Life magazine*, June 11, 1965, 97.

15. Kendall, *Balanchine & the Lost Muse*, 140.

16. Debra Craine and Judith Mackrell, *Oxford Dictionary of Dance* (Oxford: Oxford University Press, 2010), 447. For music for ballet, see http://www.balanchine.org/display. For TLC's attitude regarding Balanchine's superstitions, see chapter 15, note 27: "George worries me a little . . ."

17. Joel Lobenthal, "Tanaquil Le Clercq," *BR*, Fall 1984, 82.

18. Sally Bedell Smith, *In All His Glory: The Life of William S. Paley* (New York: Random House, 1990), 284.

19. A letter from a disgruntled woman, dated June 20, 1966, reproaches JLC for luring her to New York City in 1953 with a false promise of marriage, when he was already living with the woman who was to become his second wife (P&FP). Walter Owen, "Tanaquil Le Clercq," *Dance Magazine*, March 1950, 51.

20. Robert Sabin, "The Creative Evolution of *The Cage*: Jerome Robbins Reflects on His Most Controversial Ballet," *Dance Magazine*, August 1955, 22.

21. See note 28: "I watched the Cage . . ."

22. Sabin, "The Creative Evolution of *The Cage*," 23.

23. Ibid., 59.

24. Bocher, *The Cage*, 20–22, 26, 133.

25. Sabin, "The Creative Evolution of *The Cage*," 59; Chujoy, *The New York City Ballet*, 289.

26. TLC to JR, September 6, 1951, JRPP.

27. LK to JR, July 16, 1951, JRPP.

28. TLC to JR, undated, before her 1951 trip west, JRPP.

29. TLC to JR, August 28, 1951, JRPP.

30. JR to TLC, August 21, 1951; TLC to JR, August 28, 1951, JRPP.

31. David Vaughan, "Tanaquil Le Clercq," *The Guardian* (London), January 4, 2001, 20; Vaill, *Somewhere: The Life of Jerome Robbins*, 191 (Balanchine's reaction); Jacques d'Amboise, interview by the author, June 20, 2018.

32. d'Amboise, interview by the author, June 20, 2018; LK to JR, September 1, 1951, JRPP.

33. Vaill, *Somewhere: The Life of Jerome Robbins*, 432.

34. Ibid., 209.

35. Moore, "Tallchief and Kaye Replaced: New York Notes," *Dancing Times*, October 1954, 23.

36. Nicole Hirsch, "A Monte-Carlo: La rentrée du 'NYCB' précède la création de 'l'Hymne international Olympic," *France-Soir*, April 15, 1955 ("un peu malsaine,"); Christine De Rivoyre, "A L'Opéra de Monte-Carlo: Le New York City Ballet commencement brillamment sa tournée européenne," *Le Monde*, April 20, 1955 ("Il est toujours aussi inquiétant le mystère de cette créature sans poids, au regard de pierres précieuses, aux bras anguleux, aux arabesques que l'on croit toujours près de casser tant elles sont étirées et tant sa minceur extreme . . ." [translations by the author]). French articles, no page numbers, New York City Ballet clipping file, Paris Opera Ballet Library and Archives.

37. Joel Lobenthal, "A Conversation with Robert Barnett," *BR*, Winter 2013–14, 41.

38. Clifford Gessler, "New York City Ballet: 'Con Amore' Gets First Performance," *Oakland Tribune*, August 20, 1955, E5.

Chapter 10. Cakewalk and Convalescence

1. Tracy, *Balanchine's Ballerinas, 67*–68.

2. Reynolds, *Repertory in Review,* 121.

3. Nancy Reynolds, email to the author, April 3, 2019 (on the height difference of the two women).

4. Ruthanna Boris, "Remembering Tanny," *BR*, Fall 2001, 50.

5. Tallchief, *Maria Tallchief,* 202.

6. Boris, "Remembering Tanny," 51.

7. Boris, "Remembering Tanny," 48; Walter E. Owen, "Tanaquil Le Clercq," *Dance Magazine*, March 1950, 51 (on her reading taste).

8. Boris, "Remembering Tanny," 48.

9. Boris, "Remembering Tanny," 49, 52.

10. Boris, "Remembering Tanny," 48.

11. Walter Terry, "The Ballet: World Premiere Ruthanna Boris," *New York Herald Tribune,* June 13, 1951, 20.

12. Ruthanna Boris, "Remembering Mr. B and AGMA," *AGMA Magazine* 46, no. 1 (January 1992): 2.

13. Lynn Garafola, "Dance for a City" Revisited, exhibition materials (including GB AGMA card) from New-York Historical Society exhibit, April 20–August 15, 1999, https://academiccommons.co-lumbia.edu/doi/10.7916/D8MP6FR1); *AGMA Magazine* 1, no. 5, 6 (November 1947); *AGMA Magazine* 2, no. 8 (October 1949): 7, 5; Taper, *Balanchine: A Biography*, 13.

14. Alexander Dubé and Dorothy Kochiras, "Who's to Argue with Balanchine," *AGMA Magazine* 51, no. 3 (Fall 1997).

15. TLC to JR, undated (dictated to ELC), November 1956, JRPP.

16. TLC to JR, postcard sent to France, redirected to Tel-Aviv, Israel, postmarked July 23, 1951, JRPP.

17. TLC to JR, postcards postmarked August 7 and 20, 1951, JRPP.

18. Joel Lobenthal is the source regarding Molostwoff's closeness to ELC.

19. TLC to JR, undated, August 1951, JRPP; TLC to JR, August 28, 1951, JRPP; Tallchief, *Maria Tallchief,* 142.

20. TLC to JR, August 28, 1951, JRPP.

21. TLC to JR, undated, probably September 1951, JRPP; TLC to JR, postcard stamped received in Italy, September 11, 1951, JRPP.

22. TLC to JR, September 1951, JRPP.

23. Monción to JR, September 21, 1951, JRPP.

24. Reynolds, *Repertory in Review,* 47.

25. TLC to JR, September 6, 1951, JRPP. Since 1965 the New York Public Library (hereafter NYPL) music collection has been housed at the Library of the Performing Arts, Lincoln Center.

26. Walter E. Owen, "Ballerina, in Spare Time Is Topnotch Photographer," *Dance News,* September 1951, 7. Le Clercq's photography show was called *A Ballerina's View of the New York City Ballet.*

27. Ibid.; GB to TLC, undated, February 1952, Letters to Tanaquil Le Clercq, Balanchine, G., MS Thr 411.1, Houghton Library, Harvard University (hereafter HLH).

28. Don Langer, "Photography: Ballet Shots: Tanaquil Le Clercq, City Center Ballerina, Has Exhibit at the Music Library," *New York Herald Tribune,* February 24, 1952, D5.

29. Ibid.; TLC, "My Hobby," *Tanny: The Tanaquil Le Clercq Fan Club Semi-Annual Journal* 2 (July 1955): 7, JRDD.

30. Langer, "Photography: Ballet Shots."

31. Dr. Fredrika Borchard, "Adding Exotic Beauty to a Ballet," *St. Louis Post-Dispatch,* September 11, 1951, 3D.

32. Ibid.

33. Ibid.

34. Ibid.

35. Ibid.

36. Ibid.; TLC to JR, undated, probably October 1951, JRPP.

37. TLC to JR, postmarked October 18, 1951, JRPP.

38. JR to TLC, undated, probably late October 1951, JRPP.

39. JR to TLC, undated, probably late October 1951, JRPP.

40. TLC to JR, undated, October 1951, JRPP.

41. Lynn Garafola, curator, *Jerome Robbins and His World,* exhibit at the NYPL for the Performing Arts, March 25–June 28, 2008, Columbia Academic Commons, 22, https://academiccommons.columbia.edu/doi/10.7916/D8C83S9W.

42. Vaill, *Somewhere: The Life of Jerome Robbins,* 172–73.

43. Ibid, 193, 200, 219.

44. Reynolds, *Repertory in Review,* 133.

45. Ibid., 133–34.

46. Ibid., 133.

Chapter 11. A Reluctant Swan and a Dragonfly

1. TLC, "Jerome Robbins," with Rick Whitaker, *BR,* Summer 1998, 15; Duberman, *The Worlds of Lincoln Kirstein,* 480.

2. Volkov, *Balanchine's Tchaikovsky,* 153.

3. Reynolds, *Repertory in Review,* 130.

4. Ibid.

5. d'Amboise, *I Was a Dancer,* 272; Reynolds, *Repertory in Review,* 130; Barbara Newman, "Tanaquil LeClercq Talks about Dancing," *BR,* Fall 1982, 75, 67.

6. Newman, "Tanaquil LeClercq Talks about Dancing," 66; TLC, "Practically Anybody Can Become a Ballet Dancer," *Good Housekeeping,* August 1955, 173.

7. Faith McNulty, "Ballerina," *Cosmopolitan,* February 1953, 52.

8. John Martin, "Dancer Yesterday, a Ballerina Today," *New York Times,* February 28, 1952, Amusements, 22; Chujoy, *The New York City Ballet,* 331–32.

9. d'Amboise, *I Was a Dancer,* 272; d'Amboise at the fiftieth anniversary of the publication of *The Ballet Cook Book,* Guggenheim Museum, November 6, 2017; Joel Lobenthal, "A Conversation with Robert Barnett," *BR,* Winter 2013–14, 42.

10. Barbara Newman, "Tanaquil LeClercq Talks about Dancing," *BR,* Fall 1982, 70, 67, 66.

11. GB to TLC, February 1952, HLH.

12. GB to TLC, March 11, 1952 (includes drawing).

13. Tallchief, *Maria Tallchief,* 169; Reynolds, *Repertory in Review,* 137.

14. Reynolds, *Repertory in Review,* 138; Balanchine Catalogue, see http://www.balanchine.org, #286 (*Caracole*), #314 (*Divertimento no. 15*).

15. Chujoy, *The New York City Ballet,* 317 (deficit); Ruthanna Boris, "Remembering Tanny," *BR,* Fall 2001, 53.

16. *A Candle for St. Jude,* videorecording, directed by Paul Nickell, JRDD; "LeClercq Hailed For TV Role," *Dance News,* March 1952, 4.

17. Reynolds, *Repertory in Review,* 136.

18. Sylvester, "Robbins Is Dreamy Again with His New 'Ballade' at Center," *New York Daily News,* February 15, 1952, 407.

19. Reynolds, *Repertory in Review,* 136; Jowitt, *Jerome Robbins: His Life, His Theater, His Dance,* 209; Reynolds, *Repertory in Review,* 136.

20. TLC, "Jerome Robbins," 15; Lobenthal, "A Conversation with Robert Barnett," 44.

21. Sylvester, "Robbins Is Dreamy Again," 407.

22. Reynolds, *Repertory in Review,* 134.

23. Ibid.; LK, *Thirty Years: New York City Ballet,* 127.

24. Bocher, *The Cage.*

25. Denby, *Dance Writings,* 424; Don McDonagh, Arlene Croce, and George Dorris, "A Conversation with Edwin Denby: Parts 1 and 2," *BR* 2 no. 5 (1969): 4.

26. Bocher, *The Cage,* 135.

27. JR to RF, undated, datelined "Lausanne," JRPP; LK, *Thirty Years: New York City Ballet,* 127–28.

28. Jacques d'Amboise, interview by the author, June 14, 2018.

29. TLC to RF and Arthur Gold (hereafter AG), undated, 1952, RF&AG.

30. Newman, "Tanaquil Le Clercq Talks about Dancing," 74; TLC to RF, undated, 1952, RF&AG.

31. Jerome Robbins, interview by Deborah Jowitt, July 11, 1995, for Kennedy Center's Oral History archive, in the library of his home, JRDD.

32. JR to RF, undated, June 1952, JRPP.

33. Duberman, *The Worlds of Lincoln Kirstein,* 487.

34. Phillip Bloom, *New York City Ballet Press Book, 1956,* Paris Opera Ballet Library and Archives.

35. JR to RF, undated, June 1952, JRPP.

36. Lobenthal, *Wilde Times,* 144, 173.

37. Patricia Hancock, "Careers Demand That Ballerinas' Beauty Problems Be Solved," *Charlotte (NC) Observer,* March 29, 1956, 4B; McNulty, "Ballerina," 51; d'Amboise, from unpublished notes, edited on August 1, 2016, 2; Judith Chazin-Bennahum, interview by the author, August 28, 2018.

38. Sally MacDougall, "So You'd Like to Be a Ballerina?" *World-Telegram and Sun,* March 31, 1956; Sills, *Broadway, Balanchine & Beyond,* 75, 108–10; Arlene Croce, "Balanchine Said," https://www.newyorker.com/magazine/2009/01/26/balanchine-said.

39. Sills, *Broadway, Balanchine & Beyond,* 5.

40. Horgan, in the film *Afternoon of a Faun,* dir. Nancy Buirski (Kino Lorber, 2014); Abraham "Abe" Abdallah, email to the author, August 4, 2018. The name of the scent Balanchine chose for her is a mystery.

41. d'Amboise, *I Was a Dancer,* 42; d'Amboise, interview by the author, June 14, 2018.

42. Fisher, *In Balanchine's Company,* 16; Villella, *Prodigal Son in a World of Pain and Magic,* 43.

43. Mason, *I Remember Balanchine,* 353.

44. d'Amboise, *I Was a Dancer,* 42; Balanchine, "Mr. B. Talks about Ballet," *Life* magazine, June 11, 1965, 102; Mason, *I Remember Balanchine,* 555.

45. d'Amboise, *I Was a Dancer,* 39.

46. From a review signed "R.S." in *Music America,* December 15, 1952.

47. Schorer, *Suki Schorer on Balanchine Technique,* 30; Reynolds, *Repertory in Review,* 143; "R.S.," *Music America,* December 15, 1952. The fire also destroyed costumes for two other *lost* Balanchine ballets, *Tyl Ulenspiegel* and *Renard* (see http://www.balanchine.org, chronological title list, 289, *Metamorphoses*).

48. Holly Brubach, "Muse, Interrupted," *New York Times, T Magazine,* November 22, 1998, 63.

49. Reynolds, *Repertory in Review,* 145. *Attitude* turns are pirouettes on one raised foot with arms overhead and a high, bent leg behind the supporting leg.

50. *Concertino,* a silent 16mm black-and-white film, in JRDD, is all that remains of this performance. P. W. Manchester, "The Season in Review," *Dance News,* February 1953.

51. Brubach, "Muse, Interrupted," 63.

52. Muriel Stuart, interview by Joel Lobenthal, December 1981; Brubach, "Muse, Interrupted," 62–63.

53. Pat McBride Lousada, in the film *Afternoon of a Faun;* Jacques d'Amboise, interview by the author, June 14, 2018; Buckle, *George Balanchine, Ballet Master,* 199.

54. TLC to JR, undated, probably October 1951, JRPP.

55. Gruen, *The Private World of Ballet,* 429.

56. Taper, *Balanchine: A Biography,* 240; Toni Bentley, "Tanaquil Le Clercq," undated article from *CR Fashion Book,* 130, https://www.tonibentley.com/pdfarticles/crfashionbook/TANAQUIL.pdf.

Chapter 12. *Afternoon of a Faun*

1. Holly Brubach, "Muse, Interrupted," *New York Times, T Magazine,* November 22, 1998, 63.

2. LK, *Thirty Years: New York City Ballet,* 8.

3. Duberman, *The Worlds of Lincoln Kirstein,* 584; Reynolds, ed., *Remembering Lincoln,* 135.

4. Duberman, *The Worlds of Lincoln Kirstein,* 7; Mason, *I Remember Balanchine,* 132; Duberman, *The Worlds of Lincoln Kirstein,* 252.

5. Faith McNulty, "Ballerina," *Cosmopolitan,* February 1953, 49.

6. Ibid.; Devin Alberda, "Life in the Corps," *New York Times Magazine,* March 16, 2014, 43.

7. Allegra Kent, *Once a Dancer,* 46; Kent, "Tanaquil Le Clercq, A Great American Ballerina," *Dance Magazine,* April 2001, 62.

8. Barbara Newman, "Tanaquil Le Clercq Talks about Dancing," *BR,* Fall 1982, 66; TLC, "Practically Anybody Can Become a Ballet Dancer," *Good Housekeeping,* August 1955, 54, 173.

9. Martha Duffy, "Interview with Jerome Robbins," sound recording, disc 1, November 29, 1988.

10. GB to TLC, May 1, 1953, HLH.

11. GB to TLC, undated, May 1953, HLH.

12. Gaston Calmette, director of *Le Figaro,* noted the faun's "vils mouvements de bestialité érotique" (translated by the author), https://www.lefigaro.fr/histoire/archives/2017/05/26/26010-20170526ART-FIG00230-nijinski-deconcerte-son-public-en-1912-avec-l-apres-midi-d-un-faune.php.

13. Jowitt, *Jerome Robbins: His Life, His Theater, His Dance,* 223.

14. JLC to JR, May 16, 1953, JRPP; Jacques d'Amboise, interview by the author, June 14, 2018. The silent film was privately shot in Trieste in 1953 (see Joel Lobenthal, "Tanaquil Le Clercq," *BR,* Fall 1984, 85).

15. TLC, "Jerome Robbins," with Rick Whitaker, *BR,* Summer 1998, 18 (the description of the original set and lighting from a revival by the New York City Ballet, October 12, 2018).

16. Ibid., 18.

17. Kent, *Once a Dancer,* 94.

18. Reynolds, *Repertory in Review,* 147.

19. Jacques d'Amboise, in the film *Afternoon of a Faun,* dir. Nancy Buirski (Kino Lorber, 2014).

20. Lawrence, *Dance with Demons,* 211.

21. Ibid.

22. d'Amboise, interview by the author, June 14, 2018.

23. Ibid.

24. Ibid.

25. Christine de Rivoyre, "A L'Opéra de Monte-Carlo: Le New York City Ballet commencement brillamment sa tournée européenne," *Le Monde,* April 20, 1955 ("un très beau danseur à la fois viril et sensible . . . Ils joue cependant à des jeux très lents, très harmonieux, d'une délicatesse étrange; on dirait qu'ils se meuvent dans l'eau" [translated by the author]), NYCB Clipping File, Paris Opera Ballet Library and Archives.

26. Reynolds, *Repertory in Review,* 147; René Jouglet, "Les Américains Dansent à Paris," *Les Nouvelles Littéraires* June 16, 1955 ("méditations sur la nature du moi, essence du narcissisme . . . intellectualisme tourmenté" [translated by the author]), NYCB Clipping File, Paris Opera Ballet Library and Archives.

27. TLC, "Jerome Robbins," 18.

28. Brubach, "Muse, Interrupted," 63; Kent, *Once a Dancer,* 94.

29. Duffy, "Interview with Jerome Robbins," sound recording, disc 1, November 29, 1988, JRDD.

30. Pat McBride Lousada, in the film *Afternoon of a Faun.*

31. TLC to JR, undated, probably August 1956, from contextual evidence, JRPP.

32. http://balanchine.org/balanchine/companyitinearies.jsp.

33. TLC to RF, undated, June or early July 1953, RF&AG.

34. Ibid.

35. Duberman, *The Worlds of Lincoln Kirstein,* 504.

36. Fisher, *In Balanchine's Company,* 16.

37. Tallchief, *Tallchief: America's Prima Ballerina,* with Rosemary Wells (New York: Viking, 1999), 16. This children's book is not to be confused with Tallchief's memoir.

38. d'Amboise, email to the author (identifying photo), August 29, 2017.

Chapter 13. A Dewdrop and a Dance Hall Girl

1. Barbara Newman, "Tanaquil Le Clercq Talks about Dancing," *BR,* Fall 1982, 71.

2. Mason, *I Remember Balanchine,* 84; Teachout, *All in the Dances,* 145.

3. Reynolds, *Repertory in Review,* 157.

4. *A Belated Premiere,* film (Miris Cinema Productions, 2003), https://www.youtube.com/watch?v=GuvQYm8aqX0&list=PLGeJ66QTnvNFshish4V5u3WQB1A1Wjb6z; Mason, *I Remember Balanchine,* 12.

5. d'Amboise, *I Was a Dancer,* 193.

6. "Dewdrop among the Candy Flowers," the original name for her role, refers to an arrangement of Christmas marzipan candy in pre-Revolutionary St. Petersburg.

7. Vaill, *Somewhere: The Life of Jerome Robbins,* 231.

8. Duberman, *The Worlds of Lincoln Kirstein,* 507; Reynolds, *Repertory in Review,* 157.

9. Robert Sandla, "Over Fifty Years of Pure Magic," *Playbill,* December 3, 2007.

10. Joel Lobenthal spoke of this tutu at a symposium, "Ballerina: Fashion's Modern Muse," March 6, 2020, Fashion Institute of Technology, New York City; Allegra Kent, "Tanaquil Le Clercq, A Great American Ballerina," *Dance Magazine,* April 2001, 63; Buckle, *George Balanchine: Ballet Master,* 201; Joel Lobenthal, "Tanaquil Le Clercq," *BR,* Fall 1984, 76.

11. Kent, "Tanaquil Le Clercq, A Great American Ballerina," 63.

12. Reynolds, *Repertory in Review,* 157.

13. Tallchief, *Maria Tallchief,* 195–96. For salaries of company members on 1956 tour, see Morton Baum Papers, JRDD.

14. Robert Sylvester, "Lots of Guts in This Ballet," *New York Daily News,* January 22, 1954, 219.

15. https://www.laphil.com/musicdb/pieces/167/accompaniment-to-a-film-scene-op-34; Walter Terry, "New York City Ballet," *New York Herald Tribune,* January 21, 1954, 23; d'Amboise, *I Was a Dancer,* 207.

16. Reynolds, *Repertory in Review,* 152; Sylvester, "Lots of Guts in This Ballet," 219.

17. Fisher, *In Balanchine's Company,* 99.

18. Newman, "Tanaquil Le Clercq Talks about Dancing," 72; Reynolds, *Repertory in Review,* 152; Denby, *Dance Writings,* 459.

19. "Appendix Flattens Ballerina and Show," *The New York Daily Mirror,* February 14, 1954, Tanaquil

Le Clercq, Scrapbooks: Clippings (microfilm) 1950–1965, JRDD; "Miss Le Clercq Operated On," *New York Herald Tribune,* February 13, 1954, 9.

20. Claudia Cassidy, "On the Aisle, Balanchine's 'Scotch Symphony' and Robbins' 'Cage' at the Ballet," *Chicago Tribune,* May 29, 1954, 12.

21. d'Amboise, *I Was a Dancer,* 207.

22. Reynolds, *Repertory in Review,* 165; Holly Brubach, "Muse, Interrupted," *New York Times, T Magazine,* November 22, 1998, 63.

23. Jacques d'Amboise, interview by the author, June 14, 2018.

24. A 1964 DVD for Radio-Canada features Patricia Neary and Arthur Mitchell, a *pas de deux* Balanchine may have modified (*New York City Ballet in Montreal,* vol. 4, Video Artists International). Mitchell's movements, especially at 16:40, show the Cole influence: https://www.youtube.com/watch?v=qNDyEK7mlKc. Mason, *I Remember Balanchine,* 363.

25. Walter Terry, "Dance: The New York City Ballet," *New York Herald Tribune,* September 8, 1954, 27; NYCB website, https://www.nycballet.com/discover/ballet-repertory/western-symphony.

26. Balanchine: *New York City Ballet in Montreal,* vol. 3 (Catalogue No: DVDVA14573, VAI, Series, Radio-Canada, April 2014).

27. Reynolds, *Repertory in Review,* 170, 329–30; https://www.nycballet.com/season-and-tickets/fall-digital-season/

28. Duberman, *The Worlds of Lincoln Kirstein,* 514 (on scalpers, Paris).

29. Jacques d'Amboise, "Dinners with Tanny and Mr. B.," unpublished page edited by d'Amboise August 23, 2016 (mailed to the author July 11, 2018).

30. d'Amboise, *I Was a Dancer,* 168; d'Amboise, "Dinners with Tanny and Mr. B."

31. Walter Terry, "New York City Ballet," *New York Herald Tribune,* March 7, 1956, 18.

32. TLC, "Jerome Robbins," with Rick Whitaker, *Ballet Review,* Summer 1998, 18.

33. Reynolds, *Repertory in Review,* 173.

34. TLC to JR, postmarked Westport, April 27, 1956, JRPP. For the purchase price of land, see http://www.katzhome.com/weston_arabesque.htm. Ainsworth, "The Cat's Meow," *Weston (CT) Town Crier,* September 27, 1964, 13.

35. Abraham "Abe" Abdallah, email to the author, July 15, 2018; Randall "Randy" Bourscheidt, interview by the author (pool details), September 24, 2018.

36. Joel Lobenthal, "Muse of Many Faces," *Politico,* 7, https://www.politico.com/states/new-york/albany/story/2012/02/muse-of-many-faces-ballerina-tanaquil-le-clercqs-life-and-times-before-and-after-balanchine-remembered-and-now-novelized-067223.

37. TLC to JR, postmarked Westport, April 27, 1956, JRPP; Lobenthal, *Wilde Times,* 184.

38. Esther Brooks, interview by the author, August 28, 2018. Esther left Ballet Society in 1947 but kept in touch with friends, including Nicholas Magallanes. For details on the Puerto Rican trip, see *Dance Magazine,* May 1, 1956.

39. Deborah Jowitt, "Interview with Jerome Robbins," July 11, 1995, for Kennedy Center's Oral History archive, JRDD; Newman, "Tanaquil Le Clercq Talks about Dancing," 73–74.

40. Lynn Garafola, "The African-American Presence in Postwar American Ballet," talk delivered at the University of Santa Barbara, April 29, 2019, 8.

41. Ibid.; Arthur Mitchell, "The Stories I Could Tell: Arthur Mitchell at 75," video recording, panel moderated by Robert Greskovic, March 12, 2009, JRDD.

42. Mitchell, "The Stories I Could Tell," JRDD.

43. Ibid.

44. TLC, *The Ballet Cook Book,* 274–75.

45. Ibid.

Chapter 14. "The Royal Family" on Tour

1. Jacques d'Amboise, in the film *Afternoon of a Faun,* dir. Nancy Buirski (Kino Lorber, 2014); Jacques d'Amboise, email to the author, August 29, 2017.

2. Esther Brooks (story from Magallanes), interview by the author, August 28, 2018; Barbara Horgan, in the film *Afternoon of a Faun.*

3. Joel Lobenthal, "Muse of Many Faces," *Politico,* February 29, 2012, 7, https://www.politico.com/states/new-york/albany/story/2012/02/muse-of-many-faces-ballerina-tanaquil-le-clercqs-life-and-times-before-and-after-balanchine-remembered-and-now-novelized-067223. Lobenthal's source (confirmed by author's interview with Lobenthal, July 2020): unedited transcript of an interview with Janet Reed recorded by Robert Tracy and shared with Lobenthal by Francis Mason. The complete interview did not appear in Mason's book, *I Remember Balanchine.*

4. Mason, *I Remember Balanchine,* 133.

5. d'Amboise, *I Was a Dancer,* 271; TLC to JR, postmarked October 22, 1956, JRPP.

6. Lobenthal, *Wilde Times,* 191; TLC, "My Trip to Europe—1955," *Tanny: The Tanaquil Le Clercq Fan Club, Semi-Annual Journal,* no. 3, January 1956, 3, JRDD.

7. Lobenthal, *Wilde Times,* 191; d'Amboise, *I Was a Dancer,* 271.

8. Lobenthal, *Wilde Times,* 192.

9. Mason, *I Remember Balanchine,* 257, 261.

10. Ibid., 262, 258.

11. TLC to RF, undated, ca. September 1956, RF&AG; Lobenthal, *Wilde Times,* 192.

12. Lobenthal, "Muse of Many Faces," 8. The story was confirmed in the author's July 8, 2020, interview with Randall "Randy" Crocker, O'Brien's executor, who had heard O'Brien retell it. See also Peter Conway, "Interview with Francisco Monción," April–May 1979, transcript, 407, JRDD; and Martha Ullman West, "Afternoon of a Faun, Interrupted," *Oregon Arts Watch,* July 16, 2014, https://www.orartswatch.org/afternoon-a-a-faun-interrupted/, who heard the story from Barbara Walczak and Todd Bolender, also on that tour.

13. Fisher, *In Balanchine's Company,* 140.

14. Diana Adams to JR, postcard, September 28, 1956, JRPP. Famed stock-car racer Louise Smith, 1916–2006, was called "Fearless."

15. TLC to JR, undated, postmark blurred, but probably October 7, 1956, JRPP. (They stopped in Antwerp between Brussels and Paris.)

16. Jacques d'Amboise, interview by the author, June 14, 2018; Greg Lawrence, *Dance with Demons: The Life of Jerome Robbins,* 149; JR to TLC, February 25, 1957, JRPP.

17. Vaill, *Somewhere: The Life of Jerome Robbins,* 264. TLC to JR, undated, probably winter of 1956–57, JRPP, original missing from file.

18. JR to TLC, undated to "Dear Pocahantas," probably sent in 1956 (based on internal evidence), JRPP.

19. TLC to JR, undated. This letter ended up in the JRPP files next to an envelope addressed to JR in ELC's hand and stamped December 21, 1956, but the undated letter is not in Edith's hand nor in TLC's postpolio scrawl. The schedule she outlines is that of a dancer on tour: morning practice, lunch, postmatinee break, and after the evening performance. The reference to "summer" makes it likely that she sent it from England at the start of the tour. Holly Brubach, "Remembering Tanaquil Le Clercq," *BR,* Summer 2001, 66.

20. Robbins, Journal #10, May 23, 1974, JRPP.

21. Powell, *The Diaries of Dawn Powell 1931–1965,* entry for August 20, 1956, 362; Certificate of Marriage Registration, City of New York, Office of the City Clerk, August 20, 1956; Marjorie's stationery, letter to TLC, bears the header "Limroth Sales Corporation." Passenger manifest of Swissair Flight no. SR841 shows that JLC and Marjorie Limroth flew from New York to Geneva together on April 14,

1955. Their New York State marriage license, no. 18936, August 17, 1956, states JLC obtained a Mexican divorce from ELC, June 7, 1956, on the grounds of "incompatibility."

22. Powell, *The Diaries of Dawn Powell 1931–1965*, entry for June 3, 1954, 339.

23. Letter from unknown woman, June 20, 1966, JLC folder, P&FP; TLC to JR, undated, JRPP.

24. TLC to JR, undated postcard, artwork *An Idyll* by Francesco Bianchi Ferrari (Wallace Collection, London), sent in an envelope (missing), most likely August 1956, JRPP.

25. JR to TLC, October 8, 1956; TLC to JR, undated, August 1956, JRPP.

26. TLC to JR, undated, September or October 1956, JRPP; Mason, *I Remember Balanchine*, 497.

27. TLC to JR, undated, postmarked October 3, 1956, JRPP; Olivier Merlin, *Le Figaro Littéraire* ("maigre à faire peur"), week of September 3–9, 1964, TLC Scrapbooks. As a teen, Merlin had seen Le Clercq perform on the 1956 tour. His memory was triggered by receiving a copy of *Mourka* from her. Allegra Kent, "Tanaquil Le Clercq, a Great American Ballerina," *Dance Magazine*, April 2001, 63.

28. Mason, *I Remember Balanchine*, 411.

29. Lobenthal, *Wilde Times*, 191.

30. Villella, speaking at the Chicago Humanities Festival, "Edward Villella: An Intimate Evening," published on YouTube December 10, 2010; *Western Symphony*, film (Paris, 1956).

31. TLC to JR, undated, most likely mid-October 1956, JRPP.

32. TLC to JR, October 22, 1956, JRPP.

33. TLC to JR, October 24, 1956, JRPP.

34. Buckle, *George Balanchine: Ballet Master*, 205; Tallchief, *Maria Tallchief*, 226–27.

35. Horgan in the film *Afternoon of a Faun*; d'Amboise, *I Was a Dancer*, 180.

36. Robert Barnett, interview by Joel Lobenthal, June 16, 2011.

37. Fisher, *In Balanchine's Company*, 141–42; Holly Brubach, "Muse, Interrupted," *New York Times, T Magazine*, November 22, 1998, 64.

38. Fisher, *In Balanchine's Company*, 142.

39. Brubach, "Muse, Interrupted," 64; Mason, *I Remember Balanchine*, 186; TLC to JR, January 7, 1957, JRPP.

40. Dwight Eisenhower to LK, November 19, 1956, Morton Baum Papers, JRDD; TLC to JR, undated, 1956, JRPP.

41. Tallchief, *Maria Tallchief*, 228.

42. ELC to JR, undated, 1956, JRPP.

43. Brubach, "Muse, Interrupted," 64; TLC to JR, undated, 1956, JRPP.

44. ELC to JR, undated, postmark November 14, 1956, JRPP.

45. JR to TLC, undated, 1956; TLC to JR, November 25, 1956, JRPP.

46. ELC to JR, undated, postmark November 14, 1956, JRPP.

47. JR to TLC, December 3, 1956, JRPP.

48. Duffy, "Interview with Jerome Robbins," transcript, November 29, 1988, 12, JRDD; JR to TLC, December 12, 1956, JRPP.

49. Mason, *I Remember Balanchine*, 186; TLC to JR, January 7, 1957, JRPP.

50. TLC to JR, undated, postmarked December 31, 1956, JRPP.

51. TLC (dictated to ELC) to JR, postmarked December 21, 1956, JRPP; TLC to JR, undated letter, January 1957, JRPP.

52. TLC to JR, January 21, 1957, JRPP; TLC to JR, undated, January 1957, JRPP; TLC to JR, undated, postmark January 9, 1957, JRPP.

53. TLC to JR, probably January 1957, JRPP. Houseman had broached the idea to her in Stratford, during the 1956 festival, just before the company left on tour.

54. TLC to JR, undated, January 1957, JRPP; ELC to JR, postmarked January 20, 1957, JRPP.

55. TLC to JR, January 24, 1957, JRPP.

56. TLC to JR, undated, January 1957, JRPP.

57. TLC to JR, January 27, 1957; ELC to JR, January 28, 1957; TLC to JR, January 27, 1957, JRPP.

58. ELC to JR, January 23, 1957, JRPP.

59. TLC to JR, January 27, 1957, JRPP.

60. TLC to JR, January 21, 1957, JRPP; TLC to JR, January 29, 1957, JRPP.

61. Buckle, *George Balanchine: Ballet Master,* 207; TLC to JR, postmarked January 31, 1957, JRPP.

62. TLC to JR, February 18, 1957, JRPP.

63. TLC to JR, January 21, 1957, JRPP. (TLC to JR, February 16, 1957, expresses lack of enthusiasm about returning return home.)

64. TLC to JR, postmarked November 27, 1956, JRPP.

65. TLC to JR, postmarked November 27, 1956, JRPP.

66. TLC to JR, undated, probably January 1957, JRPP.

67. Jacques d'Amboise, in the film *Afternoon of a Faun;* TLC to JR, undated, 1956 or 1957, JRPP.

68. TLC to JR, undated, 1957, JRPP; TLC to JR, February 11, 1957, JRPP.

69. TLC to JR, February 11, 1957, JRPP.

70. JR to TLC, February 25, 1957, JRPP; TLC to JR, February 20, 1957, JRPP.

71. TLC to JR, March 1957, date partly smudged, JRPP; TLC to JR, March 3, 1957, JRPP; TLC to JR, March 12, 1957, JRPP.

Chapter 15. Warm Springs, Georgia

1. Duberman, *The Worlds of Lincoln Kirstein,* 523; ELC to JR, undated, November 1956, JRPP; Pat McBride Lousada, in the film *Afternoon of a Faun,* dir. Nancy Buirski (Kino Lorber, 2014).

2. TLC to JR, March 22, 1957, JRPP.

3. Taper, *Balanchine: A Biography,* 242.

4. TLC to JR, April 29, 1957, JRPP.

5. TLC to RF, undated, 1957, RF&AG.

6. TLC to RF, undated, 1957, RF&AG; TLC to JR, May 7, 1957, JRPP.

7. GB to TLC, May 6, 1957, HLH.

8. TLC to JR, May 22, 1957, JRPP; TLC to JR, July 6, 1957, JRPP.

9. TLC to JR, July 6, 1957, JRPP.

10. Ibid.

11. Ibid.

12. Holly Brubach, "Muse, Interrupted," *New York Times, T Magazine,* November 22, 1998, 64.

13. TLC to JR, undated, sent from Puerto Rico in 1966 (rest of postmark smudged), JRPP.

14. TLC to JR, undated, 1957, JRPP.

15. TLC to RF, undated, 1957, RF&AG.

16. TLC to JR, undated, 1957, JRPP.

17. GB to TLC, undated, 1957, HLH; TLC to GB, undated note, 1957, HLH.

18. GB to TLC, undated, 1957, HLH.

19. TLC to JR, undated letter, 1957, JRPP; TLC to JR, August 31, 1957, JRPP.

20. JLC and wife to TLC, September 11, 1957, JRPP. It's not clear how this letter, on Limroth Sales Corporation stationery, ended up in JR's possession. TLC probably sent it to him.

21. GB to TLC, undated drawings, 1957, HLH.

22. TLC to JR, undated, JRPP.

23. TLC to JR, September 16, 1957; RF to JR, September 13, 1957, JRPP.

24. TLC with Rick Whitaker, "Jerome Robbins," *BR,* Summer 1998, 18.

25. TLC to JR, October 2, 1957, JRPP.

26. Mason, *I Remember Balanchine,* 160.

27. TLC to RF, undated, 1957, RF&AG; TLC to JR, undated, 1957, JRPP.

28. TLC to JR, October 14, 1957, JRPP; TLC to JR, undated, probably November 1957, JRPP.

29. TLC to JR, November 6, 1957, JRPP.

30. d'Amboise, *I Was a Dancer,* 179; Nathan Milstein, "My Friend George Balanchine—II," *BR,* Winter 1990–91, 86, ©Nathan Milstein and Solomon Volkov.

31. Horgan, in the film *Afternoon of a Faun;* Jacques d'Amboise, in the film *Afternoon of a Faun.*

32. Mason, *I Remember Balanchine,* 186.

33. TLC to RF, undated, 1957 or 1958, RF&AG.

34. Brubach, "Muse, Interrupted," 64.

35. Holly Brubach, "Dancing around the Truth," *New York Times, T Magazine,* February 19, 2012, 115; Angela Taylor, "A Second Life for Tanaquil Le Clercq," *New York Times,* February 28, 1969, 34.

36. Taylor, "A Second Life for Tanaquil Le Clercq," 34. Joel Lobenthal was told (by a friend who heard it from a company member) that in the 1970s, Balanchine said that sometimes when TLC was calling for help, he would purposefully not respond because he knew that he would not always be there for her. In an interview with John Gruen, March 5, 1971, JRDD, Balanchine expressed pride at his ex-wife's newfound independence.

Chapter 16. A New Reality

1. Mason, *I Remember Balanchine,* 395.

2. Arthur Mitchell, "The Stories I Could Tell: Arthur Mitchell at 75," video recording, panel moderated by Robert Greskovic, March 12, 2009, JRDD.

3. "Jacques d'Amboise, Apollo at 83," *New York Times,* February 4, 2018; Jacques d'Amboise, interview by the author, July 31, 2020.

4. Arthur Mitchell, "Inspired By a Dream: the Dance Theatre of Harlem story," video recording, panel moderated by Anna Kisselgoff, February 12, 2009, JRDD.

5. Sills, *Broadway, Balanchine & Beyond,* 50. Balanchine had not changed his aesthetic by the 1970s. He still did "not like sunburns, or even suntans, on stage" (Mazo, *Dance Is a Contact Sport,* 101).

6. TLC to RF, undated, probably late 1950s, RF&AG.

7. Jacques d'Amboise, in the film *Afternoon of a Faun,* dir. Nancy Buirski (Kino Lorber, 2014).

8. Peter Conway, "Interview with Francisco Monción," April–May 1979, transcript, 306, JRDD; Gruen, *The Private World of Ballet,* 220, 116.

9. TLC to RF, undated, 1958/59, RF&AG.

10. JR to RF, August 15, 1958, JRPP.

11. JR to RF, September 25, 1958, JRPP; JR to RF, undated, October 1958, JRPP.

12. RF to JR, undated, October 1958, JRPP.

13. TLC to RF, undated, 1958, RF&AG.

14. RF to JR, undated, October 1958, JRPP; JR to RF, December 7, 1958, JRPP.

15. "Balanchine: Creator of Dances and Dancers Who Shapes Busy Art of Ballet," *Life* magazine, December 22, 1958, 101.

16. Ibid.

17. TLC to RF, undated letter, 1958/59, RF&AG.

18. RF to JR, May 19, 1960, JRPP.

19. RF to JR, June 1, 1960, JRPP.

20. JR to RF, June 5, 1960, JRPP; RF to JR, June 6, 1960, JRPP.

21. Holly Brubach, "Muse, Interrupted," *New York Times, T Magazine,* November 22, 1998, 64.

22. Mason, *I Remember Balanchine,* 411.

23. TLC to RF, undated, probably 1962, RF&AG.

24. Mason, *I Remember Balanchine,* 132; GB, Letters and telegrams, 1962, HLH.

25. TLC to JR, postmarked February 17, 1957, JRPP.

26. GB to TLC, undated, 1962, HLH.

27. d'Amboise, *I Was a Dancer,* 245; Lobenthal, *Wilde Times,* 232; Mason, *I Remember Balanchine,* 470.

28. GB to TLC, telegram, November 16, 1962, HLH; Kendall, *Balanchine & The Lost Muse,* 248n12.

29. *I, George Balanchine,* film written and directed by Nanuka Kiknadze (Neostudios, 2018), https://youtu.be/w7MMqLKkJEA.

30. From a publicity card advertising the book *Mourka,* JRPP.

31. Jeanne Thomas Fuchs, interview by the author, September 14, 2018.

32. Ibid. Russ Tallchief spoke at the symposium "Ballerina: Fashion's Modern Muse," Fashion Institute of Technology, New York, March 6, 2020.

33. Gene Palatsky, "Bravissimo to a Cat," *Newark Evening News,* August 24, 1964, 34; TLC, *Mourka: The Autobiography of a Cat,* unpaged.

34. Taper, *Balanchine, A Biography,* 244.

35. John Gruen, "Interview with George Balanchine," sound recording, at New York State Theater, March 5, 1971, JRDD.

36. Ainsworth, "The Cat's Meow," *Weston (CT) Town Crier,* September 27, 1964, 13; Barbara Siegel, "Wife of Balanchine Writes about Her Agile Cat," from a *Washington Evening Star* clipping (date missing, probably 1964–65), JRDD; Ainsworth, "The Cat's Meow," 13.

37. Robert Sabin, "Bright Victory: A Visit with Tanaquil Le Clercq," *Dance Magazine,* April 1964, 39.

38. Martha MacGregor, "The Week in Books," *New York Post,* August 16, 1964, 43.

39. Ainsworth, "The Cat's Meow," 13; Walter Terry, "City Ballet Ballerinas, 'Ivesiana,'" *New York Herald Tribune,* September 12, 1954, D5.

40. Ainsworth, "The Cat's Meow," 13; d'Amboise, in the film *Afternoon of a Faun.*

Chapter 17. Testing Times

1. d'Amboise, *I Was a Dancer,* 272.

2. Ibid.; Jacques d'Amboise, interview by the author, June 14, 2018.

3. Mason, *I Remember Balanchine,* 132. (Davidova seemed to think Adams had "left" GB in a more personal way.) d'Amboise, *I Was a Dancer,* 280–81.

4. d'Amboise, *I Was a Dancer,* 281; David Daniel, "Diana Adams on Suzanne Farrell," *BR,* Winter 1982, 14.

5. d'Amboise, *I Was a Dancer,* 281.

6. Daniel, "Diana Adams on Suzanne Farrell," 16, 14; Kent, *Once a Dancer,* 195.

7. Mason, *I Remember Balanchine,* 369; Nathan Milstein, "My Friend George Balanchine—II, *BR,* Winter 1990–91, 85.

8. Mason, *I Remember Balanchine,* 184.

9. Holly Brubach, "Muse, Interrupted," *New York Times, T Magazine,* November 22, 1998, 64.

10. Janet Reed, a dancer in the company who became its ballet mistress, later recognized his symptoms as panic attacks, but they may have been early signs of the brain-wasting disorder that killed him (see Mason, *I Remember Balanchine,* 343). Barbara Horgan, in the film *Afternoon of a Faun,* dir. Nancy Buirski (Kino Lorber, 2014); Angela Taylor, "A Second Life for Tanaquil Le Clercq," *New York Times,* February 28, 1969, 34.

11. Tallchief, *Maria Tallchief,* 292; Farrell, *Holding on to the Air,* 84–85.

12. Taper, *George Balanchine: A Biography,* 261. See also Garafola, *Dance for a City,* 18.

13. JR to Richard Buckle, April 22, 1964, JRPP.

14. Jeanne Thomas Fuchs, interview by the author, September 14, 2018.

15. Ibid.

16. Ibid.

17. Ibid.

18. Ibid.

19. Ibid.; Powell, *The Diaries of Dawn Powell 1931–1965,* entry for June 3, 1954, 339.

20. Pat McBride Lousada, in the film *Afternoon of a Faun.*

21. Fuchs, interview by the author, September 14, 2018; TLC to JR, letter postmarked March 30, 1971, JRPP.

22. Fuchs, interview by the author, September 14, 2018.

23. TLC to JR, undated letter sent from Paris, October 1956, JRPP; Fuchs, interview by the author, September 14, 2018.

24. Mason, *I Remember Balanchine,* 247; JR to TLC, undated, JRPP.

25. d'Amboise, *I Was a Dancer,* 282; Tallchief, *Maria Tallchief,* 238.·

26. Tallchief, *Maria Tallchief,* 238.

27. Daniel, "Diana Adams on Suzanne Farrell," *BR,* Winter 1982, 16.

28. Ibid., 14; Tracy, *Balanchine's Ballerinas,* 123.

29. Mason, *I Remember Balanchine,* 470.

30. Buckle, *George Balanchine: Ballet Master,* 249; "Balanchine Returns for 'Quixote' Role," *Los Angeles Times,* June 1, 1965, C16.

31. Massie, "Mr. B: 'God Creates, I Assemble,'" *Saturday Evening Post,* October 23, 1965, 35, 37.

32. Fuchs, interview by the author, September 14, 2018; Frederick M., "Balanchine Dances Again," *Shreveport (LA) Times,* May 28, 1965, 21.

33. Kent, *Once a Dancer,* 195.

34. Farrell, *Holding on to the Air,* 115; Buckle, *George Balanchine: Ballet Master,* 250.

35. Jeanne Thomas Fuchs, email to the author, September 19, 2018.

Chapter 18. A Book Launches, a Marriage Ends

1. Sills, *Broadway, Balanchine & Beyond,* 61.

2. Barbara Horgan, in the film *Afternoon of a Faun,* dir. Nancy Buirski (Kino Lorber, 2014).

3. Mason, *I Remember Balanchine,* 187; Joel Lobenthal (source on Edith's drinking) read an unedited transcript of Mason's interview with Molostwoff for *I Remember Balanchine.*

4. W. McNeill Lowry, "Suzanne's Story," *BR,* Winter 1990–91, 24.

5. Jeanne Thomas Fuchs, interview by the author, September 14, 2018.

6. Ibid.; Fuchs, interview by the author, March 28, 2021.

7. Mason, *I Remember Balanchine,* 187.

8. TLC, *The Ballet Cook Book,* 149.

9. Meryl Rosofsky, "50th Anniversary Celebration of *The Ballet Cook Book,*" event produced by *Works & Process* and presented at the Guggenheim Museum, November 5 and 6, 2017.

10. TLC, *The Ballet Cook Book,* 209–10.

11. GB to Mr. Hans Stuck at Schweizerische Bankverein, May 16, 1967, granting permission for her to draw money from his account, no amount stipulated, P&FP.

12. TLC in the film *Afternoon of a Faun.*

13. Pat McBride Lousada, "Tanaquil Le Clercq," https://www.theguardian.com/news/2001/jan/04/guardianobituaries2; Holly Brubach, "Remembering Tanaquil Le Clercq," *BR,* Summer 2001, 66.

14. TLC to JR, undated postcard, postmarked "Vosges," 1967, JRPP.

15. Menu for October 11, 1967, TLC to JR, JRPP; TLC, "Jerome Robbins," *BR,* Summer 1998, 18. See chapter 21, note 33.

16. Fuchs, interview by the author, September 14, 2018.

17. TLC to JR, undated, probably fall 1967, JRPP.

18. TLC to JR, undated letter and dated, uncashed check, November 3, 1967, JRPP.

19. Abraham "Abe" Abdallah, email to the author, July 16, 2018.

20. Fuchs, interview by the author, September 14, 2018.

21. Farrell, *Holding on to the Air*, 183.

22. Holly Brubach, "Muse, Interrupted," *New York Times, T Magazine*, November 22, 1998, 64; d'Amboise, *I Was a Dancer*, 283.

23. Abdallah, email to the author, July 16, 2018; Bourscheidt, interview by the author, August 16, 2020.

24. Vaill, *Somewhere: The Life of Jerome Robbins*, 410–11; Horgan, in the film *Afternoon of a Faun*; Farrell, *Holding on to the Air*, 185–86. (There are other accounts of these events, still a matter of controversy.)

25. Farrell, *Holding on to the Air*, 188–200.

26. Gruen, *The Private World of Ballet*, 283.

27. Ibid., 283–84.

28. Ibid., 284.

29. Mason, *I Remember Balanchine*, 481, 482.

30. Jacobs, *Celestial Bodies*, 214.

31. LK to JR, June 1, 1969, JRPP.

32. Buckle, *George Balanchine: Ballet Master*, 259.

33. d'Amboise, *I Was a Dancer*, 293–94; Farrell, *Holding on to the Air*, 213; Brubach, "Muse, Interrupted," 64; Gottlieb, *George Balanchine: The Ballet Maker*, 135.

34. Fuchs, interview by the author, September 14, 2018.

35. Abdallah, email to the author, July 15, 2018; Milstein, "My Friend George Balanchine II," *BR*, Winter 1990–91, 87.

36. TLC, *The Ballet Cook Book*, 226.

37. Ibid., 191.

38. Martha Swope, in the film *Afternoon of a Faun*.

Chapter 19. The Dance Theatre of Harlem Years

1. Pat McBride Lousada, in the film *Afternoon of a Faun*, dir. Nancy Buirski (Kino Lorber, 2014).

2. Arthur Mitchell, lecture/demonstration at the Wallach Art Gallery, New York City, February 24, 2018, for exhibit curated by Lynn Garafola, *Arthur Mitchell, Harlem's Ballet Trailblazer*, January 12 to March 11, 2018, https://exhibitions.library.columbia.edu/exhibits/show/mitchell; website of Harlem School of the Arts, 1966, https://hsanyc.org/about/history/

3. Yvonne Delaney Mitchell, "Cosmopolitan Review: Remembering Ballerina Tanaquil Le Clercq," *New York Amsterdam News*, February 20, 2014, 2.

4. Jeanne Thomas Fuchs, interview by the author, April 9, 2018; Randall "Randy" Bourscheidt, interview by the author, September 24, 2018.

5. Virginia Johnson, on the panel "Pioneering Black Ballerinas," moderated by Joel Lobenthal, Fashion Institute of Technology, New York City, February 27, 2020.

6. Delaney Mitchell, interview by the author, July 31, 2018.

7. Angela Taylor, "A Second Life for Tanaquil Le Clercq," *New York Times*, February 28, 1969, 34; Desmond W. Margetson to TLC, February 28, 1969, P&FP. For more on his life, see https://vineyard-gazette.com/obituaries/2008/06/20/desmond-w-margetson-was-engineer-inventor-athlete.

8. Zita Allen, "Arthur Mitchell's Dance Theatre of Harlem: The Early Years," for *Arthur Mitchell: Harlem's Ballet Trailblazer*, https://exhibitions.library.columbia.edu/exhibits/show/mitchell/dance-theatre-of-harlem—compa/zita-allen#_ednref33.

9. Reynolds, *Repertory in Review*, 255; LK to Robert H. Chapman, April 7, 1970, Lincoln Kirstein Papers, 1951–1999, JRDD.

10. Allen, "Arthur Mitchell's Dance Theatre of Harlem."

11. Martial Roumain, interview by the author, August 10, 2018.

12. Marcia Sells, "Dance Theatre of Harlem Dancers' Panel," moderated by Lynn Garafola, Columbia University's Wallach Art Gallery, February 24, 2018.

13. "A Place to Dance: New York City Center," lecture with panelists, Bruno Walter Auditorium, New York Public Library, November 29, 2018; Theara Ward, interview by the author, September 20, 2020; Theara Ward, "Dance Theatre of Harlem Dancers' Panel," February 24, 2018.

14. Genevieve Oswald, "Interview with Vera Stravinsky," June 14, 1976, transcript, 67, JRDD; Allen, "Arthur Mitchell's Dance Theatre of Harlem."

15. Lydia Abarca, on the panel "Pioneering Black Ballerinas," moderated by Joel Lobenthal, Fashion Institute of Technology, New York City, February 27, 2020.

16. Mitchell, informal talk following lecture/demonstration at the Wallach Art Gallery, New York City, February 24, 2018, Fashion Institute of Technology, New York City, February 27, 2020.

17. Virginia Johnson, on the panel "Pioneering Black Ballerinas," moderated by Joel Lobenthal, Fashion Institute of Technology, New York City, February 27, 2020; DTH website, https://www.dance-theatreofharlem.org/our-history/.

18. Gia Kourlas, "Louis Johnson, 90, Genre-Crossing Dancer and Choreographer, Dies," *Philadelphia Tribune,* April 10, 2020, https://www.phillytrib.com/nyt/louis-johnson-90-genre-crossing-dancer-and-choreographer-dies/article_20a1e019-e390-5fce-aadf-250960043fc5.html.

19. Virginia Johnson, "Inspired by a Dream: The Dance Theatre of Harlem Story," video recording, panel moderated by Anna Kisselgoff, February 12, 2009, JRDD.

20. Abraham "Abe" Abdallah, interviews by the author, July 2020.

21. Michael E. Stewart, interview by the author, July 17, 2020; Stewart, text from installation by Lauren Redniss, *A Gathering of Portraits from behind the Scenes at New York City Ballet,* February 2020, David H. Koch Theater, Lincoln Center, New York City.

22. Stewart, interview by the author, July 17, 2020.

23. Ibid.

24. Sells, email to the author, July 30, 2018.

25. Ibid. For more details, see https://www.npr.org/2018/11/10/666492913/major-ballet-shoe-supplier-diversifies-their-shoes.

26. John Gruen, "Interview with George Balanchine," May 29, 1971, sound disc, JRDD.

27. Reynolds, ed., *Remembering Lincoln,* 132–33 (LK's letter, May 20, 1974).

28. Gruen, "Interview with George Balanchine," May 29, 1971, sound disc, JRDD.

29. Reynolds, *Repertory in Review,* 218.

30. TLC to JR, undated, probably belongs with envelope postmarked June 23, 1966, JRPP.

31. Lynn Garafola, "The African-American Presence in Postwar American Ballet," talk delivered at the University of Santa Barbara, April 29, 2019, 12–13.

32. Ibid.

33. Ibid., 20; Singer, *First Position,* 190.

34. Kisselgoff, "Arthur Mitchell on Agon," Balanchine Foundation interview, published April 7, 2016; Barbara Newman, "Tanaquil Le Clercq Talks about Dancing," *BR,* Fall 1982, 67.

35. Author's memory, as one of JLC's students.

36. Abdallah, email to the author, July 13, 2018; Nancy Lassalle, interview by the author, April 10, 2018.

37. JLC (attorney) to ELC, August 15, 1961, P&FP.

38. Claire Nicolas White, interviews by the author, January 2019. Vittorio Rieti taught at Queens College in 1958–60 but probably met Jacques, through Balanchine, at an earlier date. Abdallah, email to the author, July 13, 2018.

39. Fuchs, interview by the author, September 14, 2018; Bourscheidt, interview by the author, August 16, 2020.

40. Abdallah, interview by the author, October 19, 2018; Bourscheidt, interview by the author, August 16, 2020; Abdallah, interview by the author, October 19, 2018.

41. Abdallah, interview by the author, October 19, 2018; Abdallah, email to the author, July 22, 2018.

42. Robbins, Journal #4, entry for December 7, 1972, JRPP.

43. Robbins, Journal #12, entry for June 26, 1975, JRPP; Abdallah, email to the author, April 15, 2019.

44. TLC to JR, March 26, 1971, JRPP.

45. Abdallah, email to the author, July 18, 2018.

46. Bourscheidt, interviews by the author, September 24, 2018, August 21, 2020.

47. Robbins, *Journal #7*, entry for July 2, 1973, JRPP. Robbins's brief home movie (JRDD) appears in the film *Afternoon of a Faun.*

48. Bourscheidt, email to the author, September 16, 2018.

49. Bourscheidt, in the film *Afternoon of a Faun;* Bourscheidt, interview by the author, September 24, 2018.

50. Bourscheidt, email to the author, September 16, 2018; Bourscheidt, interviews by the author, September 24, 2018, August 21, 2020.

51. Robbins, *Journal #7*, entry for July 3, 1973, JRPP; Bourscheidt, interview by the author, September 24, 2018.

52. Robbins, *Journal #7*, entry for July 7, 1973, JRPP; Abdallah, email to author, July 16, 2018.

53. RF to JR, July 13, 1973, JRPP.

54. Bourscheidt, interview by the author, September 24, 2018.

55. BBC website, *The Royal Variety Performance*, November 24, 1974.

56. Patricia Rosenfield and Rachel Wimpee, *The Ford Foundation: Constant Themes, Historical Variations,* Ford Foundation History Project (Sleepy Hollow, NY: Rockefeller Archive Center, 2015), 15–16, https://rockarch.org/publications/ford/overview/FordFoundationHistory1936–2001.pdfp. By 1970 the Foundation had committed 40 percent of its grant-making dollars to civil rights, but it later bowed to pressure from Congress.

57. Stewart, emails to the author, August 4–5, 2020. A *passé* involves passing the foot of the working leg past the knee of the supporting one in several directions; A *coupé* is similar but is generally performed at ankle height.

58. Stewart, interview by the author, July 17, 2020.

Chapter 20. "A Breath, a Memory, Then Gone"

1. Randall "Randy" Bourscheidt, interview by the author, September 24, 2018.

2. TLC to JR, May 1, 1957, JRPP.

3. Bourscheidt, interview by the author, September 24, 2018.

4. New York Public Library blogpost by Kathleen Leary, March 8, 2018, "Fond Reminiscences of Jerome Robbins by William James Earle," https://www.nypl.org/blog/2018/03/08/reminiscences-jerome-robbins-william-james-earle.

5. Edmund White, *City Boy—My Life in New York during the 1960s and '70s* (New York: Bloomsbury USA, 2009), 51.

6. TLC to JR, February 11, 1957, JRPP; Jacques d'Amboise, email to the author, September 5, 2018; Jacques d'Amboise, interview by the author, July 31, 2020.

7. Bourscheidt, in the film *Afternoon of a Faun,* dir. Nancy Buirski (Kino Lorber, 2014).

8. Pat McBride Lousada, in the film *Afternoon of a Faun;* Jerome Robbins Diaries, volume #4, entry for December 11, 1972, JRPP.

9. Abraham "Abe" Abdallah, interview by the author, October 31, 2018, and April 21, 2021. (For "laugh like hell," see chapter 10, note 40.)

10. Jeanne Thomas Fuchs, interview by the author, September 14, 2018; J. Alden Talbot's letter-contract with Robbins, President of Ballet Theatre, Incl, American Ballet Theatre Records, JRDD. Two years later, Lucia Chase gave him an amended licensing agreement (see Vaill, *Somewhere: The Life of Jerome Robbins,* 128).

11. JR to RF, undated, October 1982 (based on internal reference), JRPP.

12. JR to RF, undated, October 1982 (based on internal reference), JRPP; JR to RF & AG, December 2, 1982, JRPP.

13. Bourscheidt, interview by the author, September 24, 2018.

14. d'Amboise, *I Was a Dancer,* 349.

15. Lousada, in the film *Afternoon of a Faun.*

16. d'Amboise, *I Was a Dancer,* 352.

17. Ibid., 356.

18. Ibid., 356–57.

19. Ibid., 357; d'Amboise, interview by the author, June 14, 2018.

20. Farrell, *Holding on to the Air,* 267.

21. Buckle, *George Balanchine: Ballet Master,* 67; Mazo, *Dance Is a Contact Sport,* 294.

22. John Gruen, "Interview with George Balanchine," sound recording, March 5, 1971, JRDD.

23. TLC to JR, May 3, 1983, JRPP; d'Amboise, *I Was a Dancer,* 341; Vaill, *Somewhere: The Life of Jerome Robbins,* 484 (negotiation details).

24. Bourscheidt, in the film *Afternoon of a Faun.*

Chapter 21. The Final Chapter

1. Nancy Lassalle, "*First, A School:* The School of American Ballet exhibition," *BR* 11, no. 1 (Spring 1983): 17–31; Joel Lobenthal, emails to the author, June 24 & 25, 2020; Laurie Johnston, "School of American Ballet, at 50, as Rigorous as Ever," *New York Times,* January 20, 1984, B1; Jeanne Thomas Fuchs, email to the author, June 28, 2020.

2. April Stevens Neubauer, interview by the author, August 19, 2018.

3. Ibid.; Abraham "Abe" Abdallah, interview by the author, June 28, 2020; Abdallah, email to the author, October 19, 2020.

4. Neubauer, interview by the author, August 19, 2018; Norma Pane, interview by the author, September 12, 2018 (TLC remark on sparing backs).

5. Neubauer, interview by the author, August 19, 2018.

6. Ibid.

7. Ibid.

8. Abdallah, email to the author, July 14, 2008; Abdallah, interview by the author, June 28, 2020; Joel Lobenthal, "Muse of Many Faces," *Politico,* February 19, 2012, 4, 9, https://www.politico.com/states/new-york/albany/story/2012/02/muse-of-many-faces-ballerina-tanaquil-le-clercqs-life-and-times-before-and-after-balanchine-remembered-and-now-novelized-067223.

9. Randall "Randy" Bourschcidt, interview by the author, September 24, 2018; Edith Le Clercq, Last Will and Testament, June 21, 1971.

10. Abdallah, emails to the author, July 14 & 15, 2018.

11. Abdallah, interview by the author, June 28, 2020; Abdallah, email to the author, April 16, 2019.

12. Abdallah, email to the author, April 16, 2019.

13. TLC to JR, December 9, 1986, JRPP; Norma Pane, interview by the author, September 12, 2018; Bernard Taper, "Balanchine's Will," *BR,* Summer 1995, 34.

14. Pane, interview by the author, August 28, 2018.

15. Ibid.; ELC, Last Will and Testament, June 21, 1971.

16. Abdallah, email to the author, July 21, 2018; Abdallah, interview by the author, January 26, 2020.

Abe had a vivid memory of the incident (both women having talked to him about it later, each blaming the other), but Randy did not recall it.

17. Holly Brubach, "Muse, Interrupted," *New York Times, T Magazine,* November 22, 1998, 66; Abdallah, email to the author, August 2, 2018.

18. Jeanne Thomas Fuchs, interview by the author, September 14, 2018.

19. TLC to AG, January 3, 1990, RF&AG.

20. Bourscheidt, interview by the author, September 24, 2018.

21. Vaill, *Somewhere: The Life of Jerome Robbins,* 517. Karin von Aroldingen had been given the world rights to the ballet, but the final decision on the credit line was left to Tanny. Fuchs, interview by the author, September 14, 2018; Abdallah, email to the author, July 19, 2018.

22. TLC to JR, December 17, 1991, JRPP.

23. Abdallah, email to the author, July 20, 2018; Fuchs, interview by the author, September 14, 2018.

24. JR to TLC, March 12, 1993, JRPP.

25. Pane, interview by the author, August 28, 2018.

26. Abdallah, emails to the author, July 13 and 20, 2018.

27. Jennifer MacAdam, "NYCB Honors Balanchine," *St. Louis Post-Dispatch,* June 20, 1993, 4C. In 1987, Le Clercq coached Bart Cook and Maria Calegari in the *pas de deux* for a Queens College performance (see Jennifer Dunning, "Dance: Balanchine 'Divertimento' Duet in Queens," *New York Times,* December 8, 1987, C18).

28. Marilyn Hunt, "Balanchine's Divertimento: A New Life," *BR,* Fall 1985, 8, 10; d'Amboise, interview by the author, July 31, 2020.

29. Abdallah, email to the author, July 13, 2018; Abdallah, email to the author, July 24, 2018; Bourscheidt, interview by the author, September 24, 2018; TLC, "Practically Anybody Can Become a Ballet Dancer," *Good Housekeeping,* August 1955, 55.

30. TLC to JR, undated card, 1993, JRPP.

31. JR, "Dream of Tanny in Flower Market, Monday–Early A. M., 24th (March or April 1994)," Miscellaneous Notes, JRPP.

32. TLC to JR, around Memorial Day (based on internal reference to holiday and release date of *Bullworth,* the movie), 1998, JRPP; Vaill, *Somewhere: The Life of Jerome Robbins,* 521.

33. TLC, "Jerome Robbins," *BR,* Summer 1998, 18.

34. Barbara Newman, "Tanaquil Le Clercq Remembered," *BR,* Winter 2001, 51.

35. d'Amboise, *I Was a Dancer,* 415.

36. Pat McBride Lousada, "Remembering Tanaquil Le Clercq," *BR,* Summer 2001, 50.

37. Abdallah, email to the author, July 22, 2018; Nancy Lassalle, interview by the author, April 10, 2018.

38. Abdallah, email to the author, July 14, 2018.

39. Bourscheidt, interview by the author, September 24, 2018.

40. Pane, interview by the author, August 28, 2018.

41. Reynolds, *Repertory in Review,* 147.

42. https://www.youtube.com/watch?v=OYHzMxq3wrY.

Epilogue

1. Jacques d'Amboise, in the film *Afternoon of a Faun,* dir. Nancy Buirski (Kino Lorber, 2014).

2. Tobi Tobias, "Stopping Short," *New York Magazine,* January 22, 2001, 78; d'Amboise, *I Was a Dancer,* 417.

3. "Mr. B. Talks about Ballet," *Life* magazine, June 11, 1965, 102; Taper, *George Balanchine: A Biography,* 248.

4. Gottlieb, ed., *Reading DANCE,* 335–36.

5. Faith McNulty, "Ballerina," *Cosmopolitan*, February 1953, 52.

6. Singer, *First Position,* 70; "On Ballet: Fran Lebowitz and Nick Mauss/Live from the Whitney," recorded in May 2018, posted August 6, 2018, https://www.youtube.com/watch?v=g4XVhW7jPdw.

7. Abraham "Abe" Abdallah, email to the author, July 24, 2018; Barbara Newman, "Tanaquil Le Clercq Remembered," *BR,* Winter 2001, 48.

8. Newman, "Tanaquil Le Clercq Remembered," 51.

9. By 2003, TLC's estate was worth $4.6 million. The largest three shares, three-sixteenths apiece, totaled a bit more than half (TANAQUIL LECLERCQ GRANTOR TRUST, 1/23/1998, Norma R. Pane and Martin Zelner as Trustees, File No. 0512/01, Surrogate's Court of the State of New York, County of New York).

10. Joel Lobenthal, "Muse of Many Faces," *Politico,* February 29, 2012, 10, https://www.politico.com/states/new-york/albany/story/2012/02/muse-of-many-faces-ballerina-tanaquil-le-clercqs-life-and-times-before-and-after-balanchine-remembered-and-now-novelized-067223.

11. Norma Pane, interview by the author, August 28, 2018. TLC's properties were sold and divided. Abe tried to save the barn for the use of all, but he was not able to get consent from everyone. Five heirs made a gift to Randy of $100,000 (Abdallah, email to the author, August 3, 2018).

12. TLC to JR, undated, 1956–57, JRPP; Randall "Randy" Bourscheidt, in the film *Afternoon of a Faun.*

13. The building still exists but is no longer used as a restaurant.

14. Robert Gottlieb, "A Choreographer Steps Up; Farewell to a Sublime Dancer," *New York Observer,* January 15, 2001, 12.

15. Ruthanna Boris, "Remembering Tanny," *BR,* Fall 2001, 51.

16. Agnes de Mille, "Interview with Martha Swope," May 17, 1985, sound recording, JRDD; Pat McBride Lousada, "Ballet: Tanaquil Le Clercq," *The Guardian,* January 4, 2001, 20.

17. TLC, *The Ballet Cook Book,* 225–26, 232.

Bibliography

Bentley, Toni. *Costumes by Karinska.* New York: Abrams, 1995.

Bocher, Barbara. *The Cage: Dancing for Jerome Robbins and George Balanchine 1949–1954.* With Adam Darius. Self-published, 2012.

Buckle, Richard. *George Balanchine: Ballet Master.* With John Taras. New York: Random House, 1988.

Chujoy, Anatole. *The New York City Ballet.* New York: Knopf, 1953.

d'Amboise, Jacques. *I Was a Dancer.* New York: Knopf, 2011.

Danilova, Alexandra, and Holly Brubach. *Choura: The Memoirs of Alexandra Danilova.* New York: Knopf, 1986.

Decter, Jacqueline, ed. *Ballerina: Fashion's Modern Muse.* New York: Vendome, 2019.

Dee Das, Joanna. *Katherine Dunham: Dance and the African Diaspora.* New York: Oxford University Press, 2013.

Denby, Edwin. *Dance Writings.* Edited by Robert Cornfield and William MacKay. New York: Knopf, 1986.

———. *Dance Writings and Poetry.* Edited by Robert Cornfield. New Haven: Yale University Press, 1998.

Duberman, Martin. *The Worlds of Lincoln Kirstein.* New York: Knopf, 2007.

Dunning, Jennifer. *"But First a School": The First Fifty Years of the School of American Ballet.* New York: Viking, 1985.

Farrell, Suzanne. *Holding on to the Air: An Autobiography.* With Toni Bentley. 1990. Reprint, Gainesville: University Press of Florida, 2002.

Fisher, Barbara Milberg. *In Balanchine's Company: A Dancer's Memoir.* Middletown, CT: Wesleyan University Press, 2008.

Garafola, Lynn, and Eric Foner, eds. *Dance for a City—Fifty Years of the New York City Ballet.* New York: Columbia University Press, 1999.

———. *Legacies of Twentieth-Century Dance.* Middletown, CT: Wesleyan University Press, 2005.

Geva, Tamara. *Split Seconds: A Remembrance.* New York: Harper and Row, 1972.

Gottlieb, Robert. *George Balanchine: The Ballet Maker.* New York: HarperCollins, 2004.

———, ed. *Reading DANCE: A Gathering of Memoirs, Reportage, Criticism, Profiles, Interviews, and Some Uncategorizable Extras.* New York: Random House, 2008.

Greskovic, Robert. *Ballet 101: A Complete Guide to Learning and Loving the Ballet.* Milwaukee, WI: Limelight Editions, 2005.

Gruen, John. *The Private World of Ballet.* New York: Viking, 1975.

Haggin, B. H. *Discovering Balanchine.* New York: Horizon, 1981.

Homans, Jennifer. *Apollo's Angels: A History of Ballet.* New York: Random House, 2010.

Jacobs, Laura. *Celestial Bodies: How to Look at Ballet.* New York: Basic, 2018.

Jowitt, Deborah. *Jerome Robbins: His Life, His Theater, His Dance.* New York: Simon and Schuster, 2004.

Kendall, Elizabeth. *Balanchine & the Lost Muse.* New York: Oxford University Press, 2013.

Kent, Allegra. *Once a Dancer . . . : An Autobiography.* New York: St. Martin's, 1997.

Kirkland, Gelsey. *Dancing on My Grave.* New York: Berkeley Books, 1992.

Kirstein, Lincoln. *Thirty Years: New York City Ballet.* New York: Knopf, 1978.

Lawrence, Greg. *Dance with Demons: The Life of Jerome Robbins.* New York: G. P. Putnam's Sons, 2001.

Le Clercq, Tanaquil. *The Ballet Cook Book.* New York: Stein and Day, 1966.

———. *Mourka: The Autobiography of a Cat.* London: Sidgwick and Jackson, Ltd., 1965.

Lobenthal, Joel. *Wilde Times: Patricia Wilde, George Balanchine, and the Rise of New York City Ballet.* Boston: ForeEdge, Northeastern University Press, 2016.

Mason, Francis. *I Remember Balanchine: Recollections of the Ballet Master by Those Who Knew Him.* New York: Doubleday, 1991.

Mazo, Joseph H. *Dance Is a Contact Sport.* New York: Saturday Review Press; E. P. Dutton, 1974.

Milstein, Nathan, and Solomon Volkov. *From Russia to the West: The Musical Memoirs and Reminiscences of Nathan Milstein.* New York: Henry Holt, 1990.

Powell, Dawn. *The Diaries of Dawn Powell 1931–1965.* Edited by Tim Page. South Royalton, VT: Steerforth, 1995.

Preger-Simon, Marianne. *Dancing with Merce Cunningham.* Gainesville: University Press of Florida, 2019.

Reynolds, Nancy, ed. *Remembering Lincoln.* New York: The Ballet Society, 2007.

———. *Repertory in Review: 40 Years of the New York City Ballet.* New York: Dial, 1977.

Schorer, Suki. *Suki Schorer on Balanchine Technique.* With Russell Lee. Gainesville: University Press of Florida, 2006.

Sills, Bettijane. *Broadway, Balanchine & Beyond: A Memoir.* With Elizabeth McPherson. Gainesville: University Press of Florida, 2019.

Singer, Toba. *First Position: A Century of Ballet Artists.* Westport, CT: Praeger, 2007.

Tallchief, Maria. *Maria Tallchief: America's Prima Ballerina.* With Larry Kaplan. 1997. Reprint, Gainesville: University Press of Florida, 2005.

Taper, Bernard. *Balanchine: A Biography.* New York: Times Books, 1984.

Teachout, Terry. *All in the Dances: A Brief Life of George Balanchine.* Orlando, FL: Harcourt, 2004.

Tracy, Robert. *Balanchine's Ballerinas: Conversations with the Muses.* With Sharon DeLano. New York: Linden Press/Simon and Schuster, 1983.

Vaill, Amanda. *Somewhere: The Life of Jerome Robbins.* New York: Broadway, 2008.

Villella, Edward. *Prodigal Son: Dancing for Balanchine in a World of Pain and Magic.* With Larry Kaplan. New York: Simon and Schuster, 1992.

Volkov, Solomon. *Balanchine's Tchaikovsky: Interviews with George Balanchine.* New York: Simon and Schuster, 1985.

Zeller, Jessica. *Shapes of American Ballet: Teachers and Training before Balanchine.* New York: Oxford University Press, 2016.

Zorina, Vera. *Zorina.* New York: Farrar, Straus and Giroux, 1986.

Index

Page numbers in *italics* indicate illustrations.

d'Amboise, Jacques—*continued*
183, 204, 212, 216, 241–42, 244, 269, 344n13; Jack Cole, influence of, 201; JR, personality of, 87, 186–87, 216, 244; Kent, on stage, 200; King-Coit, memories of, 41–42; NYCB roles of, 3–4, 5, 72, 185–88, 195, 219, *261, 262,* 274, 330; NYCB, tours with, 75, 187, 210–11, 222, 244, 351n45; NYCB tribute to TLC, 329; SAB, classes of, 26, 32, 41, 119–20, 170; Tallchief, character of, 121, 326–27; TLC, on and off-stage, 60, 72, 81, 96–97, 158, 170, 174, 186–87, 199, 204, 210–11, 220–21, 229, 247, 260, 265, *277, 277,* 282, 312, 316, 330, 332
Dance Theatre of Harlem (DTH), 288, *289,* 290–91, *291,* 292–94, *295,* 295–96, *297,* 298–301, 306, *307, 308,* 309
Danielian, Leon, 24
Danilova, Alexandra, 37, 63, 103, 271, 284
Daughters of the American Revolution, 287
Davidova, Lucia, 179, 212, 253, 260, 367n3
Debussy, Claude, 161, 182–83
de Cuevas, Marquis, 97–98, 353n26
Dee Das, Joanna, 64, 351n22
DeLamar, Alice, 206, 310, 321
de la Renta, Oscar, 304
de Lavallade, Carmen, 208
Delibes, Léo, 202
Denby, Edwin, 4, 47, 126, 159, 163, 199–200
Dennis, MA (summer home, ELC), 26, 48
De Rivoyre, Christine, 134, 187, 356n36, 360n25
Diaghilev, Serge, 21, 36–37, 54, 100, 170, 182, 194
Divertimento (ballet, Haieff), 52–53, 326, 373n27
Divertimento No. 15 (ballet, Mozart), 160, 207, 222
Divertimento no. 15 in B-flat major (Mozart), 159, 207
Dmitriev, Vladimir Pavlovitch, 33–35, 38, 50, 89–90
Dmitriev, Vladimir Vladimirovich, 348n17
Doering, Ruth Gilbert Lawrence, 68, 83, 350n1
Dolin, Anton, 24
Don Quixote (ballet), 270–71, *272,* 273
Doubrovska, Felia, 102–3, 143, 273, 284, 290
Drew, Robert, 137
Duberman, Martin, 179, 231
Du Bois, Aline, *61*
Dunham, Katherine, 63, *65,* 67, 73, 89, 201, 300
Dunham School of Dance and Theatre, 63–64, 89, 163, 208
Dunham Technique, 63–64

Earle, William, 312
Eglevsky, André, 3, *144, 160,* 162, 173–74, 202, 344n9
Eisenhower, President Dwight, 223
Élégie (ballet), 46–47

Fancy Free (ballet), 84–85, *85,* 314, 372n10
Farmer, James, 292
Farrell, Suzanne (born Roberta Sue Ficker), 127, 257, 262–64, 269–71, *272, 273*–74, *275, 276*–77, 283–86, 292, 316, 329, 351n28
Faulkner, William, 59
Fauré, Gabriel, 274
February Revolution (Russia), 33
Festival of Two Worlds in Spoleto, Italy, 304
Few, Anne, 253
Few, Mrs. Ellen (cultural attaché spouse, sometimes spelled "Phew"), 5, 215, 233–34, 253, 344n13
Filling Station (ballet), 200
Firebird (ballet), 100, 131, 157, 178
Fire Island, NY, 102, 141, 189, *189,* 216, 226, *227,* 281, 312
Fisher, Barbara Milberg, 90, 97, 120, 170, 202, 212
Fizdale, Robert "Bobby," 2, 95, 216, 249, 281, 310, *311,* 312, 324, 329; JR, correspondence with, 164–65, 237, 239, 247–49, 252, 306, 314; TLC, correspondence with, 2, 164, 190, 214, 233, *235, 236,* 240, 247–50, 253, 305
Flair (magazine), 87–88, *88*
Forces of Rhythm (ballet), 296, *297*
Ford Foundation, The, 262, 264, 276, 292, 306, 371n56
Four Temperaments, The (ballet), 48, 50–52, 58, 97, 219, 294, *308,* 309
Françaix, Jean, 173
Francés, Esteban, 202, *203*
Franco, General Francisco, 160, 164
Fuchs, Jeanne Thomas, 107, 255, 265–69, 271, *273,* 276, 281–82, 286, 302, 314, 319, 323–25

Garafola, Lynn, 151, 300
Gauvin, Noel, 312
George Balanchine Trust, The, 324, 334
Gerstein, Jesse, 324
Gessler, Clifford, 136
Geva, Tamara (born Tamara Zheverzheeva), 3, 34–37, 62–63, 103, 120, 195, 206

OREL PROTOPOPESCU is an award-winning author, poet, and translator based in New York. Her books include *What Remains*; *A Thousand Peaks: Poems from China*; and *Thelonious Mouse*.